# TOWARD FREEDOM

## THE AUTOBIOGRAPHY OF JAWAHARLAL NEHRU

# TOWARD
# FREEDOM

## THE AUTOBIOGRAPHY OF

# JAWAHARLAL
# NEHRU

---

Beacon Press        Beacon Hill        Boston

TO

KAMALA

WHO IS NO MORE

# CONTENTS

## Introduction by JAWAHARLAL NEHRU

*This description of Nehru was first published in* The Modern Review *(Calcutta) in November 1937. Written under a pseudonym, it was not acknowledged by the writer as his own work until considerably later. It is an extraordinary and highly revealing piece of self-criticism, and the explicit reference to the Autobiography should make it even more interesting to the reader of the present volume.*

## THE RASHTRAPATI

### By "Chanakya"

"Rashtrapati Jawaharlal ki Jai!" The Rashtrapati looked up as he passed swiftly through the waiting crowds; his hands went up and were joined together in salute, and his pale hard face was lit up by a smile. It was a warm personal smile, and the people who saw it responded to it immediately and smiled and cheered in return.

The smile passed away and again the face became stern and sad, impassive in the midst of the emotion that it had roused in the multitude. Almost it seemed that the smile and the gesture accompanying it had little reality behind them; they were just tricks of the trade to gain the goodwill of the crowds whose darling he had become. Was it so?

Watch him again. There is a great procession, and tens of thousands of persons surround his car and cheer him in an ecstasy of abandonment. He stands on the seat of the car, balancing himself rather well, straight and seemingly tall, like a god, serene and unmoved by the seething multitude. Suddenly there is that smile again, or even a merry laugh, and the tension seems to break and the crowd laughs with him, not knowing what it is laughing at. He is godlike no longer, but a human being claiming kinship and comradeship with the thousands who surround him, and the crowd feels happy and friendly and takes him to its heart. But the smile is gone and the pale stern face is there again.

Is all this natural or the carefully thought out trickery of the public man? Perhaps it is both and long habit has become second nature now. The most effective pose is one in which there seems to be least of posing, and Jawaharlal has learnt well to act without the paint and powder of the actor. With his seeming carelessness and insouciance, he performs on the public stage with consummate artistry. Whither is this going to lead him and the country? What is he aiming at with all his apparent want of aim? What lies behind that mask of his, what desires, what will to power, what insatiate longings?

These questions would be interesting in any event; for Jawaharlal is a personality which compels interest and attention. But they have a vital significance for us, for he is bound up with the present in India, and probably the future, and he has the power in him to do great good to India or great injury. We must therefore seek answers to these questions.

For nearly two years now he has been President of the Congress, and some people imagine that he is just a camp-follower in the Working Committee of the Congress, suppressed or kept in check by others. And yet steadily and persistently he goes on increasing his personal prestige and influence both with the masses and with all manner of groups and people. He goes to the peasant and the worker, to the zamindar and the capitalist, to the merchant and the peddler, to the Brahmin and the untouchable, to the Muslim, the Sikh, the Parsi, the Christian, and the Jew—to all those who make up the great variety of Indian life. To all these he speaks in a slightly different language, ever seeking to win them over to his side. With an energy that is astonishing at his age, he has rushed about across this vast land of India, and everywhere he has received the most extraordinary of popular welcomes. From the far north to Cape Comorin he has gone like some triumphant Caesar passing by, leaving a trail of glory and a legend behind him. Is all this for him just a passing fancy which amuses him, or some deep design, or the play of some force which he himself does not know? Is it his will to power of which he speaks in his autobiography that is driving him from crowd to crowd and making him whisper to himself: *"I drew these tides of men into my hands and wrote my will across the sky in stars"*?

What if the fancy turn? Men like Jawaharlal, with all their capacity for great and good work, are unsafe in democracy. He calls himself a democrat and a socialist, and no doubt he does so in all earnestness, but every psychologist knows that the mind is ultimately a slave to the heart and that logic can always be made to fit in with the desires and irrepressible urges of man. A little twist and Jawaharlal might turn a dictator, sweeping aside the paraphernalia of a slow-moving democracy. He might still use the language and slogans of democracy and socialism, but we all know how fascism has fattened on this language and then cast it away as useless lumber.

Jawaharlal is certainly not a fascist either by conviction or by temperament. He is far too much of an aristocrat for the crudity and vulgarity of fascism. His very face and voice tell us that:

> Private faces in public places
> Are better and nicer than
> Public faces in private places.

The fascist face is a public face, and it is not a pleasant face in public or private. Jawaharlal's face as well as his voice are definitely private. There is no mistaking that even in a crowd, and his voice at public meetings is an intimate voice which seems to speak to individuals separately in a matter-of-fact homely way. One wonders as one hears it or sees that sensitive face what lies behind them, what thoughts and desires, what strange complexes and repressions, what passions suppressed and turned to energy, what longings which he dare not acknowledge even to himself. The train of thought holds him in public speech, but at other times his looks betray him, for his mind wanders away to strange fields and fancies, and he forgets for a moment his companion and holds inaudible converse with the creatures of his brain. Does he think of the human contacts he has missed on his life's journey, hard and tempestuous as it has been—does he long for them? Or does he dream of the future of his fashioning and of the conflicts and triumphs that he would fain have? He must know well that there is no resting by the wayside on the path he has chosen, and that even triumph itself means greater burdens. As Lawrence said to the Arabs: *"There can be no rest houses for revolt, no dividend of joy paid out."* Joy may not be for him, but something greater than joy may be his if fate and fortune are kind—the fulfillment of a life purpose.

Jawaharlal cannot become a fascist. And yet he has all the makings of a dictator in him—vast popularity, a strong will directed to a well-defined purpose, energy, pride, organizational capacity, ability, hardness, and, with all his love of the crowd, an intolerance of others and a certain contempt for the weak and inefficient. His flashes of temper are well known, and even when they are controlled the curling of the lips betrays him. His overmastering desire to get things done, to sweep away what he dislikes and build anew, will hardly brook for long the slow processes of democracy. He may keep the husk, but he will see to it that it bends to his will. In normal times he would just be an efficient and successful executive, but in this revolutionary epoch Caesarism is always at the door, and is it not possible that Jawaharlal might fancy himself as a Caesar?

Therein lies danger for Jawaharlal and for India. For it is not through Caesarism that India will attain freedom, and though she may prosper a little under a benevolent and efficient despotism she will remain stunted, and the day of the emancipation of her people will be delayed.

For two consecutive years Jawaharlal has been President of the Congress, and in some ways he has made himself so indispensable that there are many who suggest that he should be elected for a third term. But a greater disservice to India and to Jawaharlal himself can hardly be done. By electing him a third time, we shall exalt one man at the cost of the Congress and make the people think in terms of Caesarism. We shall encourage in Jawaharlal the wrong tendencies and increase his conceit and pride. He will become convinced that he alone can bear this burden or tackle India's problems. Let us remember that in spite of his apparent indifference to office he has managed to hold important offices in the Congress for the last seventeen years. He must imagine that he is indispensable, and no man must be allowed to think so. India cannot afford to have him as President of the Congress for a third year in succession.

There is a personal reason also for this. In spite of his brave talk Jawaharlal is obviously tired and stale, and he will progressively deteriorate if he continues as President. He cannot rest, for he who rides a tiger cannot dismount. But we can at least prevent him from going astray and from mental deterioration under too heavy burdens and responsibilities. We have a right to expect good work from him in the future. Let us not spoil that and spoil him by too much adulation and praise. His conceit, if any, is already formidable. It must be checked. We want no Caesars.

# AUTHOR'S PREFACE
## TO THE ORIGINAL EDITION

THIS BOOK WAS WRITTEN entirely in prison, except for the postscript and certain minor changes, from June, 1934, to February, 1935. The primary object in writing these pages was to occupy myself with a definite task, so necessary in the long solitudes of jail life, as well as to review past events in India, with which I had been connected, to enable myself to think clearly about them. I began the task in a mood of self-questioning, and, to a large extent, this persisted throughout. I was not writing deliberately for an audience, but, if I thought of an audience, it was one of my own countrymen and countrywomen. For foreign readers I would probably have written differently, or with a different emphasis, stressing certain aspects which have been slurred over in the narrative and passing over lightly certain other aspects which I have treated at some length. Many of these latter aspects may not interest the non-Indian reader, and he may consider them unimportant or too obvious for discussion or debate; but I felt that in the India of today they had a certain importance. A number of references to our internal politics and personalities may also be of little interest to the outsider.

The reader will, I hope, remember that the book was written during a particularly distressful period of my existence. It bears obvious traces of this. If the writing had been done under more normal conditions, it would have been different and perhaps occasionally more restrained. Yet I have decided to leave it as it is, for it may have some interest for others in so far as it represents what I felt at the time of writing.

My attempt was to trace, as far as I could, my own mental development, and not to write a survey of recent Indian history. The fact that this account resembles superficially such a survey is apt to mislead the reader and lead him to attach a wider importance to it than it deserves. I must warn him, therefore, that this account is wholly one-sided and, inevitably, egotistical; many important happenings have been completely ignored and many important persons, who shaped events, have hardly been mentioned. In a real survey of past events this would have been inexcusable, but a personal account can claim this indulgence. Those who want to make a proper study of our recent past will have to go to other sources. It may be, however, that this and other personal narratives will help them to fill the gaps and to provide a background for the study of hard fact.

I have discussed frankly some of my colleagues with whom I have been privileged to work for many years and for whom I have the greatest regard and affection; I have also criticized groups and individuals, sometimes perhaps rather severely. That criticism does not take away from my respect for many of them. But I have felt that those who meddle in public affairs must be frank with each other and with the public they claim to serve. A superficial courtesy and an avoidance of embarrassing and sometimes distressing questions do not help in bringing about a true understanding of each other or of the problems that face us. Real co-operation must be based on an appreciation of differences as well as common points, and a facing of facts, however inconvenient they might be. I trust, however, that nothing that I have written bears a trace of malice or ill will against any individual.

I have purposely avoided discussing the issues in India today, except vaguely and indirectly. I was not in a position to go into them with any thoroughness in prison, or even to decide in my own mind what should be done. Even after my release I did not think it worth while to add anything on this subject. It did not seem to fit in with what I had already written. And so this "autobiographical narrative" remains a sketchy, personal, and incomplete account of the past, verging on the present, but cautiously avoiding contact with it.

JAWAHARLAL NEHRU

*Badenweiler,*
*January 2, 1936.*

# TOWARD FREEDOM

The Autobiography of Jawaharlal Nehru

# I

## IN PRISON AGAIN [1]

Two of us were transferred together from the Bareilly District Jail to the Dehra Dun Jail—Govind Ballabh Pant and I. To avoid the possibility of a demonstration, we were not put on the train at Bareilly, but at a wayside station fifty miles out. We were taken secretly by motorcar at night, and, after many months of seclusion, that drive through the cool night air was a rare delight.

Before we left Bareilly Jail, a little incident took place which moved me then and is yet fresh in my memory. The superintendent of police of Bareilly, an Englishman, was present there, and, as I got into the car, he handed to me rather shyly a packet which he told me contained old German illustrated magazines. He said that he had heard that I was learning German and so he had brought these magazines for me. I had never met him before, nor have I seen him since. I do not even know his name. This spontaneous act of courtesy and the kindly thought that prompted it touched me, and I felt very grateful to him.

During that long midnight drive I mused over the relations of Englishmen and Indians, of ruler and ruled, of official and nonofficial, of those in authority and those who have to obey. What a great gulf divided the two races, and how they distrusted and disliked each other! But more than the distrust and the dislike was the ignorance of each other, and, because of this, each side was a little afraid of the other and was constantly on its guard in the other's presence. To each, the other appeared as a sour-looking, unamiable creature, and neither realized that there was decency and kindliness behind the mask. As the rulers of the land, with enormous patronage at their command, the English had attracted to themselves crowds of cringing place hunters and opportunists, and they judged of India from these unsavory specimens. The Indian saw the Englishman function only as an official with all the inhumanity of the machine and with all the passion of a vested interest trying to preserve itself. How different was the behavior of a person acting as an individual and obeying his own impulses from his behavior as an official or a unit in an army! The soldier, stiffening to attention, drops his humanity and, acting as an automaton, shoots

[1] In the original edition of this book, this chapter and the one succeeding appeared following the chapter, "In Bareilly and Dehra Dun Jails."—Ed.

3

and kills inoffensive and harmless persons who have done him no ill. So also, I thought, the police officer who would hesitate to do an unkindness to an individual would, the day after, direct a lathee charge on innocent people. He will not think of himself as an individual then, nor will he consider as individuals those crowds whom he beats down or shoots.

As soon as one begins to think of the other side as a mass or a crowd, the human link seems to go. We forget that crowds also consist of individuals, of men and women and children, who love and hate and suffer. An average Englishman, if he were frank, would probably confess that he knows some quite decent Indians but they are exceptions and as a whole Indians are a detestable crowd. The average Indian would admit that some Englishmen whom he knows are admirable, but, apart from these few, the English are an overbearing, brutal, and thoroughly bad lot. Curious how each person judges of the other race, not from the individual with whom he has come in contact, but from others about whom he knows very little or nothing at all.

Personally, I have been very fortunate and, almost invariably, I have received courtesy from my own countrymen as well as from the English. Even my jailers and the policemen who have arrested me or escorted me as a prisoner from place to place, have been kind to me, and much of the bitterness of conflict and the sting of jail life has been toned down because of this human touch. It was not surprising that my own countrymen should treat me so, for I had gained a measure of notoriety and popularity among them. Even for Englishmen I was an individual and not merely one of the mass, and, I imagine, the fact that I had received my education in England, and especially my having been to an English public school, brought me nearer to them. Because of this, they could not help considering me as more or less civilized after their own pattern, however perverted my public activities appeared to be. Often I felt a little embarrassed and humiliated because of this special treatment when I compared my lot with that of most of my colleagues.

Despite all these advantages that I had, jail was jail, and the oppressive atmosphere of the place was sometimes almost unbearable. The very air of it was full of violence and meanness and graft and untruth; there was either cringing or cursing. A person who was at all sensitive was in a continuous state of tension. Trivial occurrences would upset one. A piece of bad news in a letter, some item in the newspaper, would make one almost ill with anxiety or anger for a while. Outside there was always relief in action, and various interests and activities produced an equilibrium of the mind and body. In prison there was no outlet, and one felt bottled up and repressed; inevitably, one took one-sided and rather distorted views of happenings. Illness in jail was particularly distressing.

And yet I managed to accustom myself to the jail routine and with physical exercise and fairly hard mental work kept fit. Whatever the value of work and exercise might be outside, they are essential in jail, for without them one is apt to go to pieces. I adhered to a strict time-table, and, in order to keep up to the mark, I carried on with as many normal habits as I could, such as the daily shave (I was allowed a safety razor). I mention this minor matter because, as a rule, people gave it up and slacked in other ways. After a hard day's work, the evening found me pleasantly tired, and sleep was welcomed.

And so the days passed, and the weeks and the months. But sometimes a month would stick terribly and would not end, or so it seemed. Sometimes I would feel bored and fed up and angry with almost everything and everybody—with my companions in prison, with the jail staff, with people outside for something they had done or not done, with the British Empire (but this was a permanent feeling), and above all with myself. I would become a bundle of nerves, very susceptible to various moods caused by jail life. Fortunately I recovered soon from these.

Interview days were the red-letter days in jail. How one longed for them and waited for them and counted the days! And after the excitement of the interview there was the inevitable reaction and a sense of emptiness and loneliness. If, as sometimes happened, the interview was not a success, because of some bad news which upset me, or some other reason, I would feel miserable afterward. There were jail officials present at the interviews, of course; but two or three times at Bareilly there was in addition a Criminal Investigation Department man present with paper and pencil, eagerly taking down almost every word of the conversation. I found this exceedingly irritating, and these interviews were complete failures.

And then I gave up these precious interviews because of the brutal treatment my mother and wife had received in the course of an interview in the Allahabad Jail and afterward from the Government. For nearly seven months I had no interview. It was a dreary time for me, and, when at the end of that period I decided to resume interviews and my people came to see me, I was almost intoxicated with the joy of it. My sister's little children also came to see me, and, when a tiny one wanted to mount on my shoulder, as she used to do, it was more than my emotions could stand. That touch of home life, after the long yearning for human contacts, upset me.

When interviews stopped, the fortnightly letters from home or from some other jail (for both my sisters were in prison) became all the more precious and eagerly expected. If the letter did not come on the appointed day, I was worried. And yet, when it did come, I almost hesitated to open it. I played about with it as one does with an assured pleasure, and at the back of my mind there was also a trace of fear lest the letter contain any news or reference which might annoy me. Letter writing and receiving in jail were always serious incursions on a peaceful and unruffled existence. They produced an emotional state which was disturbing; for a day or two afterward one's mind wandered, and it was difficult to concentrate on the day's work.

In Naini Prison and Bareilly Jail I had had several companions. In Dehra Dun there were three of us to begin with—Govind Ballabh Pant, Kunwar Anand Singh of Kashipur, and I—but Pantji was discharged after a couple of months on the expiry of his six months. Two others joined us later. By the beginning of January 1933 all my companions had left me, and I was alone. For nearly eight months, till my discharge at the end of August, I lived a solitary life in Dehra Dun Jail with hardly anyone to talk to, except some member of the jail staff for a few minutes daily. This was not technically solitary confinement, but it was a near approach to it, and it was a dreary period for me. Fortunately I had resumed my interviews, and they brought some relief. As a special favor, I suppose, I was allowed to receive fresh flowers from outside and to keep a few photographs, and they cheered me greatly. Ordinarily, flowers and photographs are not permitted, and on several occasions I have not been allowed to receive the flowers that had been sent for me. Attempts to brighten up the cells were not encouraged, and I remember a superintendent of a jail once objecting to the manner in which a companion of mine, whose cell was next to mine, had arranged his toilet articles. He was told that he must not make his cell look attractive and "luxurious." The articles of luxury were: a toothbrush, tooth paste, fountain-pen ink, a bottle of hair oil, a brush and comb, and perhaps one or two other little things.

One begins to appreciate the value of the little things of life in prison. One's belongings are so few, and they cannot easily be added to or replaced; one clings to them and gathers up odd bits of things

6

which, in the world outside, would go to the wastepaper basket. The property sense does not leave one even when there is nothing worth while to own and keep.

Sometimes a physical longing would come for the soft things of life —bodily comfort, pleasant surroundings, the company of friends, interesting conversation, games with children. . . . A picture or a paragraph in a newspaper would bring the old days vividly before one, the carefree days of youth, a nostalgia would seize one, and the day would be passed in restlessness.

I used to spin a little daily, for I found some manual occupation soothing and a relief from too much intellectual work. My main occupation, however, was reading and writing. I could not have all the books I wanted, as there were restrictions and a censorship, and the censors were not always very competent for the job. Spengler's *Decline of the West* was held up because the title looked dangerous and seditious. But I must not complain, for I had, on the whole, a goodly variety of books. Again I seem to have been a favored person, and many of my colleagues (A-Class prisoners) had the greatest difficulty in getting books on current topics. In Benares Jail, I was told, even the official White Paper, containing the British Government's constitutional proposals, was not allowed in, as it dealt with political matters. The only books that British officials heartily recommended were religious books or novels. It is wonderful how dear to the heart of the British Government is the subject of religion and how impartially it encourages all brands of it.

When the most ordinary civil liberties have been curtailed in India, it is hardly pertinent to talk of a prisoner's rights. And yet the subject is worthy of consideration. If a court of law sentences a person to imprisonment, does it follow that not only his body but also his mind should be incarcerated? Why should not the minds of prisoners be free even though their bodies are not? Those in charge of the prison administrations in India will no doubt be horrified at such a question, for their capacity for new ideas and sustained thought is usually limited. Censorship is bad enough at any time and is partisan and stupid. In India it deprives us of a great deal of modern literature and advanced journals and newspapers. The list of proscribed books is extensive and is frequently added to. To add to all this, the prisoner has to suffer a second and separate censorship, and thus many books and newspapers that can be legally purchased and read outside the prison may not reach him.

7

Some time ago this question arose in the United States, in the famous Sing Sing Prison of New York, where some communist newspapers had been banned. The feeling against communists is very strong among the ruling classes in America, but in spite of this the prison authorities agreed that the inmates of the prison could receive any publication which they desired, including communist newspapers and magazines. The sole exception made by the warden was in the case of cartoons which he regarded as inflammatory.

It is a little absurd to discuss this question of freedom of mind in prison in India when, as it happens, the vast majority of the prisoners are not allowed any newspapers or writing materials. It is not a question of censorship but of total denial. Only A-Class prisoners are allowed writing materials as a matter of course, and not even all these are allowed daily newspapers. The daily newspaper allowed is of the Government's choice. For the rest, the 999 in every thousand, two or three books are permitted at a time, but conditions are such that they cannot always take advantage of this privilege. Writing or the taking of notes on books read are dangerous pastimes in which they must not indulge. This deliberate discouragement of intellectual development is curious and revealing. From the point of view of reclaiming a prisoner and of making him a fit citizen, his mind should be approached and diverted, and he should be made literate and taught some craft. But this point of view has perhaps not struck the prison authorities in India. Certainly it has been conspicuous by its absence in the United Provinces. Recently attempts have been made to teach reading and writing to the boys and young men in prison, but they are wholly ineffective, and the men in charge of them have no competence. Sometimes it is said that convicts are averse to learning. My own experience has been the exact opposite, and I found many of them, who came to me for the purpose, to have a perfect passion for learning to read and write. We used to teach such convicts as came our way, and they worked hard; and sometimes, when I woke up in the middle of the night, I was surprised to find one or two of them sitting by a dim lantern inside their barrack, learning their lessons for the next day.

So I occupied myself with my books, going from one type of reading to another, but usually sticking to "heavy" books. Novels made one feel mentally slack, and I did not read many of them. Sometimes I would weary of too much reading, and then I would take to writing. My historical series of letters to my daughter [2] kept me occupied right

[2] Now published under the title *Glimpses of World History*.

through my two-year term, and they helped me very greatly to keep mentally fit. To some extent I lived through the past I was writing about and almost forgot about my jail surroundings.

Travel books were always welcome—records of old travelers, Hiuen Tsang, Marco Polo, Ibn Battuta, and others, or moderns like Sven Hedin, with his journeys across the deserts of Central Asia, and Roerich, finding strange adventures in Tibet. Picture books also, especially of mountains and glaciers and deserts, for in prison one hungers for wide spaces and seas and mountains. I had some beautiful picture books of Mont Blanc, the Alps, and the Himalayas, and I turned to them often to gaze at the glaciers when the temperature of my cell or barrack was 115° F. or even more. An atlas was an exciting affair. It brought all manner of past memories and dreams of places we had visited and places we had wanted to go to. The longing to go again to those haunts of past days, to visit all the other inviting marks and dots that represented great cities, to cross the shaded regions that were mountains and the blue patches that were seas, to see the beauties of the world, and to watch the struggles and conflicts of a changing humanity —the longing to do all this would seize us and clutch us by the throat; we would hurriedly and sorrowfully put the atlas by and return to the well-known walls that surrounded us and the dull routine that was our daily lot.

## II

## ANIMALS IN PRISON

For fourteen and a half months I lived in my little cell or room in the Dehra Dun Jail, and I began to feel as if I were almost a part of it. I was familiar with every bit of it; I knew every mark and dent on the whitewashed walls and on the uneven floor and the ceiling with its moth-eaten rafters. In the little yard outside I greeted little tufts of grass and odd bits of stone as old friends. I was not alone in my cell, for several colonies of wasps and hornets lived there, and many lizards found a home behind the rafters, emerging in the evenings in search of prey. If thoughts and emotions leave their traces behind in the physical surroundings, the very air of that cell must be thick with them, and they must cling to every object in that little space.

I had had better cells in other prisons, but in Dehra Dun I had one

9

privilege which was very precious to me. The jail proper was a very small one, and we were kept in an old lock-up outside the jail walls, but within the jail compound. This place was so small that there was no room to walk about in it, and so we were allowed, morning and evening, to go out and walk up and down in front of the gate, a distance of about a hundred yards. We remained in the jail compound, but this coming outside the walls gave us a view of the mountains and the fields and a public road at some distance. This was not a special privilege for me; it was common for all the A- and B-Class prisoners kept at Dehra Dun. Within the compound, but outside the jail walls, there was another small building called the European Lock-up. This had no enclosing wall, and a person inside the cell could have a fine view of the mountains and the life outside. European convicts and others kept here were also allowed to walk in front of the jail gate every morning and evening.

Only a prisoner who has been confined for long behind high walls can appreciate the extraordinary psychological value of these outside walks and open views. I loved these outings, and I did not give them up even during the monsoon, when the rain came down for days in torrents and I had to walk ankle-deep in water. I would have welcomed the outing in any place, but the sight of the towering Himalayas near by was an added joy which went a long way to removing the weariness of prison. It was my good fortune that during the long period when I had no interviews, and when for many months I was quite alone, I could gaze at these mountains that I loved. I could not see the mountains from my cell, but my mind was full of them; I was ever conscious of their nearness, and a secret intimacy seemed to grow between us.

> *Flocks of birds have flown high and away;*
> *A solitary drift of cloud, too, has gone, wandering on.*
> *And I sit alone with Ching-ting Peak, towering beyond.*
> *We never grow tired of each other, the mountain and I.*

I am afraid I cannot say with the poet, Li T'ai Po, that I never grew weary, even of the mountain; but that was a rare experience, and, as a rule, I found great comfort in its proximity. Its solidity and imperturbability looked down upon me with the wisdom of a million years and mocked at my varying humors and soothed my fevered mind.

Spring was very pleasant in Dehra, and it was a far longer one than in the plains below. The winter had denuded almost all the trees of their leaves, and they stood naked and bare. Even four magnificent pipal trees, which stood in front of the jail gate, much to my surprise, dropped nearly all their leaves. Gaunt and cheerless they stood there, till the spring air warmed them up again and sent a message of life to their innermost cells. Suddenly there was a stir both in the pipals and the other trees, and an air of mystery surrounded them as of secret operations going on behind the scenes; and I would be startled to find little bits of green peeping out all over them. It was a gay and cheering sight. And then, very rapidly, the leaves would come out in their millions and glisten in the sunlight and play about in the breeze. How wonderful is the sudden change from bud to leaf!

I had never noticed before that fresh mango leaves are reddish-brown, russet colored, remarkably like the autumn tints on the Kashmir hills. But they change color soon and become green.

The monsoon rains were always welcome, for they ended the summer heat. But one could have too much of a good thing, and Dehra Dun is one of the favored haunts of the rain god. Within the first five or six weeks of the break of the monsoon we would have about fifty or sixty inches of rain, and it was not pleasant to sit cooped up in a little narrow place trying to avoid the water dripping from the ceiling or rushing in from the windows.

Autumn again was pleasant, and so was the winter, except when it rained. With thunder and rain and piercing cold winds, one longed for a decent habitation and a little warmth and comfort. Occasionally there would be a hailstorm, with hailstones bigger than marbles coming down on the corrugated iron roofs and making a tremendous noise, something like an artillery bombardment.

I remember one day particularly; it was the 24th of December, 1932. There was a thunderstorm and rain all day, and it was bitterly cold. Altogether it was one of the most miserable days, from the bodily point of view, that I have spent in jail. In the evening it cleared up suddenly, and all my misery departed when I saw all the neighboring mountains and hills covered with a thick mantle of snow. The next day—Christmas Day—was lovely and clear, and there was a beautiful view of snow-covered mountains.

Prevented from indulging in normal activities, we became more observant of nature's ways. We watched also the various animals and insects that came our way. As I grew more observant, I noticed all manner of insects living in my cell or in the little yard outside. I realized that while I complained of loneliness that yard, which seemed empty and deserted, was teeming with life. All these creeping or crawling or flying insects lived their life without interfering with me in any way, and I saw no reason why I should interfere with them. But there was continuous war between me and bedbugs, mosquitoes, and, to some extent, flies. Wasps and hornets I tolerated, and there were hundreds of them in my cell. There had been a little tiff between us when, inadvertently I think, a wasp had stung me. In my anger I tried to exterminate the lot, but they put up a brave fight in defense of their temporary home, which probably contained their eggs, and I desisted and decided to leave them in peace if they did not interfere with me any more. For over a year after that I lived in that cell surrounded by these wasps and hornets; they never attacked me, and we respected each other.

Bats I did not like, but I had to endure them. They flew soundlessly in the evening dusk, and one could just see them against the darkening sky. Eerie things; I had a horror of them. They seemed to pass within an inch of one's face, and I was always afraid that they might hit me. Higher up in the air passed the big bats, the flying foxes.

I used to watch the ants and the white ants and other insects by the hour. And the lizards too as they crept about in the evenings and stalked their prey and chased each other, wagging their tails in a most comic fashion. Ordinarily they avoided wasps, but twice I saw them stalk them with enormous care and seize them from the front. I do not know if this avoidance of the sting was intentional or accidental.

Then there were squirrels, crowds of them if trees were about. They would become very venturesome and come right near us. In Lucknow Jail I used to sit reading almost without moving for considerable periods, and a squirrel would climb up my leg and sit on my knee and have a look round. And then it would look into my eyes and realize that I was not a tree or whatever it had taken me for. Fear would disable it for a moment, and then it would scamper away. Little baby squirrels would sometimes fall down from the trees. The mother would come after them, roll them up into a little ball, and carry them off to safety. Occasionally the baby got lost. One of my companions picked up three of these lost baby squirrels and looked after them. They were so tiny that it was a problem how to feed them. The problem was, however, solved rather ingeniously. A fountain-pen filler, with a little cotton wool attached to it, made an efficient feeding bottle.

Pigeons abounded in all the jails I went to, except in the mountain prison of Almora. There were thousands of them, and in the evenings

12

the sky would be thick with them. Sometimes the jail officials would shoot them down and feed on them. There were *mainas,* of course; they are to be found everywhere. A pair of them nested over my cell door in Dehra Dun, and I used to feed them. They grew quite tame, and, if there was any delay in their morning or evening meal, they would sit quite near me and loudly demand their food. It was amusing to watch their signs and listen to their impatient cries.

In Naini there were thousands of parrots, and large numbers of them lived in the crevices of my barrack walls. Their courtship and love-making was always a fascinating sight, and sometimes there were fierce quarrels between two male parrots over a lady parrot, who sat calmly by waiting for the result of the encounter and ready to grant her favors to the winner.

Dehra Dun had a variety of birds, and there was a regular jumble of singing and lively chattering and twittering, and high above it all came the koel's plaintive call. During the monsoon and just before it the brain-fever bird visited us, and I realized soon why it was so named. It was amazing the persistence with which it went on repeating the same notes, in daytime and at night, in sunshine and in pouring rain. We could not see most of these birds; we could only hear them as a rule, as there were no trees in our little yard. But I used to watch the eagles and the kites gliding gracefully high up in the air, sometimes swooping down and then allowing themselves to be carried up by a current of air. Often a flight of wild duck would fly over our heads.

There was a large colony of monkeys in Bareilly Jail, and their antics were always worth watching. One incident impressed me. A baby monkey managed to come down into our barrack enclosure, and he could not mount up the wall again. The warder and some convict overseers and other prisoners caught hold of him and tied a bit of string round his neck. The parents (presumably) of the little one saw all this from the top of the high wall, and their anger grew. Suddenly one of them, a huge monkey, jumped down and charged almost right into the crowd which surrounded the baby monkey. It was an extraordinarily brave thing to do, for the warder and C.O.'s had sticks and lathees which they were brandishing about, and there were quite a crowd of them. Reckless courage triumphed, and the crowd of humans fled, terrified, leaving their sticks behind them! The little monkey was rescued.

We had often animal visitors that were not welcome. Scorpions were frequently found in our cells, especially after a thunderstorm. It was surprising that I was never stung by one, for I would come across them in the most unlikely places—on my bed, or sitting on a book which I had just lifted up. I kept a particularly black and poisonous-looking brute in a bottle for some time, feeding him with flies, etc.; and then, when I tied him up on a wall with a string, he managed to escape. I had no desire to meet him loose again, and so I cleaned my cell out and hunted for him everywhere, but he had vanished.

Three or four snakes were also found in my cells or near them. News of one of them got out, and there were headlines in the press. As a matter of fact I welcomed the diversion. Prison life is dull enough, and everything that breaks through the monotony is appreciated. Not that I appreciate or welcome snakes, but they do not fill me with terror as they do some people. I am afraid of their bite, of course, and would protect myself if I saw a snake. But there would be no feeling of repulsion or overwhelming fright. Centipedes horrify me much more; it is not so much fear as instinctive repulsion. In Alipore Jail in Calcutta I woke in the middle of the night and felt something crawling over my foot. I pressed a torch I had and I saw a centipede on the bed. Instinctively and with amazing rapidity I vaulted clear out of that bed and nearly hit the cell wall. I realized fully then what Pavlov's reflexes were.

In Dehra Dun I saw a new animal, or rather an animal which was new to me. I was standing at the jail gate talking to the jailer when we noticed a man outside carrying a strange animal. The jailer sent for him, and I saw something between a lizard and a crocodile, about two feet long with claws and a scaly covering. This uncouth animal, which was very much alive, had been twisted round in a most peculiar way, forming a kind of knot, and its owner had passed a pole through this knot and was merrily carrying it in this fashion. He called it a *Bo*. When asked by the jailer what he proposed to do with it, he replied with a broad smile that he would make *bhujji*—a kind of curry—out of it! He was a forest dweller. Subsequently I discovered from reading F. W. Champion's book—*The Jungle in Sunlight and Shadow*—that this animal was the pangolin.

Prisoners, especially long-term convicts, have to suffer most from emotional starvation. Often they seek some emotional satisfaction by keeping animal pets. The ordinary prisoner cannot keep them, but the convict overseers have a little more freedom and the jail staff usually do not object. The commonest pets were squirrels and, strangely, mongooses. Dogs are not allowed in jails, but cats seem to be encouraged. A little kitten made friends with me once. It belonged to a jail official, and, when he was transferred, he took it away with him. I missed it. Although dogs are not allowed, I got tied up with some dogs accidentally in Dehra Dun. A jail official had brought a bitch, and then he was transferred, and he deserted her. The poor thing became a homeless wanderer, living under culverts, picking up scraps from the warders, usually starving. As I was being kept in the lock-up, outside the jail proper, she used to come to me begging for food. I began to feed her regularly, and she gave birth to a litter of pups under a culvert. Many of these were taken away, but three remained, and I fed them. One of the puppies fell ill with a violent distemper and gave me a great deal of trouble. I nursed her with care, and sometimes I would get up a dozen times in the course of the night to look after her. She survived, and I was happy that my nursing had pulled her round.

I came in contact with animals far more in prison than I had done outside. I had always been fond of dogs and had kept some, but I could never look after them properly as other matters claimed my attention. In prison I was grateful for their company. Indians do not, as a rule, approve of animals as household pets. It is remarkable that, in spite of their general philosophy of nonviolence to animals, they are often singularly careless and unkind to them. Even the cow, that favored animal, though looked up to and almost worshiped by many Hindus and often the cause of riots, is not treated kindly. Worship and kindliness do not always go together.

Different countries have adopted different animals as symbols of their ambition or character—the eagle of the United States of America and of Germany, the lion and bulldog of England, the fighting cock of France, the bear of old Russia. How far do these patron animals mold national character? Most of them are aggressive, fighting animals, beasts of prey. The people who grow up with these examples before them appear to mold themselves consciously after them, strike up aggressive attitudes, roar, and prey on others. The Hindu is mild and nonviolent, for his patron animal is the cow.

# III

# DESCENT FROM KASHMIR

*"It is a hard and nice subject for a man to write of himself: it grates his own heart to say anything of disparagement, and the reader's ears to hear anything of praise for him."*—ABRAHAM COWLEY.

AN ONLY SON of prosperous parents is apt to be spoiled, especially so in India. And, when that son happens to have been an only child for the first eleven years of his existence, there is little hope for him to escape this spoiling. My two sisters are very much younger than I am, and between each pair of us there is a long stretch of years. And so I grew up and spent my early years as a somewhat lonely child with no companions of my age. I did not even have the companionship of children at school, for I was not sent to any kindergarten or primary school. Governesses or private tutors were supposed to be in charge of my education.

Our house itself was far from being a lonely place, for it sheltered a large family of cousins and near relations, after the manner of Hindu families. But all my cousins were much older than I was and were students at the high school or the university and considered me far too young for their work or their play. And so in the midst of that big family I felt rather lonely and was left a great deal to my own fancies and solitary games.

We were Kashmiris. Over two hundred years ago, early in the eighteenth century, our ancestor came down from that mountain valley to seek fame and fortune in the rich plains below. Those were the days of the decline of the Moghal Empire. Raj Kaul was the name of that ancestor of ours, and he had gained eminence as a Sanskrit and Persian scholar. He attracted the notice of the Emperor and, probably at his instance, the family migrated to Delhi, the imperial capital, about the year 1716. A *jagir* with a house situated on the banks of a canal had been granted to Raj Kaul, and, from the fact of this residence, "Nehru" (from *nahar,* a canal) came to be attached to his name. Kaul had been the family name; in later years, this dropped out and we became simply Nehrus.

The family experienced many vicissitudes of fortune during the unsettled times that followed, and the *jagir* dwindled and vanished away. My great-grandfather became the first vakil of the "Sarkar Company" at the shadow court of the Emperor of Delhi. My grandfather was

Kotwal of Delhi for some time before the great Revolt of 1857. He died at the early age of thirty-four in 1861.

The Revolt of 1857 put an end to our family's connection with Delhi, and all our old family papers and documents were destroyed in the course of it. The family, having lost nearly all it possessed, joined the numerous fugitives who were leaving the old imperial city and went to Agra. My father was not born then, but my two uncles were already young men and possessed some knowledge of English. This knowledge saved the younger of the two uncles, as well as some other members of the family, from a sudden and ignominious end. He was journeying from Delhi with some members of the family, among whom was his young sister, a little girl who was very fair, as some Kashmiri children are. Some English soldiers met them on the way, and they suspected this little aunt of mine to be an English girl and accused my uncle of kidnaping her. From an accusation to summary justice and punishment was usually a matter of minutes in those days, and my uncle and others of the family might well have found themselves hanging on the nearest tree. Fortunately for them, my uncle's knowledge of English delayed matters a little, and then someone who knew him passed that way and rescued him and the others.

For some years the family lived in Agra, and it was in Agra on the sixth of May, 1861, that my father was born.[1] But he was a posthumous child as my grandfather had died three months earlier. In a little painting that we have of my grandfather, he wears the Moghal court dress with a curved sword in his hand, and might well be taken for a Moghal nobleman, although his features are distinctly Kashmiri.

The burden of the family then fell on my two uncles, who were very much older than my father. The elder uncle entered the judicial department of the British Government and, being appointed to various places, was partly cut off from the rest of the family. The younger uncle entered the service of an Indian State. Later he settled down as a practicing lawyer in Agra. My father lived with him and grew up under his sheltering care. The two were greatly attached to each other, and their relation was a strange mixture of the brotherly and the paternal and filial. My father, being the last comer, was of course my grandmother's favorite son, and she was an old lady with a tremendous will of her own who was not accustomed to be ignored. It is now nearly half a century since her death, but she is still remem-

[1] An interesting coincidence: The poet, Rabindranath Tagore, was also born in this very day, month, and year.

bered among old Kashmiri ladies as a most dominating old woman and quite a terror if her will was flouted.

My uncle attached himself to the newly established High Court, and, when this court moved to Allahabad from Agra, the family moved with it. Since then Allahabad has been our home, and it was there, many years later, that I was born. My uncle gradually developed an extensive practice and became one of the leaders of the High Court Bar. Meanwhile my father was going through school and college in Cawnpore and Allahabad. His early education was confined entirely to Persian and Arabic, and he only began learning English in his early teens. But at that age he was considered to be a good Persian scholar, and knew some Arabic also, and because of this knowledge was treated with respect by much older people. But in spite of this early precocity his school and college career was chiefly notable for his numerous pranks and escapades. He was very far from being a model pupil and took more interest in games and novel adventures than in study. He was looked upon as one of the leaders of the rowdy element in the college. He was attracted to Western dress and other Western ways at a time when it was uncommon for Indians to take to them except in big cities like Calcutta and Bombay. Though he was a little wild in his behavior, his English professors were fond of him and often got him out of a scrape. They liked his spirit, and he was intelligent, and with an occasional spurt he managed to do fairly well even in class.

He got through his various university examinations without any special distinction, and then he appeared for his final, the B.A. He had not taken the trouble to work much for it, and he was greatly dissatisfied with the way he had done the first paper. Not expecting to pass the examination, as he thought he had spoiled the first paper, he decided to boycott the rest of the examination, and he spent his time instead at the Taj Mahal. (The university examinations were held then at Agra.) Subsequently his professor sent for him and was very angry with him, for he said that he (my father) had done the first paper fairly well and he had been a fool for not appearing for the other papers. Anyhow this ended my father's university career. He was never graduated.

He was keen on getting on in life and establishing himself in a profession. Naturally he looked to the law as that was the only profession then, in India, which offered any opening for talent and prizes for the successful. He also had his brother's example before him. He appeared for the High Court vakils' examination and not only passed it but topped the list and got a gold medal for it. He had found the subject after his own heart, or, rather, he was intent on success in the profession of his choice.

He started practice in the district courts of Cawnpore and, being eager to succeed, worked hard at it and soon got on well. But his love for games and other amusements and diversions continued and still took up part of his time. In particular, he was keen on wrestling. Cawnpore was famous for public wrestling matches in those days.

After serving his apprenticeship for three years at Cawnpore, father moved to Allahabad to work in the High Court. Not long after this his brother, Pandit Nand Lal, suddenly died. That was a terrible blow for my father; it was a personal loss of a dearly loved brother who had almost been a father to him, and the removal of the head and principal earning member of the family. Henceforward the burden of carrying on a large family mainly fell on his young shoulders.

He plunged into his work, bent on success, and for many months cut himself off from everything else. Nearly all of my uncle's briefs came to him, and, as he happened to do well in them, the professional success that he so ardently desired soon came his way and brought him both additional work and money. At an early age he had established himself as a successful lawyer, and he paid the price for this by becoming more and more a slave to his jealous mistress—the law. He had no time for any other activity, public or private, and even his vacations and holidays were devoted to his legal practice. The National Congress[2] was just then attracting the attention of the English-knowing middle classes, and he visited some of its early sessions and gave it a theoretical allegiance. But in those days he took no great interest in its work. He was too busy with his profession. Besides, he felt unsure of his ground in politics and public affairs; he had paid no great attention to these subjects till then and knew little about them. He had no wish to join any movement or organization where he would have to play second fiddle. The aggressive spirit of his childhood and early youth had been outwardly curbed, but it had taken a new form, a new will to power. Directed to his profession, it brought success and increased his pride and self-reliance. He loved a fight, a struggle against odds, and yet, curiously, in those days he avoided the political field. It is true that there was little of fight then in the politics of the Na-

[2] The Indian National Congress had been formed a few years before, in 1885, largely by Hindus of the student and professional classes, in protest against a number of discriminatory measures adopted by the British Government.—Ed.

tional Congress. However, the ground was unfamiliar, and his mind was full of the hard work that his profession involved. He had taken firm grip of the ladder of success, and rung by rung he mounted higher, not by anyone's favor, as he felt, not by any service of another, but by his own will and intellect.

He was, of course, a nationalist in a vague sense of the word, but he admired Englishmen and their ways. He had a feeling that his own countrymen had fallen low and almost deserved what they had got. And there was just a trace of contempt in his mind for the politicians who talked and talked without doing anything, though he had no idea at all as to what else they could do. Also there was the thought, born in the pride of his own success, that many—certainly not all—of those who took to politics had been failures in life.

An ever-increasing income brought many changes in our ways of living, for an increasing income meant increasing expenditure. The idea of hoarding money seemed to my father a slight on his own capacity to earn whenever he liked and as much as he desired. Full of the spirit of play and fond of good living in every way, he found no difficulty in spending what he earned. And gradually our ways became more and more Westernized.

Such was our home in the early days of my childhood.[3]


## IV

## CHILDHOOD

MY CHILDHOOD WAS thus a sheltered and uneventful one. I listened to the grown-up talk of my cousins without always understanding all of it. Often this talk related to the overbearing character and insulting manners of the English people, as well as Eurasians, toward Indians, and how it was the duty of every Indian to stand up to this and not to tolerate it. Instances of conflicts between the rulers and the ruled were common and were fully discussed. It was a notorious fact that whenever an Englishman killed an Indian he was acquitted by a jury of his own countrymen. In railway trains compartments were reserved for Europeans, and, however crowded the train might be—and they

[3] I was born in Allahabad on November 14, 1889, or, according to the Samvat calendar, *Margshirsh Badi 7, 1946.*

used to be terribly crowded—no Indian was allowed to travel in them, even though they were empty. Even an unreserved compartment would be taken possession of by an Englishman, and he would not allow any Indian to enter it. Benches and chairs were also reserved for Europeans in public parks and other places. I was filled with resentment against the alien rulers of my country who misbehaved in this manner; and, whenever an Indian hit back, I was glad. Not infrequently one of my cousins or one of their friends became personally involved in these individual encounters, and then of course we all got very excited over it. One of the cousins was the strong man of the family, and he loved to pick a quarrel with an Englishman, or more frequently with Eurasians, who, perhaps to show off their oneness with the ruling race, were often even more offensive than the English official or merchant. Such quarrels took place especially during railway journeys.

Much as I began to resent the presence and behavior of the alien rulers, I had no feeling whatever, so far as I can remember, against individual Englishmen. I had had English governesses, and occasionally I saw English friends of my father's visiting him. In my heart I rather admired the English.

In the evenings usually many friends came to visit father, and he would relax after the tension of the day, and the house would resound with his tremendous laughter. His laugh became famous in Allahabad. Sometimes I would peep at him and his friends from behind a curtain trying to make out what these great big people said to each other. If I was caught in the act, I would be dragged out and, rather frightened, made to sit for a while on father's knee. Once I saw him drinking claret or some other red wine. Whisky I knew. I had often seen him and his friends drink it. But the new red stuff filled me with horror, and I rushed to my mother to tell her that father was drinking blood.

I admired father tremendously. He seemed to me the embodiment of strength and courage and cleverness, far above all the other men I saw, and I treasured the hope that when I grew up I would be rather like him. But much as I admired him and loved him I feared him also. I had seen him lose his temper at servants and others; he seemed to me terrible then, and I shivered with fright, mixed sometimes with resentment, at the treatment of a servant. His temper was indeed an awful thing, and even in after years I do not think I ever came across anything to match it in its own line. But, fortunately, he had a strong sense of humor also and an iron will, and he could control himself as a rule. As he grew older this power of control grew, and it was very rare for him to indulge in anything like his old temper.

One of my earliest recollections is of this temper, for I was the victim of it. I must have been about five or six then. I noticed one day two fountain pens on his office table, and I looked at them with greed. I argued with myself that father could not require both at the same time, and so I helped myself to one of them. Later I found that a mighty search was being made for the lost pen, and I grew frightened at what I had done, but I did not confess. The pen was discovered and my guilt proclaimed to the world. Father was very angry, and he gave me a tremendous thrashing. Almost blind with pain and mortification at my disgrace, I rushed to mother, and for several days various creams and ointments were applied to my aching and quivering little body.

I do not remember bearing any ill will toward my father because of this punishment. I think I must have felt that it was a just punishment, though perhaps overdone. But, though my admiration and affection for him remained as strong as ever, fear formed a part of them. Not so with my mother. I had no fear of her, for I knew that she would condone everything I did, and, because of her excessive and indiscriminating love for me, I tried to dominate over her a little. I saw much more of her than I did of father, and she seemed nearer to me, so I would confide in her when I would not dream of doing so to father. She was petite and short of stature, and soon I was almost as tall as she was and felt more of an equal with her. I admired her beauty and loved her amazingly small and beautiful hands and feet. She belonged to a fresher stock from Kashmir, and her people had only left the homeland two generations back.

Another of my early confidants was a munshi of my father's, Munshi Mubarak Ali. He came from a well-to-do family of Badaun. The Revolt of 1857 had ruined the family, and the English troops had partly exterminated it. This affliction had made him gentle and forbearing with everybody, especially with children, and for me he was a sure haven of refuge whenever I was unhappy or in trouble. With his fine gray beard he seemed to my young eyes very ancient and full of old-time lore, and I used to snuggle up to him and listen, wideeyed, by the hour to his innumerable stories—old tales from the *Arabian Nights* or other sources, or accounts of the happenings in 1857 and 1858. It was many years later, when I was grown up, that "Munshiji" died, and the memory of him still remains with me as a dear and precious possession.

There were other stories also that I listened to, stories from the old Hindu mythology, from the epics, the *Ramayana* and the *Mahabharata,* that my mother and aunt used to tell us. My aunt, the widow of Pandit Nand Lal, was learned in the old Indian books and had an inexhaustible supply of these tales, and my knowledge of Indian mythology and folklore became quite considerable.

Of religion I had very hazy notions. It seemed to be a woman's affair. Father and my older cousins treated the question humorously and refused to take it seriously. The women of the family indulged in various ceremonies and *pujas* from time to time, and I rather enjoyed them, though I tried to imitate to some extent the casual attitude of the grown-up men of the family. Sometimes I accompanied my mother or aunt to the Ganges for a dip, sometimes we visited temples in Allahabad itself or in Benares or elsewhere, or went to see a *sanyasi* reputed to be very holy. But all this left little impression on my mind.

Then there were the great festival days—the *Holi,* when all over the city there was a spirit of revelry and we could squirt water at each other; the *Divali,* the festival of light, when all the houses were lit up with thousands of dim lights in earthen cups; the *Janmashtami,* to celebrate the birth in prison of Krishna at the midnight hour (but it was very difficult for us to keep awake till then); the *Dasehra* and *Ram Lila,* when tableaux and processions re-enacted the old story of Ramachandra and his conquest of Lanka, and vast crowds assembled to see them. All the children also went to see the *Moharram* processions with their silken *alums* and their sorrowful celebration of the tragic story of Hasan and Husain in distant Arabia. And on the two *Id* days Munshiji would dress up in his best attire and go to the big mosque for prayers, and I would go to his house and consume sweet vermicelli and other dainties. And then there were the smaller festivals, of which there are many in the Hindu calendar.

Among us and the other Kashmiris there were also some special celebrations which were not observed by most of the other Hindus. Chief of these was the *Naoroz,* the New Year's Day according to the Samvat calendar. This was always a special day for us when all of us wore new clothes, and the young people of the house got small sums of money as presents.

But more than all these festivals I was interested in one annual event in which I played the central part—the celebration of the anniversary of my birth. This was a day of great excitement for me. Early in the morning I was weighed in a huge balance against some bagfuls of wheat and other articles which were then distributed to the poor; and then I arrayed myself in new clothes and received presents, and later in the day there was a party. I felt the hero of the occasion. My chief grievance was that my birthday came so rarely. Indeed, I tried to start an agitation for more frequent birthdays. I did not realize then that a time would come when birthdays would become unpleasant reminders of advancing age.

Sometimes the whole family journeyed to a distant town to attend a marriage, either of a cousin of mine or of some more distant relation or friend. Those were exciting journeys for us children, for all rules were relaxed during these marriage festivities, and we had the free run of the place. Numerous families usually lived crowded together in the *shadi-khana,* the marriage house, where the party stayed, and there were many boys and girls and children. On these occasions I could not complain of loneliness, and we had our heart's fill of play and mischief, with an occasional scolding from our elders.

Indian marriages, both among the rich and the poor, have had their full share of condemnation as wasteful and extravagant display. They deserve all this. Even apart from the waste, it is most painful to see the vulgar display which has no artistic or aesthetic value of any kind. (Needless to say there are exceptions.) For all this the really guilty people are the middle classes. The poor are also extravagant, even at the cost of burdensome debts, but it is the height of absurdity to say, as some people do, that their poverty is due to their social customs. It is often forgotten that the life of the poor is terribly dull and monotonous, and an occasional marriage celebration, bringing with it some feasting and singing, comes to them as an oasis in a desert of soulless toil, a refuge from domesticity and the prosaic business of life. Who would be cruel enough to deny this consolation to them, who have such few occasions for laughter? Stop waste by all means, lessen the extravagance (big and foolish words to use for the little show that the poor put up in their poverty!), but do not make their life more drab and cheerless than it is.

So also for the middle classes. Waste and extravagance apart, these marriages are big social reunions where distant relations and old friends meet after long intervals. India is a big country, and it is not easy for friends to meet, and for many to meet together at the same time is still more difficult. Hence the popularity of the marriage celebrations. The only rival to them, and it has already excelled them in many ways even as a social reunion, is the political gathering, the various conferences, or the Congress!

Kashmiris have had one advantage over many others in India, especially in the north. They have never had any purdah, or seclusion of women, among themselves. Finding this custom prevailing in the Indian plains, when they came down, they adopted it, but only partly and in so far as their relations with others and non-Kashmiris were concerned. That was considered then in northern India, where most of the Kashmiris stayed, an inevitable sign of social status. But among themselves they stuck to the free social life of men and women, and every Kashmiri had the free entree into any Kashmiri house. In Kashmiri feasts and ceremonies men and women met together and sat together, though often the women would sit in one bunch. Boys and girls used to meet on a more or less equal footing. They did not, of course, have the freedom of the modern West.

So passed my early years. Sometimes, as was inevitable in a large family, there were family squabbles. When these happened to assume unusual proportions, they reached my father's ears, and he was angry and seemed to think that all such happenings were due to the folly of women. I did not understand what exactly had happened, but I saw that something was very wrong as people seemed to speak in a peculiarly disagreeable way or to avoid one another. I felt very unhappy. Father's intervention, when it took place, shook us all up.

One little incident of those early days stands out in my memory. I must have been about seven or eight then. I used to go out every day for a ride accompanied by a *sawar* from a cavalry unit then stationed in Allahabad. One evening I had a fall and my pony—a pretty animal, part Arab—returned home without me. Father was giving a tennis party. There was great consternation, and all the members of the party, headed by father, formed a procession in all kinds of vehicles and set out in search of me. They met me on the way, and I was treated as if I had performed some heroic deed!

# V

# THEOSOPHY

WHEN I WAS ten years old, we changed over to a new and much bigger house which my father named "Anand Bhawan." This house had a big garden and a swimming pool, and I was full of excitement at the fresh discoveries I was continually making. Additional buildings were put up, and there was a great deal of digging and construction, and I loved to watch the laborers at work.

There was a large swimming pool in the house, and soon I learned to swim and felt completely at home in and under the water. During the long and hot summer days I would go for a dip at all odd hours, many times a day. In the evening many friends of my father's came to the pool. It was a novelty, and the electric light that had been installed there and in the house was an innovation for Allahabad in those days. I enjoyed myself hugely during these bathing parties, and an unfailing joy was to frighten, by pushing or pulling, those who did not know how to swim. I remember, particularly, Dr. Tej Bahadur Sapru, who was then a junior at the Allahabad Bar. He knew no swimming and had no intention of learning it. He would sit on the first step in fifteen inches of water, refusing absolutely to go forward even to the second step, and shouting loudly if anyone tried to move him. My father himself was no swimmer, but he could just manage to go the length of the pool with set teeth and violent and exhausting effort.

The Boer War was then going on; this interested me, and all my sympathies were with the Boers. I began to read the newspapers for news of the fighting.

A domestic event, however, just then absorbed my attention. This was the birth of a little sister. I had long nourished a secret grievance at not having any brothers or sisters when everybody else seemed to have them, and the prospect of having at last a baby brother or sister all to myself was exhilarating. Father was then in Europe. I remember waiting anxiously in the veranda for the event. One of the doctors came and told me of it and added, presumably as a joke, that I must be glad that it was not a boy, who would have taken a share in my patrimony. I felt bitter and angry at the thought that anyone should imagine that I could harbor such a vile notion.

Father's visit to Europe led to an internal storm in the Kashmiri Brahman community in India. He refused to perform any *prayashchit* or purification ceremony on his return. Some years previously another Kashmiri Brahman had gone to England to be called to the Bar. On his return the orthodox members of the community had refused to have anything to do with him, and he was outcast, although he performed the *prayashchit* ceremony. This had resulted in the splitting up of the community into two more or less equal halves. Many Kashmiri young men went subsequently to Europe for their studies and on their return joined the reformist section, but only after a formal ceremony of purification. This ceremony itself was a bit of a farce, and there was little of religion in it. It merely signified an outward conformity and a submission to the group will. Having done so, each person indulged in all manner of heterodox activities and mixed and fed with non-Brahmans and non-Hindus.

Father went a step further and refused to go through any ceremony or to submit in any way, even outwardly and formally, to a so-called purification. A great deal of heat was generated, chiefly because of father's aggressive and rather disdainful attitude, and ultimately a considerable number of Kashmiris joined father, thus forming a third group. Within a few years these groups gradually merged into one another as ideas changed and the old restrictions fell. Large numbers of Kashmiri young men and girls have visited Europe or America for their studies, and no question has arisen of their performing any ceremonies on their return. Food restrictions have almost entirely gone, except in the case of a handful of orthodox people, chiefly old ladies, and interdining with non-Kashmiris, Moslems, and non-Indians is common. Purdah has disappeared among Kashmiris even as regards other communities. The last push to this was given by the political upheaval of 1930. Intermarriage with other communities is still not popular, although (increasingly) instances occur. Both my sisters have married non-Kashmiris, and a young member of our family has recently married a Hungarian girl. The objection to intermarriage with others is not based on religion; it is largely racial. There is a desire among many Kashmiris to preserve our group identity and our distinctive Aryan features, and a fear that we shall lose these in the sea of Indian and non-Indian humanity. We are small in numbers in this vast country.

When I was about eleven, a new resident tutor, Ferdinand T. Brooks, came and took charge of me. He was partly Irish (on his father's side), and his mother had been a Frenchwoman or a Belgian. He was a keen theosophist who had been recommended to my father

27

by Mrs. Annie Besant. For nearly three years he was with me, and in many ways he influenced me greatly. The only other tutor I had at the time was a dear old Pandit who was supposed to teach me Hindi and Sanskrit. After many years' effort the Pandit managed to teach me extraordinarily little, so little that I can only measure my pitiful knowledge of Sanskrit with the Latin I learned subsequently at Harrow. The fault no doubt was mine. I am not good at languages, and grammar has had no attraction for me whatever.

F. T. Brooks developed in me a taste for reading, and I read a great many English books, though rather aimlessly. I was well up in children's and boys' literature; the Lewis Carroll books were great favorites, and *The Jungle Books* and *Kim*. I was fascinated by Gustave Doré's illustrations to *Don Quixote,* and Fridtjof Nansen's *Farthest North* opened out a new realm of adventure to me. I remember reading many of the novels of Scott, Dickens, and Thackeray, H. G. Wells's romances, Mark Twain, and the Sherlock Holmes stories. I was thrilled by the *Prisoner of Zenda,* and Jerome K. Jerome's *Three Men in a Boat* was for me the last word in humor. Another book stands out still in my memory; it was Du Maurier's *Trilby;* also *Peter Ibbetson.* I also developed a liking for poetry, a liking which has to some extent endured and survived the many other changes to which I have been subject.

Brooks also initiated me into the mysteries of science. We rigged up a little laboratory, and there I used to spend long and interesting hours working out experiments in elementary physics and chemistry.

Apart from my studies, F. T. Brooks brought a new influence to bear upon me which affected me powerfully for a while. This was theosophy. He used to have weekly meetings of theosophists in his rooms, and I attended them and gradually imbibed theosophical phraseology and ideas. There were metaphysical arguments, and discussions about reincarnation and the astral and other supernatural bodies, and auras, and the doctrine of karma, and references not only to big books by Madame Blavatsky and other theosophists but to the Hindu scriptures, the Buddhist *Dhammapada,* Pythagoras, Apollonius Tyanaeus, and various philosophers and mystics. I did not understand much that was said, but it all sounded very mysterious and fascinating, and I felt that here was the key to the secrets of the universe. For the first time I began to think, consciously and deliberately, of religion and other worlds. The Hindu religion especially went up in my estimation; not the ritual or ceremonial part, but its great books, the *Upanishads* and the *Bhagavad Gita*. I did not understand them, of course, but they seemed very wonderful. I dreamed of astral bodies and imagined myself flying vast distances. This dream of flying high up in the air (without any appliance) has indeed been a frequent one throughout my life; and sometimes it has been vivid and realistic and the country-side seemed to lie underneath me in a vast panorama. I do not know how the modern interpreters of dreams, Freud and others, would interpret this dream.

Mrs. Annie Besant visited Allahabad in those days and delivered several addresses on theosophical subjects. I was deeply moved by her oratory and returned from her speeches dazed and as in a dream. I decided to join the Theosophical Society, although I was only thirteen then. When I went to ask father's permission, he laughingly gave it; he did not seem to attach importance to the subject either way. I was a little hurt by his lack of feeling. Great as he was in many ways in my eyes, I felt that he was lacking in spirituality. As a matter of fact he was an old theosophist, having joined the Society in its early days when Madame Blavatsky was in India. Curiosity probably led him to it more than religion, and he soon dropped out of it; but some of his friends, who had joined with him, persevered and rose high in the spiritual hierarchy of the Society.

So I became a member of the Theosophical Society at thirteen, and Mrs. Besant herself performed the ceremony of initiation, which consisted of good advice and instruction in some mysterious signs, probably a relic of freemasonry. I was thrilled. I attended the Theosophical Convention at Benares and saw old Colonel Olcott with his fine beard.

Soon after F. T. Brooks left me I lost touch with theosophy, and in a remarkably short time (partly because I went to school in England) theosophy left my life completely. But I have no doubt that those years with F. T. Brooks left a deep impress upon me, and I feel that I owe a debt to him and to theosophy. But I am afraid that theosophists have since then gone down in my estimation. Instead of the chosen ones they seem to be very ordinary folk, liking security better than risk, a soft job more than the martyr's lot. But for Mrs. Besant I always had the warmest admiration.

The next important event that I remember affecting me was the Russo-Japanese War. Japanese victories stirred up my enthusiasm, and I waited eagerly for the papers for fresh news daily. I invested in a large number of books on Japan and tried to read some of them. I felt rather lost in Japanese history, but I liked the knightly tales of old Japan and the pleasant prose of Lafcadio Hearn.

Nationalistic ideas filled my mind. I mused of Indian freedom and Asiatic freedom from the thralldom of Europe. I dreamed of brave deeds, of how, sword in hand, I would fight for India and help in freeing her.

I was fourteen. Changes were taking place in our house. My older cousins, having become professional men, were leaving the common home and setting up their own households separately. Fresh thoughts and vague fancies were floating in my mind, and I began to take a little more interest in the opposite sex. I still preferred the company of boys and thought it a little beneath my dignity to mix with groups of girls. But sometimes at Kashmiri parties, where pretty girls were not lacking, or elsewhere, a glance or a touch would thrill me.

In May 1905, when I was fifteen, we set sail for England. Father and mother, my baby sister and I, we all went together.

## VI

## HARROW AND CAMBRIDGE

ON A MAY day, toward the end of the month, we reached London, reading in the train from Dover of the great Japanese sea victory at Tsushima. I was in high good humor. The very next day happened to be Derby Day, and we went to see the race.

I was a little fortunate in finding a vacancy at Harrow, for I was slightly above the usual age for entry, being fifteen. My family went to the Continent, and after some months they returned to India.

Never before had I been left among strangers all by myself, and I felt lonely and homesick, but not for long. I managed to fit in to some extent in the life at school, and work and play kept me busy. I was never an exact fit. Always I had a feeling that I was not one of them, and the others must have felt the same way about me. I was left a little to myself. But on the whole I took my full share in the games, without in any way shining at them, and it was, I believe, recognized that I was no shirker.

I was put, to begin with, in a low form because of my small knowledge of Latin, but I was pushed higher up soon. In many subjects probably, and especially in general knowledge, I was in advance of those of my age. My interests were certainly wider, and I read both books and newspapers more than most of my fellow students. I remember writing to my father how dull most of the English boys were as they could talk about nothing but their games. But there were exceptions, especially when I reached the upper forms.

I was greatly interested in the General Election, which took place, as far as I remember, at the end of 1905 and which ended in a great Liberal victory. Early in 1906 our form master asked us about the new Government, and, much to his surprise, I was the only boy in his form who could give him much information on the subject.

Apart from politics another subject that fascinated me was the early growth of aviation. Those were the days of the Wright Brothers and Santos-Dumont (to be followed soon by Farman, Latham, and Blériot), and I wrote to father from Harrow, in my enthusiasm, that soon I might be able to pay him a week-end visit in India by air.

There were four or five Indian boys at Harrow in my time. I seldom came across those at other houses, but in our own house—the Headmaster's—we had one of the sons of the Gaekwar of Baroda. He was much senior to me and was popular because of his cricket. He left soon after my arrival. Later came the eldest son of the Maharaja of Kapurthala, Paramjit Singh, now the Tikka Sahib. He was a complete misfit and was unhappy and could not mix at all with the other boys, who often made fun of him and his ways. This irritated him greatly, and sometimes he used to tell them what he would do to them if they came to Kapurthala. Needless to say, this did not improve matters for him. He had previously spent some time in France and could speak French fluently, but oddly enough, such were the methods of teaching foreign languages in English public schools, that this hardly helped him in the French classes.

A curious incident took place once when, in the middle of the night, the housemaster suddenly visited our rooms and made a thorough search all over the house. We learned that Paramjit Singh had lost his beautiful gold-mounted cane. The search was not successful. Two or three days later the Eton and Harrow match took place at Lord's, and immediately afterward the cane was discovered in the owner's room. Evidently someone had used it at Lord's and then returned it.

There were a few Jews in our house and in other houses. They got on fairly well but there was always a background of anti-Semitic feeling. They were the "damned Jews," and soon, almost unconsciously,

31

I began to think that it was the proper thing to have this feeling. I never really felt anti-Semitic in the least, and, in later years, I had many good friends among the Jews.

I got used to Harrow and liked the place, and yet somehow I began to feel that I was outgrowing it. The university attracted me. Right through the years of 1906 and 1907 news from India had been agitating me. I got meager enough accounts from the English papers; but even that little showed that big events were happening at home. There were deportations, and Bengal seemed to be in an uproar, and Tilak's[1] name was often flashed from Poona, and there was Swadeshi[2] and boycott. All this stirred me tremendously; but there was not a soul in Harrow to whom I could talk about it. During the holidays I met some of my cousins or other Indian friends and then had a chance of relieving my mind.

A prize I got for good work at school was one of G. M. Trevelyan's Garibaldi books. This fascinated me, and soon I obtained the other two volumes of the series and studied the whole Garibaldi story in them carefully. Visions of similar deeds in India came before me, of a gallant fight for freedom, and in my mind India and Italy got strangely mixed together. Harrow seemed a rather small and restricted place for these ideas, and I wanted to go to the wider sphere of the university. So I induced father to agree to this and left Harrow after only two years' stay, which was much less than the usual period.

I was leaving Harrow because I wanted to do so myself, and yet, I well remember, that when the time came to part I felt unhappy and tears came to my eyes. I had grown rather fond of the place, and my departure for good put an end to one period in my life. And yet, I wonder, how far I was really sorry at leaving Harrow. Was it not partly a feeling that I ought to be unhappy because Harrow tradition and song demanded it? I was susceptible to these traditions, for I had deliberately not resisted them so as to be in harmony with the place.

Cambridge, Trinity College, the beginning of October 1907, my age seventeen, or rather approaching eighteen. I felt elated at being an undergraduate with a great deal of freedom, compared to school, to do what I chose. I had got out of the shackles of boyhood and felt at last that I could claim to be a grown-up. With a self-conscious air

[1] One of the great early Nationalist leaders.—Ed.
[2] Meaning literally, "of one's own country"; thus, the encouragement of Indian trade and industry, associated with the boycotting of British products.—Ed.

I wandered about the big courts and narrow streets of Cambridge, delighted to meet a person I knew.

Three years I was at Cambridge, three quiet years with little of disturbance in them, moving slowly on like the sluggish Cam. They were pleasant years, with many friends and some work and some play and a gradual widening of the intellectual horizon. I took the natural sciences tripos, my subjects being chemistry, geology, and botany, but my interests were not confined to these. Many of the people I met at Cambridge or during the vacations in London or elsewhere talked learnedly about books and literature and history and politics and economics. I felt a little at sea at first in this semihighbrow talk, but I read a few books and soon got the hang of it and could at least keep my end up and not betray too great an ignorance on any of the usual subjects. So we discussed Nietzsche (he was all the rage in Cambridge then) and Bernard Shaw's prefaces and the latest book by Lowes Dickinson. We considered ourselves very sophisticated and talked of sex and morality in a superior way, referring casually to Ivan Block, Havelock Ellis, Kraft Ebbing, or Otto Weininger. We felt that we knew about as much of the theory of the subject as anyone who was not a specialist need know.

As a matter of fact, in spite of our brave talk, most of us were rather timid where sex was concerned. At any rate I was so, and my knowledge for many years, till after I had left Cambridge, remained confined to theory. Why this was so it is a little difficult to say. Most of us were strongly attracted by sex, and I doubt if any of us attached any idea of sin to it. Certainly I did not; there was no religious inhibition. We talked of its being amoral, neither moral nor immoral. Yet in spite of all this a certain shyness kept me away, as well as a distaste for the usual methods adopted. For I was in those days definitely a shy lad, perhaps because of my lonely childhood.

My general attitude to life at the time was a vague kind of Cyrenaicism, partly natural to youth, partly the influence of Oscar Wilde and Walter Pater. It is easy and gratifying to give a long Greek name to the desire for a soft life and pleasant experiences. But there was something more in it than that, for I was not particularly attracted to a soft life. Not having the religious temper and disliking the repressions of religion, it was natural for me to seek some other standard. I was superficial and did not go deep down into anything. And so the aesthetic side of life appealed to me, and the idea of going through life worthily, not indulging it in the vulgar way, but still making the most of it and living a full and many-sided life attracted me. I enjoyed life, and I refused to see why I should consider it a thing of sin. At the same time risk and adventure fascinated me; I was always, like my father, a bit of a gambler, at first with money and then for higher stakes, with the bigger issues of life. Indian politics in 1907 and 1908 were in a state of upheaval, and I wanted to play a brave part in them, and this was not likely to lead to a soft life. All these mixed and sometimes conflicting desires led to a medley in my mind. Vague and confused it was, but I did not worry, for the time for any decision was yet far distant. Meanwhile, life was pleasant, both physically and intellectually, fresh horizons were ever coming into sight, there was so much to be done, so much to be seen, so many fresh avenues to explore. And we would sit by the fireside in the long winter evenings and talk and discuss unhurriedly deep into the night till the dying fire drove us shivering to our beds. And sometimes, during our discussions, our voices would lose their even tenor and would grow loud and excited in heated argument. But it was all make-believe. We played with the problems of human life in a mock-serious way, for they had not become real problems for us yet, and we had not been caught in the coils of the world's affairs. It was the prewar world of the early twentieth century. Soon this world was to die, yielding place to another, full of death and destruction and anguish and heart-sickness for the world s youth. But the veil of the future hid this, and we saw around us an assured and advancing order of things, and this was pleasant for those who could afford it.

I write of Cyrenaicism and the like and of various ideas that influ enced me then. But it would be wrong to imagine that I thought clearly on these subjects then or even that I thought it necessary to try to be clear and definite about them. They were just vague fancies that floated in my mind and in this process left their impress in a greater or less degree. I did not worry myself at all about these speculations. Work and games and amusements filled my life, and the only thing that disturbed me sometimes was the political struggle in India. Among the books that influenced me politically at Cambridge was Meredith Townsend's *Asia and Europe*.

From 1907 onward for several years India was seething with unrest and trouble. For the first time since the Revolt of 1857, India was showing fight and not submitting tamely to foreign rule. News of Tilak's activities and his conviction, of Aravindo Ghose and the way the masses of Bengal were taking the Swadeshi and boycott pledge stirred all of us Indians in England. Almost without an exception we were Tilakites or Extremists, as the new party was called in India.

The Indians in Cambridge had a society called the "Majlis." We discussed political problems there often but in somewhat unreal debates. More effort was spent in copying parliamentary and the University Union style and mannerisms than in grappling with the subject. Frequently I went to the Majlis, but during my three years I hardly spoke there. I could not get over my shyness and diffidence. This same difficulty pursued me in my college debating society, "The Magpie and Stump," where there was a rule that a member not speaking for a whole term had to pay a fine. Often I paid the fine.

I remember Edwin Montagu, who later became Secretary of State for India, often visiting "The Magpie and Stump." He was an old Trinity man and was then Member of Parliament for Cambridge. It was from him that I first heard the modern definition of faith: to believe in something which your reason tells you cannot be true, for, if your reason approved of it, there could be no question of blind faith. I was influenced by my scientific studies in the university and had some of the assurance which science then possessed. For the science of the nineteenth and the early twentieth centuries, unlike that of today, was very sure of itself and the world.

In the Majlis and in private talks Indian students often used the most extreme language when discussing Indian politics. They even talked in terms of admiration of the acts of violence that were then beginning in Bengal. Later I was to find that these very persons were to become members of the Indian Civil Service, High Court judges, very staid and sober lawyers, and the like. Few of these parlor firebrands took any effective part in Indian political movements subsequently.

In London there was the student center opened by the India Office. This was universally regarded by Indians, with a great deal of justification, as a device to spy on Indian students. Many Indians, however, had to put up with it, whether they wanted to or not, as it became almost impossible to enter a university without its recommendation.

The political situation in India [3] had drawn my father into more

[3] India is divided into two great parts: British India, where the British Government, through its viceroy, or governor general, exercises virtually supreme authority; and the Indian States and Agencies, which are governed by Indian rulers owing a limited responsibility to the viceroy. British India consists of a number of provinces: Ajmer-Merwara, Andaman and Nicobar Islands, Assam, Baluchistan, Bengal, Behar, Bombay, Central Provinces and Berar, Coorg, Delhi, Madras, Laccadive Islands, Northwest Frontier Province, Orissa, Punjab, Sind, and United Provinces of Agra and Oudh. The largest

active politics, and I was pleased at this although I did not agree with his politics. He had, naturally enough, joined the Moderates, whom he knew and many of whom were his colleagues in his profession. He presided over a provincial conference in his province and took up a strong line against the Extremists of Bengal and Maharashtra. He also became president of the United Provinces Provincial Congress Committee. He was present at Surat in 1907 when the Congress broke up in disorder and later emerged as a purely moderate group.

Soon after Surat, H. W. Nevinson stopped with him at Allahabad as his guest for a while and, in his book on India, he referred to father as being "moderate in everything except his generosity." This was a very wrong estimate, for father was never moderate in anything except his politics, and step by step his nature drove him from even that remnant of moderation. A man of strong feelings, strong passions, tremendous pride, and great strength of will, he was very far from the moderate type. And yet in 1907 and 1908 and for some years afterward, he was undoubtedly a moderate of Moderates, and he was bitter against the Extremists, though I believe he admired Tilak.

Why was this so? It was natural for him with his grounding in law and constitutionalism to take a lawyer's and a constitutional view of politics. His clear thinking led him to see that hard and extreme words lead nowhere unless they are followed by action appropriate to the language. He saw no effective action in prospect. The Swadeshi and boycott movements did not seem to him to carry matters far. And then the background of these movements was a religious nationalism which was alien to his nature. He did not look back to a revival in India of ancient times. He had no sympathy or understanding of them and utterly disliked many old social customs, caste and the like, which he considered reactionary. He looked to the West and felt greatly attracted by Western progress, and thought that this could come through an association with England.

Socially, the Indian national revival in 1907 was definitely reactionary. Inevitably, a new nationalism in India, as elsewhere in the East, was a religious nationalism. The Moderates thus represented a more advanced social outlook, but they were a mere handful on the top out of touch with the masses. They did not think much in terms of eco-

---

of the Indian States and Agencies are: Assam States, Baluchistan States, Central India Agency, Eastern States, Gujarat States and Baroda, Gwalior, Hyderabad, Jammu and Kashmir, Kolhapur and Deccan States, Madras States, Mysore, Northwest Frontier Agencies, Punjab States, Rajputana, Sikkim, and Western India States.—Ed.

nomics, except in terms of the new upper middle class which they partly represented and which wanted room for expansion. They advocated also petty social reforms to weaken caste and do away with old social customs which hindered growth.

Having cast his lot with the Moderates, father took an aggressive line. Most of the Extremists, apart from a few leaders in Bengal and Poona, were young men, and it irritated him to find that these youngsters dared to go their own way. Impatient and intolerant of opposition, and not suffering people whom he considered fools, he gladly pitched into them and hit out whenever he could. I remember, I think it was after I left Cambridge, reading an article of his which annoyed me greatly. I wrote him rather an impertinent letter in which I suggested that no doubt the British Government was greatly pleased with his political activities. This was just the kind of suggestion which would make him wild, and he was very angry. He almost thought of asking me to return from England immediately.

During my stay at Cambridge the question had arisen as to what career I should take up. For a little while the Indian Civil Service was contemplated; there was a glamour about it still in those days. But this idea was dropped as neither my father nor I was keen on it. The principal reason, I think, was that I was still under age for it and if I was to appear for it I would have to stay three to four years more after taking my degree. I was twenty when I took my degree at Cambridge, and the age limit for the Indian Civil Service in those days was twenty-two to twenty-four. A successful candidate had to spend an extra year in England. My people were a little tired of my long stay in England and wanted me back soon. Another reason which weighed with father was that in case I was appointed to the Indian Civil Service I would be posted in various distant places far from home. Both father and mother wanted me near them after my long absence. So the die was cast in favor of the paternal profession, the Bar, and I joined the Inner Temple.

It is curious that, in spite of my growing extremism in politics, I did not then view with any strong disfavor the idea of joining the Indian Civil Service and thus becoming a cog in the British Government's administrative machine in India. Such an idea in later years would have been repellent to me.

I left Cambridge after taking my degree in 1910. I was only moder- ately successful in my science tripos examination, obtaining second class honors. For the next two years I hovered about London. My law studies did not take up much time, and I got through the Bar examinations, one after the other, with neither glory nor ignominy. For the rest I simply drifted, doing some general reading, vaguely attracted to the Fabians and socialistic ideas, and interested in the political movements of the day. Ireland and the woman suffrage movement interested me especially. I remember also how, during a visit to Ireland in the summer of 1910, the early beginnings of Sinn Fein had attracted me.

I came across some old Harrow friends and developed expensive habits in their company. Often I exceeded the handsome allowance that father made me, and he was greatly worried on my account, fearing that I was rapidly going to the devil. But as a matter of fact I was not doing anything so notable. I was merely trying to ape to some extent the prosperous but somewhat empty-headed Englishman who is called a "man about town." This soft and pointless existence, needless to say, did not improve me in any way. My early enthusiasms began to tone down, and the only thing that seemed to go up was my conceit.

During my vacations I had sometimes traveled on the Continent. In the summer of 1909 my father and I happened to be in Berlin when Count Zeppelin arrived flying in his new airship from Friedrichshafen on Lake Constance. I believe that was his first long flight, and the occasion was celebrated by a huge demonstration and a formal welcome by the Kaiser. A vast multitude, estimated at between one and two millions, gathered in the Tempelhof Field in Berlin, and the Zeppelin arrived on time and circled gracefully above us. The Hotel Adlon presented all its residents that day with a fine picture of Count Zeppelin, and I have still got that picture.

About two months later we saw in Paris the first airplane to fly all over the city and to circle round the Eiffel Tower. The aviator's name was, I think, Comte de Lambert. Eighteen years later I was again in Paris when Lindbergh came like a shining arrow from across the Atlantic.

I had a narrow escape once in Norway, where I had gone on a pleasure cruise soon after taking my degree at Cambridge in 1910. We were tramping across the mountainous country. Hot and weary, we reached our destination, a little hotel, and demanded baths. Such a thing had not been heard of there, and there was no provision for it in the building. We were told, however, that we could wash ourselves in a neighboring stream. So, armed with table napkins or perhaps small face towels, which the hotel generously gave, two of us, a young

Englishman and I, went to this roaring torrent which was coming from a glacier near by. I entered the water; it was not deep, but it was freezing, and the bottom was terribly slippery. I slipped and fell, and the ice-cold water numbed me and made me lose all sensation or power of controlling my limbs. I could not regain my foothold and was swept rapidly along by the torrent. My companion, the Englishman, however, managed to get out, and he ran along the side and ultimately, succeeding in catching my leg, dragged me out. Later we realized the danger we were in, for about two or three hundred yards ahead of us this mountain torrent tumbled over an enormous precipice, forming a waterfall which was one of the sights of the place.

In the summer of 1912 I was called to the Bar, and in the autumn of that year I returned to India finally after a stay of over seven years in England. Twice, in between, I had gone home during my holidays. But now I returned for good, and I am afraid, as I landed at Bombay, I was a bit of a prig with little to commend me.

## VII

# BACK HOME AND WARTIME POLITICS IN INDIA

Toward the end of 1912 India was, politically, very dull. Tilak was in jail, the Extremists had been sat upon and were lying low without any effective leadership, Bengal was quiet after the unsettling of the partition of the province, and the Moderates had been effectively "rallied" to the Minto-Morley scheme of councils.[1] There was some interest in Indians overseas, especially in the condition of Indians in South Africa. The Congress was a moderate group, meeting annually, passing some feeble resolutions, and attracting little attention.

I attended the Bankipore Congress as a delegate during Christmas, 1912. It was very much an English-knowing upper-class affair where morning coats and well-pressed trousers were greatly in evidence. Essentially it was a social gathering with no political excitement or tension. Gokhale, fresh from South Africa, attended it and was the outstanding person of the session. High-strung, full of earnestness and a nervous energy, he seemed to be one of the few persons present who

[1] A "reform" put into effect in 1907-1909, increasing Indian representation in various advisory organs of government.—Ed.

took politics and public affairs seriously and felt deeply about them. I was impressed by him.

I took to the law and joined the High Court. The work interested me to a certain extent. The early months after my return from Europe were pleasant. I was glad to be back home and to pick up old threads. But gradually the life I led, in common with most others of my kind, began to lose all its freshness, and I felt that I was being engulfed in a dull routine of a pointless and futile existence. I suppose my mongrel, or at least mixed, education was responsible for this feeling of dissatisfaction with my surroundings. The habits and the ideas that had grown in me during my seven years in England did not fit in with things as I found them. Fortunately my home atmosphere was fairly congenial, and that was some help, but it was not enough. For the rest there was the Bar Library and the club, and the same people were to be found in both, discussing the same old topics, usually connected with the legal profession, over and over again. Decidedly the atmosphere was not intellectually stimulating, and a sense of the utter insipidity of life grew upon me. There were not even worth-while amusements or diversions.

The official and Service atmosphere invaded and set the tone for almost all Indian middle-class life, especially the English-knowing intelligentsia, except to some extent in cities like Calcutta and Bombay. Professional men, lawyers, doctors, and others succumbed to it, and even the academic halls of the semiofficial universities were full of it. All these people lived in a world apart, cut off from the masses and even the lower middle class. Politics was confined to this upper stratum. The nationalist movement in Bengal from 1906 onward had for the first time shaken this up and infused a new life in the Bengal lower middle class and to a small extent even the masses. This process was to grow rapidly in later years under Gandhiji's[2] leadership, but a

[2] I have referred to Mr. Gandhi or Mahatma Gandhi as "Gandhiji" throughout these pages as he himself prefers this to the addition of "Mahatma" to his name. But I have seen some extraordinary explanations of this "ji" in books and articles by English writers. Some have imagined that it is a term of endearment—Gandhiji meaning "dear little Gandhi"! This is perfectly absurd and shows colossal ignorance of Indian life. "Ji" is one of the commonest additions to a name in India, being applied indiscriminatingly to all kinds of people and to men, women, boys, girls, and children. It conveys an idea of respect, something equivalent to Mr., Mrs., or Miss. Hindustani is rich in courtly phrases and prefixes and suffixes to names and honorific titles. "Ji" is the simplest of these and the least formal of them, though perfectly correct. I learn from my brother-in-law, Ranjit S. Pandit, that this "ji" has a long and honorable ancestry. It is derived from the Sanskrit *Arya*, meaning a gentleman or noble-born (not the Nazi meaning of Aryan!). This *arya* became in Prakit *ajja*, and this led to the simple "ji."

nationalist struggle though life-giving is a narrow creed and absorbs too much energy and attention to allow of other activities.

I felt, therefore, dissatisfied with life in those early years after my return from England. My profession did not fill me with a whole-hearted enthusiasm. Politics, which to me meant aggressive nationalist activity against foreign rule, offered no scope for this. I joined the Congress and took part in its occasional meetings. When a special occasion arose, like the agitation against the Fiji indenture system for Indian workers, or the South African Indian question, I threw myself into it with energy and worked hard. But these were only temporary occupations.

I indulged in some diversions like shikar, but I had no special aptitude or inclination for it. I liked the outings and the jungle and cared little for the killing. Indeed my reputation was a singularly bloodless one, although I once succeeded, more or less by a fluke, in killing a bear in Kashmir. An incident with a little antelope damped even the little ardor that I possessed for shikar. This harmless little animal fell down at my feet, wounded to death, and looked up at me with its great big eyes full of tears. Those eyes have often haunted me since.

I was attracted in those early years to Mr. Gokhale's Servants of India Society. I never thought of joining it, partly because its politics were too moderate for me, and partly because I had no intention then of giving up my profession. But I had a great admiration for the members of the society, who had devoted themselves for a bare pittance to the country's service. Here at least, I thought, was straight and single-minded and continuous work even though this might not be on wholly right lines.

The World War absorbed our attention. It was far off and did not at first affect our lives much, and India never felt the full horror of it. Politics petered out and sank into insignificance. The Defense of India Act (the equivalent of the British Defense of the Realm Act) held the country in its grip. From the second year onward news of conspiracies and shootings came to us, and of press-gang methods to enroll recruits in the Punjab.

There was little sympathy with the British in spite of loud professions of loyalty. Moderate and Extremists alike learned with satisfaction of German victories. There was no love for Germany, of course, only the desire to see our own rulers humbled. It was the weak and helpless man's idea of vicarious revenge. I suppose most of us viewed the struggle with mixed feelings. Of all the nations involved my sympathies were probably most with France. The ceaseless and unabashed propaganda on behalf of the Allies had some effect, although we tried to discount it greatly.

Gradually political life grew again. Lokamanya Tilak came out of prison, and home rule leagues were started by him and Mrs. Besant. I joined both, but I worked especially for Mrs. Besant's league. Mrs. Besant began to play an ever-increasing part in Indian politics. The annual sessions of the Congress became a little more exciting and the Moslem League began to march with the Congress. The atmosphere became electric, and most of us young men felt exhilarated and expected big things in the near future. Mrs. Besant's internment added greatly to the excitement of the intelligentsia and vitalized the home rule movement all over the country. It stirred even the older generation, including many of the Moderate leaders. The home rule leagues were attracting not only all the old Extremists who had been kept out of the Congress since 1907 but large numbers of newcomers from the middle classes. They did not touch the masses.

Mrs. Besant's internment also resulted in my father and other Moderate leaders joining the Home Rule League. Some months later most of these Moderate members resigned from the league. My father remained in it and became the president of the Allahabad branch.

Gradually my father had been drifting away from the orthodox Moderate position. His nature rebelled against too much submission and appeal to an authority which ignored us and treated us disdainfully. But the old Extremist leaders did not attract him; their language and methods jarred upon him. The episode of Mrs. Besant's internment and subsequent events influenced him considerably, but still he hesitated before definitely committing himself to a forward line. Often he used to say in those days that moderate tactics were no good, but nothing effective could be done till some solution for the Hindu-Moslem question was found. If this was found, then he promised to go ahead with the youngest of us. The adoption by the Congress at Lucknow in 1916 of the Joint Congress-League Scheme, which had been drawn up at a meeting of the All-India Congress Committee in our house, pleased him greatly as it opened the way to a joint effort, and he was prepared to go ahead then even at the cost of breaking with his old colleagues of the Moderate group.

My own political and public activities in the early war years were modest, and I kept away from addressing public gatherings. I was still diffident and terrified of public speaking. Partly also I felt that public speeches should not be in English, and I doubted my capacity to speak at any length in Hindustani. I remember a little incident when I was induced to deliver my first public speech in Allahabad. Probably it was in 1915, but I am not clear about dates and am rather mixed up about the order of events. The occasion was a protest meeting against a new act muzzling the press. I spoke briefly and in English. As soon as the meeting was over, Dr. Tej Bahadur Sapru, to my great embarrassment, embraced and kissed me in public on the dais. This was not because of what I had said or how I had said it. His effusive joy was caused by the mere fact that I had spoken in public and thus a new recruit had been obtained for public work, for this work consisted in those days practically of speaking only.

At home, in those early years, political questions were not peaceful subjects for discussion, and references to them, which were frequent, immediately produced a tense atmosphere. Father had been closely watching my growing drift toward Extremism, my continual criticism of the politics of talk, and my insistent demand for action. What action it should be was not clear, and sometimes father imagined that I was heading straight for the violent courses adopted by some of the young men of Bengal. This worried him very much. As a matter of fact I was not attracted that way, but the idea that we must not tamely submit to existing conditions and that something must be done began to obsess me more and more. Successful action, from the national point of view, did not seem to be at all easy, but I felt that both individual and national honor demanded a more aggressive and fighting attitude to foreign rule. Father himself was dissatisfied with the Moderate philosophy, and a mental conflict was going on inside him. He was too obstinate to change from one position to another until he was absolutely convinced that there was no other way. Each step forward meant for him a hard and bitter tussle in his mind, and, when the step was taken after that struggle with part of himself, there was no going back. He had not taken it in a fit of enthusiasm but as a result of intellectual conviction, and when he had done so, all his pride prevented him from looking back.

The outward change in his politics came about the time of Mrs. Besant's internment, and from that time onward step by step he went ahead, leaving his old Moderate colleagues far behind, till the tragic happenings in the Punjab in 1919 finally led him to cut adrift from his old life and his profession and throw in his lot with the new movement started by Gandhiji.

But that was still to be, and from 1915 to 1917 he was still unsure of what to do, and the doubts in him, added to his worries about me, did not make him a peaceful talker on the public issues of the day. Often enough our talks ended abruptly by his losing his temper.

My first meeting with Gandhiji was about the time of the Lucknow Congress during Christmas, 1916. All of us admired him for his heroic fight in South Africa, but he seemed very distant and different and unpolitical to many of us young men. He refused to take part in Congress or national politics then and confined himself to the South African Indian question. Soon afterward his adventures and victory in Champaran, on behalf of the tenants of the planters, filled us with enthusiasm. We saw that he was prepared to apply his methods in India also, and they promised success.

I remember being moved also, in those days after the Lucknow Congress, by a number of eloquent speeches delivered by Sarojini Naidu in Allahabad. It was all nationalism and patriotism, and I was a pure nationalist, my vague socialist ideas of college days having sunk into the background. Roger Casement's wonderful speech at his trial in 1916 seemed to point out exactly how a member of a subject nation should feel. The Easter Week rising in Ireland by its very failure attracted, for was that not true courage which mocked at almost certain failure and proclaimed to the world that no physical might could crush the invincible spirit of a nation?

Such were my thoughts then, and yet fresh reading was again stirring the embers of socialistic ideas in my head. They were vague ideas, more humanitarian and utopian than scientific. A favorite writer of mine during the war years and after was Bertrand Russell.

These thoughts and desires produced a growing conflict within me and a dissatisfaction with my profession of the law. I carried on with it because there was nothing else to be done, but I felt more and more that it was not possible to reconcile public work, especially of the aggressive type which appealed to me, with the lawyer's job. It was not a question of principle but of time and energy. Sir Rash Behary Ghosh, the eminent Calcutta lawyer, who for some unknown reason took a fancy to me, gave me a lot of good advice as to how to get on in the profession. He especially advised me to write a book on a legal subject of my choice, as he said that this was the best way for a junior to train himself. He offered to help me with ideas in the writing of it

44

and to revise it. But all his well-meant interest in my legal career was
in vain, and few things could be more distasteful to me than to spend
my time and energy in writing legal books.


VIII

# MY WEDDING AND AN ADVENTURE
# IN THE HIMALAYAS

MY MARRIAGE TOOK place in 1916 in the city of Delhi. It was on the
*Vasanta Panchami* day which heralds the coming of spring in India.
That summer we spent some months in Kashmir. I left my family in
the valley and, together with a cousin of mine, wandered for several
weeks in the mountains and went up the Ladakh road.

This was my first experience of the narrow and lonely valleys, high
up in the world, which lead to the Tibetan plateau. From the top of
the Zoji-la Pass we saw the rich verdant mountain sides below us on
one side and the bare bleak rock on the other. We went up and up the
narrow valley bottom flanked on each side by mountains, with the
snow-covered tops gleaming on one side and little glaciers creeping
down to meet us. The wind was cold and bitter, but the sun was warm
in the daytime, and the air was so clear that often we were misled
about the distance of objects, thinking them much nearer than they
actually were. The loneliness grew; there were not even trees or vegetation to keep us company—only the bare rock and the snow and ice
and, sometimes, very welcome flowers. Yet I found a strange satisfaction in these wild and desolate haunts of nature; I was full of energy
and a feeling of exaltation.

I had an exciting experience during this visit. At one place on our
march beyond the Zoji-la Pass—I think it was called Matayan—we
were told that the cave of Amaranath was only eight miles away. It
was true that an enormous mountain all covered with ice and snow lay
in between and had to be crossed, but what did that matter? Eight
miles seemed so little. In our enthusiasm and inexperience we decided
to make the attempt. So we left our camp (which was situated at
about 11,500 feet altitude) and with a small party went up the mountain. We had a local shepherd for a guide.

We crossed and climbed several glaciers, roping ourselves up, and our troubles increased, and breathing became a little difficult. Some of our porters, lightly laden as they were, began to bring up blood. It began to snow, and the glaciers became terribly slippery; we were fagged out, and every step meant a special effort. But still we persisted in our foolhardy attempt. We had left our camp at four in the morning, and after twelve hours' almost continuous climbing we were rewarded by the sight of a huge ice field. This was a magnificent sight, surrounded as it was by snow peaks, like a diadem or an amphitheater of the gods. But fresh snow and mists soon hid the sight from us. I do not know what our altitude was, but I think it must have been about 15,000 to 16,000 feet, as we were considerably higher than the cave of Amaranath. We had now to cross this ice field, a distance probably of half a mile, and then go down on the other side to the cave. We thought that as the climbing was over, our principal difficulties had also been surmounted, and so, very tired but in good humor, we began this stage of the journey. It was a tricky business as there were many crevasses and the fresh snow often covered a dangerous spot. It was this fresh snow that almost proved to be my undoing, for, as I stepped upon it, it gave way, and down I went into a huge and yawning crevasse. It was a tremendous fissure, and anything that went right down it could be assured of safe keeping and preservation for some geological ages. But the rope held, and I clung to the side of the crevasse and was pulled out. We were shaken up by this, but still we persisted in going on. The crevasses, however, increased in number and width, and we had no equipment or means of crossing some of them. And so at last we turned back, weary and disappointed, and the cave of Amaranath remained unvisited.

The higher valleys and mountains of Kashmir fascinated me so much that I resolved to come back again soon. I made many a plan and worked out many a tour, and one, the very thought of which filled me with delight, was a visit to Manasarovar, the wonder lake of Tibet, and snow-covered Kailas near by. That was eighteen years ago, and I am still as far as ever from Kailas and Manasarovar. I have not even been to visit Kashmir again, much as I have longed to, and ever more and more I have got entangled in the coils of politics and public affairs. Instead of going up mountains or crossing the seas, I have to satisfy my wanderlust by coming to prison. But still I plan, for that is a joy that no one can deny even in prison, and besides, what else can one do in prison? And I dream of the day when I shall wander about the Himalayas and cross them to reach that lake and mountain of my desire. But meanwhile the sands of life run on, and youth passes into middle age, and that will give place to something worse, and sometimes I think that I may grow too old to reach Kailas and Manasarovar. But the journey is always worth the making even though the end may not be in sight.

## IX

## THE COMING OF GANDHI

THE END OF the World War found India in a state of suppressed excitement. Industrialization had spread, and the capitalist class had grown in wealth and power. This handful at the top had prospered and were greedy for more power and opportunity to invest their savings and add to their wealth. The great majority, however, were not so fortunate and looked forward to a lightening of the burdens that crushed them. Among the middle classes there was everywhere an expectation of great constitutional changes which would bring a large measure of self-rule and thus better their lot by opening out many fresh avenues of growth to them. Political agitation, peaceful and wholly constitutional as it was, seemed to be working itself to a head, and people talked with assurance of self-determination and self-government. Some of this unrest was visible also among the masses, especially the peasantry. In the rural areas of the Punjab the forcible methods of recruitment were still bitterly remembered, and the fierce suppression of the "Komagata Maru" people and others by conspiracy trials added to the widespread resentment. The soldiers back from active service on distant fronts were no longer the subservient robots that they used to be. They had grown mentally, and there was much discontent among them.

Among the Moslems there was anger over the treatment of Turkey and the Khilafat question, and an agitation was growing. The treaty with Turkey had not been signed yet, but the whole situation was ominous. So, while they agitated, they waited.

The dominant note all over India was one of waiting and expectation, full of hope and yet tinged with fear and anxiety. Then came the Rowlatt Bills with their drastic provisions for arrest and trial without any of the checks and formalities which the law is supposed to provide. A wave of anger greeted them all over India, and even the Moderates joined in this and opposed the measures with all their might. Indeed there was universal opposition on the part of Indians of all shades of opinion. Still the Bills were pushed through by the officials and became law, the principal concession made being to limit them to three years.

Gandhiji had passed through a serious illness early in 1919. Almost from his sick bed he begged the Viceroy not to give his consent to the Rowlatt Bills. That appeal was ignored as others had been, and then, almost against his will, Gandhiji took the leadership in his first all-India agitation. He started the *Satyagraha Sabha,* the members of which were pledged to disobey the Rowlatt Act, if it was applied to them, as well as other objectionable laws to be specified from time to time. In other words, they were to court jail openly and deliberately.

When I first read about this proposal in the newspapers, my reaction was one of tremendous relief. Here at last was a way out of the tangle, a method of action which was straight and open and possibly effective. I was afire with enthusiasm and wanted to join the *Satyagraha Sabha* immediately. I hardly thought of the consequences—law-breaking, jail-going, etc.—and if I thought of them I did not care. But suddenly my ardor was damped, and I realized that all was not plain sailing. My father was dead against this new idea. He was not in the habit of being swept away by new proposals; he thought carefully of the consequences before he took any fresh step. And the more he thought of the *Satyagraha Sabha* and its program, the less he liked it. What good would the jail-going of a number of individuals do, what pressure could it bring on the Government? Apart from these general considerations, what really moved him was the personal issue. It seemed to him preposterous that I should go to prison. The trek to prison had not then begun, and the idea was most repulsive. Father was intensely attached to his children. He was not showy in his affection, but behind his restraint there was a great love.

For many days there was this mental conflict, and because both of us felt that big issues were at stake involving a complete upsetting of our lives, we tried hard to be as considerate to each other as possible. I wanted to lessen his obvious suffering if I could, but I had no doubt in my mind that I had to go the way of *Satyagraha*. Both of us had a distressing time, and night after night I wandered about alone, tortured in mind and trying to grope my way out. Father—I discovered later —actually tried sleeping on the floor to find out what it was like, as he thought that this would be my lot in prison.

Gandhiji came to Allahabad at father's request, and they had long talks at which I was not present. As a result Gandhiji advised me not to precipitate matters or to do anything which might upset father. I was not happy at this, but other events took place in India which changed the whole situation, and the *Satyagraha Sabha* stopped its activities.

*Satyagraha* Day—all-India *hartals* and complete suspension of business—firing by the police and military at Delhi and Amritsar, and the killing of many people—mob violence in Amritsar and Ahmedabad—the massacre of Jallianwala Bagh—the long horror and terrible indignity of martial law in the Punjab. The Punjab was isolated, cut off from the rest of India; a thick veil seemed to cover it and hide it from outside eyes. There was hardly any news, and people could not go there or come out from there.

Odd individuals, who managed to escape from that inferno, were so terror-struck that they could give no clear account. Helplessly and impotently, we who were outside waited for scraps of news, and bitterness filled our hearts. Some of us wanted to go openly to the affected parts of the Punjab and defy the martial law regulations. But we were kept back, and meanwhile a big organization for relief and inquiry was set up on behalf of the Congress.

As soon as martial law was withdrawn from the principal areas and outsiders were allowed to come in, prominent Congressmen and others poured into the Punjab offering their services for relief or inquiry work. Deshbandhu Das especially took the Amritsar area under his charge, and I was deputed to accompany him there and assist him in any way he desired. That was the first occasion I had of working with him and under him, and I valued that experience very much and my admiration for him grew. Most of the evidence relating to Jallianwala Bagh and that terrible lane where human beings were made to crawl on their bellies, that subsequently appeared in the Congress Inquiry Report, was taken down in our presence. We paid numerous visits to the so-called Bagh itself and examined every bit of it carefully.

A suggestion has been made, I think by Mr. Edward Thompson, that General Dyer was under the impression that there were other exits from the Bagh and it was because of this that he continued his firing for so long. Even if that was Dyer's impression, and there were in fact some exits, that would hardly lessen his responsibility. But it seems very strange that he should have such an impression. Any person, standing on the raised ground where he stood, could have a good view of the entire space and could see how shut in it was on all sides by houses several stories high. Only on one side, for a hundred feet or so, there was no house, but a low wall about five feet high. With a murderous fire mowing them down and unable to find a way out, thousands of people rushed to this wall and tried to climb over it. The fire was then directed, it appears (both from our evidence and the innumerable bullet marks on the wall itself), toward this wall to prevent people from escaping over it. And when all was over, some of the biggest heaps of dead and wounded lay on either side of this wall.

Toward the end of that year (1919) I traveled from Amritsar to Delhi by the night train. The compartment I entered was almost full, and all the berths, except one upper one, were occupied by sleeping passengers. I took the vacant upper berth. In the morning I discovered that all my fellow passengers were military officers. They conversed with each other in loud voices which I could not help overhearing. One of them was holding forth in an aggressive and triumphant tone, and soon I discovered that he was Dyer, the hero of Jallianwala Bagh, who was describing his Amritsar experiences. He pointed out how he had the whole town at his mercy and he had felt like reducing the rebellious city to a heap of ashes, but he took pity on it and refrained. He was evidently coming back from Lahore after giving his evidence before the Hunter Committee of Inquiry. I was greatly shocked to hear his conversation and to observe his callous manner. He descended at Delhi station in pyjamas with bright pink stripes, and a dressing gown.

During the Punjab inquiry I saw a great deal of Gandhiji. Very often his proposals seemed novel to our committee, and it did not approve of them. But almost always he argued his way to their acceptance, and subsequent events showed the wisdom of his advice. Faith in his political insight grew in me.

The Punjab happenings and the inquiry into them had a profound effect on father. His whole legal and constitutional foundations were shaken by them, and his mind was gradually prepared for that change which was to come a year later. He had already moved far from his old moderate position. Dissatisfied with the leading Moderate newspaper, the *Leader* of Allahabad, he had started another daily, the *Independent,* from Allahabad early in 1919. This paper met with great success, but from the very beginning it was handicapped by quite an amazing degree of incompetence in the running of it. Almost everybody connected with it—directors, editors, managerial staff—had their share of responsibility for this. I was one of the directors, without the least experience of the job, and the troubles and the squabbles of the paper became quite a nightmare to me. Both my father and I were, however, soon dragged away to the Punjab, and during our long absence the paper deteriorated greatly and became involved in financial difficulties. It never recovered from them, and, although it had bright patches in 1920 and 1921, it began to go to pieces as soon as we went to jail. It expired finally early in 1923. This experience of newspaper proprietorship gave me a fright, and ever since I have refused to assume responsibility as a director of any newspaper. Indeed I could not do so because of my preoccupations in prison and outside.

Father presided over the Amritsar Congress during Christmas, 1919. He issued a moving appeal to the Moderate leaders or the Liberals, as they were now calling themselves, to join this session because of the new situation created by the horrors of martial law. "The lacerated heart of the Punjab" called to them, he wrote. Would they not answer that call? But they did not answer it in the way he wanted, and refused to join. Their eyes were on the new reforms that were coming as a result of the Montagu-Chelmsford recommendations. This refusal hurt father and widened the gulf between him and the Liberals.

The Amritsar Congress was the first Gandhi Congress. Lokamanya Tilak was also present and took a prominent part in the deliberations, but there could be no doubt about it that the majority of the delegates, and even more so the great crowds outside, looked to Gandhi for leadership. The slogan *Mahatma Gandhi ki jai* began to dominate the Indian political horizon. The Ali brothers, recently discharged from internment, immediately joined the Congress, and the national movement began to take a new shape and develop a new orientation.

M. Mohamad Ali went off soon on a Khilafat deputation to Europe. In India the Khilafat Committee came more and more under Gandhiji's influence and began to flirt with his ideas of nonviolent noncooperation. I remember one of the earliest meetings of the Khilafat leaders and Moulvies and Ulemas in Delhi in January 1920. A Khilafat deputation was going to wait on the Viceroy, and Gandhiji was to join it. Before he reached Delhi, however, a draft of the proposed address was, according to custom, sent to the Viceroy. When Gandhiji arrived and read this draft, he strongly disapproved of it and even said that he could not be a party to the deputation if this draft was not materially altered. His objection was that the draft was vague and wordy, and there was no clear indication in it of the absolute minimum demands which the Moslems must have. He said that this was not fair to the

Viceroy and the British Government, or to the people, or to themselves. They must not make exaggerated demands which they were not going to press, but should state the minimum clearly and without possibility of doubt, and stand by it to the death. If they were serious, this was the only right and honorable course to adopt.

This argument was a novel one in political or other circles in India. We were used to vague exaggerations and flowery language, and always there was an idea of a bargain in our minds. Gandhiji, however, carried his point; and he wrote to the private secretary of the Viceroy, pointing out the defects and vagueness of the draft address sent, and forwarding a few additional paragraphs to be added to it. These paragraphs gave the minimum demands. The Viceroy's reply was interesting. He refused to accept the new paragraphs and said that the previous draft was, in his opinion, quite proper. Gandhiji felt that this correspondence had made his own position and that of the Khilafat Committee clear, and so he joined the deputation after all.

It was obvious that the Government were not going to accept the demands of the Khilafat Committee, and a struggle was therefore bound to come. There were long talks with the Moulvies and the Ulemas, and nonviolence and nonco-operation were discussed, especially nonviolence. Gandhiji told them that he was theirs to command, but on the definite understanding that they accepted nonviolence with all its implications. There was to be no weakening on that, no temporizing, no mental reservations. It was not easy for the Moulvies to grasp this idea, but they agreed, making it clear that they did so as a policy only and not as a creed, for their religion did not prohibit the use of violence in a righteous cause.

The political and the Khilafat movements developed side by side during 1920, both going in the same direction and eventually joining hands with the adoption by the Congress of Gandhiji's nonviolent nonco-operation. The Khilafat Committee adopted this program first, and August 1 was fixed for the commencement of the campaign.

Earlier in the year a Moslem meeting (I think it was the Council of the Moslem League) was held in Allahabad to consider this program. The meeting took place in Syed Raza Ali's house. M. Mohamad Ali was still in Europe, but M. Shaukat Ali was present. I remember that meeting because it thoroughly disappointed me. Shaukat Ali was, of course, full of enthusiasm; but almost all the others looked thoroughly unhappy and uncomfortable. They did not have the courage to disagree, and yet they obviously had no intention of doing anything rash.

Were these the people to lead a revolutionary movement, I thought, and to challenge the British Empire? Gandhiji addressed them, and after hearing him they looked even more frightened than before. He spoke well in his best dictatorial vein. He was humble but also clear-cut and hard as a diamond, pleasant and soft-spoken but inflexible and terribly earnest. His eyes were mild and deep, yet out of them blazed a fierce energy and determination. This is going to be a great struggle, he said, with a very powerful adversary. If you want to take it up, you must be prepared to lose everything, and you must subject yourself to the strictest nonviolence and discipline. When war is declared, martial law prevails, and in our nonviolent struggle there will also have to be dictatorship and martial law on our side if we are to win. You have every right to kick me out, to demand my head, or to punish me whenever and howsoever you choose. But, so long as you choose to keep me as your leader, you must accept my conditions, you must accept dictatorship and the discipline of martial law. But that dictatorship will always be subject to your good will and to your acceptance and to your co-operation. The moment you have had enough of me, throw me out, trample upon me, and I shall not complain.

Something to this effect he said, and these military analogies and the unyielding earnestness of the man made the flesh of most of his hearers creep. But Shaukat Ali was there to keep the waverers up to the mark; and, when the time for voting came, the great majority of them quietly and shamefacedly voted for the proposition—for war!

As we were coming home from the meeting, I asked Gandhiji if this was the way to start a great struggle. I had expected enthusiasm, spirited language, and a flashing of eyes; instead we saw a very tame gathering of timid, middle-aged folk. And yet these people, such was the pressure of mass opinion, voted for the struggle. Of course, very few of these members of the Moslem League joined the struggle later. Many of them found a safe sanctuary in Government jobs. The Moslem League did not represent, then or later, any considerable section of Moslem opinion. It was the Khilafat Committee of 1920 that was a powerful and far more representative body, and it was this Committee that entered upon the struggle with enthusiasm.

# X

# I AM EXTERNED, AND THE CONSEQUENCES

My POLITICS HAD been those of my class, the bourgeoisie. Indeed all vocal politics then (and to a great extent even now) were those of the middle classes, and Moderate and Extremist alike represented them and, in different keys, sought their betterment. The Moderate represented especially the handful of the upper middle class who had on the whole prospered under British rule and wanted no sudden changes which might endanger their present position and interests. They had close relations with the British Government and the big landlord class. The Extremist represented also the lower ranks of the middle class. The industrial workers, their number swollen up by the war, were only locally organized in some places and had little influence. The peasantry were a blind, poverty-stricken, suffering mass, resigned to their miserable fate and sat upon and exploited by all who came in contact with them—the Government, landlords, moneylenders, petty officials, police, lawyers, priests.

In 1920 I was totally ignorant of labor conditions in factories or fields, and my political outlook was entirely bourgeois. I knew, of course, that there was terrible poverty and misery, and I felt that the first aim of a politically free India must be to tackle this problem of poverty. But political freedom, with the inevitable dominance of the middle class, seemed to me the obvious next step. I was paying a little more attention to the peasant problem since Gandhiji's agrarian movements. But my mind was full of political developments and of noncooperation, which was looming on the horizon.

Just then a new interest developed in my life which was to play an important part in later years. I was thrown, almost without any will of my own, into contact with the peasantry. This came about in a curious way.

My mother and Kamala (my wife) were both unwell, and early in May 1920 I took them up to Mussoorie. Peace negotiations were proceeding between the Afghan and British envoys (this was after the brief Afghan War in 1919 when Amanullah came to the throne) at Mussoorie, and the Afghan delegation were stopping at the same hotel. They kept to themselves, however, fed separately, and did not appear in the common rooms. I was not particularly interested in them, and for a whole month I did not see a single member of their delegation, or if I saw them I did not recognize them. Suddenly one evening I had a visit from the superintendent of police, who showed me a letter from the local government asking him to get an undertaking from me that I would not have any dealings or contacts with the Afghan delegation. This struck me as extraordinary since I had not even seen them during a month's stay and there was little chance of my doing so. The superintendent knew this, as he was closely watching the delegation, and there were literally crowds of secret service men about. But to give any undertaking went against the grain, and I told him so. He asked me to see the district magistrate, the superintendent of the Dun, and I did so. As I persisted in my refusal to give an undertaking, an order of externment was served on me, calling upon me to leave the district of Dehra Dun within twenty-four hours, which really meant within a few hours from Mussoorie. I did not like the idea of leaving my mother and wife, both of whom were ailing; and yet I did not think it right to break the order. There was no civil disobedience then. So I left Mussoorie.

My father had known Sir Harcourt Butler, who was then Governor of the United Provinces, fairly well, and he wrote to him a friendly letter saying that he was sure that he (Sir Harcourt) could not have issued such a stupid order; it must be some bright person in Simla who was responsible for it. Sir Harcourt replied that the order was quite a harmless one and Jawaharlal could easily have complied with it without any injury to his dignity. Father, in reply, disagreed with this and added that, although there was no intention of deliberately breaking the order, if my mother's or wife's health demanded it I would certainly return to Mussoorie, order or no order. As it happened, my mother's condition took a turn for the worse, and both father and I immediately started for Mussoorie. Just before starting, we received a telegram rescinding the order.

When we reached Mussoorie the next morning, the first person I noticed in the courtyard of the hotel was an Afghan who had my baby daughter in his arms! I learned that he was a minister and a member of the Afghan delegation. It transpired that immediately after my externment the Afghans had read about it in the newspapers, and they were so much interested that the head of the delegation took to sending my mother a basket of fruit and flowers every day.

As a result of the externment order from Mussoorie I spent about two weeks in Allahabad, and it was during this period that I got entangled in the *kisan* (peasant) movement. That entanglement grew

55

in later years and influenced my mental outlook greatly. I have sometimes wondered what would have happened if I had not been externed
and had not been in Allahabad just then with no other engagements.
Very probably I would have been drawn to the *kisans* anyhow, sooner
or later, but the manner of my going to them would have been different, and the effect on me might also have been different.

Early in June 1920 (so far as I can remember), about two hundred
*kisans* marched fifty miles from the interior of Partabgarh district to
Allahabad city with the intention of drawing the attention of the
prominent politicians there to their woebegone condition. They were
led by a man named Ramachandra, who himself was not a local peasant. I learned that these *kisans* were squatting on the river bank, on one
of the Jumna ghats, and, accompanied by some friends, went to see
them. They told us of the crushing exactions of the talukdars, of
inhuman treatment, and that their condition had become wholly intolerable. They begged us to accompany them back to make inquiries as
well as to protect them from the vengeance of the talukdars, who were
angry at their having come to Allahabad on this mission. They would
accept no denial and literally clung onto us. At last I promised to visit
them two days or so later.

I went there with some colleagues, and we spent three days in the
villages far from the railway and even the *pucca* road. That visit was a
revelation to me. We found the whole countryside afire with enthusiasm and full of a strange excitement. Enormous gatherings would
take place at the briefest notice by word of mouth. One village would
communicate with another, and the second with the third, and so on;
and presently whole villages would empty out, and all over the fields
there would be men and women and children on the march to the
meeting place. Or, more swiftly still, the cry of *Sita-Ram—Sita-Ra-
a-a-a-m*—would fill the air, and travel far in all directions and be
echoed back from other villages, and then people would come streaming out or even running as fast as they could. They were in miserable
rags, men and women, but their faces were full of excitement and
their eyes glistened and seemed to expect strange happenings which
would, as if by a miracle, put an end to their long misery.

They showered their affection on us and looked on us with loving
and hopeful eyes, as if we were the bearers of good tidings, the guides
who were to lead them to the promised land. Looking at them and
their misery and overflowing gratitude, I was filled with shame and
sorrow—shame at my own easygoing and comfortable life and our

56

petty politics of the city which ignored this vast multitude of semi-naked sons and daughters of India, sorrow at the degradation and overwhelming poverty of India. A new picture of India seemed to rise before me, naked, starving, crushed, and utterly miserable. And their faith in us, casual visitors from the distant city, embarrassed me and filled me with a new responsibility that frightened me.

I listened to their innumerable tales of sorrow, their crushing and ever-growing burden of rent, illegal exactions, ejectments from land and mud hut, beatings; surrounded on all sides by vultures who preyed on them—zamindar's agents, moneylenders, police; toiling all day to find what they produced was not theirs and their reward was kicks and curses and a hungry stomach. Many of those who were present were landless people who had been ejected by the landlords and had no land or hut to fall back upon. The land was rich, but the burden on it was very heavy, the holdings were small, and there were too many people after them. Taking advantage of this land hunger, the landlords, unable under the law to enhance their rents beyond a certain percentage, charged huge illegal premiums. The tenant, knowing of no other alternative, borrowed money from the moneylender and paid the premium, and then, unable to pay his debt or even the rent, was ejected and lost all he had.

This process was an old one, and the progressive pauperization of the peasantry had been going on for a long time. What had happened to bring matters to a head and rouse up the countryside? Economic conditions, of course, but these conditions were similar all over Oudh, while the agrarian upheaval of 1920 and 1921 was largely confined to three districts. This was partly due to the leadership of a remarkable person, Ramachandra.

Ramachandra was a man from Maharashtra in western India, and he had been to Fiji as an indentured laborer. On his return he had gradually drifted to these districts of Oudh and wandered about reciting Tulsidas's *Ramayana* and listening to tenants' grievances. He had little education, and to some extent he exploited the tenantry for his own benefit, but he showed remarkable powers of organization. He taught the peasants to meet frequently in *sabhas* (meetings) to discuss their own troubles and thus gave them a feeling of solidarity. Occasionally huge mass meetings were held, and this produced a sense of power. *Sita-Ram* was an old and common cry, but he gave it an almost war-like significance and made it a signal for emergencies as well as a bond between different villages.

Oudh was a particularly good area for an agrarian agitation. It was, and is, the land of the talukdars—the "Barons of Oudh" they call themselves—and the zamindari system at its worst flourished there. The exactions of the landlords were becoming unbearable, and the number of landless laborers was growing. There was on the whole only one class of tenant, and this helped united action.

India may be roughly divided into two parts—the zamindari area with its big landlords, and the area containing peasant proprietors, but there is a measure of overlapping. The three provinces of Bengal, Behar, and the United Provinces of Agra and Oudh, form the zamindari area. The peasant proprietors are comparatively better off, although even their condition is often pitiable. The mass of the peasantry in the Punjab or Gujrat (where there are peasant proprietors) is far better off than the tenants of the zamindari areas. In the greater part of the : zamindari areas there are many kinds of tenancies—occupancy tenants, nonoccupancy tenants, subtenancies, etc. The interests of various tenants often conflict with one another, and this militates against joint action. In Oudh, however, there were no occupancy tenants or even life tenants in 1920. There were only short-term tenants who were continually being ejected in favor of someone who was willing to pay a higher premium. Because there was principally one class of tenant, it was easier to organize them for joint action.

In practice there was no guarantee in Oudh for even the short term of the contract. A landlord hardly ever gave a receipt for rent received, and he could always say that the rent had not been paid and eject the tenant, for whom it was impossible to prove the contrary. Besides the rent there were an extraordinary number of illegal exactions. In one taluk I was told that there had been as many as fifty different kinds of such exactions. Probably this number was exaggerated, but it is notorious how talukdars often make their tenants pay for every special expenditure—a marriage in the family, cost of the son's education in foreign countries, a party to the Governor or other high official, a purchase of a car or an elephant. Indeed these exactions have got special names—*motrauna* (tax for purchase of motor), *hathauna* (tax for purchase of elephant), etc.

It was not surprising, therefore, that a big agrarian agitation should develop in Oudh. The agrarian movement was entirely separate from the Congress, and it had nothing to do with the nonco-operation that was taking shape. Perhaps it is more correct to say that both these widespread and powerful movements were due to the same fundamental causes.

What amazed me still more was our total ignorance in the cities of this great agrarian movement. No newspaper had contained a line about it; they were not interested in rural areas. I realized more than ever how cut off we were from our people and how we lived and worked and agitated in a little world apart from them.


## XI

## WANDERINGS AMONG THE *KISANS*

I SPENT THREE days in the villages, came back to Allahabad, and then went again. During these brief visits we wandered about a great deal from village to village, eating with the peasants, living with them in their mud huts, talking to them for long hours, and often addressing meetings, big and small. We had originally gone in a light car, and the peasants were so keen that hundreds of them, working overnight, built temporary roads across the fields so that our car could go right into the interior. Often the car got stuck and was bodily lifted out by scores of willing hands. But we had to leave the car eventually and to do most of our journeying by foot. Everywhere we went we were accompanied by policemen, Criminal Investigation Department men, and a deputy collector from Lucknow. I am afraid we gave them a bad time with our continuous marching across fields, and they were quite tired out and fed up with us and the *kisans*. The deputy collector was a somewhat effeminate youth from Lucknow, and he had turned up in patent leather pumps! He begged us sometimes to restrain our ardor, and I think he ultimately dropped out, being unable to keep up with us.

It was the hottest time of the year, June, just before the monsoon. The sun scorched and blinded. I was quite unused to going out in the sun, and ever since my return from England I had gone to the hills for part of every summer. And now I was wandering about all day in the open sun with not even a sun hat, my head being wrapped in a small towel. So full was I of other matters that I quite forgot about the heat, and it was only on my return to Allahabad, when I noticed the rich tan I had developed, that I remembered what I had gone through. I was pleased with myself, for I realized that I could stand the heat with the best of them and my fear of it was wholly unjustified. I have found that I can bear both extreme heat and great cold without much discomfort, and this has stood me in good stead in my work as well as in my periods in prison. This was no doubt due to my general physical fitness and my habit of taking exercise, a lesson I learned from my father, who was a bit of an athlete and, almost to the end of his days, continued his daily exercise. His head became covered with silvery hair, his face was deeply furrowed and looked old and weary with thought, but the rest of his body, to within a year or two of his death, seemed to be twenty years younger.

Even before my visit to Partabgarh in June 1920, I had often passed through villages, stopped there and talked to the peasants. I had seen them in their scores of thousands on the banks of the Ganges during the big *melas,* and we had taken our home rule propaganda to them. But somehow I had not fully realized what they were and what they meant to India. Like most of us, I took them for granted. This realization came to me during these Partabgarh visits, and ever since then my mental picture of India always contains this naked, hungry mass.

These peasants took away the shyness from me and taught me to speak in public. Till then I had hardly spoken at a public gathering; I was frightened at the prospect, especially if the speaking was to be done in Hindustani, as it almost always was. But I could not possibly avoid addressing these peasant gatherings, and how could I be shy of these poor unsophisticated people? I did not know the arts of oratory, and so I spoke to them, man to man, and told them what I had in my mind and in my heart. Whether the gathering consisted of a few persons or of ten thousand or more, I stuck to my conversational and rather personal method of speaking, and I found that, whatever might be lacking in it, I could at least go on. I was fluent enough. Perhaps many of them could not understand a great deal of what I said. My language or my thought was not simple enough for them. Many did not hear me when the gathering was very large, for my voice did not carry far. But all this did not matter much to them when once they had given their confidence and faith to a person.

I went back to Mussoorie to my mother and wife, but my mind was full of the *kisans,* and I was eager to be back. As soon as I returned, I resumed my visits to the villages and watched the agrarian movement grow in strength. The downtrodden *kisan* began to gain a new confidence in himself and walked straighter with head up. His fear of the landlords' agents and the police lessened, and, when there was an ejectment from a holding, no other *kisan* would make an offer for that land. Physical violence on the part of the zamindars' servants and illegal exactions became infrequent, and, whenever an instance occurred, it was immediately reported and an attempt at an inquiry was made. This checked the zamindars' agents as well as the police.

The talukdars and the big zamindars, the lords of the land, the "natural leaders of the people," as they are proud of calling themselves, are the spoiled children of the British Government; but that Government had succeeded, by the special education and upbringing it provided or failed to provide for them, in reducing them, as a class, to a state of complete intellectual impotence. They do nothing at all for their tenantry, and are complete parasites on the land and the people. Their chief activity lies in endeavoring to placate the local officials, without whose favor they could not exist for long, and demanding ceaselessly a protection of their special interests and privileges.

Right through the year 1921 I continued my visits to the rural areas, but my field of activity grew till it comprised the whole of the United Provinces. Nonco-operation had begun in earnest, and its message had reached the remotest village. A host of Congress workers in each district went about the rural areas with the new message, to which they often added, rather vaguely, a removal of *kisan* grievances. *Swaraj* was an all-embracing word to cover everything. Yet the two movements —nonco-operation and the agrarian—were quite separate, though they overlapped and influenced each other greatly in our province. As a result of Congress preaching, litigation went down with a rush and villages established their *panchayats* to deal with their disputes. Especially powerful was the influence of the Congress in favor of peace, for the new creed of nonviolence was stressed wherever the Congress worker went. This may not have been fully appreciated or understood, but it did prevent the peasantry from taking to violence.

This was no small result. Agrarian upheavals are notoriously violent, leading to *jacqueries,* and the peasants of part of Oudh in those days were desperate and at white heat. A spark would have lighted a flame. Yet they remained amazingly peaceful. The only instance of physical violence on a talukdar that I remember was when a peasant went up to him as he was sitting in his own house, surrounded by his friends, and slapped him on the face on the ground that he was immoral and inconsiderate to his own wife!

There was violence of another kind later which led to conflicts with the Government. But this conflict was bound to come, for the Government could not tolerate this growing power of a united peasantry. The *kisans* took to traveling in railway trains in large numbers without tickets, especially when they had to attend their periodical big mass meetings which sometimes consisted of sixty or seventy thousand persons. It was difficult to move them, and, unheard-of thing, they openly defied the railway authorities, telling them that the old days were gone. At whose instigation they took to the free mass traveling I do not know. Stricter railway control prevented this later.

In the autumn of 1920 a few *kisan* leaders were arrested for some petty offense. They were to be tried in Partabgarh town, but on the day of the trial a huge concourse of peasants filled the court compound and lined the route to the jail where the accused leaders were kept. The magistrate's nerve gave way, and he postponed the trial to the next day. But the crowd grew and almost surrounded the jail. The *kisans* can easily carry on for a few days on a handful of parched grain. Ultimately the *kisan* leaders were discharged, perhaps after a formal trial inside the jail. I forget how this came about, but for the *kisans* this was a great triumph, and they began to think that they could always have their way by weight of numbers alone. To the Government this position was intolerable, and soon after a similar occasion arose; this time it ended differently.

At the beginning of January 1921 I received a telegram from Rae Bareli asking me to go there immediately as trouble was expected. I left the next day. I discovered that some leading *kisans* had been arrested some days back and had been lodged in the local jail. Remembering their success at Partabgarh and the tactics they had then adopted, the peasants marched to Rae Bareli town for a mass demonstration. But this time the Government was not going to permit it, and additional police and military had been collected to stop the *kisans*. Just outside the town on the other side of a little river the main body of the *kisans* was stopped. Many of them, however, streamed in from other directions. On arrival at the station I learned of this situation, and immediately I proceeded straight to the river where the military were said to face the peasants. On the way I received a hurriedly written note from the district magistrate asking me to go back. I wrote my reply on the back of it inquiring under what law and what section he was asking me to go back and saying that till I heard from him I proposed to go on. As I reached the river, sounds of firing could be heard from the other side. I was stopped at the bridge by the military, and, as I waited there, I was suddenly surrounded by large numbers of frightened *kisans* who had been hiding in the fields on this side of the river. So I held a meeting of about a couple of thousand peasants on the spot and tried to remove their fear and lessen their excitement. It was rather an unusual situation with firing going on against their brethren within a stone's throw across a little stream and the military in evidence everywhere. But the meeting was quite successful and took away the edge from the *kisans'* fear. The district magistrate then returned from the firing line, and, at his request, I accompanied him to his house. There he kept me, under some pretext or other, for over two hours, evidently wanting to keep me away from the *kisans* and my colleagues in the city.

We found later that many men had been killed in the firing. The *kisans* had refused to disperse or to go back, but otherwise they had been perfectly peaceful. I am quite sure that if I or someone else they trusted had been there and had asked them to do so they would have dispersed. They refused to take their orders from men they did not trust. Someone actually suggested to the magistrate to wait for me a little, but he refused. He could not permit an agitator to succeed where he had failed. That is not the way of foreign governments depending on prestige.

Firing on *kisans* took place on two occasions in Rae Bareli district about that time, and then began, what was much worse, a reign of terror for every prominent *kisan* worker or member of a *panchayat*. Government had decided to crush the movement.

A little later in the year 1921, Fyzabad district had its dose of widespread repression. The trouble started there in a peculiar way. The peasants of some villages went and looted the property of a talukdar. It transpired subsequently that they had been incited to do so by the servants of another zamindar who had some kind of feud with the talukdar. The poor ignorant peasants were actually told that it was the wish of Mahatma Gandhi that they should loot, and they willingly agreed to carry out this behest, shouting *"Mahatma Gandhi ki jai"* in the process.

I was very angry when I heard of this, and within a day or two of the occurrence I was on the spot, somewhere near Akbarpur in Fyzabad district. On arrival I called a meeting for the same day, and within a few hours five or six thousand persons had collected from numerous villages within a radius of ten miles. I spoke harshly to them for the shame they had brought on themselves and our cause and said that the guilty persons must confess publicly. (I was full in those days of what I conceived to be the spirit of Gandhiji's *Satyagraha*.) I called upon those who had participated in the looting to raise their hands, and, strange to say, there in the presence of numerous police officials about two dozen hands went up. That meant certain trouble for them.

When I spoke to many of them privately later and heard their artless story of how they had been misled, I felt very sorry for them, and I began to regret having exposed these simple folk to long terms of imprisonment. But the people who suffered were not just two or three dozen. The chance was too good to be lost, and full advantage was taken of the occasion to crush the agrarian movement in that district. Over a thousand arrests were made, the district jail was overcrowded, and the trial went on for the best part of a year. Many died in prison during the trial. Many others received long sentences, and in later years, when I went to prison, I came across some of them, boys and young men, spending their youth in prison.

The Indian *kisans* have little staying power, little energy to resist for long. Famines and epidemics come and slay them in their millions. It was surprising that they had shown for a whole year great powers of resistance against the combined pressure of government and landlord. But they began to weary a little, and the determined attack of the Government on their movement ultimately broke its spirit for the time being. But it continued still in a lower key. There were not such vast demonstrations as before, but most villages contained old workers who had not been terrorized and who carried on the work in a small way.

Frightened by the agrarian movement, the Government hurried its tenancy legislation. This promised some improvement in the lot of the *kisan,* but the measure was toned down when it was found that the movement was already under control. The principal change it affected was to give a life tenancy to the *kisan* in Oudh. This sounded attractive to him but, as he has found out subsequently, his lot is in no way better.

Agrarian troubles continued to crop up in Oudh but on a smaller scale. The world depression which began in 1929, however, again created a great crisis owing to the fall in prices.

# XII

# NONCO-OPERATION

I HAVE DEALT with the Oudh agrarian upheaval in some little detail because it lifted the veil and disclosed to me a fundamental aspect of the Indian problem to which nationalists had paid hardly any attention. Agrarian troubles are frequently taking place in various parts of India, symptoms of a deep-seated unrest, and the *kisan* agitation in certain parts of Oudh in 1920 and 1921 was but one of them, though it was, in its own way, a remarkable and revealing one. In its origin it was entirely unconnected with politics or politicians, and right through its course the influence of outsiders and politicians was of the slightest. From an all-India point of view, however, it was a local affair, and very little attention was paid to it. Even the newspapers of the United Provinces largely ignored it. For their editors and the majority of their town-dwelling readers, the doings of mobs of seminaked peasants had no real political or other significance.

The Punjab and the Khilafat wrongs were the topics of the day, and nonco-operation, which was to attempt to bring about a righting of these wrongs, was the all-absorbing subject. The larger issue of national freedom, or *Swaraj*, was for the moment not stressed. Gandhiji disliked vague and big objectives; he always preferred concentrating on something specific and definite. Nevertheless, *Swaraj* was very much in the air and in people's thoughts, and frequent reference was made to it in innumerable gatherings and conferences.

In the autumn of 1920 a special session of the Congress met at Calcutta to consider what steps should be taken and, in particular, to decide about nonco-operation.

Of the prominent leaders of the older generation my father was the only one to take his stand by Gandhiji at that time. It was no easy matter for him to do so. He sensed and was much influenced by the objections that had led most of his old colleagues to oppose. He hesitated, as they did, to take a novel step toward an unknown region, where it was hardly possible to keep one's old bearings. Yet he was inevitably drawn to some form of effective action, and the proposal did embody definite action, though not exactly on the lines of his thought. It took him a long time to make up his mind.

I saw very little of father in those days before the Calcutta Special Congress. But, whenever I met him, I noticed how he was continually grappling with this problem. Quite apart from the national aspect of the question there was the personal aspect. Nonco-operation meant his withdrawing from his legal practice; it meant a total break with his past life and a new fashioning of it—not an easy matter when one is on the eve of one's sixtieth birthday. It was a break from old political colleagues, from his profession, from the social life to which he had grown accustomed, and a giving up of many an expensive habit. For the financial aspect of the question was not an unimportant one, and it was obvious that he would have to reduce his standard of living if his income from his profession vanished.

But his reason, his strong sense of self-respect, and his pride, all led him step by step to throw in his lot wholeheartedly with the new movement. The accumulated anger with which a series of events, culminating in the Punjab tragedy and its aftermath, filled him; the sense of utter wrong-doing and injustice; the bitterness of national humiliation—these had to find some way out. But he was not to be swept away by a wave of enthusiasm. It was only when his reason, backed by the trained mind of a lawyer, had weighed all the pros and cons that he took the final decision and joined Gandhiji in his campaign.

He was attracted by Gandhiji as a man, and that no doubt was a factor which influenced him. Nothing could have made him a close associate of a person he disliked, for he was always strong in his likes and dislikes. But it was a strange combination—the saint, the stoic, the man of religion, one who went through life rejecting what it offers in the way of sensation and physical pleasure, and one who had been a bit of an epicure, who accepted life and welcomed and enjoyed its many sensations, caring little for what might come in the hereafter. In the language of psychoanalysis it was a meeting of an introvert with an extrovert. Yet there were common bonds, common interests, which drew the two together and kept up, even when, in later years, their politics diverged, a close friendship between them.

This special session at Calcutta began the Gandhi era in Congress politics which has lasted since then, except for a period in the twenties when he kept in the background and allowed the *Swaraj* party, under the leadership of Deshbandhu C. R. Das and my father, to fill the picture. The whole look of the Congress changed; European clothes vanished, and soon only *khadi* was to be seen; a new class of delegate, chiefly drawn from the lower middle classes, became the type of Congressman; the language used became increasingly Hindustani, or sometimes the language of the province where the session was held, as many of the delegates did not understand English, and there was also a growing prejudice against using a foreign language in our national work; and a new life and enthusiasm and earnestness became evident in Congress gatherings.

On our way back from the Calcutta Special Congress I accompanied Gandhiji to Santiniketan on a visit to Rabindranath Tagore and his most lovable elder brother, "Boro Dada." We spent some days there, and I remember C. F. Andrews' giving me some books which interested and influenced me greatly. They dealt with the economic aspects of imperialism in Africa. One of these books—Morell's *Black Man's Burden*—moved me greatly.

About this time or a little later, C. F. Andrews wrote a pamphlet advocating independence for India. I think it was called *Independence —the Immediate Need*. This was a brilliant essay based on some of Seeley's writings on India, and it seemed to me not only to make out an unanswerable case for independence but also to mirror the inmost recesses of our hearts. The deep urge that moved us and our half-formed desires seemed to take clear shape in his simple and earnest language. There was no economic background or socialism in what he had written; it was nationalism pure and simple, the feeling of the humiliation of India and a fierce desire to be rid of it and to put an end to our continuing degradation. It was wonderful that C. F. Andrews, a foreigner and one belonging to the dominant race in India, should echo that cry of our inmost being. Nonco-operation was essentially, as Seeley had said long ago, "the notion that it was shameful to assist the foreigner in maintaining his domination." And Andrews had written that "the only way of self-recovery was through some vital upheaval from within. The explosive force needed for such an upheaval must be generated within the soul of India itself. It could not come through loans and gifts and grants and concessions and proclamations from without. It must come from within. . . . Therefore, it was with the intense joy of mental and spiritual deliverance from an intolerable burden that I watched the actual outbreak of such an inner explosive force, as that which actually occurred when Mahatma Gandhi spoke to the heart of India the *mantram*—'Be free! Be slaves no more!'—and the heart of India responded. In a sudden movement her fetters began to be loosened, and the pathway of freedom was opened."

The next three months witnessed the advancing tide of nonco-operation all over the country. The appeal for a boycott of the elections to the new legislatures was remarkably successful. It did not and

67

could not prevent everybody from going to these councils and thus keep the seats vacant. Even a handful of voters could elect, or there might be an unopposed election. But the great majority of voters abstained from voting, and all who cared for the vehemently expressed sense of the country refrained from standing as candidates.

A few old leaders, however, dropped out of the Congress after Calcutta, and among these a popular and well-known figure was that of Mr. M. A. Jinnah. Sarojini Naidu had called him the "Ambassador of Hindu-Moslem unity," and he had been largely responsible in the past for bringing the Moslem League nearer to the Congress. But the new developments in the Congress—nonco-operation and the new constitution, which made it more of a popular and mass organization—were thoroughly disapproved of by him. He disagreed on political grounds, but it was not politics in the main that kept him away. There were still many people in the Congress who were politically even less advanced than he was. But temperamentally he did not fit in at all with the new Congress. He felt completely out of his element in the *khadi*-clad crowd demanding speeches in Hindustani. The enthusiasm of the people outside struck him as mob hysteria. There was as much difference between him and the Indian masses as between Savile Row and Bond Street and the Indian village with its mud huts. He suggested once privately that only matriculates should be taken into the Congress. I do not know if he was serious in making this remarkable suggestion, but it was in harmony with his general outlook. So he drifted away from the Congress and became a rather solitary figure in Indian politics. Later, unhappily, the old Ambassador of Unity associated himself with the most reactionary elements in Moslem communalism.

The Moderates or Liberals had, of course, nothing to do with the Congress. They not only kept away from it; they merged themselves in the Government, became ministers and high officials under the new scheme, and helped in fighting nonco-operation and the Congress.

And yet the Liberals were far from happy. It is not a pleasant experience to be cut off from one's own people, to sense hostility even though one may not see it or hear it. A mass upheaval is not kind to the nonconformists, though Gandhiji's repeated warnings made nonco-operation far milder and gentler to its opponents than it otherwise would have been. But even so, the very atmosphere stifled those who opposed the movement, just as it invigorated and filled with life and energy those who supported it. Mass upheavals and real revolutionary movements always have this double effect: they encourage and bring out the personality of those who constitute the masses or side with them, and at the same time they suppress psychologically and stifle those who differ from them.

This was the reason why some people complained that nonco-operation was intolerant and tended to introduce a dead uniformity of opinion and action. There was truth in this complaint, but the truth lay in this, that nonco-operation was a mass movement, and it was led by a man of commanding personality who inspired devotion in India's millions. A more vital truth, however, lay in its effect on the masses. There was a tremendous feeling of release there, a throwing-off of a great burden, a new sense of freedom. The fear that had crushed them retired into the background, and they straightened their backs and raised their heads.

Many of us who worked for the Congress program lived in a kind of intoxication during the year 1921. We were full of excitement and optimism and a buoyant enthusiasm. We sensed the happiness of a person crusading for a cause. We were not troubled with doubts or hesitation; our path seemed to lie clear in front of us, and we marched ahead, lifted up by the enthusiasm of others, and helping to push on others. We worked hard, harder than we had ever done before, for we knew that the conflict with the Government would come soon, and we wanted to do as much as possible before we were removed.

Above all, we had a sense of freedom and a pride in that freedom. The old feeling of oppression and frustration was completely gone. There was no more whispering, no round-about legal phraseology to avoid getting into trouble with the authorities. We said what we felt and shouted it out from the housetops. What did we care for the consequences? Prison? We looked forward to it; that would help our cause still further. The innumerable spies and secret-service men who used to surround us and follow us about became rather pitiable individuals as there was nothing secret for them to discover. All our cards were always on the table.

We had not only a feeling of satisfaction at doing effective political work which was changing the face of India before our eyes and, as we believed, bringing Indian freedom very near, but also an agreeable sense of moral superiority over our opponents, in regard to both our goal and our methods. We were proud of our leader and of the unique method he had evolved, and often we indulged in fits of self-righteousness. In the midst of strife, and while we ourselves encouraged that strife, we had a sense of inner peace.

As our morale grew, that of the Government went down. They did not understand what was happening; it seemed that the old world they knew in India was toppling down. There was a new aggressive spirit abroad and self-reliance and fearlessness, and the great prop of British rule in India—prestige—was visibly wilting. Repression in a small way only strengthened the movement, and the Government hesitated for long before it would take action against the big leaders. It did not know what the consequences might be. Was the Indian Army reliable? Would the police carry out orders? As Lord Reading, the Viceroy, said in December 1921, they were "puzzled and perplexed."

The nerves of many a British official began to give way. The strain was great. There was this ever-growing opposition and spirit of defiance which overshadowed official India like a vast monsoon cloud, and yet because of its peaceful methods it offered no handle, no grip, no opportunity for forcible suppression. The average Englishman did not believe in the *bona fides* of nonviolence; he thought that all this was camouflage, a cloak to cover some vast secret design which would burst out in violent upheaval one day. Nurtured from childhood in the widespread belief that the East is a mysterious place, and in its bazaars and narrow lanes secret conspiracies are being continually hatched, the Englishman can seldom think straight on matters relating to these lands of supposed mystery. He never makes an attempt to understand that somewhat obvious and very unmysterious person, the Easterner. He keeps well away from him, gets his ideas about him from tales abounding in spies and secret societies, and then allows his imagination to run riot. So it was in the Punjab early in April 1919, when a sudden fear overwhelmed the authorities and the English people generally, made them see danger everywhere, a widespread rising, a second mutiny with its frightful massacres, and, in a blind, instinctive attempt at self-preservation at any cost, led them to that frightfulness of which Jallianwala and the Crawling Lane of Amritsar have become symbols and bywords.

The year 1921 was a year of great tension, and there was much to irritate and annoy and unnerve the official. What was actually happening was bad enough, but what was imagined was far worse. I remember an instance which illustrates this riot of the imagination. My sister Swarup's wedding, which was taking place at Allahabad, was fixed for May 10, 1921, the actual date having been calculated, as usual on such occasions, by a reference to the Samvat calendar, and an auspicious day chosen. Gandhiji and a number of leading Congressmen, including the Ali brothers, had been invited, and, to suit their convenience, a meeting of the Congress Working Committee was fixed at Allahabad about that time. The local Congressmen wanted to profit by the presence of famous leaders from outside, and so they organized a district conference on a big scale, expecting a large number of peasants from the surrounding rural areas.

There was a great deal of bustle and excitement in Allahabad on account of these political gatherings. This had a remarkable effect on the nerves of some people. I learned one day through a barrister friend that many English people were thoroughly upset and expected some sudden upheaval in the city. They distrusted their Indian servants, and carried about revolvers in their pockets. It was even said privately that the Allahabad Fort was kept in readiness for the English colony to retire there in case of need. I was much surprised and could not make out why anyone should contemplate the possibility of a rising in the sleepy and peaceful city of Allahabad just when the very apostle of nonviolence was going to visit us. Oh, it was said, May 10 (the day accidentally fixed for my sister's marriage) was the anniversary of the outbreak of the Mutiny at Meerut in 1857, and this was going to be celebrated!

Gandhiji was continually laying stress on the religious and spiritual side of the movement. His religion was not dogmatic, but it did mean a definitely religious outlook on life, and the whole movement was strongly influenced by this and took on a revivalist character so far as the masses were concerned. The great majority of Congress workers naturally tried to model themselves after their leader and even repeated his language. And yet Gandhiji's leading colleagues in the Working Committee—my father, Deshbandhu Das, Lala Lajpat Rai, and others —were not men of religion in the ordinary sense of the word, and they considered political problems on the political plane only. In their public utterances they did not bring in religion. But whatever they said had far less influence than the force of their personal example—had they not given up a great deal that the world values and taken to simpler ways of living? This in itself was taken as a sign of religion and helped in spreading the atmosphere of revivalism.

I used to be troubled sometimes at the growth of this religious element in our politics, both on the Hindu and the Moslem side. I did not like it at all. Much that Moulvies and Maulanas and Swamis and the like said in their public addresses seemed to me most unfortunate. Their history and sociology and economics appeared to me all wrong, and the religious twist that was given to everything prevented all clear thinking. Even some of Gandhiji's phrases sometimes jarred upon me—thus his frequent reference to *Rama Raj* as a golden age which was to return. But I was powerless to intervene, and I consoled myself with the thought that Gandhiji used the words because they were well known and understood by the masses. He had an amazing knack of reaching the heart of the people.

But I did not worry myself much over these matters. I was too full of my work and the progress of our movement to care for such trifles, as I thought at the time they were. A vast movement had all sorts and kinds of people in it, and, so long as our main direction was correct, a few eddies and backwaters did not matter. As for Gandhiji himself, he was a very difficult person to understand; sometimes his language was almost incomprehensible to an average modern. But we felt that we knew him quite well enough to realize that he was a great and unique man and a glorious leader, and, having put our faith in him, we gave him an almost blank check, for the time being at least. Often we discussed his fads and peculiarities among ourselves and said, half-humorously, that when *Swaraj* came these fads must not be encouraged.

Many of us, however, were too much under his influence in political and other matters to remain wholly immune even in the sphere of religion. Where a direct attack might not have succeeded, many an indirect approach went a long way to undermine the defenses. The outward ways of religion did not appeal to me, and above all I disliked the exploitation of the people by the so-called men of religion, but still I toned down toward it. I came nearer to a religious frame of mind in 1921 than at any other time since my early boyhood. Even so I did not come very near.

What I admired was the moral and ethical side of our movement and of *Satyagraha*. I did not give an absolute allegiance to the doctrine of nonviolence or accept it forever, but it attracted me more and more, and the belief grew upon me that, situated as we were in India and with our background and traditions, it was the right policy for us. The spiritualization of politics, using the word not in its narrow religious sense, seemed to me a fine idea. A worthy end should have worthy means leading up to it. That seemed not only a good ethical doctrine but sound, practical politics, for the means that are not good often defeat the end in view and raise new problems and difficulties.

And then it seemed so unbecoming, so degrading to the self-respect of an individual or a nation to submit to such means, to go through the mire. How can one escape being sullied by it? How can we march ahead swiftly and with dignity if we stoop or crawl?

Such were my thoughts then. And the nonco-operation movement offered me what I wanted—the goal of national freedom and (as I thought) the ending of the exploitation of the underdog, and the means which satisfied my moral sense and gave me a sense of personal freedom. So great was this personal satisfaction that even a possibility of failure did not count for much, for such failure could only be temporary. I did not understand or feel drawn to the metaphysical part of the *Bhagavad Gita,* but I liked to read the verses—recited every evening in Gandhiji's ashrama prayers—which say what a man should be like: Calm of purpose, serene and unmoved, doing his job and not caring overmuch for the result of his action. Not being very calm or detached myself, I suppose, this ideal appealed to me all the more.

## XIII

## FIRST IMPRISONMENT

NINETEEN TWENTY-ONE was an extraordinary year for us. There was a strange mixture of nationalism and politics and religion and mysticism and fanaticism. Behind all this was agrarian trouble and, in the big cities, a rising working-class movement. Nationalism and a vague but intense countrywide idealism sought to bring together all these various, and sometimes mutually contradictory, discontents, and succeeded to a remarkable degree. And yet this nationalism itself was a composite force, and behind it could be distinguished a Hindu nationalism, a Moslem nationalism partly looking beyond the frontiers of India, and, what was more in consonance with the spirit of the times, an Indian nationalism. For the time being they overlapped and all pulled together. It was *Hindu-Muslaman ki jai* everywhere. It was remarkable how Gandhiji seemed to cast a spell on all classes and groups of people and drew them into one motley crowd struggling in one direction. He became, indeed (to use a phrase which has been applied to another leader), "a symbolic expression of the confused desires of the people."

Even more remarkable was the fact that these desires and passions were relatively free from hatred of the alien rulers against whom they were directed. Nationalism is essentially an anti-feeling, and it feeds and fattens on hatred and anger against other national groups, and especially against the foreign rulers of a subject country. There was certainly this hatred and anger in India in 1921 against the British, but, in comparison with other countries similarly situated, it was extraordinarily little. Undoubtedly this was due to Gandhiji's insistence on the implications of nonviolence. It was also due to the feeling of release and power that came to the whole country with the inauguration of the movement and the widespread belief in success in the near future. Why be angry and full of hate when we were doing so well and were likely to win through soon? We felt that we could afford to be generous.

We were not so generous in our hearts, though our actions were circumspect and proper, toward the handful of our own countrymen who took sides against us and opposed the national movement. It was not a question of hatred or anger, for they carried no weight whatever and we could ignore them. But deep within us was contempt for their weakness and opportunism and betrayal of national honor and self-respect.

So we went on, vaguely but intensely, the exhilaration of action holding us in its grip. But about our goal there was an entire absence of clear thinking. It seems surprising now, how completely we ignored the theoretical aspects, the philosophy of our movement as well as the definite objective that we should have. Of course we all grew eloquent about *Swaraj*, but each one of us probably interpreted the word in his or her own way. To most of the younger men it meant political independence, or something like it, and a democratic form of government, and we said so in our public utterances. Many of us also thought that inevitably this would result in a lessening of the burdens that crushed the workers and the peasantry. But it was obvious that to most of our leaders *Swaraj* meant something much less than independence. Gandhiji was delightfully vague on the subject, and he did not encourage clear thinking about it either. But he always spoke, vaguely but definitely, in terms of the underdog, and this brought great comfort to many of us, although, at the same time, he was full of assurances to the top dog also. Gandhiji's stress was never on the intellectual approach to a problem but on character and piety. He did succeed amazingly in giving backbone and character to the Indian people.

It was this extraordinary stiffening-up of the masses that filled us with confidence. A demoralized, backward, and broken-up people suddenly straightened their backs and lifted their heads and took part in disciplined, joint action on a countrywide scale. This action itself, we felt, would give irresistible power to the masses. We ignored the necessity of thought behind the action; we forgot that without a conscious ideology and objective the energy and enthusiasm of the masses must end largely in smoke. To some extent the revivalist element in our movement carried us on; a feeling that nonviolence as conceived for political or economic movements or for righting wrongs was a new message which our people were destined to give to the world. We became victims to the curious illusion of all peoples and all nations that in some way they are a chosen race. Nonviolence was the moral equivalent of war and of all violent struggle. It was not merely an ethical alternative, but it was effective also. Few of us, I think, accepted Gandhiji's old ideas about machinery and modern civilization. We thought that even he looked upon them as utopian and as largely inapplicable to modern conditions. Certainly most of us were not prepared to reject the achievements of modern civilization, although we may have felt that some variation to suit Indian conditions was possible. Personally, I have always felt attracted toward big machinery and fast traveling. Still, there can be no doubt that Gandhiji's ideology influenced many people and made them critical of the machine and all its consequences. So, while some looked to the future, others looked back to the past. And, curiously, both felt that the joint action they were indulging in was worth while, and this made it easy to bear sacrifice and face self-denial.

I became wholly absorbed and wrapped in the movement, and large numbers of other people did likewise. I gave up all my other associations and contacts, old friends, books, even newspapers, except in so far as they dealt with the work in hand. I had kept up till then some reading of current books and had tried to follow the developments of world affairs. But there was no time for this now. In spite of the strength of my family bonds, I almost forgot my family, my wife, my daughter. It was only long afterward that I realized what a burden and a trial I must have been to them in those days, and what amazing patience and tolerance my wife had shown toward me. I lived in offices and committee meetings and crowds. "Go to the villages" was the slogan, and we trudged many a mile across fields and visited distant villages and addressed peasant meetings. I experienced the thrill of mass feeling, the power of influencing the mass. I began to understand a little the psychology of the crowd, the difference between the city masses and the peasantry, and I felt at home in the dust and discomfort, the pushing and jostling of large gatherings, though their want of discipline often irritated me. Since those days I have sometimes had to face hostile and angry crowds, worked up to a state when a spark would light a flame, and I found that that early experience and the confidence it begot in me stood me in good stead. Always I went straight to the crowd and trusted it, and so far I have always had courtesy and appreciation from it, even though there was no agreement. But crowds are fickle, and the future may have different experiences in store for me.

I took to the crowd, and the crowd took to me, and yet I never lost myself in it; always I felt apart from it. From my separate mental perch I looked at it critically, and I never ceased to wonder how I, who was so different in every way from those thousands who surrounded me, different in habits, in desires, in mental and spiritual outlook, had managed to gain good will and a measure of confidence from these people. Was it because they took me for something other than I was? Would they bear with me when they knew me better? Was I gaining their good will under false pretenses? I tried to be frank and straightforward to them; I even spoke harshly to them sometimes and criticized many of their pet beliefs and customs, but still they put up with me. And yet I could not get rid of the idea that their affection was meant not for me as I was, but for some fanciful image of me that they had formed. How long could that false image endure? And why should it be allowed to endure? And, when it fell down and they saw the reality, what then?

I am vain enough in many ways, but there could be no question of vanity with these crowds of simple folk. There was no posing about them, no vulgarity, as in the case of many of us of the middle classes who consider ourselves their betters. They were dull certainly, uninteresting individually; but in the mass they produced a feeling of overwhelming pity and a sense of ever-impending tragedy.

Very different were our conferences where our chosen workers, including myself, performed on the platform. There was sufficient posing there and no lack of vulgarity in our flamboyant addresses. All of us must have been to some extent guilty of this, but some of the minor Khilafat leaders probably led the rest. It is not easy to behave naturally on a platform before a large audience, and few of us had previous experience of such publicity. So we tried to look as we imagined leaders should look, thoughtful and serious, with no trace of levity or frivolity. When we walked or talked or smiled, we were conscious of thousands of eyes staring at us and we reacted accordingly. Our speeches were often very eloquent but, equally often, singularly pointless. It is difficult to see oneself as others see one. And so, unable to criticize myself, I took to watching carefully the ways of others, and I found considerable amusement in this occupation. And then the terrible thought would strike me that I might perhaps appear equally ludicrous to others.

Right through the year 1921 individual Congress workers were being arrested and sentenced, but there were no mass arrests. The Ali brothers had received long sentences for inciting the Indian Army to disaffection. Their words, for which they had been sentenced, were repeated at hundreds of platforms by thousands of persons. I was threatened in the summer with proceedings for sedition because of some speeches I had delivered. No such step, however, was taken then. The end of the year brought matters to a head. The Prince of Wales was coming to India, and the Congress had proclaimed a boycott of all the functions in connection with his visit. Toward the end of November the Congress volunteers in Bengal were declared illegal, and this was followed by a similar declaration for the United Provinces. Deshbandhu Das gave a stirring message to Bengal: "I feel the handcuffs on my wrists and the weight of iron chains on my body. It is the agony of bondage. The whole of India is a vast prison. The work of the Congress must be carried on. What matters it whether I am taken or left? What matters it whether I am dead or alive?" In the United Provinces we took up the challenge and not only announced that our volunteer organization would continue to function, but published lists of names of volunteers in the daily newspapers. The first list was headed by my father's name. He was not a volunteer but, simply for the purpose of defying the Government order, he joined and gave his name. Early in December, a few days before the Prince came to our province, mass arrests began.

We knew that matters had at last come to a head; the inevitable conflict between the Congress and the Government was about to break out. Prison was still an unknown place, the idea of going there still a novelty. I was sitting rather late one day in the Congress office at Allahabad trying to clear up arrears of work. An excited clerk told me that the police had come with a search warrant and were surrounding the office building. I was, of course, a little excited also, for it was my first experience of the kind, but the desire to show off was strong, the wish to appear perfectly cool and collected, unaffected by the comings and goings of the police. So I asked a clerk to accompany the police officer in his search round the office rooms and insisted on the rest of the staff carrying on their usual work and ignoring the police. A little later a friend and a colleague, who had been arrested just outside the office, came to me, accompanied by a policeman, to bid me good-by. I was so full of the conceit that I must treat these novel occurrences as everyday happenings that I treated my colleague in a most unfeeling manner. Casually I asked him and the policeman to wait till I had finished the letter I was writing. Soon news came of other arrests in the city. I decided at last to go home and see what was happening there. I found the inevitable police searching part of the large house and learned that they had come to arrest both father and me.

Nothing that we could have done would have fitted in so well with our program of boycotting the Prince's visit. Wherever he was taken he was met with *hartals* and deserted streets. Allahabad, when he came, seemed to be a city of the dead; Calcutta, a few days later, suddenly put a temporary stop to all the activities of a great city. It was hard on the Prince of Wales; he was not to blame, and there was no feeling against him whatever. But the Government of India had tried to exploit his personality to prop up their decaying prestige.

There was an orgy of arrests and convictions, especially in the United Provinces and in Bengal. All the prominent Congress leaders and workers in these provinces were arrested, and ordinary volunteers by the thousand went to prison. They were, at first, largely city men and there seemed to be an inexhaustible supply of volunteers for prison. The Provincial Congress Committee was arrested *en bloc* (55 members) as they were actually holding a committee meeting. Many people, who had so far taken no part in any Congress or political activity, were carried away by the wave of enthusiasm and insisted on being arrested. There were cases of Government clerks, returning from their offices in the evening, being swept away by this current and landing in jail instead of their homes. Young men and boys would crowd inside the police trucks and refuse to come out. Every evening we could hear from inside the jail, truck after truck arriving outside heralded by our slogans and shouts. The jails were crowded and the jail officials were at their wits' ends at this extraordinary phenomenon. It happened sometimes that a police truck would bring, according to the warrant accompanying it, a certain number of prisoners—no names were or could be mentioned. Actually, a larger number than that mentioned would emerge from the truck, and the jail officials did not know how to meet this novel situation. There was nothing in the Jail Manual about it.

Gradually the Government gave up the policy of indiscriminate arrests; only noted workers were picked out. Gradually also the first flush of enthusiasm of the people cooled down, and, owing to the absence in prison of all the trusted workers, a feeling of indecision and helplessness spread. But the change was superficial only; there was still thunder in the air, and the atmosphere was tense and pregnant with revolutionary possibilities. During the months of December 1921 and January 1922 it is estimated that about thirty thousand persons were sentenced to imprisonment in connection with the nonco-operation movement. But, though most of the prominent men and workers were in prison, the leader of the whole struggle, Mahatma Gandhi, was still out, issuing from day to day messages and directions which inspired the people, as well as checking many an undesirable activity. The Government had not touched him so far, for they feared the consequences, the reactions on the Indian Army and the police.

Suddenly, early in February 1922, the whole scene shifted, and we in prison learned, to our amazement and consternation, that Gandhiji had stopped the aggressive aspects of our struggle, that he had suspended civil resistance. We read that this was because of what had happened near the village of Chauri Chaura, where a mob of villagers had retaliated on some policemen by setting fire to the police station and burning half a dozen or so policemen in it.

We were angry when we learned of this stoppage of our struggle at a time when we seemed to be consolidating our position and advancing on all fronts. But our disappointment and anger in prison could do little good to anyone; civil resistance stopped, and noncooperation wilted away. After many months of strain and anxiety the Government breathed again, and for the first time had the opportunity of taking the initiative. A few weeks later they arrested Gandhiji and sentenced him for a long term of imprisonment.

# XIV

# NONVIOLENCE AND THE DOCTRINE
# OF THE SWORD

THE SUDDEN SUSPENSION of our movement after the Chauri Chaura incident was resented, I think, by almost all the prominent Congress leaders—other than Gandhiji, of course. My father (who was in jail at the time) was much upset by it. The younger people were naturally even more agitated. Our mounting hopes tumbled to the ground, and this mental reaction was to be expected. What troubled us even more were the reasons given for this suspension and the consequences that seemed to flow from them. Chauri Chaura may have been and was a deplorable occurrence and wholly opposed to the spirit of the non-violent movement; but were a remote village and a mob of excited peasants in an out-of-the-way place going to put an end, for some time at least, to our national struggle for freedom? If this was the inevitable consequence of a sporadic act of violence, then surely there was something lacking in the philosophy and technique of a nonviolent struggle. For it seemed to us to be impossible to guarantee against the occurrence of some such untoward incident. Must we train the three hundred and odd millions of India in the theory and practice of nonviolent action before we could go forward? And, even so, how many of us could say that under extreme provocation from the police we would be able to remain perfectly peaceful? But even if we succeeded, what of the numerous *agents provocateurs,* stool pigeons, and the like who crept into our movement and indulged in violence themselves or induced others to do so? If this was the sole condition of its function, then the nonviolent method of resistance would always fail.

We had accepted that method, the Congress had made that method its own, because of a belief in its effectiveness. Gandhiji had placed it before the country not only as the right method but as the most effective one for our purpose. In spite of its negative name it was a dynamic method, the very opposite of a meek submission to a tyrant's will. It was not a coward's refuge from action, but the brave man's defiance of evil and national subjection. But what was the use of the bravest and the strongest if a few odd persons—maybe even our opponents in the guise of friends—had the power to upset or end our movement by their rash behavior?

Gandhiji had pleaded for the adoption of the way of nonviolence, of peaceful nonco-operation, with all the eloquence and persuasive power which he so abundantly possessed. His language had been simple and unadorned, his voice and appearance cool and clear and devoid of all emotion, but behind that outward covering of ice there was the heat of a blazing fire and concentrated passion, and the words he uttered winged their way to the innermost recesses of our minds and hearts, and created a strange ferment there. The way he pointed out was hard and difficult, but it was a brave path, and it seemed to lead to the promised land of freedom. Because of that promise we pledged our faith and marched ahead. In a famous article—"The Doctrine of the Sword"—he had written in 1920:

"I do believe that when there is only a choice between cowardice and violence, I would advise violence. . . . I would rather have India resort to arms in order to defend her honor than that she should in a cowardly manner become or remain a helpless victim to her own dishonor. But I believe that nonviolence is infinitely superior to violence, forgiveness is more manly than punishment.

"Forgiveness adorns a soldier. But abstinence is forgiveness only when there is power to punish; it is meaningless when it pretends to proceed from a helpless creature. A mouse hardly forgives a cat when it allows itself to be torn to pieces by her. . . . But I do not believe India to be helpless, I do not believe myself to be a helpless creature. . . .

"Let me not be misunderstood. Strength does not come from physical capacity. It comes from an indomitable will. . . .

"I am not a visionary. I claim to be a practical idealist. The religion of nonviolence is not meant merely for the Rishis and saints. It is meant for the common people as well. Nonviolence is the law of our species as violence is the law of the brute. The spirit lies dormant in the brute, and he knows no law but that of physical might. The dignity of man requires obedience to a higher law—to the strength of the spirit.

"I have therefore ventured to place before India the ancient law of self-sacrifice. For *Satyagraha* and its off-shoots, nonco-operation and civil resistance, are nothing but new names for the law of suffering. The Rishis who discovered the law of nonviolence in the midst of violence, were greater geniuses than Newton. They were themselves greater warriors than Wellington. Having themselves known the use of arms, they realized their uselessness and taught a weary world that its salvation lay not through violence but through nonviolence.

"Nonviolence in its dynamic condition means conscious suffering. It does not mean meek submission to the will of the evildoer, but it means the putting of one's whole soul against the will of the tyrant. Working under this law of our being, it is possible for a single individual to defy the whole might of an unjust empire to save his honor, his religion, his soul, and lay the foundation for that empire's fall or regeneration.

"And so I am not pleading for India to practice nonviolence because it is weak. I want her to practice nonviolence being conscious of her strength and power. . . . I want India to recognize that she has a soul that cannot perish, and that can rise triumphant above any physical weakness and defy the physical combination of a whole world. . . .

"I isolate this nonco-operation from Sinn Feinism, for it is so conceived as to be incapable of being offered side by side with violence. But I invite even the school of violence to give this peaceful nonco-operation a trial. It will not fail through its inherent weakness. It may fail because of poverty of response. Then will be the time for real danger. The high-souled men, who are unable to suffer national humiliation any longer, will want to vent their wrath. They will take to violence. So far as I know, they must perish without delivering themselves or their country from the wrong. If India takes up the doctrine of the sword, she may gain momentary victory. Then India will cease to be the pride of my heart. I am wedded to India because I owe my all to her. I believe absolutely that she has a mission for the world."

We were moved by these arguments, but for us and for the National Congress as a whole the nonviolent method was not, and could not be, a religion or an unchallengeable creed or dogma. It could only be a policy and a method promising certain results, and by those results it would have to be finally judged. Individuals might make of it a religion or incontrovertible creed. But no political organization, so long as it remained political, could do so.

Chauri Chaura and its consequences made us examine these implications of nonviolence as a method, and we felt that, if Gandhiji's argument for the suspension of civil resistance was correct, our opponents would always have the power to create circumstances which would necessarily result in our abandoning the struggle. Was this the fault of the nonviolent method itself or of Gandhiji's interpretation of it? After all, he was the author and originator of it, and who could be a better judge of what it was and what it was not? And without him where was our movement?

Many years later, just before the 1930 civil disobedience movement began, Gandhiji, much to our satisfaction, made this point clear. He stated that the movement should not be abandoned because of the occurrence of sporadic acts of violence. If the nonviolent method of struggle could not function because of such almost inevitable happenings, then it was obvious that it was not an ideal method for all occasions, and this he was not prepared to admit. For him the method, being the right method, should suit all circumstances and should be able to function, at any rate in a restricted way, even in a hostile atmosphere. Whether this interpretation, which widened the scope of nonviolent action, represented an evolution in his own mind or not I do not know.

It may be that the decision to suspend civil resistance in 1922 was a right one, though the manner of doing it left much to be desired and brought about a certain demoralization.

It is possible, however, that this sudden bottling up of a great movement contributed to a tragic development in the country. The drift to sporadic and futile violence in the political struggle was stopped, but the suppressed violence had to find a way out, and in the following years this perhaps aggravated the communal trouble. The communalists of various denominations, mostly political reactionaries, had been forced to lie low because of the overwhelming mass support for the nonco-operation and civil disobedience movement. They emerged now from their retirement. Many others, secret-service agents and people who sought to please the authorities by creating communal friction, also worked on the same theme. The Moplah rising and its extraordinarily cruel suppression—what a horrible thing was the baking to death of the Moplah prisoners in the closed railway vans!—had already given a handle to those who stirred the waters of communal discord. It is just possible that if civil resistance had not been stopped and the movement had been crushed by Government, there would have been less communal bitterness and less superfluous energy left for the subsequent communal riots.

Both my father and I had been sentenced to six months' imprisonment on different charges and by different courts. The trials were farcical, and, as was our custom, we took no part in them. It was easy enough, of course, to find enough material in our speeches or other activities for a conviction. But the actual choice was amusing. Father was tried as a member of an illegal organization, the Congress volunteers, and to prove this a form with his signature in Hindu was produced. The signature was certainly his, but, as it happened, he had hardly ever signed in Hindu before, and very few persons could recognize his Hindu signature. A tattered gentleman was then produced who swore to the signature. The man was quite illiterate, and he held the signature upside down when he examined it. My daughter, aged four at the time, had her first experience of the dock during father's trial, as he held her in his arms throughout.

My offense was distributing notices for a *hartal*. This was no offense under the law then, though I believe it is one now, for we are rapidly advancing toward Dominion status. However, I was sentenced. Three months later I was informed in the prison, where I was with my father and others, that some revising authority had come to the conclusion that I was wrongly sentenced and I was to be discharged. I was surprised, as no one had taken any step on my behalf. The suspension of civil resistance had apparently galvanized the revising judges into activity. I was sorry to go out, leaving my father behind.

I decided to go almost immediately to Gandhiji in Ahmedabad. Before I arrived there, he had been arrested, and my interview with him took place in Sabarmati Prison. I was present at his trial. It was a memorable occasion, and those of us who were present are not likely ever to forget it. The judge, an Englishman, behaved with dignity and feeling. Gandhiji's statement to the court was a most moving one, and we came away, emotionally stirred, and with the impress of his vivid phrases and striking images in our mind.

I came back to Allahabad. I felt unhappy and lonely outside the prison when so many of my friends and colleagues were behind prison bars. I found that the Congress organization was not functioning well, and I tried to put it straight. In particular I interested myself in the boycott of foreign cloth. This item of our program still continued in spite of the withdrawal of civil resistance. Nearly all the cloth merchants in Allahabad had pledged themselves not to import or purchase foreign cloth, and had formed an association for the purpose. The rules of this association laid down that any infringement would be punished by a fine. I found that several of the big dealers had broken their pledges and were importing foreign cloth. This was very unfair to those who stuck to their pledges. We remonstrated with little result, and the cloth dealers' association seemed to be powerless to take action. So we decided to picket the shops of the erring merchants. Even a hint of picketing was enough for our purpose. Fines were paid, pledges were taken afresh. The money from the fines went to the cloth merchants' association.

Two or three days later I was arrested, together with a number of colleagues who had taken part in the negotiations with the merchants. We were charged with criminal intimidation and extortion! I was further charged with some other offenses, including sedition. I did not defend myself, but I made a long statement in court. I was sentenced on at least three counts, including intimidation and extortion, but the sedition charge was not proceeded with, as it was probably considered that I had already got as much as I deserved. As far as I remember there were three sentences, two of which were for eighteen months and were concurrent. In all, I think, I was sentenced to a year and nine months. That was my second sentence. I went back to prison after about six weeks spent outside it.

XV

# LUCKNOW DISTRICT JAIL

IMPRISONMENT FOR POLITICAL offenses was not a new thing in the India of 1921. From the time of the Bengal partition agitation especially, there had always been a continuous stream of men going to prison, sentenced often to very long terms. There had been internments without trial also. The greatest Indian leader of the day, Lokamanya Tilak, was sentenced in his declining years to six years' imprisonment. The Great War speeded up this process of internment and imprisonment, and conspiracy cases became frequent, usually resulting in death sentences or life terms. The Ali brothers and M. Abul Kalam Azad were among the wartime internees. Soon after the war, martial law in the Punjab took a heavy toll, and large numbers were sentenced in conspiracy cases or summary trials. So political imprisonment had become a frequent enough occurrence in India, but so far it had not been deliberately courted. It had come in the course of a person's activities, or perhaps because the secret police did not fancy him, and every effort was made to avoid it by means of a defense in the law court.

But still in 1921 prison was an almost unknown place, and very few knew what happened behind the grim gates that swallowed the new convict. Vaguely we imagined that its inhabitants were desperate peo-

85

ple and dangerous criminals. In our minds the place was associated with isolation, humiliation, and suffering, and, above all, the fear of the unknown. Frequent references to jail-going from 1920 onward, and the march of many of our comrades to prison, gradually accustomed us to the idea and took away the edge from that almost involuntary feeling of repugnance and reluctance. But no amount of previous mental preparation could prevent the tension and nervous excitement that filled us when we first entered the iron gates. Since those days, thirteen years ago, I imagine that at least three hundred thousand men and women of India have entered those gates for political offenses, although often enough the actual charge has been under some other section of the criminal code. Thousands of these have gone in and out many a time; they have got to know well what to expect inside; they have tried to adapt themselves to the strange life there, as far as one can adapt oneself to an existence full of abnormality and a dull suffering and a dreadful monotony. We grow accustomed to it, as one grows accustomed to almost anything; and yet, every time that we enter those gates again, there is a bit of the old excitement, a feeling of tension, a quickening of the pulse. And the eyes turn back involuntarily to take a last good look outside at the greenery and wide spaces, at people and conveyances moving about, at familiar faces that they may not see again for a long time.

My first term in jail, which ended rather suddenly after three months, was a hectic period both for us and the jail staff. The jail officials were half paralyzed by the influx of the new type of convict. The number itself of these newcomers, added to from day to day, was extraordinary and created an impression of a flood which might sweep away the old traditional landmarks. More upsetting still was the type of the newcomer. It belonged to all classes, but had a high proportion of the middle class. All these classes, however, had this in common: they differed entirely from the ordinary convict, and it was not easy to treat them in the old way. This was recognized by the authorities, but there was nothing to take the place of the existing rules; there were no precedents and no experience. The average Congress prisoner was not very meek and mild, and even inside the jail walls numbers gave him a feeling of strength. The agitation outside, and the new interest of the public in what transpired inside the prisons, added to this. In spite of this somewhat aggressive attitude, our general policy was one of co-operation with the jail authorities. But for our help, the troubles of the officials would have been far greater. The jailer would come to us frequently and ask us to visit some of the barracks containing our volunteers in order to soothe them or get them to agree to something.

We had come to prison of our own accord, many of the volunteers indeed having pushed their way in almost uninvited. There was thus hardly any question of any one of them trying to escape. If he had any desire to go out, he could do so easily by expressing regret for his action or giving an undertaking that he would refrain from such activity in future. An attempt to escape would only bring a measure of ignominy, and in itself was tantamount to a withdrawal from political activity of the civil resistance variety. The superintendent of our prison in Lucknow fully appreciated this and used to tell the jailer (who was a Khan Sahib) that if he could succeed in allowing some of the Congress prisoners to escape he, the superintendent, would recommend him to Government for the title of Khan Bahadur.

Most of our fellow prisoners were kept in huge barracks in the inner circle of the prison. About eighteen of us, selected I suppose for better treatment, were kept in an old weaving shed with a large open space attached. My father, two of my cousins, and I had a small shed to ourselves, about 20 feet by 16. We had considerable freedom in moving about from one barrack to another. Frequent interviews with relatives outside were allowed. Newspapers came, and the daily news of fresh arrests and the developments of our struggle kept up an atmosphere of excitement. Mutual discussions and talks took up a lot of time, and I could do little reading or other solid work. I spent the mornings in a thorough cleaning and washing of our shed, in washing father's and my own clothes, and in spinning. It was winter, the best time of year in North India. For the first few weeks we were allowed to open classes for our volunteers, or such of them as were illiterate, to teach them Hindu and Urdu and other elementary subjects. In the afternoons we played volleyball.[1]

Gradually restrictions grew. We were stopped from going outside our enclosure and visiting the part of the jail where most of our volunteers were kept. The classes naturally stopped. I was discharged about that time.

[1] A ridiculous story has appeared in the press, and, though contradicted, continues to appear from time to time. According to this, Sir Harcourt Butler, the then Governor of the United Provinces, sent champagne to my father in prison. Sir Harcourt sent my father nothing at all in prison; nobody sent him champagne or any other alcoholic drink; and indeed he had given up alcohol in 1920 after the Congress took to noncooperation, and was not taking any such drinks at that time.

I went out early in March, and six or seven weeks later, in April, I returned. I found that the conditions had greatly changed. Father had been transferred to the Naini Tal Jail, and, soon after his departure, new rules were enforced. All the prisoners in the big weaving shed, where I had been kept previously, were transferred to the inner jail and kept in the barracks (single halls) there. Each barrack was practically a jail within a jail, and no communications were allowed between different barracks. Interviews and letters were now restricted to one a month. The food was much simpler, though we were allowed to supplement it from outside.

In the barracks in which I was kept there must have been about fifty persons. We were all crowded together, our beds being about three or four feet from each other. Fortunately almost everybody in that barrack was known to me, and there were many friends. But the utter want of privacy, all day and night, became more and more difficult to endure. Always the same crowd looking on, the same petty annoyances and irritations, and no escape from them to a quiet nook. We bathed in public and washed our clothes in public, and ran round and round the barrack for exercise, and talked and argued till we had largely exhausted one another's capacity for intelligent conversation. It was the dull side of family life, magnified a hundredfold, with few of its graces and compensations, and all this among people of all kinds and tastes. It was a great nervous strain for all of us, and often I yearned for solitude. In later years I was to have enough of this solitude and privacy in prison, when for months I would see no one except an occasional jail official. Again I lived in a state of nervous tension, but this time I longed for suitable company. I thought then sometimes, almost with envy, of my crowded existence in the Lucknow District Jail in 1922, and yet I knew well enough that of the two I preferred the solitude, provided at least that I could read and write.

And yet I must say that the company was unusually decent and pleasant, and we got on well together. But all of us, I suppose, got a little bored with the others occasionally and wanted to be away from them and have a little privacy. The nearest approach to privacy that I could get was by leaving my barrack and sitting in the open part of the enclosure. It was the monsoon season, and it was usually possible to do so because of the clouds. I braved the heat and an occasional drizzle even, and spent as much time as possible outside the barrack.

Lying there in the open, I watched the skies and the clouds and I realized, better than I had ever done before, how amazingly beautiful were their changing hues.

> *To watch the changing clouds, like clime in clime;*
> *Oh! sweet to lie and bless the luxury of time.*

Time was not a luxury for us, it was more of a burden. But the time I spent in watching those ever-shifting monsoon clouds was filled with delight and a sense of relief. I had the joy of having made almost a discovery, and a feeling of escape from confinement. I do not know why that particular monsoon had that great effect on me; no previous or subsequent one has moved me in that way. I had seen and admired many a fine sunrise and sunset in the mountains and over the sea, and bathed in its glory, and felt stirred for the time being by its magnificence. Having seen it, I had almost taken it for granted and passed on to other things. But in jail there were no sunrises or sunsets to be seen, the horizon was hidden from us, and late in the morning the hot-rayed sun emerged over our guardian walls. There were no colors anywhere, and our eyes hardened and grew dull at seeing always that same drab view of mud-colored wall and barrack. They must have hungered for some light and shade and coloring, and, when the monsoon clouds sailed gaily by, assuming fantastic shapes and playing in a riot of color, I gasped in surprised delight and watched them almost as if I were in a trance. Sometimes the clouds would break, and one saw through an opening in them that wonderful monsoon phenomenon, a dark blue of an amazing depth, which seemed to be a portion of infinity.

The restrictions on us gradually grew in number, and stricter rules were enforced. The Government, having got the measure of our movement, wanted us to experience the full extent of its displeasure with our temerity in having dared to challenge it. The introduction of new rules or the manner of their enforcement led to friction between the jail authorities and the political prisoners. For several months nearly all of us—we were some hundreds at the time in that particular jail—gave up our interviews as a protest. Evidently it was thought that some of us were the troublemakers, and so seven of us were transferred to a distant part of the jail, quite cut off from the main barracks.

We were sent to a smaller enclosure, and there were some disadvantages in living there. But on the whole I was glad of the change. There was no crowding here; we could live in greater quiet and with more privacy. There was more time to read or do other work. We were cut off completely from our colleagues in other parts of the jail as well as from the outside world, for newspapers were now stopped for all political prisoners.

Newspapers did not come to us, but some news from outside trickled through, as it always manages to trickle through in prison. Our monthly interviews and letters also brought us odd bits of information. We saw that our movement was at a low ebb outside. The magic moment had passed, and success seemed to retire into the dim future. Outside, the Congress was split into two factions—the pro-changers and no-changers. The former, under the leadership of Deshbandhu Das and my father, wanted the Congress to take part in the new elections to the central and provincial councils and, if possible, to capture these legislatures; the latter, led by C. Rajagopalachari, opposed any change of the old program of nonco-operation. Gandhiji was, of course, in prison at the time. The fine ideals of the movement which had carried us forward, as on the crest of an advancing tide, were being swamped by petty squabbles and intrigues for power. We realized how much easier it was to do great and venturesome deeds in moments of enthusiasm and excitement than to carry on from day to day when the glow was past. Our spirits were damped by the news from outside, and this, added to the various humors that prison produces, increased the strain of life there. But still there remained within us an inner feeling of satisfaction, that we had preserved our self-respect and dignity, that we had acted rightly whatever the consequences. The future was dim, but, whatever shape it might take, it seemed that it would be the lot of many of us to spend a great part of our lives in prison.

We settled down to a routine of work and exercise. For exercise we used to run round and round the little enclosure, or two of us would draw water, like two bullocks yoked together, pulling a huge leather bucket from a well in our yard. In this way we watered a small vegetable garden in our enclosure. Most of us used to spin a little daily. But reading was my principal occupation during those winter days and long evenings. Almost always, whenever the superintendent visited us, he found me reading. This devotion to reading seemed to get on his nerves a little, and he remarked on it once, adding that, so far as he was concerned, he had practically finished his general reading at the age of twelve! No doubt this abstention on his part had been of use to that gallant English colonel in avoiding troublesome thoughts, and perhaps it helped him subsequently in rising to the position of Inspector-General of Prisons in the United Provinces.

The long winter evenings and the clear Indian sky attracted us to the stars, and, with the help of some charts, we spotted many of them. Nightly we would await their appearance and greet them with the satisfaction of seeing old acquaintances.

So we passed our time, and the days lengthened themselves into weeks, and the weeks became months. We grew accustomed to our routine existence. But in the world outside the real burden fell on our womenfolk, our mothers and wives and sisters. They wearied with the long waiting, and their very freedom seemed a reproach to them when their loved ones were behind prison bars.

Soon after our first arrest in December 1921 the police started paying frequent visits to Anand Bhawan, our house in Allahabad. They came to realize the fines which had been imposed on father and me. It was the Congress policy not to pay fines. So the police came day after day and attached and carried away bits of furniture. Indira, my four-year-old daughter, was greatly annoyed at this continuous process of despoliation and protested to the police and expressed her strong displeasure. I am afraid those early impressions are likely to color her future views about the police force generally.

In the jail every effort was made to keep us apart from the ordinary nonpolitical convicts, special jails being as a rule reserved for politicals. But complete segregation was impossible, and we often came into touch with those prisoners and learned from them, as well as directly, the realities of prison life in those days. It was a story of violence and widespread graft and corruption. The food was quite amazingly bad; I tried it repeatedly and found it quite uneatable. The staff was usually wholly incompetent and was paid very low salaries, but it had every opportunity to add to its income by extorting money on every conceivable occasion from the prisoners or their relatives. The duties and responsibilities of the jailer, and his assistants, and the warders, as laid down by the Jail Manual, were so many and so various that it was quite impossible for any person to discharge them conscientiously or competently. The general policy of the prison administration in the United Provinces (and probably in other provinces) had absolutely nothing to do with the reform of the prisoner or of teaching him good habits and useful trades. The object of prison labor was to harass the convict. He was to be frightened and broken into blind submission; the idea was that he should carry away from prison a fear and a horror of it, so that he might avoid crime and a return to prison in the future.

There have been some changes in recent years for the better. Food has improved a little, so also clothing and other matters. This was largely due to the agitation carried on outside by political prisoners after their discharge. Nonco-operation also resulted in a substantial increase in the warders' salaries to give them an additional inducement to remain loyal to the *sarkar*. A feeble effort is also made now to teach reading and writing to the boys and younger prisoners. But all these changes, welcome as they are, barely scratch the problem, and the old spirit remains much the same.

The great majority of the political prisoners had to put up with this regular treatment for ordinary prisoners. They had no special privileges or other treatment, but, being more aggressive and intelligent than the others, they could not easily be exploited, nor could money be made out of them. Because of this they were naturally not popular with the staff, and, when occasion offered itself, a breach of jail discipline by any of them was punished severely. For such a breach a young boy of fifteen or sixteen, who called himself Azad, was ordered to be flogged. He was stripped and tied to the whipping triangle, and as each stripe fell on him and cut into his flesh, he shouted, *"Mahatma Gandhi ki jai."* Every stripe brought forth the slogan till the boy fainted. Later, that boy was to become one of the leaders of the group of terrorists in North India.

## XVI

## OUT AGAIN

ONE MISSES MANY things in prison, but perhaps most of all one misses the sound of women's voices and children's laughter. The sounds one usually hears are not of the pleasantest. The voices are harsh and minatory, and the language brutal and largely consisting of swear words. Once I remember being struck by a new want. I was in the Lucknow District Jail, and I realized suddenly that I had not heard a dog bark for seven or eight months.

On the last day of January 1923 all of us politicals in the Lucknow Jail were discharged. There is always a feeling of relief and a sense of glad excitement in coming out of the prison gate. The fresh air and open expanses, the moving street scene, and the meeting with old friends, all go to the head and slightly intoxicate. Almost, there is a touch of hysteria in one's first reactions to the outer world. We felt exhilarated, but this was a passing sensation, for the state of Congress politics was discouraging enough. In the place of ideals there were intrigues, and various cliques were trying to capture the Congress machinery by the usual methods which have made politics a hateful word to those who are at all sensitive.

On my return home from jail the first letter that met my eyes was one from Sir Grimwood Mears, the then Chief Justice of the Allahabad High Court. The letter had been written before my discharge, but evidently in the knowledge that it was coming. I was a little surprised at the cordiality of his language and his invitation to me to visit him frequently. I hardly knew him. He had just come to Allahabad in 1919 when I was drifting away from legal practice. I think I argued only one case before him, and that was my last one in the High Court. For some reason or other he developed a partiality for me without knowing much about me. He had an idea—he told me so later—that I would go far, and he wanted to be a wholesome influence on me to make me appreciate the British viewpoint. His method was subtle. He was of opinion, and there are many Englishmen who still think so, that the average "extremist" politician in India had become anti-British because in the social sphere he had been treated badly by Englishmen. This had led to resentment and bitterness and extremism. There is a story, which has been repeated by responsible persons, to the effect that my father was refused election to an English club and this made him anti-British and extremist. The story is wholly without foundation and is a distortion of an entirely different incident. But to many an English-man such instances, whether true or not, afford a simple and sufficient explanation of the origins of the nationalist movement. As a matter of fact neither my father nor I had any particular grievance on this score. As individuals we had usually met with courtesy from the English-man, and we got on well with him, though, like all Indians, we were no doubt racially conscious of subjection, and resented it bitterly. I must confess that even today I get on very well with an Englishman, unless he happens to be an official and wants to patronize me, and even then there is no lack of humor in our contacts. Probably I have more in common with him than the Liberals or others who co-operate with him politically in India.

Sir Grimwood's idea was to root out this original cause of bitterness by friendly intercourse and frank and courteous treatment. I saw him several times. On the pretext of objecting to some municipal tax he would come to see me and discuss other matters. On one occasion he made quite an onslaught on the Indian Liberals—timid, weak-kneed opportunists with no character or backbone, he called them, and his language was stronger and full of contempt. "Do you think we have any respect for them?" he said. I wondered why he spoke to me in this way; probably because he thought that this kind of talk might please me. And then he led up the conversation to the new councils and their ministers and the opportunities these ministers had for serving their country. Education was one of the most vital problems before the country. Would not an Education Minister, with freedom to act as he chose, have a worthy opportunity to mold the destinies of millions, the chance of a lifetime? Suppose, he went on, a man like you, with intelligence, character, ideals, and the energy to push them through, was in charge of education for the province, could you not perform wonders? And he assured me, adding that he had seen the Governor recently, that I would be given perfect freedom to work out my policy. Then, realizing, perhaps, that he had gone too far, he said that he could not, of course, commit anybody officially, and the suggestion he had made was a personal one.

I was diverted by Sir Grimwood's diplomatic and roundabout approach to the proposal he had made. The idea of my associating myself with the Government as a Minister was unthinkable for me; indeed, it was hateful to me. But I have often yearned, then as well as in later years, for a chance to do some solid, positive, constructive work. Destruction and agitation and nonco-operation are hardly normal activities for human beings. And yet, such is our fate, that we can only reach the land where we can build after passing through the deserts of conflict and destruction. And it may be that most of us will spend our energies and our lives in struggling and panting through those shifting sands, and the building will have to be done by our children or our children's children.

I occupied myself with many activities and sought thereby to keep away from the problems that troubled me. But there was no escape from them, no getting away from the questions that were always being formed in my mind and to which I could find no satisfactory answer. Action now was partly an attempt to run away from myself; no longer was it a wholehearted expression of the self as it had been in 1920 and 1921. I came out of the shell that had protected me then and looked round at the Indian scene as well as at the world outside. I found many changes that I had not so far noticed, new ideas, new conflicts, and instead of light I saw a growing confusion. My faith in Gandhiji's leadership remained, but I began to examine some parts of his program more critically. But he was in prison and beyond our reach, and his advice could not be taken.

From 1923 onward I found a great deal of solace and happiness in family life, though I gave little time to it. I have been fortunate in my family relationships, and in times of strain and difficulty they have soothed me and sheltered me. I realized, with some shame at my own unworthiness in this respect, how much I owed to my wife for her splendid behavior since 1920. Proud and sensitive as she was, she had not only put up with my vagaries but brought me comfort and solace when I needed them most.

Our style of living had undergone some change since 1920. It was much simpler, and the number of servants had been greatly reduced. Even so, it was not lacking in any essential comfort. Partly to get rid of superfluities and partly to raise money for current expenditures, many things had been sold off—horses and carriages, and household articles which did not fit in with our new style of living. Part of our furniture had been seized and sold by the police. For lack of furniture and gardeners, our house lost its prim and clean appearance, and the garden went wild. For nearly three years little attention had been paid to house or garden. Having become accustomed to a lavish scale of expenditure, father disliked many economies. He decided therefore to go in for chamber practice in his spare time and thus earn some money. He had very little spare time, but, even so, he managed to earn a fair amount.

I felt uncomfortable and a little unhappy at having to depend financially on father. Ever since I had given up my legal practice, I had practically no income of my own, except a trifle from some dividends on shares. My wife and I did not spend much. Indeed, I was quite surprised to find how little we spent. This was one of the discoveries made by me in 1921 which brought me great satisfaction. *Khadi* clothes and third-class railway traveling demand little money. I did not fully realize then, living as we did with father, that there are innumerable other household expenses which mount up to a considerable figure. Anyhow, the fear of not having money has never troubled me; I suppose I could earn enough in case of necessity, and we can do with relatively little.

We were not much of a burden on father, and even a hint of this kind would have pained him greatly. Yet I disliked my position, and for the next three years I thought over the problem without finding a solution. There was no great difficulty in my finding paying work, but the acceptance of any such work necessitated my giving up or, at any rate, my curtailing the public work I was doing. So far I had given all my working time to Congress work and municipal work. I did not like to withdraw from them for the sake of making money. So I refused offers, financially very advantageous, from big industrial firms. Probably they were willing to pay heavily, not so much for my competence as for the opportunity to exploit my name. I did not like the idea of being associated with big industry in this way. To go back to the profession of law was also out of the question for me. My dislike for it had grown and kept on growing.

A suggestion was made in the 1924 Congress that the general secretaries should be paid. I happened to be one of the secretaries then, and I welcomed the proposal. It seemed to me quite wrong to expect whole-time work from anyone without paying him a maintenance allowance at least. Otherwise some person with private means has to be chosen, and such gentlemen of leisure are not perhaps always politically desirable, nor can they be held responsible for the work. The Congress would not have paid much; our rates of payment were low enough. But there is in India an extraordinary and thoroughly unjustified prejudice against receiving salaries from public funds (though not from the State), and my father strongly objected to my doing so. My co-secretary, who was himself in great need of money, also considered it below his dignity to accept it from the Congress. And so I, who had no dignity in the matter and was perfectly prepared to accept a salary, had to do without it.

Once only I spoke to father on the subject and told him how I disliked the idea of my financial dependence. I put it to him as gently and indirectly as possible so as not to hurt him. He pointed out to me how foolish it would be of me to spend my time, or most of it, in earning a little money, instead of doing public work. It was far easier for him to earn with a few days' work all that my wife and I would require for a year. The argument was weighty, but it left me unsatisfied. However, I continued to act in consonance with it.

## XVII

# AN INTERLUDE AT NABHA

IMMEDIATELY AFTER THE Congress at Delhi in the autumn of 1923 I had a strange and unexpected adventure.

The Sikhs, and especially the Akalis among them, had been coming into repeated conflict with the Government in the Punjab. The incident to which I am going to refer had little to do with this general Sikh movement, but there is no doubt that it occurred because of the Sikh upheaval. The rulers of two Sikh states in the Punjab, Patiala and Nabha, had a bitter, personal quarrel which resulted ultimately in the deposition of the Maharaja of Nabha by the Government of India. A British Administrator was appointed to rule the Nabha State. This deposition was resented by the Sikhs, and they agitated against it both in Nabha and outside. In the course of this agitation, a religious ceremony, at a place called Jaito in Nabha State, was stopped by the new Administrator. To protest against this, and with the declared object of continuing the interrupted ceremony, the Sikhs began sending *jathas* (batches of men) to Jaito. These *jathas* were stopped, beaten by the police, arrested, and usually carried to an out-of-the-way place in the jungle and left there. I had been reading accounts of these beatings from time to time, and, when I learned at Delhi, immediately after the Special Congress, that another *jatha* was going and I was invited to come and see what happened, I gladly accepted the invitation. It meant the loss of only a day to me, as Jaito was near Delhi. Two of my Congress colleagues—A. T. Gidwani and K. Santanum of Madras —accompanied me. The *jatha* marched most of the way. It was arranged that we should go to the nearest railway station and then try to reach by road the Nabha boundary near Jaito just when the *jatha* was due to arrive there. We arrived in time, having come in a country cart, and followed the *jatha,* keeping apart from it. On arrival at Jaito the *jatha* was stopped by the police, and immediately an order was served on me, signed by the English Administrator, calling upon me not to enter Nabha territory and, if I had entered it, to leave it immediately. A similar order was served on Gidwani and Santanum, but without their names being mentioned, as the Nabha authorities did not know them. My colleagues and I told the police officer that we were there not as part of the *jatha* but as spectators, and it was not our intention to break any of the Nabha laws. Besides, when we were

97

already in the Nabha territories, there could be no question of our not entering them, and obviously we could not vanish suddenly into thin air. Probably the next train from Jaito went many hours later. So for the present, we told him, we proposed to remain there. We were immediately arrested and taken to the lock-up. After our removal the *jatha* was dealt with in the usual manner.

We were kept the whole day in the lock-up, and in the evening we were marched to the station. Santanum and I were handcuffed together, his left wrist to my right one, and a chain attached to the handcuff was held by the policeman leading us. Gidwani, also handcuffed and chained, brought up the rear. This march of ours down the streets of Jaito town reminded me forcibly of a dog being led on by a chain. We felt somewhat irritated to begin with, but the humor of the situation dawned upon us, and on the whole we enjoyed the experience. We did not enjoy the night that followed. This was partly spent in crowded third-class compartments in slow-moving trains, with, I think, a change at midnight, and partly in a lock-up at Nabha. All this time, till the forenoon of next day, when we were finally delivered up at the Nabha Jail, the joint handcuff and the heavy chain kept us company. Neither of us could move at all without the other's co-operation. To be handcuffed to another person for a whole night and part of a day is not an experience I should like to repeat.

In Nabha Jail we were all three kept in a most unwholesome and insanitary cell. It was small and damp, with a low ceiling which we could almost touch. At night we slept on the floor, and I would wake up with a start, full of horror, to find that a rat or a mouse had just passed over my face.

Two or three days later we were taken to court for our case, and the most extraordinary and Gilbertian proceedings went on there from day to day. The magistrate or judge seemed to be wholly uneducated. He knew no English, of course, but I doubt if he knew how to write the court language, Urdu. We watched him for over a week, and during all this time he never wrote a line. If he wanted to write anything, he made the court reader do it. We put in a number of small applications. He did not pass any orders on them at the time. He kept them and produced them the next day with a note written by somebody else on them. We did not formally defend ourselves. We had got so used to not defending cases in court during the nonco-operation movement that the idea of defense, even when it was manifestly permissible, seemed almost indecent. But I gave the court a long statement containing the facts, as well as my own opinion about Nabha ways, especially under British administration.

Our case was dragging on from day to day although it was a simple enough affair. Suddenly there was a diversion. One afternoon after the court had risen for the day we were kept waiting in the building; and late in the evening, at about 7 P.M., we were taken to another room where a person was sitting by a table and there were some other people about. One man, our old friend, the police officer who had arrested us at Jaito, was there, and he got up and began making a statement. I inquired where we were and what was happening. I was informed that it was a courtroom and we were being tried for conspiracy. This was an entirely different proceeding from the one we had so far attended, which was for breach of the order not to enter Nabha territory. It was evidently thought that the maximum sentence for this breach, being only six months, was not enough punishment for us and a more serious charge was necessary. Apparently three were not enough for conspiracy, and so a fourth man, who had absolutely nothing to do with us, was arrested and put on his trial with us. This unhappy man, a Sikh, was not known to us, but we had just seen him in the fields on our way to Jaito.

The lawyer in me was rather taken aback by the casualness with which a conspiracy trial had been started. The case was a totally false one, but decency required that some formalities should be observed. I pointed out to the judge that we had had no notice whatever and that we might have wanted to make arrangements for our defense. This did not worry him at all. It was the Nabha way. If we wanted to engage a lawyer for our defense we could chose someone in Nabha. When I suggested that I might want some lawyer from outside, I was told that this was not permitted under the Nabha rules. We were further enlightened about the peculiarities of Nabha procedure. In some disgust we told the judge to do what he liked, but so far as we were concerned we would take no part in the proceedings. I could not wholly adhere to this resolve. It was difficult to listen to the most astounding lies about us and remain silent, and so occasionally we expressed our opinion, briefly but pointedly, about the witnesses. We also gave the court a statement in writing about the facts. This second judge, who tried the conspiracy case, was more educated and intelligent than the other one.

Both these cases went on and we looked forward to our daily visits to the two courtrooms, for that meant a temporary escape from the foul cell in jail. Meanwhile, we were approached, on behalf of the Administrator, by the superintendent of the jail and told that if we would express our regret and give an undertaking to go away from Nabha, the proceedings against us would be dropped. We replied that there was nothing to express regret about, so far as we were concerned; it was for the administration to apologize to us. We were also not prepared to give any undertaking.

About a fortnight after our arrest the two trials at last ended. All this time had been taken up by the prosecution, for we were not defending. Much of it had been wasted in long waits, for every little difficulty that arose necessitated an adjournment or a reference to some authority behind the scenes—probably the English Administrator. On the last day, when the prosecution case was closed, we handed in our written statements. The first court adjourned and, to our surprise, returned a little later with a bulky judgment written out in Urdu. Obviously this huge judgment could not have been written during the interval. It had been prepared before our statements had been handed in. The judgment was not read out; we were merely told that we had been awarded the maximum sentence of six months for breach of the order to leave Nabha territory.

In the conspiracy case we were sentenced the same day to either eighteen months or two years, I forget which. This was to be in addition to the sentence for six months. Thus we were given in all either two years or two and a half years.

Right through our trial there had been any number of remarkable incidents which gave us some insight into the realities of Indian state administration, or rather the British administration of an Indian state. The whole procedure was farcical. Because of this I suppose no newspaperman or outsider was allowed in court. The police did what they pleased, and often ignored the judge or magistrate and actually disobeyed his directions. The poor magistrate meekly put up with this, but we saw no reason why we should do so. On several occasions I had to stand up and insist on the police behaving and obeying the magistrate. Sometimes there was an unseemly snatching of papers by the police, and, the magistrate being incapable of action or of introducing order in his own court, we had partly to do his job! The poor magistrate was in an unhappy position. He was afraid of the police, and he seemed to be a little frightened of us, too, for our arrest had been noised in the press. If this was the state of affairs when more or less prominent politicians like us were concerned, what, I wonder, would be the fate of others less known?

My father knew something of Indian states, and so he was greatly upset at my unexpected arrest in Nabha. Only the fact of arrest was known; little else in the way of news could leak out. In his distress he even telegraphed to the Viceroy for news of me. Difficulties were put in the way of his visiting me in Nabha, but he was allowed at last to interview me in prison. He could not be of any help to me, as I was not defending myself, and I begged him to go back to Allahabad and not to worry. He returned, but he left a young lawyer colleague of ours, Kapil Dev Malaviya, in Nabha to watch the proceedings. Kapil Dev's knowledge of law and procedure must have been considerably augmented by his brief experience of the Nabha courts. The police tried to deprive him forcibly in open court of some papers that he had.

Most of the Indian states are well known for their backwardness and their semifeudal conditions. They are personal autocracies, devoid even of competence or benevolence. Many a strange thing occurs there which never receives publicity. And yet their very inefficiency lessens the evil in some ways and lightens the burden on their unhappy people. For this is reflected in a weak executive, and it results in making even tyranny and injustice inefficient. That does not make tyranny more bearable, but it does make it less far-reaching and widespread. The assumption of direct British control over an Indian state has a curious result in changing this equilibrium. The semifeudal conditions are retained, autocracy is kept, the old laws and procedure are still supposed to function, all the restrictions on personal liberty and association and expression of opinion (and these are all-embracing) continue, but one change is made which alters the whole background. The executive becomes stronger, while a measure of efficiency is introduced, and this leads to a tightening-up of all the feudal and autocratic bonds. In course of time the British administration would no doubt change some of the archaic customs and methods, for they come in the way of efficient government as well as commercial penetration. But to begin with they take full advantage of them to tighten their hold on the people, who have now to put up not only with feudalism and autocracy, but with an efficient enforcement of them by a strong executive.

I saw something of this in Nabha. The state was under a British Administrator, a member of the Indian Civil Service, and he had the full powers of an autocrat, subject only to the Government of India.

And yet at every turn we were referred to Nabha laws and procedure to justify the denial of the most ordinary rights. We had to face a combination of feudalism and the modern bureaucratic machine with the disadvantages of both and the advantages of neither.

So our trial was over and we had been sentenced. We did not know what the judgments contained, but the solid fact of a long sentence had a sobering effect. We asked for copies of the judgments, and were told to apply formally for them.

That evening in jail the superintendent sent for us and showed us an order of the Administrator under the Criminal Procedure Code suspending our sentences. There was no condition attached, and the legal result of that order was that the sentences ended so far as we were concerned. The superintendent then produced a separate order called an executive order, also issued by the Administrator, asking us to leave Nabha and not to return to the state without special permission. I asked for the copies of the two orders, but they were refused. We were then escorted to the railway station and released there. We did not know a soul in Nabha, and even the city gates had been closed for the night. We found that a train was leaving soon for Ambala, and we took this. From Ambala I went on to Delhi and Allahabad.

From Allahabad I wrote to the Administrator requesting him to send me copies of his two orders, so that I might know exactly what they were, also copies of the two judgments. He refused to supply any of these copies. I pointed out that I might decide to file an appeal, but he persisted in his refusal. In spite of repeated efforts I have never had the opportunity to read these judgments, which sentenced me and my two colleagues to two years or two and half years. For aught I know, these sentences may still be hanging over me, and may take effect whenever the Nabha authorities or the British Government so choose.

The three of us were discharged in this "suspended" way, but I could never find out what had happened to the fourth member of the alleged conspiracy, the Sikh who had been tacked on to us for the second trial. Very likely he was not discharged. He had no powerful friends or public interest to help him, and, like many another person, he sank into the oblivion of a state prison. He was not forgotten by us. We did what we could, and this was very little, and, I believe, the Gurdwara Committee interested itself in his case also.

All three of us—Gidwani, Santanum, and I—brought an unpleasant companion with us from our cell in Nabha Jail. This was the typhus bacillus, and each one of us had an attack of typhoid. Mine was severe, and for a while dangerous enough, but it was the lightest of the three, and I was only bedridden for about three or four weeks, but the other two were very seriously ill for long periods.

There was yet another sequel to this Nabha episode. Probably six months or more later, Gidwani was acting as the Congress representative in Amritsar, keeping in touch with the Sikh Gurdwara Committee. The Committee sent a special *jatha* of five hundred persons to Jaito, and Gidwani decided to accompany it as an observer to the Nabha border. He had no intention of entering Nabha territory. The *jatha* was fired on by the police near the border, and many persons were, I believe, killed and wounded. Gidwani went to the help of the wounded when he was pounced upon by the police and taken away. No proceedings in court were taken against him. He was simply kept in prison for the best part of a year when, utterly broken in health, he was discharged.

Gidwani's arrest and confinement seemed to me to be a monstrous abuse of executive authority. I wrote to the Administrator (who was still the same English member of the Indian Civil Service) and asked him why Gidwani had been treated in this way. He replied that Gidwani had been imprisoned because he had broken the order not to enter Nabha territory without permission. I challenged the legality of this as well as, of course, the propriety of arresting a man who was giving succor to the wounded, and I asked the Administrator to send me or publish a copy of the order in question. He refused to do so. I felt inclined to go to Nabha myself and allow the Administrator to treat me as he had treated Gidwani. Loyalty to a colleague seemed to demand it. But many friends thought otherwise and dissuaded me. I took shelter behind the advice of friends, and made of it a pretext to cover my own weakness. For, after all, it was my weakness and disinclination to go to Nabha Jail again that kept me away, and I have always felt a little ashamed of thus deserting a colleague. As often with us all, discretion was preferred to valor.

# XVIII

# M. MOHAMAD ALI, MY FATHER, AND GANDHIJI

IN DECEMBER 1923 the annual session of the Congress was held at Co-conada in the south, Maulana Mohamad Ali was the president, and, as was his wont, he delivered an enormously long presidential address. But it was an interesting one. He traced the growth of political and communal feeling among the Moslems and showed how the famous Moslem deputation to the Viceroy in 1908, under the leadership of the Aga Khan, which led to the first official declaration in favor of separate electorates, was a command performance and had been engineered by the Government itself.

Mohamad Ali induced me, much against my will, to accept the All-India Congress secretaryship for his year of presidency. I had no desire to accept executive responsibility, when I was not clear about future policy. But I could not resist Mohamad Ali, and both of us felt that some other secretary might not be able to work as harmoniously with the new president as I could. He had strong likes and dislikes, and I was fortunate enough to be included in his "likes." A bond of affection and mutual appreciation tied us to each other. He was deeply and, as I considered, most irrationally religious, and I was not, but I was attracted by his earnestness, his overflowing energy, and keen intelligence. He had a nimble wit, but sometimes his devastating sarcasm hurt, and he lost many a friend thereby. It was quite impossible for him to keep a clever remark to himself, whatever the consequences might be.

We got on well together during his year of office, though we had many little points of difference. I introduced in the office of the All-India Congress Committee a practice of addressing all our members by their names only, without any prefixes or suffixes, honorific titles and the like. There are so many of these in India—Mahatma, Maulana, Pandit, Shaikh, Syed, Munshi, Moulvi, and latterly Sriyut and Shri, and, of course, Mr. and Esquire—and they are so abundantly and often unnecessarily used that I wanted to set a good example. But I was not to have my way. Mohamad Ali sent me a frantic telegram directing me "as president" to revert to our old practice and, in particular, always to address Gandhiji as Mahatma.

Another frequent subject for argument between us was the Almighty. Mohamad Ali had an extraordinary way of bringing in some reference to God even in Congress resolutions, either by way of expressing gratitude or some kind of prayer. I used to protest, and then he would shout at me for my irreligion. And yet, curiously enough, he would tell me later that he was quite sure that I was fundamentally religious, in spite of my superficial behavior or my declarations to the contrary. I have often wondered how much truth there was in his statement. Perhaps it depends on what is meant by religion and religious.

I avoided discussing this subject of religion with him, because I knew we would only irritate each other, and I might hurt him. It is always a difficult subject to discuss with convinced believers of any creed. With most Moslems it is probably an even harder matter for discussion, since no latitude of thought is officially permitted to them. Ideologically, theirs is a straight and narrow path, and the believer must not swerve to the right or the left. Hindus are somewhat different, though not always so. In practice they may be very orthodox; they may, and do, indulge in the most out-of-date, reactionary, and even pernicious customs, and yet they will usually be prepared to discuss the most radical ideas about religion. I imagine the modern Arya Samajists have not, as a rule, this wide intellectual approach. Like the Moslems, they follow their own straight and narrow path. There is a certain philosophical tradition among the intelligent Hindus, which, though it does not affect practice, does make a difference to the ideological approach to a religious question. Partly, I suppose, this is due to the wide and often conflicting variety of opinions and customs that are included in the Hindu fold. It has, indeed, often been remarked that Hinduism is hardly a religion in the usual sense of the word. And yet, what amazing tenacity it has got, what tremendous power of survival! One may even be a professing atheist—as the old Hindu philosopher, Charvaka, was—and yet no one dares say that he has ceased to be a Hindu. Hinduism clings on to its children, almost despite them. A Brahman I was born, and a Brahman I seem to remain whatever I might say or do in regard to religion or social custom. To the Indian world I am "Pandit" so and so, in spite of my desire not to have this or any other honorific title attached to my name. I remember meeting a Turkish scholar once in Switzerland, to whom I had sent previously a letter of introduction in which I had been referred to as "Pandit Jawaharlal Nehru." He was surprised and a little disappointed to see me, for, as he told me, the "Pandit" had led him to expect a reverend and scholarly gentleman of advanced years.

I met Mohamad Ali for the last time on the occasion of the Lahore

Congress in December 1929. He was not pleased with some parts of my presidential address, and he criticized it vigorously. He saw that the Congress was going ahead, and becoming politically more aggressive. He was aggressive enough himself, and, being so, he disliked taking a back seat and allowing others to be in the front. He gave me solemn warning: "I warn you, Jawahar, that your present colleagues will desert you. They will leave you in the lurch in a crisis. Your own Congressmen will send you to the gallows." A dismal prophecy!

Soon after my return from Coconada, in January 1924, I had a new kind of experience in Allahabad. I write from memory, and I am likely to get mixed up about dates. But I think that was the year of the *Kumbh,* or the *Ardh-Kumbh,* the great bathing *mela* held on the banks of the Ganges at Allahabad. Vast numbers of pilgrims usually turn up, and most of them bathe at the confluence of the Ganges and the Jumna—the *Triveni,* it is called, as the mythical Saraswati is also supposed to join the other two. The Ganges river bed is about a mile wide, but in winter the river shrinks and leaves a wide expanse of sand exposed, which is very useful for the camps of the pilgrims. Within this river bed, the Ganges frequently changes its course. In 1924 the current of the Ganges was such that it was undoubtedly dangerous for crowds to bathe at the *Triveni.* With certain precautions, and the control of the numbers bathing at a time, the danger could be greatly lessened.

I was not at all interested in this question, as I did not propose to acquire merit by bathing in the river on the auspicious days. But I noticed in the press that a controversy was going on between Pandit Madan Mohan Malaviya and the Provincial Government, the latter (or the local authorities) having issued orders prohibiting all bathing at the junction of the rivers. This was objected to by Malaviyaji, as, from the religious point of view, the whole point was to bathe at that confluence. The Government was perfectly justified in taking precautions to prevent accidents and possible serious loss of life, but, as usual, it set about its work in the most wooden and irritating way possible.

On the big day of the *Kumbh,* I went down to the river early in the morning to see the *mela,* with no intention of bathing. On arrival at the river bank, I learned that Malaviyaji had sent some kind of polite ultimatum to the district magistrate, asking him for permission to bathe at the *Triveni.* Malaviyaji was agitated, and the atmosphere was tense. The magistrate refused permission. Thereupon Malaviyaji decided to offer *Satyagraha,* and, accompanied by about two hundred others, he marched toward the junction of the rivers. I was interested in these developments and, on the spur of the moment, joined the *Satyagraha* band. A tremendous barrier had been erected right across the open space, to keep away people from the confluence. When we reached this high palisade, we were stopped by the police, and a ladder we had was taken away from us. Being nonviolent *Satyagrahis,* we sat down peacefully on the sands near the palisade. And there we sat for the whole morning and part of the afternoon. Hour after hour went by, the sun became stronger, the sand hotter, and all of us hungrier. Foot and mounted police stood by on both sides of us. I think the regular cavalry was also there. Most of us grew impatient and said that something should be done. I believe the authorities also grew impatient, and decided to force the pace. Some order was given to the cavalry, who mounted their horses. It struck me (I do not know if I was right) that they were going to charge us and drive us away in this fashion. I did not fancy the idea of being chased by mounted troopers, and, anyhow, I was fed up with sitting there. So I suggested to those sitting near me that we might as well cross over the palisade, and I mounted it. Immediately scores of others did likewise, and some even pulled out a few stakes, thus making a passageway. Somebody gave me a national flag, and I stuck it on top of the palisade, where I continued to sit. I grew rather excited and thoroughly enjoyed myself, watching the people clambering up or going through and the mounted troopers trying to push them away. I must say that the cavalry did their work as harmlessly as possible. They waved about their wooden staffs and pushed people with them but refrained from causing much injury. Faint memories of revolutionary barricades came to me.

At last I got down on the other side and, feeling very hot after my exertions, decided to have a dip in the Ganges. On coming back, I was amazed to find that Malaviyaji and many others were still sitting on the other side of the palisade as before. But the mounted troopers and the foot police now stood shoulder to shoulder between the *Satyagrahis* and the palisade. So I went (having got out by a roundabout way) and sat down again near Malaviyaji. For some time we sat on, and I noticed that Malaviyaji was greatly agitated; he seemed to be trying to control some strong emotion. Suddenly, without a hint to anyone, he dived in the most extraordinary way through the policemen and the horses. For anyone that would have been a surprising dive, but for an old and physically weak person like Malaviyaji, it was astounding. Anyhow, we all followed him; we all dived. After some effort to keep us back, the cavalry and the police did not interfere. A little later they were withdrawn.

We half expected some proceedings to be taken against us by the Government, but nothing of the kind happened. Government probably did not wish to take any steps against Malaviyaji, and so the smaller fry got off too.

Early in 1924 there came suddenly the news of the serious illness of Gandhiji in prison, followed by his removal to a hospital and an operation. India was numbed with anxiety; we held our breaths almost and waited, full of fear. The crisis passed, and a stream of people began to reach Poona from all parts of the country to see him. He was still in hospital, a prisoner under guard, but he was permitted to see a limited number of friends. Father and I visited him in the hospital.

He was not taken back from the hospital to the prison. As he was convalescing, Government remitted the rest of his sentence and discharged him. He had then served about two years out of the six years to which he had been sentenced. He went to Juhu, by the seaside near Bombay, to recuperate.

Our family also trekked to Juhu, and established itself in a tiny little cottage by the sea. We spent some weeks there, and I had, after a long gap, a holiday after my heart, for I could indulge in swimming and running and riding on the beach. The main purpose of our stay, however, was not holiday-making, but discussions with Gandhiji. Father wanted to explain to him the *Swarajist* position, and to gain his passive co-operation at least, if not his active sympathy. I was also anxious to have some light thrown on the problems that were troubling me. I wanted to know what his future program of action was going to be.

The Juhu talks, so far as the *Swarajists* were concerned, did not succeed in winning Gandhiji, or even in influencing him to any extent. Behind all the friendly talk and the courteous gestures, the fact remained that there was no compromise. They agreed to differ, and statements to this effect were issued to the press.

I also returned from Juhu a little disappointed, for Gandhiji did not resolve a single one of my doubts. As is usual with him, he refused to look into the future, or lay down any long-distance program.

Ever since Gandhiji appeared on the Indian political scene, there has been no going back in popularity for him, so far as the masses are concerned. There has been a progressive increase in his popularity, and this process still continues. They may not carry out his wishes, for human nature is often weak, but their hearts are full of good will for him. When objective conditions help, they rise in huge mass movements; otherwise they lie low. A leader does not create a mass movement out of nothing, as if by a stroke of the magician's wand. He can take advantage of the conditions themselves when they arise; he can prepare for them, but not create them.

There is a waning and a waxing of Gandhiji's popularity among the intelligentsia. In moments of forward-going enthusiasm they follow him; when the inevitable reaction comes, they grow critical. But even so the great majority of them bow down to him. Partly this has been due to the absence of any other effective program. The Liberals and various groups resembling them do not count; those who believe in terroristic violence are completely out of court in the modern world and are considered ineffective and out of date. The socialist program is still little known, and it frightens the upper-class members of the Congress.

After a brief political estrangement in the middle of 1924, the old relations between my father and Gandhiji were resumed and they grew even more cordial. However much they differed from one another, each had the warmest regard and respect for the other. What was it that they so respected? Father has given us a glimpse into his mind in a brief foreword he contributed to a booklet called *Thought Currents,* containing selections from Gandhiji's writings:

"I have heard," he writes, "of saints and supermen, but have never had the pleasure of meeting them, and must confess to a feeling of skepticism about their real existence. I believe in men and things manly. The 'Thought Currents' preserved in this volume have emanated from a man and are things manly. They are illustrative of two great attributes of human nature—Faith and Strength. . . .

"'What is all this going to lead to?' asks the man with neither faith nor strength in him. The answer 'to victory or death' does not appeal to him. . . . Meanwhile the humble and lowly figure standing erect . . . on the firm footholds of faith unshakable and strength unconquerable, continues to send out to his countrymen his message of sacrifice and suffering for the motherland. That message finds echo in millions of hearts. . . ."

And he finishes up by quoting Swinburne's lines:

*Have we not men with us royal,*
*Men the masters of things? . . .*

Evidently he wanted to stress the fact that he did not admire Gandhiji as a saint or a Mahatma, but as a man. Strong and unbending himself, he admired strength of spirit in him. For it was clear that this little man of poor physique had something of steel in him, something rocklike which did not yield to physical powers, however great they might be. And in spite of his unimpressive features, his loincloth and bare body, there was a royalty and a kingliness in him which compelled a willing obeisance from others. Consciously and deliberately meek and humble, yet he was full of power and authority, and he knew it, and at times he was imperious enough, issuing commands which had to be obeyed. His calm, deep eyes would hold one and gently probe into the depths; his voice, clear and limpid, would purr its way into the heart and evoke an emotional response. Whether his audience consisted of one person or a thousand, the charm and magnetism of the man passed on to it, and each one had a feeling of communion with the speaker. This feeling had little to do with the mind, though the appeal to the mind was not wholly ignored. But mind and reason definitely had second place. This process of "spell-binding" was not brought about by oratory or the hypnotism of silken phrases. The language was always simple and to the point, and seldom was an unnecessary word used. It was the utter sincerity of the man and his personality that gripped; he gave the impression of tremendous inner reserves of power. Perhaps also it was a tradition that had grown up about him which helped in creating a suitable atmosphere. A stranger, ignorant of this tradition and not in harmony with the surroundings, would probably not have been touched by that spell, or, at any rate, not to the same extent. And yet one of the most remarkable things about Gandhiji was, and is, his capacity to win over, or at least to disarm, his opponents.

Gandhiji had little sense of beauty or artistry in man-made objects, though he admired natural beauty. The Taj Mahal was for him an embodiment of forced labor and little more. His sense of smell was feeble. And yet in his own way he had discovered the art of living and had made of his life an artistic whole. Every gesture had meaning and grace, without a false touch. There were no rough edges or sharp corners about him, no trace of vulgarity or commonness, in which, unhappily, our middle classes excel. Having found an inner peace, he radiated it to others and marched through life's tortuous ways with firm and undaunted step.

How different was my father from him! But in him too there was strength of personality and a measure of kingliness, and the lines of Swinburne he had quoted would apply to him also. In any gathering in which he was present he would inevitably be the center and the hub. Whatever the place where he sat at table, it would become, as an eminent English judge said later, the head of the table. He was neither meek nor mild, and, again unlike Gandhiji, he seldom spared those who differed from him. Consciously imperious, he evoked great loyalty as well as bitter opposition. It was difficult to feel neutral about him; one had to like him or dislike him. With a broad forehead, tight lips, and a determined chin, he had a marked resemblance to the busts of the Roman emperors in the museums in Italy. Many friends in Italy who saw his photograph with us remarked on this resemblance. In later years especially, when his head was covered with silver hair—unlike me, he kept his hair to the end—there was a magnificence about him and a grand manner, which is sadly to seek in this world of today. I suppose I am partial to him, but I miss his noble presence in a world full of pettiness and weakness. I look round in vain for that grand manner and splendid strength that was his.

I remember showing Gandhiji a photograph of father sometime in 1924, when he was having a tug-of-war with the *Swaraj* party. In this photograph father had no mustache, and, till then, Gandhiji had always seen him with a fine mustache. He started almost on seeing this photograph and gazed long at it, for the absence of the mustache brought out the hardness of the mouth and the chin; and he said, with a somewhat dry smile, that now he realized what he had to contend against. The face was softened, however, by the eyes and by the lines that frequent laughter had made. But sometimes the eyes glittered.

In December 1924 the Congress session was held at Belgaum, and Gandhiji was president. For him to become the Congress president was something in the nature of an anticlimax, for he had long been the permanent superpresident. I did not like his presidential address. It struck me as being very uninspiring. At the end of the session I was again elected, at Gandhiji's instance, the working secretary of the All-India Congress Committee for the next year. In spite of my own wishes in the matter, I was gradually becoming a semipermanent secretary of the Congress.

# XIX

# COMMUNALISM RAMPANT

My ILLNESS IN the autumn of 1923, after my return from Nabha Prison, when I had a bout with the typhus germ, was a novel experience for me. I was unused to illness or lying in bed with fever or physical weakness. I was a little proud of my health, and I objected to the general valetudinarian attitude that was fairly common in India. My youth and good constitution pulled me through, but, after the crisis was over, I lay long in bed in an enfeebled condition, slowly working my way to health. And during this period I felt a strange detachment from my surroundings and my day-to-day work, and I viewed all this from a distance, apart. I felt as if I had extricated myself from the trees and could see the wood as a whole; my mind seemed clearer and more peaceful than it had previously been. I suppose this experience, or something like it, is common enough to those who have passed through severe illness. But for me it was in the nature of a spiritual experience—I use the word not in a narrow religious sense—and it influenced me considerably. I felt lifted out of the emotional atmosphere of our politics and could view the objectives and the springs that had moved me to action more clearly. With this clarification came further questioning for which I had no satisfactory answer. But more and more I moved away from the religious outlook on life and politics. I cannot write much about that experience of mine; it was a feeling I cannot easily express. It was eleven years ago, and only a faded impression of it remains in the mind now. But I remember well that it had a lasting effect on me and on my way of thinking, and for the next two years or more I went about my work with something of that air of detachment.

Partly, no doubt, this was due to developments which were wholly outside my control and with which I did not fit in. I have referred already to some of the political changes. Far more important was the progressive deterioration of Hindu-Moslem relations, in North India especially. In the bigger cities a number of riots took place, brutal and callous in the extreme. The atmosphere of distrust and anger bred new causes of dispute which most of us had never heard of before. Previously a fruitful source of discord had been the question of cow sacrifice, especially on the *Bakr-id* day. There was also tension when Hindu and Moslem festivals clashed.

But now a fresh cause of friction arose, something that was ever present, ever recurring. This was the question of music before mosques. Objection was taken by the Moslems to music or any noise which interfered with their prayers in their mosques. In every city there are many mosques, and five times every day they have prayers, and there is no lack of noises and processions (including marriage and funeral processions). So the chances of friction were always present. In particular, objection was taken to processions and noises at the time of the sunset prayer in the mosques. As it happens, this is just the time when evening worship takes place in the Hindu temples, and gongs are sounded and the temple bells ring. *Arti,* this is called, and *arti-namaz* disputes now assumed major proportions.

It seems amazing that a question which could be settled with mutual consideration for each other's feelings and a little adjustment should give rise to great bitterness and rioting. But religious passions have little to do with reason or consideration or adjustments, and they are easy to fan when a third party in control can play off one group against another.

One is apt to exaggerate the significance of these riots in a few northern cities. Most of the towns and cities and the whole of rural India carried on peacefully, little affected by these happenings, but the newspapers naturally gave great prominence to every petty communal disturbance.[1] It is perfectly true, however, that communal tension and bitterness increased in the city masses. This was pushed on by the communal leaders at the top, and it was reflected in the stiffening-up of the political communal demands. Because of the communal tension, Moslem political reactionaries, who had taken a back seat during all these years of nonco-operation, emerged into prominence, helped in the process by the British Government. From day to day new and more far-reaching communal demands appeared on their behalf, striking at the very root of national unity and Indian freedom. On the Hindu side also political reactionaries were among the principal communal leaders, and, in the name of guarding Hindu interests, they played definitely into the hands of the Government. They did not succeed, and indeed they could not, however much they tried by their methods, in gaining any of the points on which they laid stress; they succeeded only in raising the communal temper of the country.

The Congress was in a quandary. Sensitive to and representative

[1] The term "communalism" in Indian usage connotes the opposition of religious groups within the state on political and other matters.—Ed.

of national feeling as it was, these communal passions were bound to affect it. Many a Congressman was a communalist under his national cloak. But the Congress leadership stood firm and, on the whole, refused to side with either communal party, or rather with any communal group, for now the Sikhs and other smaller minorities were also loudly voicing their particular demands. Inevitably this led to denunciation from both the extremes.

Long ago, right at the commencement of nonco-operation or even earlier, Gandhiji had laid down his formula for solving the communal problem. According to him, it could only be solved by good will and the generosity of the majority group, and so he was prepared to agree to everything that the Moslems might demand. He wanted to win them over, not to bargain with them. With foresight and a true sense of values he grasped at the reality that was worth while; but others, who thought they knew the market price of everything and were ignorant of the true value of anything, stuck to the methods of the market place. They saw the cost of purchase with painful clearness, but they had no appreciation of the worth of the article they might have bought.

It is easy to criticize and blame others, and the temptation is almost irresistible to find some excuse for the failure of one's plans. Was not the failure due to the deliberate thwarting of others, rather than to an error in one's own way of thinking or acting? We cast the blame on the Government and the communalists; the latter blame the Congress. Of course, there was thwarting of us, deliberate and persistent thwarting, by the Government and their allies. Of course, British governments in the past and the present have based their policy on creating divisions in our ranks. Divide and rule has always been the way of empires, and the measure of their success in this policy has been also the measure of their superiority over those whom they thus exploit. We cannot complain of this, or, at any rate, we ought not to be surprised at it. To ignore it and not to provide against it is in itself a mistake in one's thought.

How are we to provide against it? Not, surely, by bargaining and haggling and generally adopting the tactics of the market place, for whatever offer we make, however high our bid might be, there is always a third party which can bid higher and, what is more, give substance to its words. If there is no common national or social outlook, there will not be common action against the common adversary. If we think in terms of the existing political and economic structure and merely wish to tamper with it here and there, to reform it, to "Indianize" it, then all real inducement for joint action is lacking. The object then becomes one of sharing in the spoils, and the third and controlling party inevitably plays the dominant role and hands out its gifts to the prize boys of its choice. Only by thinking in terms of a different political framework—and even more so a different social framework—can we build up a stable foundation for joint action. The whole idea underlying the demand for independence was this: to make people realize that we were struggling for an entirely different political structure and not just an Indianized edition (with British control behind the scenes) of the present order, which Dominion status signifies. Political independence meant, of course, political freedom only, and did not include any social change or economic freedom for the masses. But it did signify the removal of the financial and economic chains which bind us to the City of London, and this would have made it easier for us to change the social structure. So I thought then. I would add now that I do not think it is likely that real political freedom will come to us by itself. When it comes, it will bring a large measure of social freedom also.

But almost all our leaders continued to think within the narrow steel frame of the existing political, and of course the social, structure. They faced every problem—communal or constitutional—with this background, and, inevitably, they played into the hands of the British Government, which controlled completely that structure. They could not do otherwise, for their whole outlook was essentially reformist and not revolutionary, in spite of occasional experiments with direct action. But the time had gone by when any political or economic or communal problem in India could be satisfactorily solved by reformist methods. Revolutionary outlook and planning and revolutionary solutions were demanded by the situation. But there was no one among the leaders to offer these.

The want of clear ideals and objectives in our struggle for freedom undoubtedly helped the spread of communalism. The masses saw no clear connection between their day-to-day sufferings and the fight for *Swaraj*. They fought well enough at times by instinct, but that was a feeble weapon which could be easily blunted or even turned aside for other purposes. There was no reason behind it, and in periods of reaction it was not difficult for the communalists to play upon this feeling and exploit it in the name of religion. It is never-theless extraordinary how the bourgeois classes, both among the Hindus and the Moslems, succeeded, in the sacred name of religion, in getting a measure of mass sympathy and support for programs and demands which had absolutely nothing to do with the masses, or even the lower middle class. Every one of the communal demands put forward by any communal group is, in the final analysis, a demand for jobs, and these jobs could only go to a handful of the upper middle class. There is also, of course, the demand for special and additional seats in the legislatures, as symbolizing political power, but this too is looked upon chiefly as the power to exercise patronage. These narrow political demands, benefiting at the most a small number of the upper middle classes, and often creating barriers in the way of national unity and progress, were cleverly made to appear the demands of the masses of that particular religious group. Religious passion was hitched on to them in order to hide their barrenness.

In this way political reactionaries came back to the political field in the guise of communal leaders, and the real explanation of the various steps they took was not so much their communal bias as their desire to obstruct political advance. We could only expect opposition from them politically, but still it was a peculiarly distressing feature of an unsavory situation to find to what lengths they would go in this respect. Moslem communal leaders said the most amazing things and seemed to care not at all for Indian nationalism or Indian freedom; Hindu communal leaders, though always speaking apparently in the name of nationalism, had little to do with it in practice and, incapable of any real action, sought to humble themselves before the Government, and did that too in vain. Both agreed in condemning socialistic and suchlike "subversive" movements; there was a touching unanimity in regard to any proposal affecting vested interests. Moslem communal leaders said and did many things harmful to political and economic freedom, but as a group and individually they conducted themselves before the Government and the public with some dignity. That could hardly be said of the Hindu communal leaders.

The Delhi Unity Conference of 1924 was hardly over when a Hindu-Moslem riot broke out in Allahabad. It was not a big riot, as such riots go, in so far as casualties were concerned; but it was painful to have these troubles in one's home town. I rushed back with others from Delhi to find that the actual rioting was over; but the aftermath, in the shape of bad blood and court cases, lasted a long time. I forget why the riot had begun. That year, or perhaps later, there was also some trouble over the *Ram Lila* celebrations at Allahabad. Probably because of restrictions about music before mosques, these celebrations, involving huge processions as they did, were abandoned as a protest. For about eight years now the *Ram Lila* has not been held in Allahabad, and the greatest festival of the year for hundreds of thousands in the Allahabad district has almost become a painful memory. How well I remember my visits to it when I was a child! How excited we used to get! And the vast crowds that came to see it from all over the district and even from other towns. It was a Hindu festival, but it was an open-air affair, and Moslems also swelled the crowds, and there was joy and lightheartedness everywhere. Trade flourished. Many years afterward, when, as a grown-up, I visited it, I was not excited, and the procession and the tableaux rather bored me. My standards of art and amusement had gone up. But even then, I saw how the great crowds appreciated and enjoyed the show. It was carnival time for them. And now, for eight or nine years, the children of Allahabad, not to mention the grown-ups, have had no chance of seeing this show and having a bright day of joyful excitement in the dull routine of their lives. And all because of trivial disputes and conflicts! Surely religion and the spirit of religion have much to answer for. What kill-joys they have been!

## XX

## MUNICIPAL WORK

FOR TWO YEARS I carried on, but with an ever-increasing reluctance, with the Allahabad municipality. My term of office as chairman was for three years. Before the second year was well begun, I was trying to rid myself of the responsibility. I had liked the work and given a great deal of my time and thought to it. I had met with a measure of success and gained the good will of all my colleagues. Even the Provincial Government had overcome its political dislike of me to the extent of commending some of my municipal activities. And yet I found myself hedged in, obstructed, and prevented from doing anything really worth while.

It was not deliberate obstruction on anybody's part; indeed, I had a surprising amount of willing co-operation. But on the one side, there was the Government machine; on the other, the apathy of the members of the municipality as well as the public. The whole steel frame of municipal administration, as erected by Government, prevented radical growth or innovation. The financial policy was such that the municipality was always dependent on the Government. Most radical schemes of taxation or social development were not permissible under the existing municipal laws. Even such schemes as were legally permissible had to be sanctioned by Government; and only the optimists, with a long stretch of years before them, could confidently ask for and await this sanction. It amazed me to find out how slowly and laboriously and inefficiently the machinery of Government moved when any job of social construction, or of nation building was concerned. There was no slowness or inefficiency, however, when a political opponent had to be curbed or struck down. The contrast was marked.

The department of the Provincial Government dealing with local self-government was presided over by a Minister; but, as a rule, this presiding genius was supremely ignorant of municipal affairs or, indeed, of any public affairs. Indeed, he counted for little and was largely ignored by his own department, which was run by the permanent officials of the Indian Civil Service. These officials were influenced by the prevailing conception of high officials in India that government was primarily a police function. Some idea of authoritarian paternalism colored this conception, but there was hardly any appreciation of the necessity of social services on a large scale.

Year after year government resolutions and officials and some newspapers criticize municipalities and local boards, and point out their many failings. And from this the moral is drawn that democratic institutions are not suited to India. Their failings are obvious enough, but little attention is paid to the framework within which they have to function. This framework is neither democratic nor autocratic; it is a cross between the two, and has the disadvantages of both. That a central government should have certain powers of supervision and control may be admitted, but this can only fit in with a popular local body if the central government itself is democratic and responsive to public needs. Where this is not so, there will either be a tussle between the two or a tame submission to the will of the central authority, which thus exercises power without in any way shouldering responsibility. This is obviously unsatisfactory, and it takes away from the reality of popular control. Even the members of the municipal board look more to the central authority than to their constituents, and the public also often ignores the board. Real social issues hardly ever come before the board, chiefly because they lie outside its functions, and its most obvious activity is tax collecting, which does not make it excessively popular.

Whatever the reasons, the fact remains that our local bodies are not, as a rule, shining examples of success and efficiency, though they might, even so, compare with some municipalities in advanced democratic countries. They are not usually corrupt; they are just inefficient, and their weak point is nepotism, and their perspectives are all wrong. All this is natural enough; for democracy, to be successful, must have a background of informed public opinion and a sense of responsibility. Instead, we have an all-pervading atmosphere of authoritarianism, and the accompaniments of democracy are lacking. There is no mass educational system, no effort to build up public opinion based on knowledge. Inevitably public attention turns to personal or communal or other petty issues.

The main interest of Government in municipal administration is that "politics" should be kept out. Any resolution of sympathy with the national movement is frowned upon; textbooks which might have a nationalist flavor are not permitted in the municipal schools, even pictures of national leaders are not allowed there. A national flag has to be pulled down on pain of suppression of the municipality.

These few instances show how much freedom our municipal and district boards have, how little democratic they are. The attempt to keep out political opponents from all municipal and local services—of course they did not go in for direct government service—deserves a little attention. It is estimated that above three hundred thousand persons have gone to prison at various times during the past fourteen years; and there can be no doubt that, politics apart, these three hundred thousand included some of the most dynamic and idealistic, the most socially minded and selfless people in India. They had push and energy and the ideal of service to a cause. They were thus the best material from which a public department or utility service could draw its employees. And yet Government has made every effort, even to the extent of passing laws, to keep out these people, and so to punish them and those who sympathized with them. It prefers and pushes on the lap-dog breed, and then complains of the inefficiency of our local bodies. And, although politics are said to be outside the province of local bodies, Government has no objection whatever to their indulging in politics in support of itself. Teachers in local board schools have been practically compelled, for fear of losing their jobs, to go out in the villages to do propaganda on behalf of Government.

During the last fifteen years Congress workers have had to face many difficult positions; they have shouldered heavy responsibilities; they have, after all, combated, not without success, a powerful and entrenched Government. This hard course of training has given them self-reliance and efficiency and strength to persevere; it has provided them with the very qualities of which a long and emasculating course of authoritarian government had deprived the Indian people. Of course, the Congress movement, like all mass movements, had, and has, many undesirables—fools, inefficients, and worse. But I have no doubt whatever that an average Congress worker is likely to be far more efficient and dynamic than another person of similar qualifications.

There is one aspect of this matter which Government and its advisers perhaps do not appreciate. The attempt to deprive Congress workers of all jobs and to shut avenues of employment to them is welcomed by the real revolutionary. The average Congressman is notoriously not a revolutionary, and after a period of semirevolutionary action he resumes his humdrum life and activities. He gets entangled either in his business or profession or in the mazes of local politics. Larger issues seem to fade off in his mind, and revolutionary ardor, such as it was, subsides. Muscle turns to fat, and spirit to a love of security. Because of this inevitable tendency of middle-class workers, it has always been the effort of advanced and revolutionary-minded Congressmen to prevent their comrades from entering the constitutional mazes of the legislatures and the local bodies, or accepting whole-time jobs which prevent them from effective action. The Government has, however, now come to their help to some extent by making it a little more difficult for the Congress worker to get a job, and it is thus likely that he will retain some of his revolutionary ardor or even add to it.

After a year or more of municipal work I felt that I was not utilizing my energies to the best advantage there. The most I could do was to speed up work and make it a little more efficient. I could not push through any worth-while change. I wanted to resign from the chairmanship, but all the members of the board pressed me to stay. I had received uniform kindness and courtesy from them, and I found it hard to refuse. At the end of my second year, however, I finally resigned.

This was in 1925. In the autumn of that year my wife fell seriously ill, and for many months she lay in a Lucknow hospital. The Congress was held that year at Cawnpore, and, somewhat distracted, I rushed backward and forward between Allahabad, Cawnpore, and Lucknow. (I was still general secretary of the Congress.)

Further treatment in Switzerland was recommended for my wife. I welcomed the idea, for I wanted an excuse to go out of India myself. My mind was befogged, and no clear path was visible; and I thought that, perhaps, if I was far from India I could see things in better perspective and lighten up the dark corners of my mind.

At the beginning of March 1926 we sailed, my wife, our daughter, and I, from Bombay for Venice. With us on the same boat went also my sister and brother-in-law, Ranjit S. Pandit. They had planned their European trip long before the question of our going had arisen.

## XXI

## IN EUROPE

I WAS GOING back to Europe after more than thirteen years—years of war, and revolution, and tremendous change. The old world I knew had expired in the blood and horror of the war, and a new world awaited me. I expected to remain in Europe for six or seven months or, at most, till the end of the year. Actually our stay lengthened out to a year and nine months.

It was a quiet and restful period for both my mind and body. We spent it chiefly in Switzerland, in Geneva, and in a mountain sanatorium at Montana. My younger sister, Krishna, came from India and joined us early in the summer of 1926, and remained with us till the end of our stay in Europe. I could not leave my wife for long, and so I could only pay brief visits to other places. Later, when my wife was better, we traveled a little in France, England, and Germany. On our mountaintop, surrounded by the winter snow, I felt completely cut off from India as well as the European world. India, and Indian happenings, seemed especially far away. I was a distant onlooker, reading, watching, following events, gazing at the new Europe, its politics, economics, and the far freer human relationships, and trying to understand them. When we were in Geneva I was naturally interested in the activities of the League of Nations and the International Labor Office.

But with the coming of winter, the winter sports absorbed my attention; for some months they were my chief occupation and interest. I had done ice skating previously, but skiing was a new experience, and I succumbed to its fascination. It was a painful experience for a long time, but I persisted bravely, in spite of innumerable falls, and I came to enjoy it.

Life was very uneventful on the whole. The days went by and my wife gradually gained strength and health. We saw few Indians; indeed, we saw few people apart from the little colony living in that mountain resort. But in the course of the year and three-quarters that we spent in Europe, we came across some Indian exiles and old revolutionaries whose names had been familiar to me.

I must say that I was not greatly impressed by most of the Indian political exiles that I met abroad, although I admired their sacrifice, and sympathized with their sufferings and present difficulties, which are very real. I did not meet many of them; there are so many spread out all over the world. Only a few are known to us even by reputation, and the others have dropped out of the Indian world and been forgotten by their countrymen whom they sought to serve.

There were many other Indians floating about the face of Europe, talking a revolutionary language, making daring and fantastic suggestions, asking curious questions. They seemed to have the impress of the British Secret Service upon them.

We met, of course, many Europeans and Americans. From Geneva we went on a pilgrimage many a time (the first time with a letter of introduction from Gandhiji) to the Villa Olga at Villeneuve, to see Romain Rolland. Another precious memory is that of Ernst Toller, the young German poet and dramatist; and of Roger Baldwin, of the Civil Liberties Union of New York. In Geneva we also made friends with Dhan Gopal Mukerji, the author.

Before going to Europe I had met Frank Buchman, of the Oxford Group Movement, in India. He had given me some of the literature of his movement, and I had read it with amazement. Sudden conversions and confessions, and a revivalist atmosphere generally, seemed to me to go ill with intellectuality. I could not make out how some persons, who seemed obviously intelligent, should experience these strange emotions and be affected by them to a great extent. I grew curious. I met Frank Buchman again, in Geneva, and he invited me to one of his international house parties, somewhere in Rumania, I think, this one was. I was sorry I could not go and look at this new emotionalism at close quarters. My curiosity has thus remained unsatisfied, and the more I read of the growth of the Oxford Group Movement the more I wonder.

Soon after our arrival in Switzerland, the General Strike broke out in England. I was vastly excited, and my sympathies were naturally all on the strikers' side. The collapse of the strike, after a few days, came almost as a personal blow. Some months later I happened to visit England for a few days. The miners' struggle was still on, and London lay in semidarkness at night. I paid a brief visit to a mining area—I think it was somewhere in Derbyshire. I saw the haggard and pinched faces of the men and women and children, and, more revealing still, I saw many of the strikers and their wives being tried in the local or county court. The magistrates were themselves directors or managers of the coal mines, and they tried the miners and sentenced them for trivial offenses under certain emergency regulations. One case especially angered me: three or four women, with babies in their arms, were brought up in the dock for the offense of having jeered at the blacklegs. The young mothers (and their babies) were obviously miserable and undernourished; the long struggle had told upon them and enfeebled them, and embittered them against the scabs who seemed to take the bread from their mouths.

One reads often about class justice, and in India nothing is commoner than this, but somehow I had not expected to come across such a flagrant example of it in England. It came as a shock. Another fact that I noticed with some surprise was the general atmosphere of fear among the strikers. They had definitely been terrorized by the police and the authorities, and they put up very meekly, I thought, with rather offensive treatment. It is true that they were thoroughly exhausted after a long struggle, their spirit was near breaking point, their comrades of other trade-unions had long deserted them. But still, compared to the poor Indian worker, there was a world of difference. The British miners had still a powerful organization, the sympathy of a nationwide, and indeed worldwide, trade-union movement, publicity, and resources of many kinds. All these were lacking to the Indian worker. And yet that frightened and terrorized look in the two had a strange resemblance.

Toward the end of 1926 I happened to be in Berlin, and I learned there of a forthcoming Congress of Oppressed Nationalities, which was to be held at Brussels. The idea appealed to me, and I wrote home, suggesting that the Indian National Congress might take official part in the Brussels Congress. My suggestion was approved, and I was appointed the Indian Congress representative for this purpose.

The Brussels Congress was held early in February 1927. I do not know who originated the idea. Berlin was at the time a center which attracted political exiles and radical elements from aboard; it was gradually catching up Paris in that respect. The communist element was also strong there. Ideas of some common action between oppressed nations *inter se,* as well as between them and the labor left wing, were very much in the air. It was felt more and more that the struggle for freedom was a common one against the thing that was imperialism; and joint deliberation and, where possible, joint action were desirable. The colonial Powers—England, France, Italy, etc.—were naturally hostile to any such attempts being made; but Germany was, since the war, no longer a colonial Power, and the German Government viewed with a benevolent neutrality the growth of agitation in the colonies and dependencies of other Powers. This was one of the reasons which made Berlin a center for advanced and disaffected elements from abroad. Among these the most prominent and active were the Chinese belonging to the left wing of the Kuomintang, which was then sweeping across China, the old feudal elements rolling down before its irresistible advance. Even the imperialist Powers lost their aggressive habits and minatory tone before this new phenomenon. It appeared that the solution of the problem of China's unity and freedom could not long be delayed. The Kuomintang was flushed with success, but it knew the difficulties that lay ahead, and it wanted to strengthen itself by international propaganda. Probably it was the left wing of the party, cooperating with communists and near-communists abroad, that laid stress on this propaganda, both to strengthen China's national position abroad and its own position in the party ranks at home. The party had not split up at the time into two or more rival and bitterly hostile groups, and presented, to all outward seeming, a united front.

The European representatives of the Kuomintang, therefore, welcomed the idea of the Congress of Oppressed Nationalities; perhaps they even originated the idea jointly with some other people. Some communists and near-communists were also at the back of the proposal right from the beginning, but, as a whole, the communist element kept in the background. Active support and help also came from Latin America, which was then chafing at the economic imperialism of the United States. Mexico, with a radical President and policy, was eager to take the lead in a Latin-American *bloc* against the United States;

and Mexico, therefore, took great interest in the Brussels Congress. Officially the Government could not take part, but it sent one of its leading diplomats to be present as a benevolent observer.

There were also present at Brussels representatives from the national organizations of Java, Indo-China, Palestine, Syria, Egypt, Arabs from North Africa, and African Negroes. Then there were many left-wing labor organizations represented; and several well-known men who had played a leading part in European labor struggles for a generation, were present. Communists were there also, and they took an important part in the proceedings; they came not as communists but as representatives of trade-unions or similar organizations.

George Lansbury was elected president, and he delivered an elo-quent address. That in itself was proof that the Congress was not so rabid after all, nor was it merely hitched on to the star of communism. But there is no doubt that the gathering was friendly toward the communists, and, even though agreement might be lacking on some matters, there appeared to be several common grounds for action.

Mr. Lansbury agreed to be president also of the permanent organization that was formed—the League against Imperialism. But he repented of his rash behavior soon, or perhaps his colleagues of the British Labour party did not approve of it. The Labour party was "His Majesty's Opposition" then, soon to blossom out as "His Majesty's Government," and future Cabinet Ministers cannot dabble in risky and revolutionary politics. Mr. Lansbury resigned from the presidency on the ground of being too busy for it; he even resigned from the membership of the League. I was hurt by this sudden change in a person whose speech I had admired only two or three months earlier.

The League against Imperialism had, however, quite a number of distinguished persons as its patrons. Einstein was one of them, and Madame Sun Yat-sen, and I think, Romain Rolland. Many months later Einstein resigned, as he disagreed with the pro-Arab policy of the League in the Arab-Jewish quarrels in Palestine.

The Brussels Congress, as well as the subsequent Committee meetings of the League, which were held in various places from time to time, helped me to understand some of the problems of colonial and dependent countries. They gave me also an insight into the inner conflicts of the Western labor world. I knew something about them already; I had read about them, but there was no reality behind my knowledge, as there had been no personal contacts. I had some such contacts now, and sometimes had to face problems which reflected these inner conflicts. As between the labor worlds of the Second International and the Third International, my sympathies were with the latter. The whole record of the Second International from the war onward filled me with distaste, and we in India had had sufficient personal experience of the methods of one of its strongest supports—the British Labour party. So I turned inevitably with good will toward communism, for, whatever its faults, it was at least not hypocritical and not imperialistic. It was not a doctrinal adherence, as I did not know much about the fine points of communism, my acquaintance being limited at the time to its broad features. These attracted me, as also the tremendous changes taking place in Russia. But communists often irritated me by their dictatorial ways, their aggressive and rather vulgar methods, their habit of denouncing everybody who did not agree with them. This reaction was no doubt due, as they would say, to my own bourgeois education and up-bringing.

It was curious how, in our League against Imperialism committee meetings, I would usually be on the side of the Anglo-American members on petty matters of argument. There was a certain similarity in our outlook in regard to method at least. We would both object to declamatory and long-winded resolutions, which resembled manifestos. We preferred something simpler and shorter, but the Continental tradition was against this. There was often difference of opinion between the communist elements and the non-communists. Usually we agreed on a compromise. Later on, some of us returned to our homes and could not attend any further committee meetings.

The Brussels Congress was viewed with some consternation by the foreign and colonial offices of the imperialist Powers. The Congress itself was probably full of international spies, many of the delegates even representing various secret services. We had an amusing instance of this. An American friend of mine, who was in Paris, had a visit from a Frenchman who belonged to the French secret service. It was quite a friendly visit to inquire about certain matters. When he had finished his inquiries he asked the American if he did not recognize him, for they had met previously. The American looked hard, but he had to admit that he could not place him at all. The secret service agent then told him that he had met him at the Brussels Congress as a Negro delegate, with his face, hands, etc., all blacked over!

One of the meetings of the Committee of the League against Imperialism took place at Cologne, and I attended it. After the meeting was over, we were asked to go to Düsseldorf, near by, to attend a

Sacco-Vanzetti meeting. As we were returning from that meeting, we were asked to show our passports to the police. Most of the people had their passports with them, but I had left mine at the hotel in Cologne as we had only come for a few hours to Düsseldorf. I was thereupon marched to a police station. Fortunately for me I had companions in distress—an Englishman and his wife, who also had left their passport in Cologne. After about an hour's wait, during which probably telephonic inquiries were made, the police chief was graciously pleased to allow us to depart.

The League against Imperialism veered more toward communism in later years, though at no time, so far as I know, did it lose its individual character. I could only remain in distant touch with it by means of correspondence. In 1931, because of my part in the Delhi truce between the Congress and the Government of India, it grew exceedingly angry with me, and excommunicated me with bell, book, and candle—or, to be more accurate, it expelled me by some kind of a resolution. I must confess that it had great provocation, but it might have given me some chance of explaining my position.

In the summer of 1927 my father came to Europe. I met him at Venice, and during the next few months we were often together. All of us—my father, my wife, my young sister, and I—paid a brief visit to Moscow in November during the tenth anniversary celebrations of the Soviet. It was a very brief visit, just three or four days in Moscow, decided upon at the last moment. But we were glad we went, for even that glimpse was worth while. It did not, and could not, teach us much about the new Russia, but it did give us a background for our reading. To my father all such Soviet and collectivist ideas were wholly novel. His whole training had been legal and constitutional, and he could not easily get out of that framework. But he was definitely impressed by what he saw in Moscow.

Our stay in Europe had been unduly prolonged. Probably we would have returned home sooner but for father's visiting Europe. It was our intention to spend some time in southeastern Europe and Turkey and Egypt on our way back. But there was no time for this then, and I was eager to be back in time for the next Congress session, which was going to be held in Madras at Christmastime. We sailed from Marseilles, my wife, sister, daughter, and I, early in December for Colombo. My father remained in Europe for another three months.

# XXII

## EXPERIENCE OF LATHEE CHARGES

I WAS RETURNING from Europe in good physical and mental condition. My wife had not yet wholly recovered, but she was far better, and that relieved me of anxiety on her score. I felt full of energy and vitality, and the sense of inner conflict and frustration that had oppressed me so often previously was, for the time being, absent. My outlook was wider, and nationalism by itself seemed to me definitely a narrow and insufficient creed. Political freedom, independence, were no doubt essential, but they were steps only in the right direction; without social freedom and a socialistic structure of society and the State, neither the country nor the individual could develop much. I felt I had a clearer perception of world affairs, more grip on the present-day world, ever changing as it was. I had read largely, not only on current affairs and politics, but on many other subjects that interested me, cultural and scientific. I found the vast political, economic, and cultural changes going on in Europe and America a fascinating study. Soviet Russia, despite certain unpleasant aspects, attracted me greatly, and seemed to hold forth a message of hope to the world. Europe, in the middle twenties, was trying to settle down in a way; the great depression was yet to come. But I came back with the conviction that this settling down was superficial only, and big eruptions and mighty changes were in store for Europe and the world in the near future.

To train and prepare our country for these world events—to keep in readiness for them, as far as we could—seemed to be the immediate task. The preparation was largely an ideological one. First of all, there should be no doubt about the objective of political independence. This should be clearly understood as the only possible political goal for us; something radically different from the vague and confusing talk of Dominion status. Then there was the social goal. It would be too much, I felt, to expect the Congress to go far in this direction just then. The Congress was a purely political and nationalistic body, unused to thinking on other lines. But a beginning might be made. Outside the Congress, in labor circles and among the young, the idea could be pushed on much further. For this purpose I wanted to keep myself free from Congress office, and I had a vague idea also of spending some months in remote rural areas to study their conditions. But this was not to be, and events were to drag me again into the heart of Congress politics.

Immediately on our arrival in Madras I was caught in the whirl. I presented a bunch of resolutions to the Working Committee—resolutions on independence, war danger, association with the League against Imperialism, etc.—and nearly all of these were accepted and made into official Working Committee resolutions. I had to put them forward at the open session of the Congress, and, to my surprise, they were all almost unanimously adopted. The Independence resolution was supported even by Mrs. Annie Besant. This all-round support was very gratifying, but I had an uncomfortable feeling that the resolutions were either not understood for what they were, or were distorted to mean something else. That this was so became apparent soon after the Congress, when a controversy arose on the meaning of the Independence resolution.

These resolutions of mine were somewhat different from the usual Congress resolutions; they represented a new outlook. Many Congressmen no doubt liked them, some had a vague dislike for them, but not enough to make them oppose. Probably the latter thought that they were academic resolutions, making little difference either way, and the best way to get rid of them was to pass them and move on to something more important. The Independence resolution thus did not represent then, as it did a year or two later, a vital and irrepressible urge on the part of the Congress; it represented a widespread and growing sentiment.

Gandhiji was in Madras, and he attended the open Congress sessions, but he did not take any part in the shaping of policy. He did not attend the meetings of the Working Committee, of which he was a member. That had been his general political attitude in the Congress since the dominance of the *Swaraj* party. But he was frequently consulted, and little of importance was done without his knowledge. I do not know how far the resolutions I put before the Congress met with his approval. I am inclined to think that he disliked them, not so much because of what they said, but because of their general trend and outlook. He did not, however, criticize them on any occasion.

The unreality of the Independence resolution came out in that very session of the Congress, when another resolution condemning the Simon Commission and appealing for its boycott was considered. As a corollary to this it was proposed to convene an All-Parties Conference, which was to draw up a constitution for India. It was manifest that the moderate groups, with whom co-operation was sought, could never think in terms of independence. The very utmost they could go to was some form of Dominion status.

I stepped back into the Congress secretaryship. There were personal considerations—the desire of the president for the year, Dr. M. A. Ansari, who was an old and dear friend—and the fact that, as many of my resolutions had been passed, I ought to see them through. It was true that the resolution on the All-Parties Conference had partly neutralized the effect of my resolutions. Still, much remained. The real reason for my accepting office again was my fear that the Congress might, through the instrumentality of the All-Parties Conference, or because of other reasons, slide back to a more moderate and compromising position. It seemed to be in a hesitant mood, swinging alternately from one extreme to another. I wanted to prevent, as far as I could, the swing back to moderation and to hold on to the independence objective.

The National Congress always attracts a large number of side shows at its annual sessions. One of the side shows at Madras was a Republican Conference which held its first (and last) sessions that year. I was asked to preside. The idea appealed to me, as I considered myself a republican. But I hesitated, as I did not know who was at the back of the new venture, and I did not want to associate myself with mushroom growths. I presided, eventually, but later I repented of this, for the Republican Conference turned out to be, like so many others, a still-born affair. For several months I tried, and tried in vain, to get the text of the resolutions passed by it. It is amazing how many of our people love to sponsor new undertakings and then ignore them and leave them to shift for themselves. There is much in the criticism that we are not a persevering lot.

I have been accused by some leaders of the Hindu *Mahasabha* of my ignorance of Hindu sentiments because of my defective education and general background of "Persian" culture. What culture I possess, or whether I possess any at all, is a little difficult for me to say. Persian, as a language, unhappily, I do not even know. But it is true that my father had grown up in an Indo-Persian cultural atmosphere, which was the legacy in north India of the old Delhi court, and of which, even in these degenerate days, Delhi and Lucknow are the two chief centers. Kashmiri Brahmans had a remarkable capacity for adaptation, and coming down to the Indian plains and finding that this Indo-Persian culture was predominant at the time, they took to it, and produced a number of fine scholars in Persian and Urdu. Later they adapted themselves with equal rapidity to the changing order, when a knowledge of English and the elements of European culture became necessary.

The year 1928 was, politically, a full year, with plenty of activity all over the country. There seemed to be a new impulse moving the people forward, a new stir that was equally present in the most varied groups. Probably the change had been going on gradually during my long absence from the country; it struck me as very considerable on my return. Early in 1926, India was still quiescent, passive, perhaps not fully recovered from the effort of 1919-1922; in 1928 she seemed fresh, active, and full of suppressed energy. Everywhere there was evidence of this: among the industrial workers, the peasantry, middle-class youth, and the intelligentsia generally. The trade-union movement had grown greatly, and the All-India Trade-Union Congress, established seven or eight years previously, was already a strong and representative body. The peasantry was also astir. This was noticeable in the United Provinces and especially in Oudh, where large gatherings of protesting tenants became common. Another very noticeable feature of the India of 1928 was the growth of the youth movement. Everywhere youth leagues were being established, youth conferences were being held.

Wherever the Commission went it was greeted by hostile crowds and the cry of "Simon, go back," and thus vast numbers of the Indian masses became acquainted not only with Sir John Simon's name but with two words of the English language, the only two they knew. These words must have become a hated obsession for the members of the Commission. The story is related that once, when they were staying at the Western Hostel in New Delhi, the refrain seemed to come to them in the night out of the darkness. They were greatly irritated at being pursued in this way, even at night. As a matter of fact, the noise that disturbed them came from the jackals that infest the waste places of the imperial capital.

The All-Parties Conference met at Lucknow to consider the report of their committee. Again some of us were in a dilemma, for we did not wish to come in the way of a communal settlement, if that was possible, and yet we were not prepared to yield on the question of independence. We begged that the conference leave this question open so that each constituent part could have liberty of action on this issue— the Congress adhering to independence and the more moderate groups to Dominion status. But my father had set his heart on the report, and he would not yield, nor perhaps could he under the circumstances. I was thereupon asked by our independence group in the Conference—and this was a large one—to make a statement to the Conference on its behalf, dissociating ourselves completely from everything that lowered the objective of independence. But we made it further clear that we would not be obstructive as we did not wish to come in the way of the communal statement.

This was not a very effective line to adopt on such a major issue; at best it was a negative gesture. A positive side was given to our attitude by our founding that very day the Independence for India League.

The Simon Commission was moving about, pursued by black flags and hostile crowds shouting, "Go back." Occasionally there were minor conflicts between the police and the crowds. Lahore brought matters to a head and suddenly sent a thrill of indignation throughout the country. The anti-Simon Commission demonstration there was headed by Lala Lajpat Rai; and, as he stood by the roadside in front of the thousands of demonstrators, he was assaulted and beaten on his chest with a baton by a young English police officer. There had been no attempt whatever on the part of the crowd, much less on the part of Lalaji, to indulge in any methods of violence. Even so, as he stood peacefully by, he and many of his companions were severely beaten by the police. Anyone who takes part in street demonstrations runs the risk of a conflict with the police, and, though our demonstrations were almost always perfectly peaceful, Lalaji must have known of this risk and taken it consciously. But still, the manner of the assault, the needless brutality of it, came as a shock to vast numbers of people in India. Those were the days when we were not used to lathee charges by the police; our sensitiveness had not been blunted by repeated brutality. To find that even the greatest of our leaders, the foremost and most popular man in the Punjab, could be so treated seemed little short of monstrous, and a dull anger spread all over the country, especially in north India. How helpless we were, how despicable when we could not even protect the honor of our chosen leaders!

The physical injury to Lalaji had been serious enough, as he had been hit on the chest and he had long suffered from heart disease. Probably, in the case of a healthy young man the injury would not have been great, but Lalaji was neither young nor healthy. What effect this physical injury had on his death a few weeks later it is hardly possible to say definitely, though his doctors were of opinion that it hastened the end. But I think that there can be no doubt that the mental shock which accompanied the physical injury had a tremendous effect on Lalaji. He felt angry and bitter, not so much at the personal humiliation, as at the national humiliation involved in the assault on him.

It was this sense of national humiliation that weighed on the mind of India, and when Lalaji's death came soon after, inevitably it was connected with the assault, and sorrow itself gave pride of place to anger and indignation. It is well to appreciate this, for only so can we have some understanding of subsequent events, of the phenomenon of Bhagat Singh, and of his sudden and amazing popularity in north India. It is very easy and very fatuous to condemn persons or acts without seeking to understand the springs of action, the causes that underlie them. Bhagat Singh was not previously well known; he did not become popular because of an act of violence, an act of terrorism. Terrorists have flourished in India, off and on, for nearly thirty years, and at no time, except in the early days in Bengal, did any of them attain a fraction of that popularity which came to Bhagat Singh. This is a patent fact which cannot be denied; it has to be admitted. And another fact, which is equally obvious, is that terrorism, in spite of occasional recrudescence, has no longer any real appeal for the youth of India. Fifteen years' stress on nonviolence has changed the whole background in India and made the masses much more indifferent to, and even hostile to, the idea of terrorism as a method of political action. Even the classes from which the terrorists are usually drawn, the lower middle-classes and intelligentsia, have been powerfully affected by the Congress propaganda against methods of violence. Their active and impatient elements, who think in terms of revolutionary action, also realize fully now that revolution does not come through terrorism, and that terrorism is an outworn and profitless method which comes in the way of real revolutionary action. Terrorism is a dying thing in India and elsewhere, not because of Government coercion, which can only suppress and bottle up, not eradicate, but because of basic causes and world events. Terrorism usually represents the infancy of a revolutionary urge in a country. That stage passes, and with it passes terrorism as an important phenomenon. Occasional outbursts may continue because of local causes or individual suppressions. India has undoubtedly passed that stage, and no doubt even the occasional outbursts will gradually die out. But this does not mean that all people in India have ceased to believe in methods of violence. They have, very largely, ceased to believe in individual violence and terrorism, but many, no doubt, still think that a time may come when organized, violent methods may be necessary for gaining freedom, as they have often been necessary in other countries. That is today an academic issue which time alone will put to the test; it has nothing to do with terroristic methods.

Bhagat Singh thus did not become popular because of his act of terrorism, but because he seemed to vindicate, for the moment, the honor of Lala Lajpat Rai, and through him of the nation. He became a symbol; the act was forgotten, the symbol remained, and within a few months each town and village of the Punjab, and to a lesser extent in the rest of northern India, resounded with his name. Innumerable songs grew up about him, and the popularity that the man achieved was something amazing.

The assault on Lala Lajpat Rai, and his subsequent death, increased the vigor of the demonstrations against the Simon Commission in the places which it subsequently visited. It was due in Lucknow, and the local Congress committee made extensive preparations for its "reception." Huge processions, meetings, and demonstrations were organized many days in advance, both as propaganda and as rehearsals for the actual show. I went to Lucknow and was present at some of these. The success of these preliminary demonstrations, which were perfectly orderly and peaceful, evidently nettled the authorities, and they began to obstruct and issue orders against the taking out of processions in certain areas. It was in this connection that I had a new experience, and my body felt the baton and lathee blows of the police.

Processions had been prohibited, ostensibly to avoid any interference with the traffic. We decided to give no cause for complaint on this score, and arranged for small groups of sixteen, as far as I can remember, to go separately, along unfrequented routes to the meeting place. Technically, this was no doubt a breach of the order, for sixteen with a flag were a procession. I led one of the groups of sixteen and, after a big gap, came another such group under the leadership of my colleague, Govind Ballabh Pant. My group had gone perhaps about two hundred yards—the road was a deserted one—when we heard the clatter of horses' hoofs behind us. We looked back to find a bunch of mounted police, probably two or three dozen in number, bearing down upon us at a rapid pace. They were soon right upon us, and the impact of the horses broke up our little column of sixteen. The mounted policemen then started belaboring our volunteers with huge batons or truncheons, and, instinctively, the volunteers sought refuge on the sidewalks, and some even entered the petty shops. They were pursued and beaten down. My own instinct had urged me to seek safety when I saw the horses charging down upon us; it was a discouraging sight. But then, I suppose, some other instinct held me to my place, and I survived the first charge, which had been checked by the volunteers behind me. Suddenly I found myself alone in the middle of the road; a few yards away from me, in various directions, were the policemen beating down our volunteers. Automatically, I began moving slowly to the side of the road to be less conspicuous, but again I stopped and had a little argument with myself, and decided that it would be unbecoming for me to move away. All this was a matter of a few seconds only, but I have the clearest recollections of that conflict within me and the decision, prompted by my pride, I suppose, which could not tolerate the idea of my behaving like a coward. Yet the line between cowardice and courage was a thin one, and I might well have been on the other side. Hardly had I so decided, when I looked round to find that a mounted policeman was trotting up to me, brandishing his long new baton. I told him to go ahead, and turned my head away—again an instinctive effort to save the head and face. He gave me two resounding blows on the back. I felt stunned, and my body quivered all over, but, to my surprise and satisfaction, I found that I was still standing. The police force was withdrawn soon after and made to block the road in front of us. Our volunteers gathered together again, many of them bleeding and with split skulls, and we were joined by Pant and his lot, who had also been belabored, and all of us sat down facing the police. So we sat for an hour or so, and it became dark. On the one side, various high officials gathered; on the other, large crowds began to assemble as the news spread. Ultimately, the officials agreed to allow us to go by our original route, and we went that way with the mounted policemen, who had charged us and belabored us, going ahead of us as a kind of escort.

I have written about this petty incident in some detail because of its effect on me. The bodily pain I felt was quite forgotten in a feeling of exhilaration that I was physically strong enough to face and bear lathee blows. And a thing that surprised me was that right through the incident, even when I was being beaten, my mind was quite clear and I was consciously analyzing my feelings. This rehearsal stood me in good stead the next morning, when a stiffer trial was in store for us. For the next morning was the time when the Simon Commission was due to arrive, and our great demonstration was going to take place.

My father was at Allahabad at the time, and I was afraid that the news of the assault on me, when he read about it in the next morning's papers, would upset him and the rest of the family. So I telephoned to him late in the evening to assure him that all was well and that he should not worry. But he did worry, and, finding it difficult to sleep over it, he decided at about midnight to come over to Lucknow. The last train had gone, and so he started by motorcar. He had some bad luck on the way, and it was nearly five in the morning by the time he had covered the journey of 146 miles and reached Lucknow, tired out and exhausted.

That was about the time when we were getting ready to go in procession to the station. The previous evening's incidents had the effect of rousing up Lucknow more than anything that we could have done, and, even before the sun was out, vast numbers of people made their way to the station. Innumerable little processions came from various parts of the city, and from the Congress office started the main procession, consisting of several thousands, marching in fours. We were in this main procession. We were stopped by the police as we approached the station. There was a huge open space, about half a mile square, in front of the station (this has now been built over by the new station) and we were made to line up on one side of this *maidan,* and there our procession remained, making no attempt to push our way forward. The place was full of foot and mounted police, as well as the military. The crowd of sympathetic onlookers swelled up, and many of these persons managed to spread out in twos and threes in the open space. Suddenly we saw in the far distance a moving mass. It was two or three long lines of cavalry or mounted police, covering the entire area, galloping down toward us, and striking and riding down the numerous stragglers that dotted the *maidan.* That charge of galloping horsemen was a fine sight, but for the tragedies that were being enacted on the way, as harmless and very much surprised sight-seers went under the horses' hoofs. Behind the charging lines these people lay on the ground, some still unable to move, others writhing in pain, and the whole appearance of that *maidan* was that of a battlefield. But we did not have much time for gazing on that scene or for reflections; the horsemen were soon upon us, and their front line clashed almost at a gallop with the massed ranks of our processionists. We held our ground, and, as we appeared to be unyielding, the horses had to pull up at the last moment and reared up on their hind legs with their front hoofs quivering in the air over our heads. And then began a beating of us, and battering with lathees and long batons both by the mounted and the foot police. It was a tremendous hammering, and the clearness of vision that I had had the evening before left me. All I knew was that I had to stay where I was and must not yield or go back. I felt half blinded with the blows, and sometimes a dull anger seized me and a desire to hit out. I thought how easy it would be to pull down the police officer in front of me from his horse and to mount up myself, but long training and discipline held, and I did not raise a hand, except to protect my face from a blow. Besides, I knew well enough that any aggression on our part would result in a ghastly tragedy, the shooting down of large numbers of our men.

After what seemed a tremendous length of time, but was probably only a few minutes, our line began to yield slowly, step by step, without breaking up. This left me somewhat isolated, and more exposed at the sides. More blows came, and then I was suddenly lifted off my feet from behind and carried off, to my great annoyance. Some of my younger colleagues, thinking that a dead set was being made at me, had decided to protect me in this summary fashion.

Our processionists lined up again about a hundred feet behind our original line. The police also withdrew and stood in a line, fifty feet apart from us. So we remained, when the cause of all this trouble, the Simon Commission, secretly crept away from the station in the far distance, more than half a mile away. But, even so, they did not escape the back flags or demonstrators. Soon after, we came back in full procession to the Congress office and there dispersed, and I went on to father, who was anxiously waiting for us.

Now that the excitement of the moment had passed, I felt pains all over my body and great fatigue. Almost every part of me seemed to ache, and I was covered with contused wounds and marks of blows. But fortunately I was not injured in any vital spot. Many of our companions were less fortunate, and were badly injured. Govind Ballabh Pant, who stood by me, offered a much bigger target, being six foot odd in height, and the injuries he received then have resulted in a painful and persistent malady which prevented him for a long time from straightening his back or leading an active life. I emerged with a somewhat greater conceit of my physical condition and powers of endurance. But the memory that endures with me, far more than that of the beating itself, is that of many of the faces of those policemen, and especially of the officers, who were attacking us. Most of the real beating and battering was done by European sergeants; the

Indian rank and file were milder in their methods. And those faces, full of hate and blood-lust, almost mad, with no trace of sympathy or touch of humanity! Probably the faces on our side just then were equally hateful to look at, and the fact that we were mostly passive did not fill our minds and hearts with love for our opponents, or add to the beauty of our countenances. And yet, we had no grievance against each other; no quarrel that was personal, no ill will. We happened to represent, for the time being, strange and powerful forces which held us in thrall and cast us hither and thither, and, subtly gripping our minds and hearts, roused our desires and passions and made us their blind tools. Blindly we struggled, not knowing what we struggled for and whither we went. The excitement of action held us; but, as it passed, immediately the question arose: To what end was all this? To what end?

## XXIII
## THUNDER IN THE AIR

As WORKING GENERAL secretary of the Congress, I was busy in looking after and strengthening its organization, and I was particularly interested in directing people's attention to social and economic changes. I traveled a great deal and addressed many important gatherings. I presided, I think, over four provincial conferences in 1928 as well as over youth leagues and students' conferences. From time to time I visited rural areas, and occasionally I addressed industrial workers. The burden of my speeches was always much the same, though the form varied according to local circumstances and the stress depended on the kind of audience I happened to be addressing. Everywhere I spoke on political independence and social freedom and made the former a step toward the attainment of the latter. I wanted to spread the ideology of socialism especially among Congress workers and the intelligentsia; for these people, who were the backbone of the national movement, thought largely in terms of the narrowest nationalism. Their speeches laid stress on the glories of old times; the injuries, material and spiritual, caused by alien rule; the sufferings of our people; the indignity of foreign domination over us and our national honor demanding that we should be free; the necessity for sacrifice at the altar of the motherland. They were familiar themes which found an echo in every Indian heart, and the nationalist in me responded to them and was moved by them (though I was never a blind admirer of ancient times in India or elsewhere). But, though the truth in them remained, they seemed to grow a little thin and threadbare with constant use, and their ceaseless repetition prevented the consideration of other problems and vital aspects of our struggle. They only fostered emotion and did not encourage thought.

I was by no means a pioneer in the socialist field in India. Indeed, I was rather backward, and I had only advanced painfully, step by step, where many others had gone ahead blazing a trail. The workers' trade-union movement was, ideologically, definitely socialist, and so were the majority of the youth leagues. A vague, confused socialism was already part of the atmosphere of India when I returned from Europe in December 1927, and even earlier than that there were many individual socialists. Mostly they thought along utopian lines, but Marxian theory was influencing them increasingly, and a few considered themselves as hundred per cent Marxists. This tendency was strengthened in India, as in Europe and America, by developments in the Soviet Union, and particularly the Five-Year Plan.

Such importance as I possessed as a socialist worker lay in the fact that I happened to be a prominent Congressman holding important Congress offices. There were many other well-known Congressmen who were beginning to think likewise. This was most marked in the United Provinces Provincial Congress Committee, and in this Committee we even tried, as early as 1926, to draw up a mild socialist program. We declared that the existing land system must go and that there should be no intermediaries between the State and the cultivator. We had to proceed cautiously, as we were moving in an atmosphere which was, till then, unused to such ideas.

In the second half of 1928 and in 1929 there was frequent talk of my arrest. I do not know what reality lay behind the press references and the numerous private warnings I received from friends who seemed to be in the know, but the warnings produced a feeling of uncertainty in me, and I felt I was always on the verge of it. I did not mind this particularly as I knew that, whatever the future held for me, it could not be a settled life of routine. The sooner I got used to uncertainty and sudden changes and visits to prison the better. I think that on the whole I succeeded in getting used to the idea ( and to a much lesser extent my people also succeeded); whenever arrest came I took it more casually than I might otherwise have done. So rumors of arrest were not without compensation; they gave a certain excitement and a bite to my daily existence. Every day of freedom was something precious, a day gained. As a matter of fact, I had a long innings in 1928 and 1929, and arrest came at last as late as April 1930. Since then my brief periods outside prison have had a measure of unreality about them, and I have lived in my house as a stranger on a short visit, or moved about uncertainly, not knowing what the morrow would hold for me, and with the constant expectation of a call back to jail.

As 1928 approached its appointed end, the Calcutta Congress drew near. My father was to preside over it. He was full of the All-Parties Conference and of his report to it and wanted to push this through the Congress. To this he knew that I was not agreeable, because I was not prepared to compromise on the independence issue, and this irritated him. We did not argue about the matter much, but there was a definite feeling of mental conflict between us, an attempt to pull different ways. Differences of opinion we had often had before, vital differences which had kept us in different political camps. But I do not think that at any previous or subsequent occasion the tension had been so great. Both of us were rather unhappy about it. In Calcutta matters came to this, that my father made it known that if he could not have his way in the Congress—that is, if he could not have a majority for the resolution in favor of the All-Parties Report—he would refuse to preside over the Congress. That was a perfectly reasonable and constitutional course to adopt. Nonetheless it was disconcerting to many of his opponents who did not wish to force the issue to this extent.

There were negotiations between the two groups, and a compromise formula was announced. Then this fell through. It was all rather confusing and not very edifying. The main resolution of the Congress, as it was finally adopted, accepted the All-Parties Report but intimated that if the British Government did not agree to that constitution within a year the Congress would revert to independence. It was an offer of a year's grace and a polite ultimatum. The resolution was no doubt a come-down from the ideal of independence, for the All-Parties Report did not even ask for full Dominion status. And yet it was probably a wise resolution in the sense that it prevented a split when no one was ready for it, and kept the Congress together for the struggle that began in 1930. It was clear enough that the British Government were not going to accept the All-Parties Constitution within a year. The struggle was inevitable; and, as matters stood in the country, no such struggle could be at all effective without Gandhiji's lead.

I had opposed the resolution in the open Congress, though I did so half-heartedly. And yet I was again elected general secretary. In the Congress sphere I seemed to act the part of the famous Vicar of Bray. Whatever president sat on the Congress throne, still I was secretary in charge of the organization.

A few days before the Calcutta Congress, the All-India Trade-Union Congress was held at Jharia, the center of the coal mine area. I attended and participated in it for the first two days and then had to go away to Calcutta. It was my first trade-union congress, and I was practically an outsider, though my activities among the peasantry, and lately among the workers, had gained for me a measure of popularity with the masses. I found the old tussle going on between the reformists and the more advanced and revolutionary elements.

My own sympathies at Jharia were with the advanced group but, being a newcomer, I felt a little at sea in these domestic conflicts of the Trade-Union Congress, and I decided to keep aloof from them. After I had left Jharia, the annual Trade-Union Congress elections took place, and I learned at Calcutta that I had been elected president for the next year. I had been put forward by the moderate group, probably because they felt that I stood the best chance of defeating the other candidate, who was an actual worker (on the railways) and who had been put forward by the radical group. If I had been present at Jharia on the day of the election, I am sure that I would have withdrawn in favor of the worker candidate. It seemed to me positively indecent that a newcomer and nonworker should be suddenly thrust into the presidency. This was in itself a measure of the infancy and weakness of the trade-union movement in India.

In March 1929 the Government struck suddenly at organized labor by arresting some of its most prominent workers from the advanced groups. The leaders of the Bombay Girni Kamgar Union were taken, as well as labor leaders from Bengal, the United Provinces, and the Punjab. Some of these were communists, others were near-communists, yet others were just trade-unionists. This was the beginning of the famous Meerut trial which lasted for four years and a half.

The Meerut Case Defense Committee (of which I was a member) did not have an easy time with the accused. There were different kinds of people among these, with different types of defenses, and often there was an utter absence of harmony among them. After some months we wound up the formal committee, but we continued to help in our individual capacities. The development of the political situation was absorbing more and more of our attention, and in 1930 all of us were ourselves in jail.

Gandhiji was still keeping away from politics, except for the part he played at the Calcutta Congress. He was, however, in full touch with developments and was often consulted by the Congress leaders. His main activity for some years had been *khadi* propaganda, and with this object he had undertaken extensive tours all over India. He took each province by turn and visited every district and almost every town of any consequence, as well as remote rural areas. Everywhere he attracted enormous crowds, and it required a great deal of previous staff work to carry through his program. In this manner he has repeatedly toured India and got to know every bit of the vast country from the north to the far south, from the eastern mountains to the western sea. I do not think any other human being has ever traveled about India as much as he has done.

In the past there were great wanderers who were continually on the move, pilgrim souls with the wanderlust; but their means of locomotion were slow, and a lifetime of such wandering could hardly compete with a year by railway and motorcar. Gandhiji went by railway and automobile, but he did not confine himself to them; he tramped also. In this way he gathered his unique knowledge of India and her people, and in this way also scores of millions saw him and came into personal touch with him.

He came to the United Provinces in 1929 on his *khadi* tour, and spent many weeks in these provinces during the hottest part of the year. I accompanied him occasionally for a few days at a time and, despite previous experience, could not help marveling at the vast crowds he attracted. This was especially noticeable in our eastern districts, like Gorakhpur, where the swarms of human beings reminded one of hordes of locusts. As we motored through the rural areas, we would have gatherings of from ten thousand to twenty-five thousand every few miles, and the principal meeting of the day might even exceed a hundred thousand. There were no broadcasting facilities, except rarely in a few big cities, and it was manifestly impossible to be heard by these crowds. Probably they did not expect to hear anything; they were satisfied if they saw the Mahatma. Gandhiji usually addressed them briefly, avoiding undue strain; it would have been quite impossible to carry on otherwise in this fashion from hour to hour and day to day.

I did not accompany him throughout his United Provinces tour as I could be of no special use to him and there was no point in my adding to the number of the touring party. I had no objection to crowds, but there was not sufficient inducement to get pushed and knocked about and my feet crushed—the usual fate of people accompanying Gandhiji. I had plenty of other work to do and had no desire to confine myself to *khadi* propaganda, which seemed to me a relatively minor activity in view of the developing political situation. To some extent I resented Gandhiji's preoccupation with nonpolitical issues, and I could never understand the background of his thought. In those days he was collecting funds for *khadi* work, and he would say frequently that he wanted money for *Daridranarayan,* the "Lord of the Poor," or "God that resides in the poor"; meaning thereby, presumably, that he wanted it to help the poor to find employment and work in cottage industries. But behind that word there seemed to be a glorification of poverty; God was especially the Lord of the poor; they were His chosen people. That, I suppose, is the usual religious attitude everywhere. I could not appreciate it, for poverty seemed to me a hateful thing, to be fought and rooted out and not to be encouraged in any way. This inevitably led to an attack on a system which tolerated and produced poverty, and those who shrunk from this had of necessity to justify poverty in some way. They could only think in terms of scarcity and could not picture a world abundantly supplied with the necessaries of life; probably, according to them, the rich and the poor would always be with us.

Whenever I had occasion to discuss this with Gandhiji, he would lay stress on the rich treating their riches as a trust for the people; it was a viewpoint of considerable antiquity, and one comes across it frequently in India as well as medieval Europe. I confess that I have always been wholly unable to understand how any person can reasonably expect this to happen, or imagine that therein lies the solution of the social problem.

The Legislative Assembly and the provincial councils had long ceased to interest anyone, except the handful who moved in their sacred orbits. They carried on in their humdrum way, providing some kind of a cloak—a torn and tattered affair—to the authoritarian and despotic nature of the Government, an excuse to some people to talk of India's parliament, and allowances to their members.

A rude awakening came to the Assembly one day when Bhagat Singh and B. K. Dutt threw two bombs from the visitors' gallery on to the floor of the house. No one was seriously hurt, and probably the bombs were intended, as was stated by the accused later, to make a noise and create a stir, and not to injure.

They did create a stir both in the Assembly and outside. Other activities of terrorists were not so innocuous. A young English police officer, who was alleged to have hit Lala Lajpat Rai, was shot down and killed in Lahore. In Bengal and elsewhere there seemed to be a recrudescence of terrorist activity. A number of conspiracy cases were launched, and the number of *détenus*—people kept in prison or otherwise detained without trial or conviction—rapidly increased.

In the Lahore conspiracy case some extraordinary scenes were enacted in the court by the police, and a great deal of public attention was drawn to the case because of this. As a protest against the treatment given to them in court and in prison, there was a hunger strike on the part of most of the prisoners. I forget the exact reason why it began, but ultimately the question involved became the larger one of treatment of prisoners, especially politicals. This hunger strike went on from week to week and created a stir in the country. Owing to the physical weakness of the accused, they could not be taken to court, and the proceedings had to be adjourned repeatedly. The Government of India thereupon initiated legislation to allow court proceedings to continue even in the absence of the accused or their counsel. The question of prison treatment had also to be considered by them.

I happened to be in Lahore when the hunger strike was already a month old. I was given permission to visit some of the prisoners in the prison, and I availed myself of this. I saw Bhagat Singh for the first time, and Jatindranath Das and a few others. They were all very weak and bedridden, and it was hardly possible to talk to them much. Bhagat Singh had an attractive, intellectual face, remarkably calm and peaceful. There seemed to be no anger in it. He looked and talked with great gentleness, but then I suppose that anyone who has been fasting for a month will look spiritual and gentle. Jatin Das looked milder still, soft and gentle like a young girl. He was in considerable pain when I saw him. He died later, as a result of fasting, on the sixty-first day of the hunger strike.

Jatin Das's death created a sensation all over the country. It brought the question of the treatment of political prisoners to the front, and Government appointed a committee on the subject. As a result of the deliberations of this committee, new rules were issued creating three classes of prisoners. No special class of political prisoners was created. These new rules, which seemed to promise a change for the better, as a matter of fact made little difference, and the position remained, and still remains, highly unsatisfactory.

The 1929 Congress was going to be held in Lahore. After ten years it had come back to the Punjab. Much had happened during this decade, and India's face had changed, but there was no lack of parallels. Political tension was growing; the atmosphere of struggle was developing fast. The long shadow of the conflict to come lay over the land.

As the summer and monsoon months gradually shaded off into the autumn, the provincial Congress committees busied themselves with the election of the president for the Lahore session of the Congress. There was almost unanimity in favor of Gandhiji.

So he was recommended for the presidency by the provincial committees. But he would have none of it. His refusal, though emphatic, seemed to leave some room for argument, and it was hoped that he would reconsider it. A meeting of the All-India Congress Committee was held in Lucknow to decide finally, and almost to the last hour all of us thought that he would agree. But he would not do so, and at the last moment he pressed my name forward. The All-India Congress Committee was somewhat taken aback by his final refusal, and a little irritated at being placed in a difficult and invidious position. For want of any other person, and in a spirit of resignation, they finally elected me.

I have seldom felt quite so annoyed and humiliated as I did at that election. It was not that I was not sensible of the honor, for it was a great honor, and I would have rejoiced if I had been elected in the ordinary way. But I did not come to it by the main entrance or even a side entrance; I appeared suddenly by a trap door and bewildered the audience into acceptance. They put a brave face on it and, like a necessary pill, swallowed me. My pride was hurt, and I almost felt like handing back the honor. Fortunately I restrained myself from making an exhibition of myself and stole away with a heavy heart.

Probably the person who was happiest about this decision was my father. He did not wholly like my politics, but he liked me well enough, and any good thing that came my way pleased him. Often he would criticize me and speak a little curtly to me, but no person who cared to retain his good will could run me down in his presence.

My election was indeed a great honor and a great responsibility for me; it was unique in that a son was immediately following his father in the presidential chair. It was often said that I was the youngest president of the Congress—I was just forty when I presided. This was not true. I think Gokhale was about the same age, and Maulana Abul Kalam Azad (though he is a little older than me) was probably just under forty when he presided. But Gokhale was considered one of the elder statesmen even when he was in his late thirties, and Abul Kalam Azad has especially cultivated a look of venerable age to give a suitable background to his great learning. As statesmanship has seldom been considered one of my virtues, and no one has accused me of possessing an excess of learning, I have escaped so far the accusation of age, though my hair has turned gray and my looks betray me.

The Lahore Congress drew near. Meanwhile events were marching, step by step, inevitably, pushed onward, so it seemed, by some motive force of their own. Individuals, for all the brave show they put up, played a very minor role. One had the feeling of being a cog in a great machine which swept on relentlessly.

Hoping perhaps to check this onward march of destiny, the British Government took a forward step, and the Viceroy, Lord Irwin, made an announcement about a forthcoming Round Table Conference. It was an ingeniously worded announcement, which could mean much or very little, and it seemed to many of us obvious that the latter was the more likely contingency. And in any event, even if there was more in the announcement, it could not be anywhere near what we wanted. Hardly had this viceregal announcement been made, when, almost with indecent haste, so it seemed, a "Leaders' Conference" was arranged at Delhi, and people from various groups were invited to it. Gandhiji was there, so was my father; Vithalbhai Patel (still president of the Assembly) was also there, and Moderate leaders like Dr. Tej Bahadur Sapru and others. A joint resolution or manifesto was agreed to, accepting the Viceroy's declaration subject to some conditions, which, it was stated, were vital and must be fulfilled. If these conditions were accepted by Government, then co-operation was to be offered. These conditions [1] were solid enough and would have made a difference.

It was a triumph to get such a resolution agreed to by representatives of all the groups, moderate and advanced. For the Congress it was a comedown; as a common measure of agreement it was high. But there was a fatal catch in it. The conditions were looked upon from at least two different viewpoints. The Congress people considered them to be essential, the *sine qua non*, without which there could be no co-opera-

---

[1] The conditions were:

(1) All discussions at the proposed conference to be on the basis of full Dominion status for India.

(2) There should be a predominant representation of Congressmen at the conference.

(3) A general amnesty of political prisoners.

(4) The Government of India to be carried on from now onward, as far as is possible under existing conditions, on the lines of a Dominion government.

tion. For them they represented the minimum required. For the Moderate groups they were a desirable maximum which should be stated, but which could not be insisted on to the point of refusal of co-operation.

And so it happened that later on, though none of these conditions were satisfied and most of us lay in jail, together with scores of thousands of others, our Moderate friends, who had signed that manifesto with us, gave their full co-operation to our jailers.

Most of us suspected that this would happen—though hardly to the extent it did happen—but there was some hope that this joint action, whereby the Congress people had to some extent curbed themselves, would also result in curbing the propensities of the Liberals and others to indiscriminate and almost invariable co-operation with the British Government. A more powerful motive for some of us, who heartily disliked the compromising resolution, was to keep our own Congress ranks well knit together. On the eve of a big struggle we could not afford to split up the Congress. It was well known that Government was not likely to accept the conditions laid down by us, and our position would thus be stronger and we could easily carry our Right wing with us. It was only a question of a few weeks; December and the Lahore Congress were near.

And yet that joint manifesto was a bitter pill for some of us. To give up the demand for independence, even in theory and even for a short while, was wrong and dangerous; it meant that it was just a tactical affair, something to bargain with, not something which was essential and without which we could never be content. So I hesitated and refused to sign the manifesto, but, as was not unusual with me, I allowed myself to be talked into signing. Even so, I came away in great distress, and the very next day I thought of withdrawing from the Congress presidency, and wrote accordingly to Gandhiji. I do not suppose that I meant this seriously, though I was sufficiently upset. A soothing letter from Gandhiji and three days of reflection calmed me.

Just prior to the Lahore Congress, a final attempt was made to find some basis of agreement between Congress and the Government. An interview with Lord Irwin, the Viceroy, was arranged. I do not know who took the initiative in arranging this interview, but I imagine that Vithalbhai Patel was the prime mover. Gandhiji and my father were present at the interview, representing the Congress viewpoint. The interview came to nothing; there was no common ground, and the two main parties—the Government and Congress—were far apart from each other. So now nothing remained but for the Congress to go ahead. The year of grace given at Calcutta was ending; independence was to be declared once for all the objective of the Congress, and the necessary steps taken to carry on the struggle to attain it.

During these final weeks prior to the Lahore Congress I had to attend to important work in another field. The All-India Trade-Union Congress was meeting at Nagpur, and, as president for the year, I had to preside over it. It was very unusual for the same person to preside over both the National Congress and the Trade-Union Congress within a few weeks of each other. I had hoped that I might be a link between the two and bring them closer to each other—the National Congress to become more socialistic, more proletarian, and organized labor to join the national struggle.

It was, perhaps, a vain hope, for nationalism can only go far in a socialistic or proletarian direction by ceasing to be nationalism. Yet I felt that, bourgeois as the outlook of the National Congress was, it did represent the only effective revolutionary force in the country. As such, labor ought to help it and co-operate with it and influence it, keeping, however, its own identity and idealogy distinct and intact. And I hoped that the course of events and the participation in direct action would inevitably drive the Congress to a more radical ideology and to face social and economic issues. The development of the Congress during recent years had been in the direction of the peasant and the village. If this development continued, it might in course of time become a vast peasant organization, or, at any rate, an organization in which the peasant element predominated.

Many Congressmen took prominent part in labor activities. The advanced sections of labor, however, fought shy of the National Congress. They mistrusted its leaders, and considered its ideology bourgeois and reactionary, which indeed it was, from the labor point of view. The Congress was, as its very name implied, a nationalist organization.

I played a very undistinguished role at the Nagpur Trade-Union Congress. Being a newcomer in the labor field and still feeling my way, I was a little hesitant. Generally, I expressed my views in favor of the more advanced groups, but I avoided acting with any group and played the part more of an impartial speaker than a directing president. I was thus an almost passive spectator of the breaking-up of the Trade-Union Congress and the formation of a new moderate organization. Personally, I felt that the Right groups were not justified in breaking away, and yet some of the leaders of the Left had forced the pace and given them every pretext to depart. Between the quarrels of the Right and

Left, a large Center group felt a little helpless. Perhaps given a right lead, it could have curbed the two and avoided the break-up of the Trade Union Congress, and, even if the break came, it would not have had the unfortunate consequences which resulted.

I was out of all this from 1930 onward, as I was mostly in prison.

## XXIV

## INDEPENDENCE AND AFTER

THE LAHORE CONGRESS remains fresh in my memory—a vivid patch. That is natural, for I played a leading role there and, for a moment, occupied the center of the stage; and I like to think sometimes of the emotions that filled me during those crowded days. I can never forget the magnificent welcome that the people of Lahore gave me, tremendous in its volume and its intensity. I knew well that this overflowing enthusiasm was for a symbol and an idea, not for me personally; yet it was no little thing for a person to become that symbol, even for a while, in the eyes and hearts of great numbers of people, and I felt exhilarated and lifted out of myself. But my personal reactions were of little account, and there were big issues at stake. The whole atmosphere was electric and surcharged with the gravity of the occasion. Our decisions were not going to be mere criticisms or protests or expressions of opinion, but a call to action which was bound to convulse the country and affect the lives of millions.

What the distant future held for us and our country, none dared prophesy; the immediate future was clear enough, and it held the promise of strife and suffering for us and those who were dear to us. This thought sobered our enthusiasms and made us very conscious of our responsibility. Every vote that we gave became a message of farewell to ease, comfort, domestic happiness, and the intercourse of friends, and an invitation to lonely days and nights and physical and mental distress.

The main resolution on independence, and the action to be taken in furtherance of our freedom struggle, was passed almost unanimously, barely a score of persons, out of many thousands, voting against it. The All-India Congress Committee had been authorized to plan and carry out our campaign, but all knew that the real decision lay with Gandhiji.

The Lahore Congress was attended by large numbers of people from the Frontier Province near by. Individual delegates from this province had always come to the Congress sessions, and for some years past Khan Abdul Ghaffar Khan had been attending and taking part in our deliberations. In Lahore for the first time a large batch of earnest young men from the Frontier came into touch with all-India political currents. Their fresh minds were impressed, and they returned with a sense of unity with the rest of India in the struggle for freedom and full of enthusiasm for it. They were simple but effective men of action, less given to talk and quibbling than the people of any other province in India, and they started organizing their people and spreading the new ideas. They met with success, and the men and women of the Frontier, the latest to join in India's struggle, played an outstanding and remarkable part from 1930 onward.

Immediately after the Lahore Congress, and in obedience to its mandate, my father called upon the Congress members of the Legislative Assembly and the provincial councils to resign from their seats. Nearly all of them came out in a body, a very few refusing to do so, although this involved a breach of their election promises.

Still we were vague about the future. In spite of the enthusiasm shown at the Congress session, no one knew what the response of the country would be to a program of action. We had burned our boats and could not go back, but the country ahead of us was an almost strange and uncharted land. To give a start to our campaign, and partly also to judge the temper of the country, January 26 was fixed as Independence Day, when a pledge of independence was to be taken all over the country.

And so, full of doubt about our program, but pushed on by enthusiasm and the desire to do something effective, we waited for the march of events. I was in Allahabad during the early part of January; my father was mostly away. It was the time of the great annual fair, the *Magh Mela*; probably it was the special *Kumbh* year, and hundreds of thousands of men and women were continually streaming into Allahabad, or holy Prayag, as it was to the pilgrims. They were all kinds of people, chiefly peasants, also laborers, shopkeepers, artisans, merchants, businessmen, professional people—indeed, it was a cross section of Hindu India. As I watched these great crowds and the unending streams of people going to and from the river, I wondered how they would react to the call for civil resistance and peaceful direct action. How many of them knew or cared for the Lahore decisions? How amazingly powerful was that faith which had for thousands of years brought them and their forbears from every corner of India to bathe in the holy Ganga! Could they not divert some of this tremendous energy to political and economic action to better their own lot? Or were their minds too full of the trappings and traditions of their religion to leave room for other thoughts? I knew, of course, that these other thoughts were already there, stirring the placid stillness of ages. It was the movement of these vague ideas and desires among the masses that had caused the upheavals of the past dozen years and had changed the face of India. There was no doubt about their existence and of the dynamic energy behind them. But still doubt came and questions arose to which there was no immediate answer. How far had these ideas spread? What strength lay behind them, what capacity for organized action, for long endurance?

Our house attracted crowds of pilgrims. It lay conveniently situated near one of the places of pilgrimage, Bharadwaj, where in olden times there was a university, and on the days of the *mela* an endless stream of visitors would come to us from dawn to dusk. Curiosity, I suppose, brought most of them, and the desire to see well-known persons they had heard of, especially my father. But a large proportion of those who came were politically inclined and asked questions about the Congress and what it had decided and what was going to happen; also they were full of their own economic troubles and wanted to know what they should do about them. Our political slogans they knew well, and all day the house resounded with them. I started the day by saying a few words to each group of twenty or fifty or a hundred as it came, one after the other; but soon this proved an impossible undertaking, and I silently saluted them when they came. There was a limit to this, too, and then I tried to hide myself. It was all in vain. The slogans became louder and louder, the verandas of the house were full of these visitors of ours, each door and window had a collection of prying eyes. It was impossible to work or talk or feed or, indeed, do anything. This was not only embarrassing, it was annoying and irritating. Yet there they were, these people looking up with shining eyes full of affection, with generations of poverty and suffering behind them, and still pouring out their gratitude and love and asking for little in return, except fellow feeling and sympathy. It was impossible not to feel humbled and awed by this abundance of affection and devotion.

A dear friend of ours was staying with us at the time, and often it became impossible to carry on any conversation with her, for every five minutes or less I had to go out to say a word or two to a crowd that had assembled, and in between we listened to the slogans and shouting outside. She was amused at my plight and a little impressed, I think, by what she considered my great popularity with the masses. (As a matter of fact the principal attraction was my father, but, as he was away, I had to face the music.) She turned to me suddenly and asked me how I liked this hero worship. Did I not feel proud of it? I hesitated a little before answering, and this led her to think that she had, perhaps, embarrassed me by too personal a question. She apologized. She had not embarrassed me in the least, but I found the question difficult to answer. My mind wandered away, and I began to analyze my own feelings and reactions. They were very mixed.

It was true that I had achieved, almost accidentally as it were, an unusual degree of popularity with the masses; I was appreciated by the intelligentsia; to young men and women I was a bit of a hero, and a halo of romance seemed to surround me in their eyes. Songs had been written about me, and the most impossible and ridiculous legends had grown up. Even my opponents had often put in a good word for me and patronizingly admitted that I was not lacking in competence or in good faith.

Only a saint, perhaps, or an inhuman monster could survive all this, unscathed and unaffected, and I can place myself in neither of these categories. It went to my head, intoxicated me a little, and gave me confidence and strength. I became (I imagine so, for it is a difficult task to look at oneself from outside) just a little bit autocratic in my ways, just a shade dictatorial. And yet I do not think that my conceit increased markedly. I had a fair measure of my abilities, I thought, and I was by no means humble about them. But I knew well enough that there was nothing at all remarkable about them, and I was very conscious of my failings. A habit of introspection probably helped me to retain my balance and view many happenings connected with myself in a detached manner. Experience of public life showed me that popularity was often the handmaiden of undesirable persons; it was certainly not an invariable sign of virtue or intelligence. Was I popular, then, because of my failings or my accomplishments? Why, indeed, was I popular?

Not because of intellectual attainments, for they were not extraordinary, and, in any event, they do not make for popularity. Not because of so-called sacrifices, for it is patent that hundreds and thousands in our own day in India have suffered infinitely more, even to the point of the last sacrifice. My reputation as a hero is entirely a bogus one; I do not feel at all heroic, and generally the heroic attitude or the dramatic pose in life strikes me as silly. As for romance, I should say that I am the least romantic of individuals. It is true that I have some physical and mental courage, but the background of that is probably pride—personal, group, and national—and a reluctance to be coerced into anything.

I had no satisfactory answer to my question. Then I proceeded along a different line of inquiry. I found that one of the most persistent legends about my father and myself was to the effect that we used to send our linen weekly from India to a Paris laundry. We have repeatedly contradicted this, but the legend persists. Anything more fantastic and absurd it is difficult for me to imagine, and, if anyone is foolish enough to indulge in this wasteful snobbery, I should have thought he would get a special mention for being a prize fool.

Another equally persistent legend, often repeated in spite of denial, is that I was at school with the Prince of Wales. The story goes on to say that when the Prince came to India in 1921 he asked for me; I was then in jail. As a matter of fact, I was not only not at school with him, but I have never had the advantage of meeting him or speaking to him.

I do not mean to imply that my reputation or popularity, such as they are, depend on these or similar legends. They may have a more secure foundation, but there is no doubt that the superstructure has a thick covering of snobbery, as is evidenced by these stories. At any rate, there is the idea of mixing in high society and living a life of luxury and then renouncing it all; renunciation has always appealed to the Indian mind. As a basis for a reputation this does not at all appeal to me. I prefer the active virtues to the passive ones, and renunciation and sacrifice for their own sakes have little appeal for me. I do value them from another point of view—that of mental and spiritual training—just as a simple and regular life is necessary for the athlete to keep in good physical condition. And the capacity for endurance and persever-ance in spite of hard knocks is essential for those who wish to dabble in great undertakings. But I have no liking or attraction for the ascetic view of life, the negation of life, the terrified abstention from its joys and sensations. I have not consciously renounced anything that I really valued; but then, values change.

The question that my friend had asked me still remained unan-swered: did I not feel proud of this hero worship of the crowd? I disliked it and wanted to run away from it, yet I had got used to it;

when it was wholly absent, I rather missed it. Neither way brought satisfaction, but, on the whole, the crowd had filled some inner need of mine. The notion that I could influence them and move them to action gave me a sense of authority over their minds and hearts; this satisfied, to some extent, my will to power. On their part, they exercised a subtle tyranny over me, for their confidence and affection moved inner depths within me and evoked emotional responses. Individualist as I was, sometimes the barriers of individuality seemed to melt away, and I felt that it would be better to be accursed with these unhappy people than to be saved alone. But the barriers were too solid to disappear, and I peeped over them with wondering eyes at this phenomenon which I failed to understand.

Conceit, like fat on the human body, grows imperceptibly, layer upon layer, and the person whom it affects is unconscious of the daily accretion. Fortunately the hard knocks of a mad world tone it down or even squash it completely, and there has been no lack of these hard knocks for us in India during recent years. The school of life has been a difficult one for us, and suffering is a hard taskmaster.

I have been fortunate in another respect also—the possession of family members and friends and comrades, who have helped me to retain a proper perspective and not to lose my mental equilibrium. Public functions, addresses by municipalities, local boards, and other public bodies, processions, and the like, used to be a great strain on my nerves and my sense of humor and reality. The most extravagant and pompous language would be used, and everybody would look so solemn and pious that I felt an almost uncontrollable desire to laugh, or to stick out my tongue, or stand on my head, just for the pleasure of shocking and watching the reactions on the faces at that august assembly! Fortunately for my reputation and for the sober respectability of public life in India, I have suppressed this mad desire and usually behaved with due propriety. But not always. Sometimes there has been an exhibition on my part in a crowded meeting, or more often in processions, which I find extraordinarily trying. I have suddenly left a procession, arranged in our honor, and disappeared in the crowd, leaving my wife or some other person to carry on, perched up in a car or carriage, with that procession.

This continuous effort to suppress one's feelings and behave in public is a bit of a strain, and the usual result is that one puts on a glum and solid look on public occasions. Perhaps because of this I was once described in an article in a Hindi magazine as resembling a

Hindu widow! I must say that, much as I admire Hindu widows of the old type, this gave me a shock. The author evidently meant to praise me for some qualities he thought I possessed—a spirit of gentle resignation and renunciation and a smileless devotion to work. I had hoped that I possessed—and, indeed, I wish that Hindu widows would possess—more active and aggressive qualities and the capacity for humor and laughter. Gandhiji once told an interviewer that if he had not had the gift of humor he might have committed suicide, or something to this effect. I would not presume to go so far, yet life certainly would have been almost intolerable for me but for the humor and light touches that some people gave to it.

My very popularity and the brave addresses that came my way, full (as is, indeed, the custom of all such addresses in India) of choice and flowery language and extravagant conceits, became subjects for raillery in the circle of my family and intimate friends. The high-sounding and pompous words and titles that were often used for all those prominent in the national movement, were picked out by my wife and sisters and others and bandied about irreverently. I was addressed as *Bharat Bhushan*—"Jewel of India," *Tyagamurti*—"O Embodiment of Sacrifice"; this light-hearted treatment soothed me, and the tension of those solemn public gatherings, where I had to remain on my best behavior, gradually relaxed. Even my little daughter joined in the game. Only my mother insisted on taking me seriously, and she never wholly approved of any sarcasm or raillery at the expense of her darling boy. Father was amused; he had a way of quietly expressing his deep understanding and sympathy.

But all these shouting crowds, the dull and wearying public functions, the interminable arguments, and the dust and tumble of politics touched me on the surface only, though sometimes the touch was sharp and pointed. My real conflict lay within me, a conflict of ideas, desires, and loyalties, of subconscious depths struggling with outer circumstances, of an inner hunger unsatisfied. I became a battleground, where various forces struggled for mastery. I sought an escape from this; I tried to find harmony and equilibrium, and in this attempt I rushed into action. That gave me some peace; outer conflict relieved the strain of the inner struggle.

Why am I writing all this sitting here in prison? The quest is still the same, in prison or outside, and I write down my past feelings and experiences in the hope that this may bring me some peace and psychic satisfaction.

# XXV

# CIVIL DISOBEDIENCE BEGINS

INDEPENDENCE DAY CAME, January 26, 1930, and it revealed to us, as in a flash, the earnest and enthusiastic mood of the country. There was something vastly impressive about the great gatherings everywhere, peacefully and solemnly taking the pledge of independence [1] without any speeches or exhortation. This celebration gave the necessary impetus to Gandhiji, and he felt, with his sure touch on the pulse of the people, that the time was ripe for action. Events followed then in quick succession, like a drama working up to its climax.

As civil disobedience approached and electrified the atmosphere, our thoughts went back to the movement of 1921-22 and the manner of its sudden suspension after Chauri Chaura. The country was more disciplined now, and there was a clearer appreciation of the nature of the struggle. The technique was understood to some extent, but more important still from Gandhiji's point of view, it was fully realized by everyone that he was terribly in earnest about nonviolence. There could be no doubt about that now, as there probably was in the minds of some people ten years before. Despite all this, how could we possibly be certain that an outbreak of violence might not occur in some locality either spontaneously or as the result of an intrigue? And, if such an incident occurred, what would be its effect on our civil disobedience movement? Would it be suddenly wound up as before? That prospect was most disconcerting.

Gandhiji probably thought over this question also in his own way, though the problem that seemed to trouble him, as far as I could gather from scraps of conversation, was put differently.

The nonviolent method of action to bring about a change for the better was to him the only right method and, if rightly pursued, an infallible method. Must it be said that this method required a specially favorable atmosphere for its functioning and success, and that it should not be tried if outward conditions were not suited to it? That led to the conclusion that the nonviolent method was not meant for all contingencies, and was thus neither a universal nor an infallible method. This conclusion was intolerable for Gandhiji, for he firmly believed that it was a universal and infallible method. Therefore, necessarily, it must function even though the external conditions were unfavorable,

[1] This pledge is given in Appendix A.

and even in the midst of strife and violence. The way of its functioning might be varied to suit varying circumstances, but to stop it would be a confession of failure of the method itself.

Perhaps his mind worked in some such way, but I cannot be sure of his thoughts. He did give us the impression that there was a slightly different orientation to his thinking, and that civil disobedience, when it came, need not be stopped because of a sporadic act of violence. If, however, the violence became in any way part of the movement itself, then it ceased to be a peaceful civil disobedience movement, and its activities had to be curtailed or varied. This assurance went a long way in satisfying many of us. The great question that hung in the air now was—how? How were we to begin? What form of civil disobedience should we take up that would be effective, suited to the circumstances, and popular with the masses? And then the Mahatma gave the hint.

Salt suddenly became a mysterious word, a word of power. The salt tax was to be attacked, the salt laws were to be broken. We were bewildered and could not quite fit in a national struggle with common salt. Another surprising development was Gandhiji's announcement of his "Eleven Points." What was the point of making a list of some political and social reforms—good in themselves, no doubt—when we were talking in terms of independence? Did Gandhiji mean the same thing when he used this term as we did, or did we speak a different language? We had no time to argue, for events were on the move. They were moving politically before our eyes from day to day in India; and, hardly realized by us at the time, they were moving fast in the world and holding it in the grip of a terrible depression. Prices were falling, and the city dwellers welcomed this as a sign of the plenty to come, but the farmer and the tenant saw the prospect with alarm.

Then came Gandhiji's correspondence with the Viceroy and the beginning of the Dandi Salt March from the Ashrama at Sabarmati. As people followed the fortunes of this marching column of pilgrims from day to day, the temperature of the country went up. A meeting of the All-India Congress Committee was held at Ahmedabad to make final arrangements for the struggle that was now almost upon us. The leader in the struggle was not present, for he was already tramping with his pilgrim band to the sea, and he refused to return. The All-India Congress Committee planned what should be done in case of arrests, and large powers were given to the president to act on behalf of the Committee, in case it could not meet, to nominate members of the Working Committee in place of those arrested, and to nominate a successor for himself with the same powers. Similar powers were given by provincial and local Congress committees to their presidents.

Thus was inaugurated a regime when so-called "dictators" flourished and controlled the struggle on behalf of the Congress. Secretaries of state for India and viceroys and governors have held up their hands in horror and proclaimed how vicious and degraded was the Congress because it believed in dictatorships; they, of course, being convinced adherents of democracy. Occasionally the Moderate press in India has also preached to us the virtues of democracy. We listened to all this in silence (because we were in prison) and in amazement. Brazen-faced hypocrisy could hardly go further. Here was India being governed forcibly under an absolute dictatorship under ordinances and suppression of every kind of civil liberty, and yet our rulers talked unctuously of democracy. Even normally, where was the shadow of democracy in India? It was no doubt natural for the British Government to defend its power and vested interests in India and to suppress those who sought to challenge its authority. But its assertion that all this was the democratic method was worthy of record for future generations to admire and ponder over.

The Congress had to face a situation in which it would be impossible for it to function normally; when it would be declared an unlawful organization, and its committees could not meet for consultation or any action, except secretly. Secrecy was not encouraged by us, as we wanted to keep our struggle a perfectly open one, and thus to keep up our tone and influence the masses. But even secret work did not take us far. All our leading men and women at the center, as well as in the provinces and in local areas, were bound to be arrested. Who was then to carry on? The only course open to us was, after the fashion of an army in action, to make arrangements for new commanders to be appointed as old ones were disabled. We could not sit down in the field of battle and hold committee meetings. Indeed, we did so sometimes, but the object of this, and the inevitable result, was to have the whole committee arrested *en bloc*. We did not even have the advantage of a general staff sitting safely behind the lines, or a civilian cabinet in still greater safety elsewhere. Our general staffs and cabinets had to keep, by the very nature of our struggle, in the most advanced and exposed positions, and they were arrested and removed in the early stages. And what was the power we conferred on our "dictators"? It was an honor for them to be put forward as symbols of the national determination to carry on the struggle; but the actual authority they had was largely confined to "dictating" themselves to prison. They could only function at all when the committee they represented could not meet on account of *force majeure*; and wherever and whenever that committee could meet, the "dictator" lost his individual authority, such as it was. He or she could not tackle any basic problems or principles; only minor and superficial phases of the movement could be affected by the "dictator." Congress "dictatorships" were really steppingstones to prison; and from day to day this process went on, new persons taking the place of those who were disabled.

And so, having made our final preparations, we bade good-by to our comrades of the All-India Congress Committee at Ahmedabad, for none knew when or how we would meet again, or whether we would meet at all. We hastened back to our posts to give the finishing touches to our local arrangements, in accordance with the new directions of the All-India Congress Committee, and, as Sarojini Naidu said, to pack up our toothbrushes for the journey to prison.

On our way back, father and I went to see Gandhiji. He was at Jambusar with his pilgrim band, and we spent a few hours with him there and then saw him stride away with his party to the next stage in the journey to the salt sea. That was my last glimpse of him then as I saw him, staff in hand, marching along at the head of his followers, with firm step and a peaceful but undaunted look. It was a moving sight.

At Jambusar my father had decided, in consultation with Gandhiji, to make a gift of his old house in Allahabad to the nation and to rename this Swaraj Bhawan. On his return to Allahabad he made the announcement, and actually handed over charge to the Congress people; part of the large house being converted into a hospital. He was unable to go through the legal formalities at the time, and, a year and a half later, I created a trust of the property, in accordance with his wishes.

April came, and Gandhiji drew near to the sea, and we waited for the word to begin civil disobedience by an attack on the salt laws. For months past we had been drilling our volunteers, and Kamala and Krishna (my wife and sister) had both joined them and donned male attire for the purpose. The volunteers had, of course, no arms or even sticks. The object of training them was to make them more efficient in their work and capable of dealing with large crowds. The 6th of April was the first day of the National Week, which is celebrated annually in memory of the happenings in 1919, from *Satyagraha* Day to Jallianwala Bagh. On that day Gandhiji began the breach of the salt laws at Dandi beach, and three or four days later permission was given to all Congress organizations to do likewise and begin civil disobedience in their own areas.

It seemed as though a spring had been suddenly released; all over the country, in town and village, salt manufacture was the topic of the day, and many curious expedients were adopted to produce salt. We knew precious little about it, and so we read it up where we could and issued leaflets giving directions; we collected pots and pans and ultimately succeeded in producing some unwholesome stuff, which we waved about in triumph and often auctioned for fancy prices. It was really immaterial whether the stuff was good or bad; the main thing was to commit a breach of the obnoxious salt law, and we were successful in that, even though the quality of our salt was poor. As we saw the abounding enthusiasm of the people and the way salt-making was spreading like a prairie fire, we felt a little abashed and ashamed for having questioned the efficacy of this method when it was first proposed by Gandhiji. And we marveled at the amazing knack of the man to impress the multitude and make it act in an organized way.

I was arrested on the 14th of April as I was entraining for Raipur in the Central Provinces, where I was going to attend a conference. That very day I was tried in prison and sentenced to six months' imprisonment under the Salt Act. In anticipation of arrest I had nominated (under the new powers given to me by the All-India Congress Committee) Gandhiji to act as Congress president in my absence, but, fearing his refusal, my second nomination was for father. As I expected, Gandhiji would not agree, and so father became the acting president of the Congress. He was in poor health; nevertheless he threw himself into the campaign with great energy; and, during those early months, his strong guidance and enforcement of discipline was of tremendous benefit to the movement. The movement benefited greatly, but it was at the cost of such health and physical fitness as had remained in him.

Those were days of stirring news—processions and lathee charges and firing, frequent *hartals* to celebrate noted arrests, and special observances, like Peshawar Day, Garhwali Day, etc. For the time being the boycott of foreign cloth and all British goods was almost complete. When I heard that my aged mother and, of course, my sisters used to stand under the hot summer sun picketing before foreign cloth shops, I was greatly moved. Kamala did so also, but she did something more. She threw herself into the movement in Allahabad city and district with an energy and determination which amazed me, who thought I had known her so well for so many years. She forgot her ill-health and rushed about the whole day in the sun, and showed remarkable powers of organization. I heard of this vaguely in jail. Later, when my father joined me there, I was to learn from him how much he had himself appreciated Kamala's work, and especially her organizing capacity. He did not at all fancy my mother or the girls rushing about in the hot sun, but, except for an occasional remonstrance, he did not interfere.

The biggest news of all that came to us in those early days was of the occurrences in Peshawar on April 23,[2] and subsequently all over the Frontier Province. Anywhere in India such a remarkable exhibition of disciplined and peaceful courage before machine-gun firing would have stirred the country. In the Frontier Province it had an additional significance, for the Pathans, noted for their courage, were not noted for their peaceful nature; and these Pathans had set an example which was unique in India. In the Frontier Province also occurred the famous incident of the refusal to fire on the civil population by the Garhwali soldiers. They refused to fire because of a soldier's distaste for firing on an unarmed crowd, and because, no doubt, of sympathy with the crowd. But even sympathy is not usually enough to induce a soldier to take the grave step of refusing to obey his officer's orders. He knows the consequences. The Garhwalis probably did so (in common with some other regiments elsewhere whose disobedience did not receive publicity) because of a mistaken notion that the British power was collapsing. Only when such an idea takes possession of the soldier does he dare to act according to his own sympathies and inclinations. Probably for a few days or weeks the general commotion and civil disobedience led some people to think that the last days of British rule had come, and this influenced part of the Indian Army. Soon it became obvious that no such thing was going to happen in the near future, and then there was no more disobedience in the army. Care was also taken not to put them in compromising positions.

Many strange things happened in those days, but undoubtedly the most striking was the part of the women in the national struggle. They came out in large numbers from the seclusion of their homes and, though unused to public activity, threw themselves into the heart of the struggle. The picketing of foreign cloth and liquor shops they made their preserve. Enormous processions consisting of women alone were taken out in all the cities; and, generally, the attitude of the women

[2] When British machine-guns and airplanes as well quelled a mass protest against certain governmental measures.—Ed.

was more unyielding than that of the men. Often they became Congress "dictators" in provinces and in local areas.

The breach of the Salt Act soon became just one activity, and civil resistance spread to other fields. This was facilitated by the promulgation of various ordinances by the Viceroy prohibiting a number of activities. As these ordinances and prohibitions grew, the opportunities for breaking them also grew, and civil resistance took the form of doing the very thing that the ordinance was intended to stop. The initiative definitely remained with the Congress and the people; and, as each ordinance law failed to control the situation from the point of view of government, fresh ordinances were issued by the Viceroy. Many of the Congress Working Committee members had been arrested, but it continued to function with new members added on to it, and each official ordinance was countered by a resolution of the Working Committee giving directions as to how to meet it. These directions were carried out with surprising uniformity all over this country—with one exception, the one relating to the publication of newspapers.

When an ordinance was issued for the further control of the press and the demand of security from newspapers, the Working Committee called upon the nationalist press to refuse to give any security, and to stop publication instead. This was a hard pill to swallow for the newspapermen, for just then the public demand for news was very great. Still the great majority of newspapers—some Moderate papers excepted —stopped publication, with the result that all manner of rumors began to spread. But they could not hold out for long; the temptation was too great, and the sight of their Moderate rivals picking up their business too irritating. So most of them drifted back to publication.

Gandhiji had been arrested on May 5. After his arrest big raids on the salt pans and depots were organized on the west coast. There were very painful incidents of police brutality during these raids. Bombay then occupied the center of the picture with its tremendous *hartals* and processions and lathi charges. Several emergency hospitals grew up to treat the victims of these lathee charges. Much that was remarkable happened in Bombay, and, being a great city, it had the advantage of publicity. Occurrences of equal importance in small towns and the rural areas received no publicity.

In the latter half of June my father went to Bombay, and with him went my mother and Kamala. They had a great reception, and during their stay there occurred some of the fiercest of the lathee charges. These were, indeed, becoming frequent occurrences in Bombay. A fortnight or so later an extraordinary all-night ordeal took place there, when Malaviyaji and members of the Working Committee, at the head of a huge crowd, spent the night facing the police, who blocked their way.

On his return from Bombay father was arrested on June 30, and Syed Mahmud was arrested with him. They were arrested as acting president and secretary of the Working Committee, which was declared unlawful. Both of them were sentenced to six months. My father's arrest was probably due to his having issued a statement defining the duties of a soldier or policeman in the event of an order to fire on civil populations being given. The statement was strictly a legal affair, and contained the present British Indian law on this point. Nevertheless, it was considered a provocative and dangerous document.

The Bombay visit had been a great strain on father; from early morning to late at night he was kept busy, and he had to take the responsibility for every important decision. He had long been unwell, but now he returned fagged out, and decided, at the urgent advice of his doctors, to take complete rest immediately. He arranged to go to Mussoorie and packed up for it, but the day before he intended leaving for Mussoorie, he appeared before us in our barrack in Naini Central Prison.


## XXVI

## IN NAINI PRISON

I HAD GONE back to jail after nearly seven years, and memories of prison life had somewhat faded. I was in Naini Central Prison, one of the big prisons of the province, and I was to have the novel experience of being kept by myself. My enclosure was apart from the big enclosure containing the jail population of between 2200 and 2300. It was a small enclosure, circular in shape, with a diameter of about one hundred feet, and with a circular wall about fifteen feet high surrounding it. In the middle of it was a drab and ugly building containing four cells. I was given two of these cells, connecting with each other, one to serve as a bathroom and lavatory. The others remained unoccupied for some time.

After the exciting and very active life I had been leading outside, I felt rather lonely and depressed. I was tired out, and for two or three days I slept a great deal. The hot weather had already begun, and I was permitted to sleep at night in the open, outside my cell in the narrow space between the inner building and the enclosing wall. My bed was heavily chained up, lest I might take it up and walk away, or, more probably, to avoid the bed's being used as a kind of scaling ladder to climb the wall of the enclosure. The nights were full of strange noises. The convict overseers, who guarded the main wall, frequently shouted to each other in varying keys, sometimes lengthening out their cries till they sounded like the moaning of a distant wind; the night watchmen in the barracks were continually counting away in a loud voice the prisoners under their charge and shouting out that all was well; and several times a night some jail official, going his rounds, visited our enclosure and shouted an inquiry to the warder on duty. As my enclosure was some distance away from the others, most of these voices reached me indistinctly, and I could not make out at first what they were. At times I felt as if I were on the verge of the forest, and the peasantry were shouting to keep the wild animals away from their fields; sometimes it seemed the forest itself and the beasts of the night were keeping up their nocturnal chorus.

Was it my fancy, I wonder, or is it a fact that a circular wall reminds one more of captivity than a rectangular one? The absence of corners and angles adds to the sense of oppression. In the daytime that wall even encroached on the sky and only allowed a glimpse of a narrow-bounded portion. With a wistful eye I looked

> *Upon that little tent of blue*
> *Which prisoners call the sky,*
> *And at every drifting cloud that went*
> *With sails of silver by.*

At night that wall enclosed me all the more, and I felt as if I were at the bottom of a well. Or else that part of the star-lit sky that I saw ceased to be real and seemed part of an artificial planetarium.

My barrack and enclosure were popularly known throughout the jail as the *Kuttaghar*—the Dog House. This was an old name which had nothing to do with me. The little barrack had been built originally, apart from all others, for especially dangerous criminals who had to be isolated. Latterly it had been used for political prisoners, *détenus,* and the like who could thus be kept apart from the rest of the jail. In front of the enclosure, some distance away, was an erection that gave me a shock when I first had a glimpse of it from my barrack. It looked like a huge cage, and men went round and round inside it. I found out later that it was a water pump worked by human labor, as many as sixteen persons being employed at a time. I got used to it, as one gets used to everything; but it has always seemed to me one of the most foolish and barbarous ways of utilizing human labor power. And, whenever I pass it, I think of the zoo.

For some days I was not permitted to go outside my enclosure for exercise or any other purpose. I was later allowed to go out for half an hour in the early mornings, when it was almost dark, and to walk or run under the main wall. That early morning hour had been fixed for me so that I might not come in contact with, or be seen by, the other prisoners. I liked that outing, and it refreshed me tremendously. In order to compress as much open-air exercise as I could in the short time at my disposal, I took to running and gradually increased this to over two miles daily.

I used to get up very early in the morning, about four, or even half-past three, when it was quite dark. Partly this was due to going to bed early, as the light provided was not good for much reading. I liked to watch the stars, and the position of some well-known constellation would give me the approximate time. From where I lay I could just see the pole star peeping over the wall, and, as it was always there, I found it extraordinarily comforting. Surrounded by a revolving sky, it seemed to be a symbol of cheerful constancy and perseverence.

For a month I had no companion, but I was not alone, as I had the warder and the convict overseers and a convict cook and cleaner in my enclosure. Occasionally other prisoners came there on some business, most of them being convict overseers—C.O.'s—serving out long sentences. "Lifers"—convicts sentenced for life—were common. Usually a life sentence was supposed to terminate after twenty years, or even less, but there were many in prison then who had served more than twenty years already. I saw one very remarkable case in Naini. Prisoners carry about, attached to their clothes at the shoulder, little wooden boards giving information about their convictions and mentioning the date when release is due. On the board of one prisoner I read that his date of release was 1996! He had already, in 1930, served out several years, and he was then a person of middle age. Probably he had been given several sentences, and they had been added up one after the other; the total, I think, amounting to seventy-five years.

For years and years many of these "lifers" do not see a child or woman, or even animals. They lose touch with the outside world completely, and have no human contacts left. They brood and wrap themselves in angry thoughts of fear and revenge and hatred; forget the good of the world, the kindness and joy, and live only wrapped up in the evil, till gradually even hatred loses its edge and life becomes a soulless thing, a machinelike routine. Like automatons they pass their days, each exactly like the other, and have few sensations except one —fear! From time to time the prisoner's body is weighed and measured. But how is one to weigh the mind and the spirit which wilt and stunt themselves and wither away in this terrible atmosphere of oppression? People argue against the death penalty, and their arguments appeal to me greatly. But when I see the long-drawn-out agony of a life spent in prison, I feel that it is perhaps better to have that penalty rather than to kill a person slowly and by degrees. One of the "lifers" came up to me once and asked me: "What of us 'lifers'? Will *Swaraj* take us out of this hell?"

Who are these "lifers"? Many of them come in gang cases, when large numbers, as many as fifty or a hundred, may be convicted *en bloc*. Some of these are probably guilty, but I doubt if most of those convicted are really guilty; it is easy to get people involved in such cases. An approver's evidence, a little identification, is all that is needed. Dacoits are increasing nowadays, and the prison population goes up year by year. If people starve, what are they to do? Judges and magistrates wax eloquent about the increase of crime but are blind to the obvious economic causes of it.

Then there are the agriculturists who have a little village riot over some land dispute, lathis fly about, and somebody dies—result, many people in jail for life or for a long term. Often all the menfolk in a family will be imprisoned in this way, leaving the women to carry on as best they can. Not one of these is a criminal type. Generally they are fine young men, considerably above the average villager, both physically and mentally. A little training, some diversion of interest to other subjects and jobs, and these people would be valuable assets to the country.

Indian prisons contain, of course, hardened criminals, persons who are aggressively antisocial and dangerous to the community. But I have been amazed to find large numbers of fine types in prison, boys and men, whom I would trust unhesitatingly. I do not know what the proportion of real criminals to noncriminal types is, and probably no one in the prison department has ever even thought of this distinction. A more sensible economic policy, more employment, more education would soon empty out our prisons. But of course to make that successful, a radical plan, affecting the whole of our social fabric, is essential. The only other real alternative is what the British Government is doing: increasing its police forces and enlarging its prisons in India. The number of persons sent to jail in India is appalling. In a recent report issued by the secretary of the All-India Prisoners' Aid Society, it is stated that in the Bombay Presidency alone 128,000 persons were sent to jail in 1933, and the figure for Bengal for the same year was 124,000. I do not know the figures for all the provinces, but if the total for two provinces exceeds a quarter of a million, it is quite possible that the all-India total approaches the million mark. This figure does not, of course, represent the permanent jail population, for a large number of persons get short sentences. The permanent population will be very much less, but still it must be enormous. Some of the major provinces in India are said to have the biggest prison administrations in the world. The United Provinces are among those supposed to have this doubtful honor, and very probably they have, or had, one of the most backward and reactionary administrations. Not the least effort is made to consider the prisoner as an individual, a human being, and to improve or look after his mind. The one thing the United Provinces administration excels in is keeping its prisoners. There are remarkably few attempts to escape, and I doubt if one in ten thousand succeeds in escaping.

One of the most saddening features of the prisons is the large number of boys, from fifteen upward, who are to be found in them. Most of them are bright-looking lads who, if given the chance, might easily make good. Lately some beginnings have been made to teach them the elements of reading and writing but, as usual, these are absurdly inadequate and inefficient. There are very few opportunities for games or recreation, no newspapers of any kind are permitted nor are books encouraged. For twelve hours or more all prisoners are kept locked up in their barracks or cells with nothing whatever to do in the long evenings.

Interviews are only permitted once in three months, and so are letters —a monstrously long period. Even so, many prisoners cannot take advantage of them. If they are illiterate, as most are, they have to rely on some jail official to write on their behalf; and the latter, not being keen on adding to his other work, usually avoids it. Or, if a letter is written, the address is not properly given, and the letter does not arrive. Interviews are still more difficult. Often prisoners are transferred to different jails, and their people cannot trace them. I have met many prisoners who had lost complete touch with their families for years and did not know what had happened. Interviews, when they do take place after three months or more, are most extraordinary. A number of prisoners and their interviewers are placed together on either side of a barrier, and they all try to talk simultaneously. There is a great deal of shouting at each other, and the slight human touch that might have come from the interview is entirely absent.

A very small number of prisoners, ordinarily not exceeding one in a thousand (Europeans excepted), are given some extra privileges in the shape of better food and more frequent interviews and letters. During a big political civil resistance movement, when scores of thousands of political prisoners go to jail, this figure of special class prisoners goes up slightly, but even so it is very low. About 95 per cent of these political prisoners, men and women, are treated in the ordinary way and are not given even these facilities.

Some individuals, sentenced for revolutionary activities for life or long terms of imprisonment, are often kept in solitary confinement for long periods. In the United Provinces, I believe, all such persons are automatically kept in solitary cellular confinement. Ordinarily, this solitary confinement is awarded as a special punishment for a prison offense. But in the case of these persons—usually young boys—they are kept alone although their behavior in jail might be exemplary. Thus an additional and very terrible punishment is added by the jail department to the sentence of the court, without any reason therefor. This seems very extraordinary, and hardly in conformity with any rule of law. Solitary confinement, even for a short period, is a most painful affair; for it to be prolonged for years is a terrible thing. It means the slow and continuous deterioration of the mind, till it begins to border on insanity; and the appearance of a look of vacancy, or a frightened animal type of expression. It is the killing of the spirit by degrees, the slow vivisection of the soul. Even if a man survives it, he becomes abnormal and an absolute misfit in the world. And the question always arises—was this man guilty at all of any act or offense? Police methods in India have long been suspect; in political matters they are doubly so.

European or Eurasian prisoners, whatever their crime or status, are automatically placed in a higher class and get better food, lighter work, and more interviews and letters. A weekly visit from a clergyman keeps them in touch with outside affairs. The parson brings them foreign illustrated and humorous papers, and communicates with their families when necessary.

No one grudges the European convicts these privileges, for they are few enough, but it is a little painful to see the utter absence of any human standard in the treatment of others—men and women. The convict is not thought of as an individual human being, and so he or she is seldom treated as such. One sees in prison the inhuman side of the State apparatus of administrative repression at its worst. It is a machine which works away callously and unthinkingly, crushing all that come in its grip, and the jail rules have been purposely framed to keep this machine in evidence. Offered to sensitive men and women, this soulless regime is a torture and an anguish of the mind. I have seen long-term convicts sometimes breaking down at the dreariness of it all, and weeping like little children. And a word of sympathy and encouragement, so rare in this atmosphere, has suddenly made their faces light up with joy and gratitude.

And yet among the prisoners themselves there were often touching instances of charity and good comradeship. A blind "habitual" prisoner was once discharged after thirteen years. After this long period he was going out, wholly unprovided for, into a friendless world. His fellow convicts were eager to help him, but they could not do much. One gave his shirt deposited in the jail office, another some other piece of clothing. A third had that very morning received a new pair of *chappals* (leather sandals), and he had shown them to me with some pride. It was a great acquisition in prison. But, when he saw this blind companion of many years going out barefooted, he willingly parted with his new *chappals*. I thought then that there appeared to be more charity inside the jail than outside it.

That year 1930 was full of dramatic situations and inspiring happenings; what surprised most was the amazing power of Gandhiji to inspire and enthuse a whole people. There was something almost hypnotic about it, and we remembered the words used by Gokhale about him: how he had the power of making heroes out of clay. Peaceful civil disobedience as a technique of action for achieving great national ends seemed to have justified itself, and a quiet confidence grew in the country, shared by friend and opponent alike, that we were marching toward victory. A strange excitement filled those who were active in the movement, and some of this even crept inside the jail. "*Swaraj* is coming!" said the ordinary convicts; and they waited impatiently for it, in the selfish hope that it might do them some good. The warders, coming in contact with the gossip of the bazaars, also expected that *Swaraj* was near; the petty jail official grew a little more nervous.

We had no daily newspapers in prison, but a Hindi weekly brought us some news, and often this news would set our imaginations afire. Daily lathee charges, sometimes firing, martial law at Sholapur with sentences of ten years for carrying the national flag. We felt proud of our people, and especially of our womenfolk, all over the country. I had a special feeling of satisfaction because of the activities of my mother, wife, and sisters, as well as many girl cousins and friends; and, though I was separated from them and was in prison, we grew nearer to each other, bound by a new sense of comradeship in a great cause. The family seemed to merge into a larger group, and yet to retain its old flavor and intimacy. Kamala surprised me, for her energy and enthusiasm overcame her physical ill-health, and, for some time at least, she kept well in spite of strenuous activities.

The thought that I was having a relatively easy time in prison, at a time when others were facing danger and suffering outside, began to oppress me. I longed to go out; and, as I could not do that, I made my life in prison a hard one, full of work. I used to spin daily for nearly three hours on my own *charkha;* for another two or three hours I did *newar* weaving, which I had especially asked for from the jail authorities. I liked these activities. They kept me occupied without undue strain or requiring too much attention, and they soothed the fever of my mind. I read a great deal, and otherwise busied myself with cleaning up, washing my clothes, etc. The manual labor I did was of my own choice, as my imprisonment was "simple."

And so, between thought of outside happenings and my jail routine, I passed my days in Naini Prison. As I watched the working of an Indian prison, it struck me that it was not unlike the British government of India. There is great efficiency in the apparatus of government, which goes to strengthen the hold of the Government on the country, and little or no care for the human material of the country. Outwardly the prison must appear efficiently run, and to some extent this was true. But no one seemed to think that the main purpose of the prison must be to improve and help the unhappy individuals who come to it. Break them!—that is the idea, so that by the time they go out, they may not have the least bit of spirit left in them. And how is the prison controlled, and the convicts kept in check and punished? Very largely with the help of the convicts themselves, some of whom are made convict warders (C.W.'s) or convict overseers (C.O.'s), and are induced to co-operate with the authorities because of fear, and in the hope of rewards and special remissions. There are relatively few paid non-convict warders; most of the guarding inside the prison is done by convict warders and C.O.'s. A widespread system of spying pervades the prison, convicts being encouraged to become stool pigeons and to spy on one another; and no combination or joint action is, of course, permitted among the prisoners. This is easy to understand, for only by keeping them divided up could they be kept in check.

Outside, in the government of our country, we see much the same, on a larger, though less obvious, scale. But there the C.W.'s or C.O.'s are known differently. They have impressive titles, and their liveries of office are more gorgeous. And behind them, as in prison, stands the armed guard with weapons ever ready to enforce conformity.

How important and essential is a prison to the modern State! The prisoner at least begins to think so, and the numerous administrative and other functions of the Government appear almost superficial before the basic functions of the prison, the police, the army. In prison one begins to appreciate the Marxian theory, that the State is really the coercive apparatus meant to enforce the will of a group that controls the government.

For a month I was alone in my barrack. Then a companion came—Narmada Prasad Singh—and his coming was a relief. Two and a half months later, on the last day of June 1930, our little enclosure was the scene of unusual excitement. Unexpectedly early in the morning, my father and Dr. Syed Mahmud were brought there. They had both been arrested in Anand Bhawan, while they were actually in their beds, that morning.

## XXVII

## THE NO-TAX CAMPAIGN IN THE UNITED PROVINCES

MY FATHER'S ARREST was accompanied by, or immediately preceded by, the declaration of the Congress Working Committee as an unlawful body. This led to a new development outside—the Committee would be arrested *en bloc* when it was having a meeting. Substitute members were added to it, under the authority given to the acting presidents, and in this way several women became acting members. Kamala was one of them.

Father was in very poor health when he came to jail, and the conditions in which he was kept there were of extreme discomfort. This was not intentional on the part of the Government, for they were prepared to do what they could to lessen those discomforts. But they could not do much in Naini Prison. Four of us were now crowded together in the four tiny cells of my barrack. It was suggested by the superintendent of the prison that father might be kept in some other part of the jail where he might have a little more room, but we preferred to be together, so that some of us could attend personally to his comforts.

The monsoon was just beginning, and it was not particularly easy to keep perfectly dry even inside the cells, for the rainwater came through the roof occasionally and dripped in various places. At night it was always a problem where to put father's bed in the little ten-foot by five-foot veranda attached to our cell, in order to avoid the rain. Sometimes he had fever. The jail authorities ultimately decided to build an additional veranda, a fine broad one, attached to our cell. This veranda was built, and it was a great improvement, but father did not profit by it much, as he was discharged soon after it was ready. Those of us who continued to live in that barrack took full advantage of it later.

Toward the end of July there was a great deal of talk about Dr. Tej Bahadur Sapru and Mr. M. R. Jayakar endeavoring to bring about peace between the Congress and the Government. We heard that there had been some correspondence between Lord Irwin and Messrs. Sapru and Jayakar, and that the "peacemakers" had visited Gandhiji. Later, we were told, a brief statement that father had agreed to in Bombay a few days before his arrest had encouraged them. Mr. Slocombe (a correspondent of the London *Daily Herald* then in India) had drafted this statement after a conversation with my father, and father had approved it. It envisaged the possibility of suspending civil disobedience if the Government agreed to a number of conditions. I remember father mentioning it to me in Naini, after his arrest, and adding that he was rather sorry that he had given such a vague statement in a hurry, as it was possible that it might be misunderstood. It was indeed misunderstood, as even the most exact and explicit statements are likely to be, by people whose way of thinking is entirely different.

Dr. Tej Bahadur Sapru and Mr. Jayakar suddenly descended on us in Naini Prison, on July 27, with a note from Gandhiji. We had long interviews with them, which were very exhausting for father as he was actually feverish then. We talked and argued in a circle, hardly understanding one another's language or thought, so great was the difference in political outlook. It was obvious to us that there was not the faintest chance of any peace. We refused to make any suggestions without first consulting our colleagues of the Working Committee, especially Gandhiji. And we wrote something to this effect to Gandhiji.

Eleven days later, on August 8, Dr. Sapru came to see us again with the Viceroy's reply. The Viceroy had no objection to our going to Yeravda, the prison in Poona where Gandhiji was kept; but he and his Council could not allow us to meet members of the Working Committee who were outside and were still carrying on an active campaign against the Government.

Two days later, on August 10, the three of us—father, Mahmud, and I—were sent by a special train from Naini to Poona. Our train did not stop at the big stations; we rushed past them, stopping at the small wayside ones. Still, news of us traveled ahead, and large crowds gathered both at the stations where we stopped and at those where we did not stop. We reached Kirkee, near Poona, late at night on the 11th.

Our conferences in the prison office with Messrs. Sapru and Jayakar lasted three days, the 13th, 14th, and 15th of August, and we exchanged letters giving expression to our views and indicating the minimum conditions necessary to enable us to withdraw civil disobedience and offer co-operation to the Government. These letters were subsequently published in the newspapers.

The strain of these conferences had told on father, and on the 16th he suddenly got high fever. This delayed our return, and we started back on the night of the 19th, again by special train, for Naini. Every effort was made by the Bombay Government to provide a comfortable journey for father, and even in Yeravda, during our brief stay there, his comforts were studied. I remember an amusing incident on the night of our arrival at Yeravda. Colonel Martin, the superintendent, asked father what kind of food he would like. Father told him that he took very simple and light food, and then he enumerated his various requirements from early morning tea in bed to dinner at night. (In Naini we used to get food for him daily from home.) The list father gave in all innocence and simplicity consisted certainly of light foods, but it was impressive. Very probably at the Ritz or the Savoy it would have been considered simple and ordinary food, as father himself was convinced that it was. But in Yeravda Prison it seemed strange and far away and most inappropriate. Mahmud and I were highly amused to watch the expression on Colonel Martin's face as he listened to father's numerous and expensive requirements in the way of food. For a long time he had had in his keeping the greatest and most famous of India's leaders, and all that he had required in the way of food was goat's milk, dates, and perhaps oranges occasionally. The new type of leader that had come to him was very different.

During our journey back from Poona to Naini we again rushed by the big stations and stopped in out-of-the-way places. But the crowds were larger still, filling the platforms and sometimes even swarming over the railway lines, especially at Harda, Itarsi, and Sohagpur. Accidents were narrowly averted.

Father's condition was rapidly deteriorating. Many doctors came to examine him, his own doctors as well as doctors sent on behalf of the Provincial Government. It was obvious that jail was the worst place for him, and there could be no proper treatment there. And yet, when a suggestion was made by some friend in the press that he should be released because of his illness, he was irritated, as he thought that people might think that the suggestion came from him. He even went to the length of sending a telegram to Lord Irwin, saying that he did not want to be released as a special favor. But his condition was growing worse from day to day; he was losing weight rapidly, and physically he was a shadow of himself. On the 8th of September he was discharged after exactly ten weeks of prison.

Our barrack became a dull and lifeless place after his departure. There was so much to be done when he was with us, little services to add to his comfort, and all of us—Mahmud, Narmada Prasad, and I— filled our days with this joyful service. I had given up *newar* weaving, I spun very little, and I did not have much time for books either. And now that he was gone, we reverted rather heavily and joylessly to the old routine. Even the daily newspaper stopped after father's release. Four or five days later my brother-in-law, Ranjit S. Pandit, was arrested, and he joined us in our barrack.

A month later, on October 11, I was discharged on the expiry of six months' sentence. I knew I would have little freedom, for the struggle was going on and becoming more intense. The attempts of the "peacemakers"—Messrs. Sapru and Jayakar—had failed. On the very day I was discharged one or two more ordinances were announced. I was glad to be out and eager to do something effective during my short spell of freedom.

Kamala was in Allahabad then, busy with her Congress work; father was under treatment at Mussoorie, and my mother and sisters were with him. I spent a busy day and a half in Allahabad before going up to Mussoorie myself with Kamala. The great question before us then was whether a no-tax campaign in the rural areas should be started or not. The time for rent collection and payment of revenue was close at hand, and, in any event, collections were going to be difficult because of the tremendous fall in the prices of agricultural produce. The world slump was now very evident in India.

It seemed an ideal opportunity for a no-tax campaign, both as a part of the general civil disobedience movement and, independently, on its own merits. It was manifestly impossible both for landlords and tenants to pay up the full demand out of that year's produce. They had to fall back on old reserves, if they had any, or borrow. The zamindars usually had something to fall back upon, or could borrow more easily. The average tenant, always on the verge of destitution and starvation, had nothing to fall back upon. In any democratic country, or where the agriculturists were properly organized and had influence, it would have been quite impossible, under those circumstances, to make them pay much. In India their influence was negligible, except in so far as the Congress, in some parts of the country, stood for them; and except, of course, for the ever-present fear of peasant risings when the situation became intolerable for them. But they had become accustomed for generations past to stand almost anything without much murmuring.

When I came out of jail in October, both political and economic conditions seemed to me to be crying out for a no-tax campaign in rural areas. The economic difficulties of the agriculturists were obvious enough. Politically, our civil disobedience activities, though still flourishing everywhere, were getting a bit stale. People went on going to jail in small numbers, and sometimes in large groups, but the sting had gone from the atmosphere. The cities and the middle classes were a bit tired of the *hartals* and processions. Obviously something was needed to liven things up, a fresh infusion of blood was necessary. Where could this come from except from the peasantry?—and the reserve stocks there were enormous. It would again become a mass movement touching the vital interests of the masses and, what was to me very important, would raise social issues.

We discussed these matters, my colleagues and I, during the brief day and a half I was at Allahabad. At short notice we convened a meeting there of the executive of our Provincial Congress Committee, and, after long debate, we decided to sanction a no-tax campaign, making it permissive for any district to take it up. We did not declare it ourselves in any part of the province, and the Executive Council made it apply to zamindars as well as tenants, to avoid the class issue if possible. We knew, of course, that the main response would come from the peasantry.

Having got this permission to go ahead, our district of Allahabad wanted to take the first step. We decided to convene a representative *kisan* or peasants' conference of the district a week later, to give the new campaign a push. I felt that I had done a good first day's work after release from jail. I added to it a big mass meeting in Allahabad city, where I spoke at length. It was for this speech that I was subsequently convicted again.

And then, on October 13, Kamala and I went off to Mussoorie to spend three days with father. He was looking just a little better, and I was happy to think that he had turned the corner and was getting well. I remember those quiet and delightful three days well; it was good to be back in the family. Indira, my daughter, was there; and my three little nieces, my sister's daughters. I would play with the children, and sometimes we would march bravely round the house in a stately procession, led, flag in hand, by the youngest, aged three or four, singing *Jhanda uncha rahe hamara,* our flag song. And those three days were the last I was to have with father before his fatal illness came to snatch him away from me.

Expecting my rearrest soon, and desiring perhaps to see a little more of me, father suddenly decided to return to Allahabad also. Kamala and I were going down from Mussoorie on October 17 to be in time for the peasant conference at Allahabad on the 19th. Father arranged to start with the others on the 18th, the day after us.

We had a somewhat exciting journey back, Kamala and I. At Dehra Dun an order under Section 144, Criminal Procedure Code was served on me almost as I was leaving. At Lucknow we got off for a few hours, and I learned that another order under Section 144 awaited me there, but it was not actually served on me, as the police officer could not reach me owing to the large crowds. I was presented with an address by the municipality, and then we left by car for Allahabad, stopping at various places en route to address some peasant gatherings. We reached Allahabad on the night of the 18th.

The morning of the 19th brought yet another order under Section 144 for me! The Government was evidently hot on my trail, and my hours were numbered. I was anxious to attend the *kisan* conference before my rearrest. We called this conference a private one of delegates only, and so it was, and did not allow outsiders to come in. It was very representative of Allahabad district, and, as far as I remember, about sixteen hundred delegates were present. The conference decided very enthusiastically to start the no-tax campaign in the district. There was some hesitation among our principal workers, some doubt about the success of such a venture, for the influence and the power of the big zamindars to terrorize, backed as this was by the Government, was very great, and they wondered if the peasantry would be able to withstand this. But there was no hesitation or doubt in the minds of the sixteen hundred and odd peasants of all degrees who were present—or at any rate it was not apparent. I was one of the speakers at the conference. I do not know if thereby I committed a breach of the Section 144 order which had forbidden me from speaking in public.

I then went to the station to receive my father and the rest of the family. The train was late, and, immediately after their arrival, I left them to attend a public meeting, a joint affair of the peasants, who had come from the surrounding villages, and the townspeople. Kamala and I were returning from this meeting, thoroughly tired out, after 8 P.M. I was looking forward to a talk with father, and I knew that he was waiting for me, for we had hardly spoken to each other since his return. On our way back our car was stopped almost in sight of our house, and I was arrested and carried off across the River Jumna to my old quarters in Naini. Kamala went on, alone, to Anand Bhawan to inform the waiting family of this new development; and, at the stroke of nine, I re-entered the great gate of Naini Prison.

After eight days' absence I was back again in Naini, and I rejoined Syed Mahmud, Narmada Prasad, and Ranjit Pandit in the same old barrack. Some days afterward I was tried in prison on a number of charges, all based on various parts of that one speech I had delivered at Allahabad, the day after my discharge. As usual with us, I did not defend myself, but made a brief statement in court. I was sentenced for sedition under Section 124A to eighteen months' rigorous imprisonment and a fine of five hundred rupees; under the Salt Act of 1882 to six months and a fine of one hundred rupees; and under Ordinance VI of 1930 (I forget what this ordinance was about) also to six months and a fine of one hundred rupees. As the last two were concurrent, the total sentence was two years' rigorous imprisonment and, in addition, five months in default of fines. This was my fifth term.

My rearrest and conviction had some effect on the tempo of the civil disobedience movement for a while; it put on a little spurt and showed greater energy. This was largely due to father. When news was brought to him by Kamala of my arrest, he had a slightly unpleasant shock. Almost immediately he pulled himself together and banged a table in front of him, saying that he had made up his mind to be an invalid no longer. He was going to be well and to do a man's work, and not to submit weakly to illness. It was a brave resolve, but unhappily no strength of will could overcome and crush that deep-seated disease that was eating into him. Yet for a few days it worked a marked change, to the surprise of those who saw him. For some months past, ever since he had been at Yeravda, he had been bringing up blood in his sputum. This stopped quite suddenly after this resolve of his, and for some days it did not reappear. He was pleased about it, and he came to see me in prison and mentioned this fact to me in some triumph. It was unfortunately a brief respite, for the blood came later in greater quantities, and the disease reasserted itself. During this interval he worked with his old energy and gave a push to the civil disobedience movement all over India. He conferred with many people from various places and issued detailed instructions. He fixed one day (it was my birthday in November!) for an all-India celebration at which the offending passages from my speech, for which I had been convicted, were read out at public meetings. On that day there were numerous lathee charges and forcible dispersals of processions and meetings, and it was estimated that, on that day alone, about five thousand arrests were made all over the country. It was a unique birthday celebration.

Ill as he was, this assumption of responsibility and pouring out of energy was very bad for father, and I begged of him to take absolute rest. I realized that such rest might not be possible for him in India, for his mind would always be occupied with the ups and downs of our struggle, and, inevitably, people would go to him for advice. So I suggested to him to go for a short sea voyage toward Rangoon, Singapore, and the Dutch Indies, and he rather liked the idea. It was arranged that a doctor friend might accompany him on the voyage. With this object in view he went to Calcutta, but his condition grew slowly worse, and he was unable to go far. In a Calcutta suburb he remained for seven weeks, and the whole family joined him there, except Kamala, who remained in Allahabad for most of the time, doing Congress work.

My rearrest had probably been hastened because of my activities in connection with the no-tax campaign. As a matter of fact few things could have been better for that campaign than my arrest on that particular day, immediately after the *kisan* conference, while the peasant delegates were still in Allahabad. Their enthusiasm grew because of it, and they carried the decisions of the conference to almost every village in the district. Within a couple of days the whole district knew that the no-tax campaign had been inaugurated, and everywhere there was a joyful response to it.

Our chief difficulty in those days was one of communication, of getting people to know what we were doing or what we wanted them to do. Newspapers would not publish our news for fear of being penalized and suppressed by Government; printing presses would not print our leaflets and notices; letters and telegrams were censored and often stopped. The only reliable method of communication open to us was to send couriers with dispatches, and even so our messengers were sometimes arrested. The method was an expensive one and required a great deal of organization. It was organized with some success, and the provincial centers were in constant touch with headquarters as well as with their principal district centers. It was not difficult to spread any information in the cities. Many of these issued unauthorized news sheets, usually cyclostyled, daily or weekly, and there was always a great demand for them. For our public notifications, one of the city methods was by beat of drum; this resulted usually in the arrest of the drummer. This did not matter, as arrests were sought, not avoided. All these methods suited the cities and were not easily applicable to the rural areas. Some kind of touch was kept up with principal village centers by means of messengers and cyclostyled notices, but this was not satisfactory, and it took time for our instructions to percolate to distant villages.

The *kisan* conference at Allahabad got over this difficulty. Delegates had come to it from practically every important village in the district, and, when they dispersed, they carried the news of the fresh decisions affecting the peasantry, and of my arrest in connection with them, to every part of the district. They became, sixteen hundred of them, effective and enthusiastic propagandists for the no-tax campaign. The initial success of the movement thus became assured, and there was no doubt that the peasantry as a whole in that area would not pay their rent to begin with, and not at all unless they were frightened into doing so. No one, of course, could say what their powers of endurance would be in face of official or zamindari violence and terrorism. Our appeal had been addressed both to zamindars and tenants not to pay; in theory it was not a class appeal. In practice most of the zamindars did pay their revenue, even some who sympathized with the national struggle. The pressure on them was great, and they had more to lose. The tenantry, however, stood firm and did not pay, and our campaign thus became practically a no-rent campaign.

Government repression grew. Local Congress committees, youth leagues, etc., which had rather surprisingly carried on so far, were declared illegal and suppressed. The treatment of political prisoners in jails became worse. Government was especially irritated when people returned to jail for a second sentence soon after their discharge. This failure to bend in spite of punishment hurt the morale of the rulers. In November or early December 1930 there were some cases of flogging of political prisoners in United Provinces prisons, apparently for offenses against jail discipline. News of this reached us in Naini Prison and upset us—since then we have got used to this, as well as many worse happenings in India—for flogging seemed to me to be an undesirable infliction, even on hardened criminals of the worst type. For young, sensitive boys and for technical offenses of discipline, it was barbarous. We four in our barrack wrote to the Government about it, and, not receiving any reply for about two weeks, we decided to take some definite step to mark our protest at the floggings and our sympathy with the victims of this barbarity. We undertook a complete fast for three days—seventy-two hours. This was not much as fasts go, but none of us was accustomed to fasting and did not know how we would stand it. My previous fasts had seldom exceeded twenty-four hours.

We went through that fast without any great difficulty, and I was glad to find out that it was not such an ordeal as I feared. Very foolishly I carried on my strenuous exercises—running, jerks, etc.—right through that fast. I do not think that did me much good, especially as I had been feeling a little unwell previously. Each one of us lost seven to eight pounds in weight during those three days. This was in addition to the fifteen to twenty-six pounds that each had lost in the previous months in Naini.

Except for these occasional alarms, we lived a quiet life in prison. The weather was agreeable, for winter in Allahabad is very pleasant. Ranjit Pandit was an acquisition to our barrack, for he knew much about gardening, and soon that dismal enclosure of ours was full of flowers and gay with color. He even arranged in that narrow, restricted space a miniature golf course!

One of the welcome excitements of our prison existence at Naini was the passage of airplanes over our heads. Allahabad is one of the ports of call for all the great air lines between East and West, and the giant planes going to Australia, Java, and French Indo-China would pass almost directly above our heads at Naini. Most stately of all were the Dutch liners flying to and from Batavia. Sometimes, if we were lucky, we saw a plane in the early winter morning, when it was still dark and the stars were visible. The great liner was brightly lit up, and at both ends it had red lights. It was a beautiful sight, as it sailed by, against the dark background of the early-morning sky.

The New Year's Day, the first of January 1931, brought us the news of Kamala's arrest. I was pleased, for she had so longed to follow many of her comrades to prison. Ordinarily, if they had been men, both she and my sister and many other women would have been arrested long ago. But at that time the Government avoided, as far as possible, arresting women, and so they had escaped for so long. And now she had her heart's desire! How glad she must be, I thought. But I was apprehensive, for she was always in weak health, and I feared that prison conditions might cause her much suffering.

As she was arrested, a pressman who was present asked her for a message, and, on the spur of the moment and almost unconsciously, she gave a little message that was characteristic of her: "I am happy beyond measure and proud to follow in the footsteps of my husband. I hope the people will keep the flag flying." Probably she would not have said just that if she had thought over the matter, for she considered herself a champion of woman's rights against the tyranny of man!

My father was in Calcutta and far from well, but news of Kamala's arrest and conviction shook him up, and he decided to return to Allahabad. He sent on my sister Krishna immediately to Allahabad and followed himself, with the rest of the family, a few days later. On the 12th of January he came to see me in Naini. I saw him after nearly two months, and I had a shock which I could conceal with difficulty. He seemed to be unaware of the dismay that his appearance had produced in me, and told me that he was much better than he had lately been in Calcutta. His face was swollen, and he seemed to think that this was due to some temporary cause.

That face of his haunted me. It was so utterly unlike him. For the first time a fear began to creep in my mind that there was real danger for him ahead. I had always associated him with strength and health, and I could not think of death in connection with him. He had always laughed at the idea of death, made fun of it, and told us that he proposed to live for a further long term of years. Latterly I had noticed that whenever an old friend of his youth died, he had a sense of loneliness, of being left by himself in strange company, and even a hint of an approaching end. But generally this mood passed, and his overflowing vitality asserted itself; we of his family had grown so used to his rich personality and the all-embracing warmth of his affection that it was difficult for us to think of the world without him.

I was troubled by that look of his, and my mind was full of forebodings. Yet I did not think that any danger to him lay in the near future. I was myself, for some unknown reason, keeping poor health just then.

Those were the last days of the first Round Table Conference, and we were a little amused—and I am afraid our amusement had a touch of disdain in it. In the hour of our country's sorest trial, and when our men and women had behaved so wonderfully, there were some of our countrymen who were prepared to ignore our struggle and give their moral support to the other side. It became clearer to us than it had been before how, under the deceptive cover of nationalism, conflicting economic interests were at work, and how those with vested interests were trying to preserve them for the future in the name of this very nationalism. The Round Table Conference was an obvious collection of these vested interests.

We did not really mind or care what the Round Table Conference did. It was far away, unreal and shadowy, and the struggle lay here in our towns and villages. We had no illusions about the speedy termination of our struggle or about the dangers ahead, and yet the events of 1930 had given us a certain confidence in our national strength and stamina, and with that confidence we faced the future.

What filled our minds most was the approach of January 26, the first anniversary of Independence Day, and we wondered how this would be celebrated. It was observed, as we learned subsequently, all over the country by the holding of mass meetings which confirmed the resolution of independence, and passed an identical resolution called the "Resolution of Remembrance." The organization of this celebration was a remarkable feat, for newspapers and printing presses were not available, nor could the post or telegraph be utilized. And yet an identical resolution, in the particular language of the province concerned, was passed at large gatherings held at more or less the same times at innumerable places, urban and rural, throughout the country. Most of these gatherings were held in defiance of the law and were forcibly dispersed by the police.

January 26 found us in Naini Prison musing of the year that was past and of the year that was to come. In the forenoon I was told suddenly that my father's condition was serious and that I must go home immediately. On inquiry, I was informed that I was being discharged. Ranjit also accompanied me.

That evening, many other persons were discharged from various prisons throughout India. These were the original and substitute members of the Congress Working Committee. The Government was giving us a chance to meet and consider the situation. So, in any event, I would have been discharged that evening. Father's condition hastened my release by a few hours. Kamala also was discharged that day from her Lucknow prison after a brief jail life of 26 days. She too was a substitute member of the Working Committee.

## XXVIII

## DEATH OF MY FATHER

I saw father after two weeks, for he had visited me at Naini on January 12, when his appearance had given me a shock. He had now changed for the worse, and his face was even more swollen. He had some little difficulty in speaking, and his mind was not always quite clear. But his old will remained, and this held on and kept the body and mind functioning.

He was pleased to see Ranjit and me. A day or two later Ranjit (who did not come in the category of Working Committee members) was taken back to Naini Prison. This upset father, and he was continually asking for him and complaining that when so many people were coming to see him from distant parts of India, his own son-in-law was kept away. The doctors were worried by this insistence, and it was obvious that it was doing father no good. After three or four days, I think at the doctors' suggestion, the United Provinces Government released Ranjit.

On January 26, the same day that I was discharged, Gandhiji was also discharged from Yeravda Prison. I was anxious to have him in

Allahabad, and, when I mentioned his release to father, I found that he was eager to see him. The very next day Gandhiji started from Bombay after a stupendous mass meeting of welcome there, such as even Bombay had not seen before. He arrived at Allahabad late at night, but father was lying awake, waiting for him, and his presence and the few words he uttered had a markedly soothing effect on father. To my mother also his coming brought solace and relief.

The various Working Committee members, original and substitute, who had been released were meanwhile at a loose end and were waiting for directions about a meeting. Many of them, anxious about father, wanted to come to Allahabad immediately. It was decided therefore to summon them all forthwith to a meeting at Allahabad. Two days later thirty or forty of them arrived, and their meetings took place in Swaraj Bhawan next to our house. I went to these meetings from time to time, but I was much too distraught to take any effective part in them, and I have at present no recollection whatever of what their decisions were. I suppose they were in favor of a continuance of the civil disobedience movement.

All these old friends and colleagues who had come, many of them freshly out of prison and expecting to go back again soon, wanted to visit father and to have what was likely to be a last glimpse and a last farewell of him. They came to him in twos and threes in the mornings and evenings, and father insisted on sitting up in an easy chair to receive his old comrades. There he sat, massively and rather expressionlessly, for the swelling on his face prevented much play of expression. But, as one old friend came after another and comrade succeeded comrade, there was a glitter in his eye and recognition of them, and his head bowed a little, and his hands joined in salutation. And though he could not speak much, sometimes he would say a few words, and even then his old humor did not leave him. There he sat like an old lion mortally wounded and with his physical strength almost gone, but still very leonine and kingly. As I watched him, I wondered what thoughts passed through his head, or whether he was past taking interest in our activities. He was evidently often struggling with himself, trying to keep a grip of things which threatened to slip away from his grasp. To the end this struggle continued, and he did not give in, occasionally speaking to us with extreme clarity. Even when a constriction in his throat made it difficult for him to make himself understood, he took to writing on slips of paper what he wanted to say.

He took practically no interest in the Working Committee meetings which were taking place next door. A fortnight earlier they would have excited him, but now he felt that he was already far away from such happenings. "I am going soon, Mahatmaji," he said to Gandhiji, "and I shall not be here to see *Swaraj*. But I know that you have won it and will soon have it."

Most of the people who had come from other cities and provinces departed. Gandhiji remained, and a few intimate friends and near relatives, and the three eminent doctors, old friends of his, to whom, he used to say, he had handed over his body for safekeeping—M. A. Ansari, Bidhan Chandra Roy, and Jivraj Mehta. On the morning of February 4 he seemed to be a little better, and it was decided to take advantage of this and remove him to Lucknow, where there were facilities for deep X-ray treatment which Allahabad did not possess. That very day we took him by car, Gandhiji and a large party following us. We went slowly, but he was nevertheless exhausted. The next day he seemed to be getting over the fatigue, and yet there were some disquieting symptoms. Early next morning, February 6, I was watching by his bedside. He had had a troublesome and restless night; suddenly I noticed that his face grew calm and the sense of struggle vanished from it. I thought that he had fallen asleep, and I was glad of it. But my mother's perceptions were keener, and she uttered a cry. I turned to her and begged her not to disturb him as he had fallen asleep. But that sleep was his last long sleep, and from it there was no awakening.

We brought his body that very day by car to Allahabad. I sat in that car and Ranjit drove it, and there was Hari, father's favorite personal servant. Behind us came another car containing my mother and Gandhiji, and then other cars. I was dazed all that day, hardly realizing what had happened, and a succession of events and large crowds kept me from thinking. Great crowds in Lucknow, gathered together at brief notice—the swift dash from Lucknow to Allahabad sitting by the body, wrapped in our national flag, and with a big flag flying above—the arrival at Allahabad, and the huge crowds that had gathered for miles to pay homage to his memory. There were some ceremonies at home, and then the last journey to the Ganges with a mighty concourse of people. As evening fell on the river bank on that winter day, the great flames leaped up and consumed that body which had meant so much to us who were close to him as well as to millions in India. Gandhiji said a few moving words to the multitude, and then all of us crept silently home. The stars were out and shining brightly when we returned, lonely and desolate.

Many thousands of messages of sympathy came to my mother and to me. Lord and Lady Irwin also sent my mother a courteous message. This tremendous volume of good will and sympathy took away somewhat the sting from our sorrow, but it was, above all, the wonderfully soothing and healing presence of Gandhiji that helped my mother and all of us to face that crisis in our lives.

I found it difficult to realize that he had gone. Three months later I was in Ceylon with my wife and daughter, and we were spending a few quiet and restful days at Nuwara Eliya. I liked the place, and it struck me suddenly that it would suit father. Why not send for him? He must be tired out, and rest would do him good. I was on the point of sending a telegram to him to Allahabad.

On our return to Allahabad from Ceylon the post brought one day a remarkable letter. The envelope was addressed to me in father's handwriting, and it bore innumerable marks and stamps of different post offices. I opened it in amazement to find that it was, indeed, a letter from father to me, only it was dated February 28, 1926. It was delivered to me in the summer of 1931, thus having taken five and a half years in its journey. The letter had been written by father at Ahmedabad on the eve of my departure for Europe with Kamala in 1926. It was addressed to me to Bombay care of the Italian Lloyd steamer on which we were traveling. Apparently it just missed us there, and then it visited various places, and perhaps lay in many pigeonholes till some enterprising person sent it on to me. Curiously enough, it was a letter of farewell.

XXIX

# THE DELHI PACT

ON THE DAY and almost at the very hour of my father's death, a large group of the Indian members of the Round Table Conference landed in Bombay. Mr. Srinivasa Sastri and Sir Tej Bahadur Sapru, and perhaps some others whom I do not remember, came direct to Allahabad. Gandhiji and some members of the Congress Working Committee were already there. There were some private meetings at our house at which an account was given of what the Round Table Conference had done.

The Round Table delegates did not tell us anything of importance about the Round Table Conference that we did not know already. They did tell us of various intrigues behind the scenes, of what Lord So-and-So said or Sir Somebody did in private. Our Liberal friends in India have always seemed to me to attach more importance to private talks and gossip with and about high officials than to principles or to the realities of the Indian situation. Our informal discussions with the Liberal leaders did not lead to anything, and our previous opinions were only confirmed that the Round Table Conference decisions had not the least value. Someone then suggested—I forget who he was—that Gandhiji should write to the Viceroy and ask for an interview and have a frank talk with him. He agreed to do so, although I do not think that he expected much in the way of result.

Gandhiji always welcomed a meeting with those who disagreed with him. But it was one thing to deal with individuals on personal or minor issues; it was quite another matter to come up against an impersonal thing like the British Government representing triumphant imperialism. Realizing this, Gandhiji went to the interview with Lord Irwin with no high expectation. The civil disobedience movement was still going on, though it had toned down because there was much talk of *pourparlers* with Government.

The interview was arranged without delay, and Gandhiji went off to Delhi, telling us that if there were any serious conversations with the Viceroy regarding a provisional settlement, he would send for the members of the Working Committee. A few days later we were all summoned to Delhi. For three weeks we remained there, meeting daily and having long and exhausting discussions. Gandhiji had frequent interviews with Lord Irwin, but sometimes there was a gap of three or four days, probably because the Government of India was communicating with the India Office in London. Sometimes apparently small matters or even certain words would hold up progress. One such word was "suspension" of civil disobedience. Gandhiji had all along made it clear that civil disobedience could not be finally stopped or given up, as it was the only weapon in the hands of the people. It could, however, be suspended. Lord Irwin objected to this word and wanted finality about the word, to which Gandhiji would not agree. Ultimately the word "discontinued" was used.

Delhi attracted in those days all manner of people. There were many foreign journalists, especially Americans, and they were somewhat annoyed with us for our reticence. They would tell us that they got much more news about the Gandhi-Irwin conversations from the New

Delhi Secretariat than from us, which was a fact. Then there were many people of high degree who hurried to pay their respects to Gandhiji, for was not the Mahatma's star in the ascendant? It was very amusing to see these people, who had kept far away from Gandhiji and the Congress and often condemned them, now hastening to make amends. The Congress seemed to have made good, and no one knew what the future might hold. Anyway, it was safer to keep on good terms with the Congress and its leaders. A year later yet another change was witnessed in them, and they were shouting again their deep abhorrence of the Congress and all its works and their utter dissociation from it.

Even the communalists were stirred by events, and sensed with some apprehension that they might not occupy a very prominent place in the coming order. And so, many of them came to the Mahatma and assured him that they were perfectly willing to come to terms on the communal issue, and, if only he would take the initiative, there would be no difficulty about a settlement.

The very prosperous gentlemen who came to visit Gandhiji showed us another side of human nature, and a very adaptable side, for wherever they sensed power and success, they turned to it and welcomed it with the sunshine of their smiles. Many of them were stanch pillars of the British Government in India. It was comforting to know that they would become equally stanch pillars of any other government that might flourish in India.

Often in those days I used to accompany Gandhiji in his early morning walks in New Delhi. That was usually the only time one had a chance of talking to him, for the rest of the day was cut up into little bits, each minute allotted to somebody or something. Even the early morning walk was sometimes given over to an interviewer, usually from abroad, or to a friend, come for a personal consultation. We talked of many matters, of the past, of the present, and especially of the future. I remember how he surprised me with one of his ideas about the future of the Congress. I had imagined that the Congress, as such, would automatically cease to exist with the coming of freedom. He thought that the Congress should continue, but on one condition: that it passed a self-denying ordinance, laying it down that none of its members could accept a pay job under the State, and, if anyone wanted such a post of authority in the State, he would have to leave the Congress. I do not at present remember how he worked this out, but the whole idea underlying it was that the Congress, by its detachment and having no ax to grind, could exercise tremendous moral pressure on the Executive as well as other departments of the Government, and thus keep them on the right track.

Now this is an extraordinary idea which I find difficult to grasp, and innumerable difficulties present themselves. It seems to me that such an assembly, if it could be conceived, would be exploited by some vested interest. But, practicality apart, it does help one to understand a little the background of Gandhiji's thought.

Gandhiji's conception of democracy has nothing to do with numbers or majority or representation in the ordinary sense. It is based on service and sacrifice, and it uses moral pressure. He claims to be "a born democrat." "I make that claim, if complete identification with the poorest of mankind, longing to live no better than they, and a corresponding conscious effort to approach that level to the best of one's ability, can entitle one to make it." This is his definition of a democrat. He says further:

"Let us recognize the fact that the Congress enjoys the prestige of a democratic character and influence not by the number of delegates and visitors it has drawn to its annual function, but by an ever-increasing amount of service it has rendered. Western democracy is on its trial, if it has not already proved a failure. May it be reserved to India to evolve the true science of democracy by giving a visible demonstration of its success.

"Corruption and hypocrisy ought not to be the inevitable products of democracy, as they undoubtedly are today. Nor is bulk a true test of democracy. True democracy is not inconsistent with a few persons representing the spirit, the hope, and the aspirations of those whom they claim to represent. I hold that democracy cannot be evolved by forcible methods. The spirit of democracy cannot be imposed from without; it has to come from within."

This is certainly not Western democracy, as he himself says; but, curiously enough, there is some similarity to the communist conception of democracy. A few communists will claim to represent the real needs and desires of the masses, even though the latter may themselves be unaware of them. The similarity, however, is slight and does not take us far; the differences in outlook and approach are far greater, notably in regard to methods and force.

Whether Gandhiji is a democrat or not, he does represent the peasant masses of India; he is the quintessence of the conscious and subconscious will of those millions. It is perhaps something more than representation; for he is the idealized personification of those vast millions. Of course, he is not the average peasant. A man of the keenest intellect, of fine feeling and good taste, wide vision; very human, and yet essentially the ascetic who has suppressed his passions and emotions, sublimated them and directed them in spiritual channels; a tremendous personality, drawing people to himself like a magnet, and calling out fierce loyalties and attachments—all this so utterly unlike and beyond a peasant. And yet withal he is the greatest peasant, with a peasant's outlook on affairs, and with a peasant's blindness to some aspects of life. But India is peasant India, and so he knows his India well, reacts to her slightest tremors, gauges a situation accurately and almost instinctively, and has a knack of acting at the psychological moment.

What a problem and a puzzle he has been not only to the British Government but to his own people and his closest associates! Perhaps in every other country he would be out of place today, but India still seems to understand, or at least appreciate, the prophetic-religious type of man, talking of sin and salvation and nonviolence. Indian mythology is full of stories of great ascetics, who, by the rigor of their sacrifices and self-imposed penance, built up a "mountain of merit" which threatened the dominion of some of the lesser gods and upset the established order. These myths have often come to my mind when I have watched the amazing energy and inner power of Gandhiji, coming out of some inexhaustible spiritual reservoir. He was obviously not of the world's ordinary coinage; he was minted of a different and rare variety, and often the unknown stared at us through his eyes.

India, even urban India, even the new industrial India, had the impress of the peasant upon her; and it was natural enough for her to make this son of hers, so like her and yet so unlike, an idol and a beloved leader. He revived ancient and half-forgotten memories, and gave her glimpses of her own soul. Crushed in the dark misery of the present, she had tried to find relief in helpless muttering and in vague dreams of the past and the future, but he came and gave hope to her mind and strength to her much-battered body, and the future became an alluring vision. Two-faced like Janus, she looked both backward into the past and forward into the future, and tried to combine the two.

Many of us had cut adrift from this peasant outlook, and the old ways of thought and custom and religion had become alien to us. We called ourselves moderns and thought in terms of "progress," and industrialization and a higher standard of living and collectivization. We considered the peasant's viewpoint reactionary; and some, a growing number, looked with favor toward socialism and communism. How came we to associate ourselves with Gandhiji politically, and to become, in many instances, his devoted followers? The question is hard to answer, and to one who does not know Gandhiji, no answer is likely to satisfy. Personality is an indefinable thing, a strange force that has power over the souls of men, and he possesses this in ample measure, and to all who come to him he often appears in a different aspect. He attracted people, but it was ultimately intellectual conviction that brought them to him and kept them there. They did not agree with his philosophy of life, or even with many of his ideals. Often they did not understand him. But the action that he proposed was something tangible which could be understood and appreciated intellectually. Any action would have been welcome after the long tradition of inaction which our spineless politics had nurtured; brave and effective action with an ethical halo about it had an irresistible appeal, both to the intellect and the emotions. Step by step he convinced us of the rightness of the action, and we went with him, although we did not accept his philosophy. To divorce action from the thought underlying it was not perhaps a proper procedure and was bound to lead to mental conflict and trouble later. Vaguely we hoped that Gandhiji, being essentially a man of action and very sensitive to changing conditions, would advance along the line that seemed to us to be right. And in any event the road he was following was the right one thus far; and, if the future meant a parting, it would be folly to anticipate it.

All this shows that we were by no means clear or certain in our minds. Always we had the feeling that, while we might be more logical, Gandhiji knew India far better than we did, and a man who could command such tremendous devotion and loyalty must have something in him that corresponded to the needs and aspirations of the masses. If we could convince him, we felt that we could also convert these masses. And it seemed possible to convince him; for, in spite of his peasant outlook, he was the born rebel, a revolutionary out for big changes, whom no fear of consequences could stop.

How he disciplined our lazy and demoralized people and made them work—not by force or any material inducement, but by a gentle look and a soft word and, above all, by personal example! In the early days of *Satyagraha* in India, as long ago as 1919, I remember how Umar Sobani of Bombay called him the "beloved slave-driver." Much had happened in the dozen years since then. Umar had not lived to see these changes, but we who had been more fortunate looked back from those early months of 1931 with joy and elation. Nineteen-thirty had, indeed, been a wonder year for us, and Gandhiji seemed to have changed the face of our country with his magic touch. No one was foolish enough to think that we had triumphed finally over the British Government. Our feeling of elation had little to do with the Government. We were proud of our people, of our womenfolk, of our youth, of our children for the part they had played in the movement. It was a spiritual gain, valuable at any time and to any people, but doubly so to us, a subject and downtrodden people. And we were anxious that nothing should happen to take this away from us.

To me, personally, Gandhiji had always shown extraordinary kindness and consideration, and my father's death had brought him particularly near to me. He had always listened patiently to whatever I had to say and had made every effort to meet my wishes. This had, indeed, led me to think that perhaps some colleagues and I could influence him continuously in a socialist direction, and he had himself said that he was prepared to go step by step as he saw his way to do so. It seemed to me almost inevitable then that he would accept the fundamental socialist position, as I saw no other way out from the violence and injustice and waste and misery of the existing order. He might disagree about the methods but not about the ideal. So I thought then, but I realize now that there are basic differences between Gandhiji's ideals and the socialist objective.

On the night of the 4th of March we waited till midnight for Gandhiji's return from the Viceroy's house. He came back about 2 A.M., and we were wakened and told that an agreement had been reached. We saw the draft. I knew most of the clauses, for they had been often discussed, but, at the very top, Clause 2[1] with its reference to safeguards, etc., gave me a tremendous shock. I was wholly unprepared for it. I said nothing then, and we all retired.

There was nothing more to be said. The thing had been done, our leader had committed himself; and, even if we disagreed with him, what could we do? Throw him over? Break from him? Announce our

[1] Clause 2 of the Delhi Settlement (dated March 5, 1931): "As regards constitutional questions, the scope of future discussion is stated, with the assent of His Majesty's Government, to be with the object of considering further the scheme for the constitutional Government of India discussed at the Round Table Conference. Of the scheme there outlined, Federation is an essential part; so also are Indian responsibility and reservations or safeguards in the interests of India, for such matters as, for instance, defense; external affairs; the position of minorities; the financial credit of India; and the discharge of obligations."

disagreement? That might bring some personal satisfaction to an individual, but it made no difference to the final decision. The civil disobedience movement was ended for the time being at least, and not even the Working Committee could push it on now, when the Government could declare that Mr. Gandhi had already agreed to a settlement. I was perfectly willing, as were our other colleagues, to suspend civil disobedience and to come to a temporary settlement with the Government. It was not an easy matter for any of us to send our comrades back to jail, or to be instrumental in keeping many thousands in prison who were already there. Prison is not a pleasant place to spend our days and nights, though many of us may train ourselves for it and talk light-heartedly of its crushing routine. Besides, three weeks or more of conversations between Gandhiji and Lord Irwin had led the country to expect that a settlement was coming, and a final break would have been a disappointment. So all of us in the Working Committee were decidedly in favor of a provisional settlement (for obviously it could be nothing more), provided that thereby we did not surrender any vital position.

Two matters interested me above all others. One was that our objective of independence should in no way be toned down, and the second was the effect of the settlement on our United Provinces agrarian situation. Gandhiji had made this point quite clear to Lord Irwin. The peasants were unable to pay the taxes demanded by the Government. He had stated that, while the no-tax campaign would be withdrawn, we could not advise the peasantry to pay beyond their capacity.

The question of our objective, of independence, also remained. I saw in that Clause 2 of the settlement that even this seemed to be jeopardized. Was it for this that our people had behaved so gallantly for a year? Were all our brave words and deeds to end in this? The independence resolution of the Congress, the pledge of January 26, so often repeated? So I lay and pondered on that March night, and in my heart there was a great emptiness as of something precious gone, almost beyond recall.

> *This is the way the world ends,*
> *Not with a bang, but a whimper.*

Gandhiji learned indirectly of my distress, and the next morning he asked me to accompany him in his usual walk. We had a long talk, and he tried to convince me that nothing vital had been lost, no surrender of principle made. He interpreted Clause 2 of the agreement in a particular way so as to make it fit in with our demand for independence, relying chiefly on the words in it: "in the interests of India." The interpretation seemed to me to be a forced one, and I was not convinced, but I was somewhat soothed by his talk. The merits of the agreement apart, I told him that his way of springing surprises upon us frightened me; there was something unknown about him which, in spite of the closest association for fourteen years, I could not understand at all and which filled me with apprehension. He admitted the presence of this unknown element in him, and said that he himself could not answer for it or foretell what it might lead to.

For a day or two I wobbled, not knowing what to do. There was no question of opposing or preventing that agreement then. That stage was past, and all I could do was to dissociate myself theoretically from it, though accepting it as a matter of fact. That would have soothed my personal vanity, but how did it help the larger issue? Would it not be better to accept gracefully what had been done, and put the most favorable interpretation upon it, as Gandhiji had done? In an interview to the press immediately after the agreement he had stressed that interpretation and that we stood completely by independence. He went to Lord Irwin and made this point quite clear, so that there might be no misapprehension then or in the future. In the event of the Congress sending any representative to the Round Table Conference, he told him, it could only be on this basis and to advance this claim. Lord Irwin could not, of course, admit the claim, but he recognized the right of the Congress to advance it.

So I decided, not without great mental conflict and physical distress, to accept the agreement and work for it wholeheartedly. There appeared to me to be no middle way.

In the course of Gandhiji's interviews with Lord Irwin prior to the agreement, as well as after, he had pleaded for the release of political prisoners other than the civil disobedience prisoners. The latter were going to be discharged as part of the agreement itself. But there were thousands of others, both those convicted after trial and *détenus* kept without any charge, trial, or conviction. Many of these *détenus* had been kept so for years, and there had always been a great deal of resentment all over India, and especially in Bengal, which was most affected, at this method of imprisonment without trial. Gandhiji had pleaded for their release, not necessarily as part of the agreement, but as eminently desirable in order to relieve political tension and establish a more normal atmosphere in Bengal. But the Government was not agreeable to this.

I left Delhi soon after the provisional settlement was arrived at and went to Lucknow. We had taken immediate steps to stop civil disobedience all over the country, and the whole Congress organization had responded to our new instructions with remarkable discipline. We had many people in our ranks who were dissatisfied, many firebrands; and we had no means of compelling them to desist from the old activities. But without a single exception known to me, the huge organization accepted in practice the new role, though many criticized it. Our first job was to see that the civil disobedience prisoners were discharged. Thousands of these were discharged from day to day, and after some time only a number of disputed cases were left in prison; apart, of course, from the thousands of *détenus* and those convicted for violent activities, who were not released.

These discharged prisoners, when they went home to their towns or villages, were naturally welcomed back by their people. There were often decorations and buntings, and processions, and meetings, and speeches and addresses of welcome. It was all very natural and to be expected, but the change was sudden from the time when the police lathee was always in evidence, and meetings and processions were forcibly dispersed. The police felt rather uncomfortable, and probably there was a feeling of triumph among many of our people who came out of jail. There was little enough reason to be triumphant, but a coming out of jail always brings a feeling of elation (unless the spirit has been crushed in jail), and mass jail deliveries add very much to this exhilaration.

I mention this fact here, because in later months great exception was taken by the Government to this "air of triumph," and it was made a charge against us! Brought up and living always in an authoritarian atmosphere, with a military notion of government and with no roots or supports in the people, nothing is more painful to them than a weakening of what they consider their prestige. None of us, so far as I know, had given the least thought to the matter, and it was with great surprise that we learned later that Government officials, from the heights of Simla to the plains below, were simmering with anger and wounded pride at this impudence of the people. These outbursts on the part of the Government and its friends in the press, came as a revelation to us. They showed what a state of nerves they had been in, what suppressions they had put up with, resulting in all manner of complexes. It was extraordinary that a few processions and a few speeches of our rank-and-file men should so upset them.

As a matter of fact there was in Congress ranks then, and even less in the leadership, no idea of having "defeated" the British Government. But there was a feeling of triumph among us at our own people's sacrifices and courage.

I had a little breakdown in health soon after the Delhi Pact. Even in jail I had been unwell, and then the shock of father's death, followed immediately by the long strain of the Delhi negotiations, proved too much for my physical health. I recovered somewhat for the Karachi Congress.

The Karachi Congress was an even greater personal triumph for Gandhiji than any previous Congress had been. The president, Sardar Vallabhbhai Patel, was one of the most popular and forceful men in India with the prestige of victorious leadership in Gujrat, but it was the Mahatma who dominated the scene.

The principal resolution dealt with the Delhi Pact and the Round Table Conference. I accepted it, of course, as it emerged from the Working Committee; but, when I was asked by Gandhiji to move it in the open Congress, I hesitated. It went against the grain, and I refused at first, and then this seemed a weak and unsatisfactory position to take up. Either I was for it or against it, and it was not proper to prevaricate or leave people guessing in the matter. Almost at the last moment, a few minutes before the resolution was taken up in the open Congress, I decided to sponsor it. In my speech I tried to lay before the great gathering quite frankly what my feelings were and why I had wholeheartedly accepted that resolution and pleaded with them to accept it. That speech, made on the spur of the moment and coming from the heart, and with little of ornament or fine phrasing in it, was probably a greater success than many of my other efforts which had followed a more careful preparation.

I spoke on other resolutions, too, notably on the Bhagat Singh resolution and the one on fundamental rights and economic policy. The latter resolution interested me especially, partly because of what it contained, and even more so because it represented a new outlook in the Congress. So far the Congress had thought along purely nationalist lines, and had avoided facing economic issues, except in so far as it encouraged cottage industries and Swadeshi generally. In the Karachi resolution it took a step, a very short step, in a socialist direction by advocating nationalization of key industries and services, and various other measures to lessen the burden on the poor and increase it on the rich. This was not socialism at all, and a capitalist state could easily accept almost everything contained in that resolution.

This very mild and prosaic resolution evidently made the big people of the Government of India furiously to think. Perhaps they even pictured, with their usual perspicacity, the red gold of the Bolsheviks stealing its way into Karachi and corrupting the Congress leaders. Living in a kind of political harem, cut off from the outer world, and surrounded by an atmosphere of secrecy, their receptive minds love to hear tales of mystery and imagination. And then these stories are given out in little bits in a mysterious manner, through favored newspapers, with a hint that much more could be seen if only the veil were lifted. In this approved and well-practiced manner, frequent references have been made to the Karachi resolution on Fundamental Rights, etc., and I can only conclude that they represent the Government view of this resolution. The story goes that a certain mysterious individual with communist affiliations drew up this resolution, or the greater part of it, and thrust it down upon me at Karachi; that thereupon I issued an ultimatum to Mr. Gandhi to accept this or to face my opposition on the Delhi Pact issue, and Mr. Gandhi accepted it as a sop to me and forced it down on a tired Subjects Committee and Congress on the concluding day.

So far as Mr. Gandhi is concerned, I have had the privilege of knowing him pretty intimately for the last twenty-one years, and the idea of my presenting ultimatums to him or bargaining with him seems to me monstrous. We may accommodate ourselves to each other; or we may, on a particular issue, part company; but the methods of the market place can never affect our mutual dealings.

## XXX

## A SOUTHERN HOLIDAY

MY DOCTORS URGED me to take some rest and go for a change, and I decided to spend a month in Ceylon. India, huge as the country is, did not offer a real prospect of change or mental rest, for wherever I might go, I would probably come across political associates and the same problems would pursue me. Ceylon was the nearest place within reach of

India, and so to Ceylon we went—Kamala, Indira, and I. That was the first holiday I had had since our return from Europe in 1927, the first time since then that my wife and daughter and I holidayed together peacefully with little to distract our attention. There has been no repetition of that experience, and sometimes I wonder if there will be any.

And yet we did not really have much rest in Ceylon, except for two weeks at Nuwara Eliya. We were fairly overwhelmed by the hospitality and friendliness of all classes of people there. It was very pleasant to find all this good will, but it was often embarrassing also. At Nuwara Eliya groups of laborers, tea-garden workers and others, would come daily, walking many miles, bringing gracious gifts with them—wild flowers, vegetables, homemade butter. We could not, as a rule, even converse together; we merely looked at each other and smiled. Our little house was full of those precious gifts of theirs, which they had given out of their poverty, and we passed them on to the local hospital and orphanages.

We visited many of the famous sights and historical ruins of the island, and Buddhist monasteries, and the rich tropical forests. At Anuradhapura I liked greatly an old seated statue of the Buddha. A year later, when I was in Dehra Dun Jail, a friend in Ceylon sent me a picture of this statue, and I kept it on my little table in my cell. It became a precious companion for me, and the strong, calm features of Buddha's statue soothed me and gave me strength and helped me to overcome many a period of depression.

Buddha has always had a great appeal for me. It is difficult for me to analyze this appeal, but it is not a religious appeal, and I am not interested in the dogmas that have grown up round Buddhism. It is the personality that has drawn me. So also the personality of Christ has attracted me greatly.

I saw many Buddhist *bhikkus* (monks) in their monasteries and on the highways, meeting with respect wherever they went. The dominant expression of almost all of them was one of peace and calm, a strange detachment from the cares of the world. They did not have intellectual faces, as a rule, and there was no trace of the fierce conflicts of the mind on their countenances. Life seemed to be for them a smooth-flowing river moving slowly to the great ocean. I looked at them with some envy, with just a faint yearning for a haven; but I knew well enough that my lot was a different one, cast in storms and tempests. There was to be no haven for me, for the tempests within me were as stormy as those outside. And if perchance I found myself in a safe harbor, protected from the fury of the winds, would I be contented or happy there?

For a little while the harbor was pleasant, and one could lie down and dream and allow the soothing and enervating charm of the tropics to steal over one. Ceylon fitted in with my mood then, and the beauty of the island filled me with delight. Our month of holiday was soon over, and it was with real regret that we bade good-by. So many memories come back to me of the land and her people; they have been pleasant companions during the long, empty days in prison. One little incident lingers in my memory; it was near Jaffna, I think. The teachers and boys of a school stopped our car and said a few words of greeting. The ardent, eager faces of the boys stood out, and then one of their number came to me, shook hands with me, and without question or argument, said: "I will not falter." That bright young face with shining eyes, full of determination, is imprinted in my mind. I do not know who he was; I have lost trace of him. But somehow I have the conviction that he will remain true to his word and will not falter when he has to face life's difficult problems.

From Ceylon we went to south India, right to the southern tip at Cape Comorin. Amazingly peaceful it was there. And then through Travancore, Cochin, Malabar, Mysore, Hyderabad—mostly Indian States, some the most progressive of their kind, some the most backward. Travancore and Cochin educationally far in advance of British India; Mysore probably ahead industrially; Hyderabad almost a perfect feudal relic. We received courtesy and welcome everywhere, both from the people and the authorities; but behind that welcome I could sense the anxiety of the latter lest our visit might lead the people to think dangerously.

In Bangalore, in the Mysore State, I had hoisted at a great gathering a national flag on an enormous iron pole. Not long after my departure this pole was broken up into bits, and the Mysore Government made the display of the flag an offense. This ill-treatment and insult of the flag I had hoisted pained me greatly.

In Travancore even the Congress had been made an unlawful association, and no one can enroll ordinary members for it, although in British India it is now lawful since the withdrawal of civil disobedience. Hyderabad had no necessity for going back or withdrawing facilities, for it had never moved forward at all or given any facility of the kind. Political meetings are unknown in Hyderabad; even social and religious gatherings are looked upon with suspicion, and special permission has to be taken for them. There are no newspapers worthy of the name issued there, and, in order to prevent the germs of corruption from coming from outside, a large number of newspapers published in other parts of India are prevented entry.

In Cochin we visited the quarter of the "White Jews," as they are called, and saw one of the services in their old tabernacle. The little community is very ancient and very unique. It is dwindling in numbers. The part of Cochin they live in, we were told, resembles ancient Jerusalem. It certainly has an ancient look about it.

We also visited, along the backwaters of Malabar, some of the towns inhabited chiefly by Christians belonging to the Syrian churches. Few people realize that Christianity came to India as early as the first century after Christ, long before Europe turned to it, and established a firm hold in south India. Although these Christians have their religious head in Antioch or somewhere else in Syria, their Christianity is practically indigenous and has few outside contacts.

To my surprise, we also came across a colony of Nestorians in the south; I was told by their bishop that there were ten thousand of them. I had labored under the impression that the Nestorians had long been absorbed in other sects, and I did not know that they had ever flourished in India. But I was told that at one time they had a fairly large following in India, extending as far north as Benares.

We had gone to Hyderabad especially to pay a visit to Mrs. Sarojini Naidu and her daughters, Padmaja and Leilamani. During our stay with them a small *purdanashin* gathering of women assembled at their house to meet my wife, and Kamala apparently addressed them. Probably she spoke of women's struggle for freedom against man-made laws and customs (a favorite topic of hers) and urged the women not to be too submissive to their menfolk. There was an interesting sequel to this two or three weeks later, when a distracted husband wrote to Kamala from Hyderabad and said that since her visit to that city his wife had behaved strangely. She would not listen to him and fall in with his wishes, as she used to, but would argue with him and even adopt an aggressive attitude.

Seven weeks after we had sailed from Bombay for Ceylon we were back in that city, and immediately I plunged again into the whirlpool of Congress politics.

# XXXI

# FRICTION AND THE ROUND TABLE CONFERENCE

SHOULD GANDHIJI GO to London for the second Round Table Conference or not? Again and again the question arose, and there was no definite answer. No one knew till the last moment—not even the Congress Working Committee or Gandhiji himself. For the answer depended on many things, and new happenings were constantly giving a fresh turn to the situation. Behind that question and answer lay real and difficult problems.

We were told repeatedly, on behalf of the British Government and their friends, that the first Round Table Conference had already laid down the framework of the constitution, that the principal lines of the picture had been drawn, and all that remained was the filling in of this picture. But the Congress did not think so; so far as it was concerned, the picture had to be drawn or painted from the very beginning on an almost blank canvas. It was true that by the Delhi agreement the federal basis had been approved and the idea of safeguards accepted. But a federation had long seemed to many of us the best solution of the Indian constitutional problem, and our approval of this idea did not mean our acceptance of the particular type of federation envisaged by the first Round Table Conference.

The gulf between the Congress viewpoint and that of the British Government was immense, and it seemed exceedingly unlikely that it could be bridged at that stage. Very few Congressmen expected any measure of agreement between the Congress and the Government at the second Round Table Conference, and even Gandhiji, optimistic as he always is, could not look forward to much. And yet he was never hopeless and was determined to try to the very end. All of us felt that, whether success came or not, the effort had to be made, in pursuance of the Delhi agreement. But there were two vital considerations which might have barred our participation in the second Round Table Conference. We could only go if we had full freedom to place our viewpoint in its entirety before the Round Table Conference, and were not prevented from doing so by being told that the matter had already been decided, or for any other reason. We could also be prevented from being represented at the Round Table Conference by conditions in India. A situation might have developed here which precipitated a conflict with the Government, or in which we had to face severe repression. If this took place in India and our very house was on fire, it would have been singularly out of place for any representative of ours to ignore the fire and talk academically of constitutions and the like in London.

The situation was developing swiftly in India. In Bengal the Delhi agreement had made little difference, and the tension continued and grew worse. Some civil disobedience prisoners were discharged, but thousands of politicals, who were technically not civil disobedience prisoners, remained in prison. The *détenus* also continued in jail or detention camps. Fresh arrests were frequently made for "seditious" speeches or other political activities, and generally it was felt that the Government offensive had continued without any abatement.

The Congress Working Committee felt very helpless before this intricate problem of Bengal. In the United Provinces the agrarian situation was becoming worse.

In the Frontier Province, too, the Delhi Pact brought no peace. There was a permanent state of tension there, and government was a military affair, with special laws and ordinances and heavy punishments for trivial offenses. To oppose this state of affairs, Abdul Ghaffar Khan led a great agitation, and he soon became a bugbear to the Government. From village to village he went striding along, carrying his six-feet-three of Pathan manhood, and establishing centers of the "Redshirts." Wherever he or his principal lieutenants went, they left a trail of their "Redshirts" behind, and the whole province was soon covered by branches of the *Khudai Khidmatgar*. They were thoroughly peaceful and, though vague allegations of violence have been made against them, not a single definite charge has been established. But, whether they were peaceful or not, they had the tradition of war and violence behind them, they lived near the turbulent frontier, and this rapid growth of a disciplined movement, closely allied to the Indian national movement, thoroughly upset the Government. I do not suppose they ever believed in its professions of peace and nonviolence. But, even if they had done so, their reactions to it would only have been of fright and annoyance. It represented too much of actual and potential powers for them to view it with equanimity.

Of this great movement the unquestioned head was Khan Abdul Ghaffar Khan—"*Fakhr-e-Afghan*," "*Fakr-e-Pathan*," the "Pride of the Pathans," "*Gandhi-e-Sarhad*," the "Frontier Gandhi," as he came to be known. He had attained an amazing popularity in the Frontier Province by sheer dint of quiet, persevering work, undaunted by difficulties or Government action. He was, and is, no politician as politicians go; he knows nothing of the tactics and maneuvers of politics. A tall, straight man, straight in body and mind, hating fuss and too much talk, looking forward to freedom for his Frontier Province people within the framework of Indian freedom, but vague about, and uninterested in, constitutions and legal talk. Action was necessary to achieve anything, and Mahatma Gandhi had taught a remarkable way of peaceful action which appealed to him. For action, organization was necessary; therefore, without further argument or much drafting of rules for his organization, he started organizing—and with remarkable success.

He was especially attracted to Gandhiji. At first his shyness and desire to keep in the background made him keep away from him. Later they had to meet to discuss various matters, and their contacts grew. It was surprising how this Pathan accepted the idea of nonviolence, far more so in theory than many of us. And it was because he believed in it that he managed to impress his people with the importance of remaining peaceful in spite of provocation.

Abdul Ghaffar Khan has been known and liked for many years in Congress circles. But he has grown to be something more than an individual comrade; more and more he has come to be, in the eyes of the rest of India, the symbol of the courage and sacrifice of a gallant and indomitable people, comrades of ours in a common struggle.

Long before I had heard of Abdul Ghaffar Khan, I knew his brother, Dr. Khan Sahib. He was a student at St. Thomas's Hospital in London when I was at Cambridge, and later, when I was eating my Bar dinners at the Inner Temple, he and I became close friends; and hardly a day went by, when I was in London, when we did not meet. I returned to India, leaving him in England, and he stayed on for many more years, serving as a doctor in wartime. I saw him next in Naini Prison.

It was Gandhiji's wish to go to the Frontier Province immediately after the Karachi Congress, but the Government did not encourage this at all. Repeatedly, in later months, when Government officials complained of the doings of the "Redshirts," he pressed to be allowed to go there to find out for himself, but to no purpose. Nor was my going there approved. In view of the Delhi agreement, it was not considered desirable by us to enter the Frontier Province against the declared wish of the Government.

From all over the country we were continually receiving complaints from local Congress Committees pointing out breaches of the Delhi Pact by local officials. The more important of these were forwarded by us to the Government, which, in its turn, brought charges against Congressmen of violation of the Pact. So charges and countercharges were made, and later they were published in the press. Needless to say, this did not result in the improvement of the relations between the Congress and the Government.

And yet this friction on petty matters was by itself of no great importance. Its importance lay in its revealing the development of a more fundamental conflict, something which did not depend on individuals but arose from the very nature of our national struggle and the want of equilibrium of our agrarian economy, something that could not be liquidated or compromised away without a basic change. Our national movement had originally begun because of the desire of our upper middle classes to find means of self-expression and self-growth, and behind it there was the political and economic urge. It spread to the lower middle classes and became a power in the land; and then it began to stir the rural masses, who were finding it more and more difficult to keep up, as a whole, even their miserable rock-bottom standard of living. The old self-sufficient village economy had long ceased to exist. Auxiliary cottage industries, ancillary to agriculture, which had relieved somewhat the burden on the land, had died off, partly because of State policy, but largely because they could not compete with the rising machine industry. The burden on land grew, and the growth of Indian industry was too slow to make much difference to this. Ill-equipped and almost unawares, the overburdened village was thrown into the world market and was tossed about hither and thither. It could not compete on even terms. It was backward in its methods of production, and its land system, resulting in a progressive fragmentation of holdings, made radical improvement impossible. So the agricultural classes, both landlords and tenants, went downhill, except during brief periods of boom. The landlords tried to pass on the burden to their tenantry, and the growing pauperization of the peasantry—both the petty landholders and the tenants—drew them to the national movement. The agricultural proletariat, the large numbers of landless laborers in rural areas, were also attracted; and for all these rural classes nationalism or *Swaraj* meant fundamental changes in the land system which would relieve or lessen their burdens and provide land for the landless. These desires found no clear expression either in the peasantry or in the middle-class leaders of the national movement.

The civil disobedience movement of 1930 happened to fit in unbeknown to its own leaders at first, with the great world slump in industry and agriculture. The rural masses were powerfully affected by this slump, and they turned to the Congress and civil disobedience. For them it was not a matter of a fine constitution drawn up in London or elsewhere, but of a basic change in the land system, especially in the zamindari areas. The zamindari system, indeed, seemed to have outlived its day and had no stability left in it. But the British Government, situated as it was, could not venture to undertake a radical change of this land system. Even when it had appointed the Royal Agricultural Commission, the terms of reference to it barred a discussion of the question of ownership of land or the system of land tenure.

The British Government, like most governments I suppose, has an idea that much of the trouble in India is due to "agitators." It is a singularly inept notion. India has had a great leader during the past fifteen years who has won the affection and even adoration of her millions and has seemed to impose his will on her in many ways. He has played a vitally important part in her recent history, and yet more important than he were the people themselves who seemed to follow blindly his behests. The people were the principal actors, and behind them, pushing them on, were great historical urges which prepared them and made them ready to listen to their leader's piping. But for that historical setting and political and social urges, no leaders or agitators could have inspired them to action. It was Gandhiji's chief virtue as a leader that he could instinctively feel the pulse of the people and know when conditions were ripe for growth and action.

In 1930 the national movement in India fitted in for a while with the growing social forces of the country, and because of this a great power came to it, a sense of reality, as if it were indeed marching step by step with history. The Congress represented that national movement, and this power and strength were reflected in the growth of Congress prestige. This was something vague, incalculable, indefinable, but nevertheless very much present. The peasantry, of course, turned to the Congress and gave it its real strength; the lower middle-class formed the backbone of its fighting ranks. Even the upper *bourgeoisie,* troubled by this new atmosphere, thought it safer to be friendly with the Congress. The great majority of the textile mills in India signed undertakings prescribed by the Congress and were afraid of doing things which might bring on them the displeasure of the Congress. While people argued fine legal points in London at the first Round

Table Conference, the reality of power seemed to be slowly and imperceptibly flowing toward the Congress as representing the people.

This vague sense of a dual authority growing in the country was naturally most irritating to the Government. The sense of conflict grew, and we could feel the hardening on the side of Government. Soon after the Delhi Pact, Lord Irwin had left India, and Lord Willingdon had come in his place as Viceroy. A legend grew up that the new Viceroy was a hard and stern person and not so amenable to compromise as his predecessor. Many of our politicians have inherited a "liberal" habit of thinking of politics in terms of persons rather than of principles. They do not realize that the broad imperial policy of the British Government does not depend on the personal views of the Viceroys. The change of Viceroys, therefore, did not and could not make any difference, but, as it happened, the policy of Government gradually changed owing to the development of the situation. The Civil Service hierarchy had not approved of pacts and dealings with the Congress; all their training and authoritarian conceptions of government were opposed to this. They had an idea that they had added to the Congress influence and Gandhiji's prestige by dealing with him almost as an equal and it was about time that he was brought down a peg or two. The notion was a very foolish one, but then the Indian Civil Service is not known for the originality of its conceptions. Whatever the reason, the Government stiffened its back and tightened its hold, and it seemed to tell us, in the words of the old prophet: My little finger is thicker than my father's loins. Whereas he chastised you with whips, I will chastise you with scorpions.

But the time for chastisement was not yet. If possible the Congress was to be represented at the second Round Table Conference. Twice Gandhiji went to Simla to have long conversations with the Viceroy and other officials.

His first visit to Simla was inconclusive. The second visit took place in the last week of August. A final decision had to be taken one way or the other, but still he found it difficult to make up his mind to leave India. In Bengal, in the Frontier Province, and in the United Provinces, he saw trouble ahead, and he did not want to go unless he had some assurance of peace in India. At last some kind of an agreement was arrived at with the Government, embodied in a statement and some letters that were exchanged. This was done at the very last moment to enable him to travel by the liner that was carrying the delegates to the Round Table Conference. Indeed, it was after the last moment, in a sense, as the last train had gone. A special train from Simla to Kalka was arranged, and other trains were delayed to make the connections.

I accompanied him from Simla to Bombay, and there, one bright morning toward the end of August, I waved good-by to him as he was carried away to the Arabian Sea and the far West. That was my last glimpse of him for two years.

Gandhiji went to London as the sole representative of the Congress to the Round Table Conference. We had decided, after long debate, not to have additional representatives. Partly this was due to our desire to have our best men in India at a very critical time, when the most tactful handling of the situation was necessary. We felt that, in spite of the Round Table Conference meeting in London, the center of gravity lay in India, and developments in India would inevitably have their reactions in London. We wanted to check untoward developments, and to keep our organization in proper condition. This was, however, not the real reason for our sending only one representative.

We were not joining the Round Table Conference to talk interminably about the petty details of a constitution. We were not interested in those details at that stage, and they could only be considered when some agreement on fundamental matters had been arrived at with the British Government. The real question was how much power was to be transferred to a democratic India. If by a strange chance a basis of agreement was found on those fundamentals, the rest followed easily enough. It had been settled between us that, in case of such an agreement, Gandhiji would immediately summon to London some or even all the members of the Working Committee, so that we could then share the work of detailed negotiation.

The British Government had, however, no intention of falling in with our wishes in the matter. Their policy was to postpone the consideration of fundamental questions and to make the Conference exhaust itself, more or less, on minor and immaterial matters. Even when major matters were considered, the Government held its hand, refused to commit itself, and promised to express its opinion after mature consideration later on. Their trump card was, of course, the communal issue, and they played it for all it was worth. It dominated the Conference.

The great majority of the Indian members of the Conference fell in, most of them willingly, some unwillingly, with this official maneuvering. They were a motley assembly. Few of them represented any but themselves. Some were able and respected; of many others this could not be said. As a whole they represented, politically and socially, the most reactionary elements in India. So backward and reactionary were they that the Indian Liberals, so very moderate and cautious in India, shone as progressives in their company.

It was fitting that in this assembly of vested interests—imperialist, feudal, financial, industrial, religious, communal—the leadership of the British Indian delegation should usually fall to the Aga Khan, who in his own person happened to combine all these interests in some degree. Closely associated as he has been with British imperialism and the British ruling class for over a generation, he could thoroughly appreciate and represent our rulers' interests and viewpoint. He was an able representative of Imperialist England at that Round Table Conference. The irony of it was that he was supposed to represent India.

The scales were terribly loaded against us at that Conference, and, little as we expected from it, we watched its proceedings with amazement and ever-growing disgust. We saw the pitiful and absurdly inadequate attempts to scratch the surface of national and economic problems, the pacts and intrigues and maneuvers, the joining of hands of some of our own countrymen with the most reactionary elements of the British Conservative party, the endless talk over petty issues, the deliberate shelving of all that really mattered, the continuous playing into the hands of the big vested interests and especially British imperialism, the mutual squabbles, varied by feasting and mutual admiration. It was all jobbery—big jobs, little jobs, jobs and seats for the Hindus, for the Moslems, for the Sikhs, for the Anglo-Indians, for the Europeans; but all jobs for the upper classes—the masses had no look-in. Opportunism was rampant, and different groups seemed to prowl about like hungry wolves waiting for their prey—the spoils under the new constitution. The very conception of freedom had taken the form of large-scale jobbery—"Indianization" it was called—more jobs for Indians in the army, in the civil services, etc. No one thought in terms of independence, of real freedom, of a transfer of power to a democratic India, of the solution of any of the vital and urgent economic problems facing the Indian people. Was it for this that India had struggled so manfully? Must we exchange this murky air for the rare atmosphere of fine idealism and sacrifice?

Gandhiji was in an extraordinarily difficult position in that Conference, and we wondered from afar how he could tolerate it. But with amazing patience he carried on and made attempt after attempt to find some basis of agreement. One characteristic gesture he made, which suddenly showed up how communalism really covered political reaction. He did not like many of the communal demands put forward on behalf of the Moslem delegates to the Conference; he thought, and his own Moslem nationalist colleagues thought so, that some of these demands were a bar to freedom and democracy. But still he offered to accept the whole lot of them, without question or argument, if the Moslem delegates there joined forces with him and the Congress on the political issue, that is, on independence.

The offer, however, was not accepted, and indeed it is a little difficult to imagine the Aga Khan standing for Indian independence. This demonstrated that the real trouble was not communal, although the communal issue loomed large before the Conference. It was political reaction that barred all progress and sheltered itself behind the communal issue. By careful selection of its nominees for the Conference, the British Government had collected these reactionary elements, and, by controlling the procedure, they had made the communal issue the major issue, and an issue on which no agreement was possible between the irreconcilables gathered there.

The British Government succeeded in its endeavor, and thereby demonstrated that it still has, not only the physical strength to uphold its Empire, but also the cunning and statecraft to carry on the imperial tradition for a while longer.

The Conference itself, with all its scheming and opportunism and futile meandering, was no failure for India. It was constituted so as to fail, and the people of India could hardly be made responsible for its failing. But it succeeded in diverting world attention from real issues in India, and, in India itself, it produced disillusion and depression and a sense of humiliation. It gave a handle to reactionary forces to raise their heads again.

Success or failure was to come to the people of the country by events in India itself. The powerful nationalist movement could not fade away, because of distant maneuvering in London. Nationalism represented a real and immediate need of the middle classes and peasantry, and by its means they sought to solve their problems. The movement could thus either succeed, fulfil its function, and give place to some other movement, which would carry the people further on the road to progress and freedom, or else it could be forcibly suppressed for the time being. That struggle was to come in India soon after and was to result in temporary disablement. The second Round Table Conference could not affect this struggle much, but it did create an atmosphere somewhat unfavorable to it.

## XXXII

## ARRESTS, ORDINANCES, PROSCRIPTIONS

SOME TIME AFTER Gandhiji had gone to London two incidents suddenly concentrated all-India attention on the situation in Bengal. These two took place in Hijli and Chittagong.

Hijli was a special detention camp jail for *détenus*. It was officially announced that a riot had taken place inside the camp, the *détenus* had attacked the staff, and the latter had been forced to fire on them. Two *détenus* were killed by this firing, and many were wounded. A local official inquiry, held immediately after, absolved the staff from all blame for this firing and its consequences. But there were many curious features; some facts leaked out which did not fit in with the official version, and vehement demands were made for a fuller inquiry. Contrary to the usual official practice in India, the Government of Bengal appointed an inquiring committee consisting of high judicial officers. It was a purely official committee, but it took evidence and considered the matter fully, and its findings were against the staff of the detention camp jail. It was held that the fault was largely that of the staff and the firing was unjustified. The previous Government communiqués issued on the subject were thus entirely falsified.

There was nothing very extraordinary about the Hijli occurrence. Unhappily, such incidents are not rare in India, and one frequently reads of "jail riots" and of the gallant suppression of unarmed and helpless prisoners within the jail by armed warders and others. Hijli was unusual in so far as it exposed, and exposed officially, the utter one-sidedness, and even the falsity, of Government communiqués on such occurrences.

The Chittagong affair was much more serious. A terrorist shot down and killed a Moslem police inspector. This was followed by a Hindu-Moslem riot, or so it was called. It was patent, however, that it was something much more than that, something different from the usual communal riot. It was obvious that the terrorist's act had nothing to do with communalism; it was directed against a police officer, regardless of whether he was a Hindu or Moslem. Yet it is true that there was some Hindu-Moslem rioting afterward. How this started, what was the occasion for it, has not been cleared up, although very serious charges have been made by responsible public men. Another feature of the rioting was the part taken by definite groups of other people, Anglo-Indians, chiefly railway employees, and other Government employees, who are alleged to have indulged in reprisals on a large scale. J. M. Sen-Gupta and other noted leaders of Bengal made specific allegations in regard to the occurrences in Chittagong, and challenged an inquiry or even a suit for defamation, but the Government preferred to take no such step.

The Chittagong murder of a police official by a terrorist, and its consequences, made one realize very vividly the dangerous possibilities of terroristic activity and the enormous harm it might do to the cause of Indian unity and freedom. The reprisals that followed also showed us that fascist methods had appeared in India. Since then there have been many instances, notably in Bengal, of such reprisals, and the fascist spirit has undoubtedly spread in the European and Anglo-Indian community. Some of the Indian hangers-on of British imperialism have also imbibed it.

I went to Calcutta for a few days in November 1931. I had a very crowded program and, apart from meeting individuals and groups privately, addressed a number of mass meetings. In all these meetings I discussed the question of terrorism and tried to show how wrong and futile and harmful it was for Indian freedom. I did not abuse the terrorists, nor did I call them "dastardly" or "cowardly," after the fashion of some of our countrymen who have themselves seldom, if ever, yielded to the temptation of doing anything brave or involving risk. It has always seemed to me a singularly stupid thing to call a man or woman who is constantly risking his life a coward. And the reaction of it on that man is to make him a little more contemptuous of his timid critics who shout from a distance and are incapable of doing anything.

On my last evening in Calcutta, a little before I was due to go to the station for my departure, two young men called on me. They were very young, about twenty, with pale, nervous faces and brilliant eyes. I did not know who they were, but soon I guessed their errand. They were very angry with me for my propaganda against terroristic violence. They said that it was producing a bad effect on young men, and they could not tolerate my intrusion in this way. We had a little argument; it was a hurried one, for the time of my departure was at hand. I am afraid our voices and our tempers rose, and I told them some hard things; and, as I left them, they warned me finally that if I continued to misbehave in the future they would deal with me as they had dealt with others.

And so I left Calcutta, and, as I lay in my berth in the train that night, I was long haunted by the excited faces of these two boys. Full of life and nervous energy they were; what good material if only they turned the right way! I was sorry that I had dealt with them hurriedly and rather brusquely, and wished I had had the chance of a long conversation with them. Perhaps I could have convinced them to apply their bright young lives to other ways, ways of serving India and freedom, in which there was no lack of opportunity for daring and self-sacrifice. Often I have thought of them in these afteryears. I never found out their names, nor did I have any other trace of them; and I wonder, sometimes, if they are dead or in some cell in the Andaman Islands.

It was December. The second Peasant Conference took place in Allahabad, and then I hurried south to the Karnataka to fulfill an old promise made to my old comrade of the Hindustani Seva Dal, Doctor N. S. Hardiker. The Seva Dal, the volunteer wing of the national movement, had all along been an auxiliary of the Congress, though its organization was quite separate. In the summer of 1931, however, the Working Committee decided to absorb it completely into the Congress organization, and to make it the volunteer department of the Congress. This was done, and Hardiker and I were put in charge of it.

On my way to the Karnataka from Allahabad I had gone to Bombay with Kamala. She was again ill, and I arranged for her treatment in Bombay. It was in Bombay, almost immediately after our arrival from Allahabad, that we learned that the Government of India had promulgated a special ordinance for the United Provinces. They had decided not to wait for Gandhiji's arrival, although he was already on the high seas and due in Bombay soon. The ordinance was supposed to deal with the agrarian agitation, but it was so extraordinarily wide-flung and far-reaching that it made all political or public activity impossible. It provided even for the punishment of parents and guardians for the sins of their children and wards—a reversal of the old biblical practice.

I was eager to go back to Allahabad and to give up the Karnataka tour. I felt that my place was with my comrades in the United Provinces, and to be far away when so much was happening at home was an ordeal. I decided, however, in favor of adhering to the Karnataka program. On my return to Bombay some friends advised me to stay on for Gandhiji's arrival, which was due exactly a week later. But this was impossible. From Allahabad came news of Purushottam Das Tandon's arrest and other arrests. There was, besides, our Provincial Conference which had been fixed at Etawah for that week. And so I decided to go to Allahabad and to return to Bombay six days later, if I were free, to meet Gandhiji and to attend a meeting of the Working Committee. I left Kamala bedridden in Bombay.

Even before I had reached Allahabad, at Chheoki station, an order under the new ordinance was served on me. At Allahabad station another attempt was made to serve a duplicate of that order on me; at my house a third attempt was made by a third person. Evidently no risks were being taken. The order interned me within the municipal limits of Allahabad, and I was told that I must not attend any public meeting or function, or speak in public, or write anything in a newspaper or leaflet. There were many other restrictions. I found that a similar order had been served on many of my colleagues, including Tasadduq Sherwani. The next morning I wrote to the district magistrate (who had issued the order) acknowledging receipt of it and informing him that I did not propose to take my orders from him as to what I was to do or not to do. I would carry on with my ordinary work in the ordinary way, and in the course of this work I proposed to return to Bombay soon to meet Mr. Gandhi and take part in the meeting of the Working Committee, of which I was the secretary.

A new problem confronted us. I had come from Bombay with the intention of suggesting a postponement of the Provincial Conference, as it clashed somewhat with Gandhiji's arrival, and in order to avoid conflict with the Government. But before my return to Allahabad a peremptory message had come from the United Provinces Government to our president, Sherwani, inquiring if our Conference would consider the agrarian question, for if so, they would prohibit the Conference itself. It was patent that the main purpose of the Conference was to discuss the agrarian question, which was agitating the whole province; to meet and not to discuss it would be the height of absurdity and self-stultification. And in any event our president or anyone else had no authority to tie down the Conference. Quite apart from the Government's threat, it was the intention of some of us to postpone the Conference, but this threat made a difference. Many of us were rather obstinate in such matters, and the idea of being dictated to by

Government was not pleasant. After long argument we decided to swallow our pride and to postpone the Conference. We did so because almost at any cost we wanted still to avoid the development of the conflict, which had already begun, till Gandhiji's arrival. We did not want him to be confronted with a situation in which he was powerless to take the helm. In spite of our postponement of our Provincial Conference there was a great display of the police and military at Etawah, some stray delegates were arrested, and the Swadeshi Exhibition there was seized by the military.

Sherwani and I decided to leave Allahabad for Bombay on the morning of December 26. As we got into the train we read in the morning's papers of the new Frontier Province ordinance and the arrest of Abdul Ghaffar Khan and Doctor Khan Sahib and others. Very soon our train, the Bombay Mail, came to a sudden halt at a wayside station, Iradatganj, which is not one of its usual stopping places, and police officials mounted up to arrest us. A Black Maria waited by the railway line, and Sherwani and I were taken in this closed prisoners' van away to Naini. The superintendent of police, an Englishman, who had arrested us on that morning of Boxing Day looked glum and unhappy. I am afraid we had spoiled his Christmas.

And so to prison!

Two days after our arrest Gandhiji landed in Bombay, and it was only then that he learned of the latest developments. Some of his closest colleagues in the Frontier Province and the United Provinces had been arrested. The die seemed to be cast and all hope of peace gone, but still he made an effort to find a way out, and sought an interview with the Viceroy, Lord Willingdon, for the purpose. The interview, he was informed from New Delhi, could only take place on certain conditions—these conditions being that he must not discuss recent events in Bengal, the United Provinces, and the Frontier, the new ordinances, and the arrests under them. (I write from memory, and have not got the text of the viceregal reply before me.) What exactly Gandhiji or any Congress leader was officially supposed to discuss with the Viceroy, apart from these forbidden subjects which were agitating the country, passes one's comprehension. It was absolutely clear now that the Government of India had determined to crush the Congress and would have no dealings with it. The Working Committee had no choice left but to resort to civil disobedience. They expected arrest at any moment, and they wanted to give a lead to the country before their enforced departure. Even so, the civil disobedience resolution was passed tentatively, and another attempt was made by Gandhiji to see the Viceroy, and he sent him a second telegram asking for an unconditional interview. The reply of the Government was to arrest Gandhiji as well as the Congress president, and to press the button which was to let loose fierce repression all over the country. It was clear that whoever else wanted or did not want the struggle, the Government was eager and overready for it.

We were in jail, of course, and all this news came to us vaguely and disjointedly. Our trial was postponed to the New Year, and so we had, as undertrials, more interviews than a convict could have. We heard of the great discussion that was going on as to whether the Viceroy should or should not have agreed to the interview, as if it really mattered either way. This question of the interview shadowed all other matters. It was stated that Lord Irwin would have agreed to the interview and if he and Gandhiji had met all would have been well. I was surprised at the extraordinarily superficial view that the Indian press took of the situation and how they ignored realities. Was the inevitable struggle between Indian nationalism and British imperialism—in the final analysis, two irreconcilables—to be reduced to the personal whims of individuals? Could the conflict of two historical forces be removed by smiles and mutual courtesy? Gandhiji was driven to act in one way, because Indian nationalism could not commit hara-kiri or submit willingly to foreign dictation in vital matters; the British Viceroy of India had to act in a particular way to meet the challenge of this nationalism and to endeavor to protect British interests, and it made not the slightest difference who the Viceroy was at the time. Lord Irwin would have acted exactly as Lord Willingdon did, for either of them was but the instrument of British imperialist policy and could only make some minor deviations from the line laid down. Lord Irwin, indeed, was subsequently a member of the British Government, and he associated himself fully with the official steps taken in India. To praise or condemn individual Viceroys for British policy in India seems to me a singularly inept thing to do, and our habit of indulging in this pastime can only be due to an ignorance of the real issues or to a deliberate evasion of them.

January 4, 1932, was a notable day. It put a stop to argument and discussion. Early that morning Gandhiji and the Congress president, Vallabhbhai Patel, were arrested and confined without trial as State prisoners. Four new ordinances were promulgated giving the most far-reaching powers to magistrates and police officers. Civil liberty ceased to exist, and both person and property could be seized by the authorities. It was a declaration of a kind of state of siege for the whole of India, the extent and intensity of application being left to the discretion of the local authorities.[1]

On that 4th of January also our trial took place in Naini Prison under the United Provinces Emergency Powers Ordinance, as it was called. Sherwani was sentenced to six months' rigorous imprisonment and a fine of one hundred and fifty rupees; I was sentenced to two years' rigorous imprisonment and a fine of five hundred rupees (in default six months more). Our offenses were identical; we had been served with identical orders of internment in Allahabad city; we had committed the same breach of them by attempting to go together to Bombay; we had been arrested and tried together under the same section, and yet our sentences were very dissimilar. There was, however, one difference: I had written to the district magistrate and informed him of my intention to go to Bombay in defiance of the order; Sherwani had given no such formal notice, but his proposed departure was equally well known, and had been mentioned in the press. Immediately after the sentence Sherwani asked the trying magistrate, to the amusement of those present and the embarrassment of the magistrate, if his smaller sentence was due to communal considerations.

Quite a lot happened on that fateful day, January 4, all over the country. Not far from where we were, in Allahabad city, huge crowds came in conflict with the police and military, and there were the usual lathee charges involving deaths and other casualties. The jails began to fill with civil disobedience prisoners. To begin with, these prisoners went to the district jails, and Naini and the other great central prisons received only the overflows. Later, all the jails filled up, and huge temporary camp jails were established.

The Congress had been declared illegal—the Working Committee at the top, the provincial committees, and innumerable local committees. Together with the Congress all manner of allied or sympathetic or advanced organizations had been declared unlawful—*kisan sabhas* and peasant unions, youth leagues, students' associations, advanced political organizations, national universities and schools, hospitals,

---

[1] Sir Samuel Hoare, Secretary of State for India, stated in the House of Commons on March 24, 1932: "I admit that the ordinances that we have approved are very drastic and severe. They cover almost every activity of Indian life."

Swadeshi concerns, libraries. The lists were indeed formidable, and contained many hundreds of names for each major province. The all-India total must have run into several thousands, and this very number of outlawed organizations was in itself a tribute to the Congress and the national movement.

My wife lay in Bombay, ill in bed, fretting at her inability to take part in civil disobedience. My mother and both my sisters threw themselves into the movement with vigor, and soon both the sisters were in jail with a sentence of a year each. Odd bits of news used to reach us through newcomers to prison or through the local weekly paper that we were permitted to read. We could only guess much that was happening, for the press censorship was strict, and the prospect of heavy penalties always faced newspapers and news agencies. In some provinces it was an offense even to mention the name of a person arrested or sentenced.

So we sat in Naini Prison cut off from the strife outside, and yet wrapped up in it in a hundred ways; busying ourselves with spinning or reading or other activities, talking sometimes of other matters, but thinking always of what was happening beyond the prison walls. We were out of it, and yet in it. Sometimes the strain of expectation was very great; or there was anger at something wrongly done; disgust at weakness or vulgarity. At other times we were strangely detached, and could view the scene calmly and dispassionately and feel that petty individual errors or weaknesses mattered little when vast forces were at play and the mills of the gods were grinding. We would wonder what the morrow would bring of strife and tumult, and gallant enthusiasm and cruel repression and hateful cowardice—and what was all this leading to? Whither were we going? The future was hid from us, and it was as well that it was hidden; even the present was partly covered by a veil, so far as we were concerned. But this we knew: that there was strife and suffering and sacrifice in the present and on the morrow.

# XXXIII

# BALLYHOO

THOSE EARLY MONTHS of 1932 were remarkable, among other things, for an extraordinary exhibition of ballyhoo on the part of the British authorities. Officials, high and low, shouted out how virtuous and peaceful they were, and how sinful and pugnacious was the Congress. They stood for democracy while the Congress favored dictatorships. Was not its president called a dictator? In their enthusiasm for a righteous cause they forgot trifles like ordinances, and suppression of all liberties, and muzzling of newspapers and presses, imprisonment of people without trial, seizure of properties and moneys, and the many other odd things that were happening from day to day. They forgot also the basic character of British rule in India. Ministers of Government (our own countrymen) grew eloquent on how Congressmen were "grinding their axes"—in prison—while they labored for the public good on paltry salaries of a few thousand rupees per month. The lower magistracy not only sentenced us to heavy terms but lectured to us in the process, and sometimes abused the Congress and individuals connected with it. Even Sir Samuel Hoare, from the serene dignity of his high office as Secretary of State for India, announced that "though dogs may bark the caravan passes on." Most surprising of all, the Cawnpore Communal Riots were laid at the door of the Congress. The horrors of these truly horrible riots were laid bare, and it was repeatedly stated that the Congress was responsible for them. As it happened, the Congress had played the only decent part in them, and one of its noblest sons lay dead, mourned by every group and community in Cawnpore. No doubt, in this and other matters, the truth will prevail in the end, but sometimes the lie has a long start.

It was all very natural, I suppose, this exhibition of a hysterical war mentality; and no one could expect truth or restraint under the circumstances. But it did seem to go beyond expectation and was surprising in its intensity and abandon. It was some indication of the state of nerves of the ruling group in India, and of how they had been repressing themselves in the past. Probably the anger was not caused by anything we had done or said, but by the realization of their own previous fear of losing their empire. Rulers who are confident of their own strength do not give way in this manner.

It was evident that the Government had long prepared its blow, and it wanted it to be as thorough and staggering as possible right at the beginning. In 1930 it was always attempting, by fresh ordinances, to catch up an ever-worsening situation. The initiative remained then with Congress. The 1932 methods were different, and Government began with an offensive all along the line. Every conceivable power was given and taken under a batch of all-India and provincial ordinances; organizations were outlawed; buildings, property, automobiles, bank accounts were seized; public gatherings and processions forbidden; and newspapers and printing presses fully controlled. India lived practically under martial law, and Congress never really got back the initiative or any freedom of action. The first blows stunned it and most of its bourgeois sympathizers who had been its principal supporters in the past. Their pockets were hit, and it became obvious that those who joined the civil disobedience movement, or were known to help it in any way, stood to lose not only their liberty, but perhaps all their property.

I do not think any Congressman has a right to object to the procedure adopted by the Government, although the violence and coercion used by the Government against an overwhelmingly nonviolent movement was certainly most objectionable from any civilized standards. If we choose to adopt revolutionary direct-action methods, however nonviolent they might be, we must expect every resistance. We cannot play at revolution in a drawing room, but many people want to have the advantage of both. For a person to dabble in revolutionary methods, he must be prepared to lose everything he possesses. The prosperous and the well-to-do are therefore seldom revolutionaries, though individuals may play the fool in the eyes of the worldly wise and be dubbed traitors to their own class.

The new environment in India tolerated no neutral hues, and so some of our countrymen appeared in the brightest of approved colors, and, with song and feasting, they declared their love and admiration for our rulers. They had nothing to fear from the ordinances and the numerous prohibitions and inhibitions and curfew orders and sunset laws; for had it not been officially stated that all this was meant for the disloyal and the seditious, and the loyal need have no cause for alarm?

The Government had somehow got hold of the idea that Congress was going to exploit women in the struggle by filling the jails with them, in the hope that women would be well treated or would get light sentences. It was a fantastic notion, as if anyone likes to push his womenfolk into prison. Usually, when girls or women took an active part in the campaign, it was in spite of their fathers or brothers or husbands, or at any rate not with their full co-operation. Government, however, decided to discourage women by long sentences and bad treatment in prison. Soon after my sisters' arrest and conviction, a number of young girls, mostly 15 or 16 years old, met in Allahabad to discuss what they could do. They had no experience but were full of enthusiasm and wanted advice. They were arrested as they were meeting in a private house, and each of them was sentenced to two years' rigorous imprisonment. This was a minor incident, one of many that were occurring all over India from day to day. Most of the girls and women who were sentenced had a very bad time in prison, even worse than the men had. I heard of many painful instances, but the most extraordinary account that I saw was one prepared by Miraben (Madeleine Slade) giving her experiences, together with those of other civil disobedience prisoners, in a Bombay jail.

The response of the peasantry in some of the principal districts of the United Provinces to the call for civil disobedience, which inevitably got mixed up with the dispute about fair rent and remissions, was very fine. It was a far bigger and more disciplined response than in 1930. To begin with, there was good humor about it too. A delightful story came to us of a visit of a police party to the village Bakulia in Rae Bareli district. They had gone to attach goods for nonpayment of rent. The village was relatively prosperous, and its residents were men of some spirit. They received the revenue and police officials with all courtesy and, leaving the doors of all the houses open, invited them to go wherever they wanted to. Some attachments of cattle, etc., were made. The villages then offered *pan supari* to the police and revenue officials, who retired looking very small and rather shamefaced! But this was a rare and unusual occurrence, and very soon there was little of humor or charity or human kindness to be seen. Poor Bakulia could not escape punishment for its spirit because of its humor.

Swaraj Bhawan had been seized by the Government, in common with numerous other buildings all over the country. All the valuable equipment and material belonging to the Congress hospital, which was functioning in Swaraj Bhawan, was also seized. For a few days the hospital ceased functioning altogether, but then an open-air dispensary was established in a park near by. Later the hospital, or rather dispensary, moved to a small house adjoining Swaraj Bhawan, and there it functioned for nearly two and a half years.

There was some talk of our dwelling house, Anand Bhawan, also being taken possession of by the Government, for I had refused to pay a large amount due as income tax. This tax had been assessed on father's income in 1930, and he had not paid it that year because of civil disobedience. In 1931, after the Delhi Pact, I had an argument with the income tax authorities about it, but ultimately I agreed to pay and did pay an installment. Just then came the ordinances, and I decided to pay no more. It seemed to me utterly wrong, and even immoral, for me to ask the peasants to withhold payment of rent and revenue and to pay income tax myself. I expected, therefore, that our house would be attached by the Government. I disliked this idea intensely, as it would have meant my mother being turned out; our books, papers, goods and chattels, and many things that we valued for personal and sentimental reasons going into strange hands and perhaps being lost; and our national flag being pulled down and the Union Jack put up instead. At the same time I was attracted to the idea of losing the house. I felt that this would bring me nearer to the peasantry, who were being dispossessed, and would hearten them. From the point of view of our movement it was certainly a desirable thing. But the Government decided otherwise and did not touch the house, perhaps because of consideration for my mother, perhaps because they judged rightly that it would give an impetus to civil disobedience. Many months afterward some odd railway shares of mine were discovered and attached, for nonpayment of income tax. My motorcar, as well as my brother-in-law's, had been previously attached and sold.

One feature of these early months pained me greatly. This was the hauling down of our national flag by various municipalities and public bodies, and especially by the Calcutta Corporation, which was said to have a majority of Congress members. The flag was taken down under pressure from the police and the Government, which threatened severe action in case of noncompliance. This action would have probably meant a suspension of the municipality or punishment of its members. Organizations with vested interests are apt to be timid, and perhaps it was inevitable that they should act as they did; but nevertheless it hurt. That flag had become a symbol to us of much that we held dear, and under its shadow we had taken many a pledge to protect its honor. To pull it down with our own hands, or to have it pulled down at our behest, seemed not only a breaking of that pledge but almost a sacrilege. It was a submission of the spirit, a denial of the truth in one; an affirmation, in the face of superior physical might, of the false. And those who submitted in this way lowered the morale of the nation, and injured its self-respect.

It was not that they were expected to behave as heroes and rush into the fire. It was wrong and absurd to blame anyone for not being in the front rank and courting prison, or other suffering or loss. Each one had many duties and responsibilities to shoulder, and no one else had a right to sit in judgment on him. But to sit or work in the background is one thing; to deny the truth, or what one conceives to be the truth, is a more serious matter. It was open to members of municipalities, when called upon to do anything against the national interest, to resign from their seats. As a rule they preferred to remain in those seats. No one knows how he will behave in a similar crisis when the primeval instincts overpower reason and restraint. So we may not blame. But that should not prevent us from noting that falling away from right conduct, and from taking care in future that the steering wheel of the ship of the nation is not put in hands that tremble and fail when the need is greatest. Worse still is the attempt to justify this failure and call it right conduct. That, surely, is a greater offense than the failure itself.

The months went by bringing their daily toll of good news and bad, and we adapted ourselves in our respective prisons, to our dull and monotonous routine. The National Week came—April 6 to 13—and we knew that this would witness many an unusual happening. Much, indeed, happened then; but for me everything else paled before one occurrence. In Allahabad my mother was in a procession which was stopped by the police and later charged with lathees. When the procession had been halted, someone brought her a chair, and she was sitting on this on the road at the head of the procession. Some people who were especially looking after her, including my secretary, were arrested and removed, and then came the police charge. My mother was knocked down from her chair and was hit repeatedly on the head with canes. Blood came out of an open wound in the head; she fainted and lay on the roadside, which had now been cleared of the processionists and public. After some time she was picked up and brought by a police officer in his car to Anand Bhawan.

That night a false rumor spread in Allahabad that my mother had died. Angry crowds gathered together, forgot about peace and non-violence, and attacked the police. There was firing by the police, resulting in the death of some people.

When the news of all this came to me some days after the occurrence (for we had a weekly paper), the thought of my frail old mother lying bleeding on the dusty road obsessed me, and I wondered how I would have behaved if I had been there. How far would my non-violence have carried me? Not very far, I fear, for that sight would have made me forget the long lesson I had tried to learn for more than a dozen years; and I would have recked little of the consequences, personal or national.

Slowly she recovered, and, when she came to see me next month in Bareilly Jail, she was still bandaged up. But she was full of joy and pride at having shared with our volunteer boys and girls the privilege of receiving cane and lathi blows. Her recovery, however, was more apparent than real, and it seems that the tremendous shaking that she received at her age upset her system entirely and brought into prominence deep-seated troubles, which a year later assumed dangerous proportions.

XXXIV

## IN BAREILLY AND DEHRA DUN JAILS

AFTER SIX WEEKS in Naini Prison I was transferred to the Bareilly District Jail. I was again keeping indifferent health, and, much to my annoyance, I used to get a daily rise in temperature. After four months spent in Bareilly, when the summer temperature was almost at its highest, I was again transferred, this time to a cooler place, Dehra Dun Jail, at the foot of the Himalayas. There I remained, without a break, for fourteen and a half months, almost to the end of my two-year term. News reached me, of course, from interviews and letters and selected newspapers, but I was wholly out of touch with much that was happening and had only a hazy notion of the principal events.

When I was out of prison for five months I was kept busy with personal affairs as well as the political situation as I found it then. I was back in prison again. For three years I have been mostly in prison and out of touch with events, and I have had little opportunity of making myself acquainted in any detail with all that has happened during this period.

Gradually, the civil disobedience movement declined; though it still carried on, not without distinction. Progressively it ceased to be a mass movement. Apart from the severity of Government repression, the first

223

severe blow to it came in September 1932, when Gandhiji fasted for the first time on the Harijan issue.[1] That fast roused mass consciousness, but it diverted it from the main political issue. Civil disobedience was finally killed for all practical purposes by the suspension of it in May 1933. It continued after that more in theory than in practice. It is no doubt true that, even without that suspension, it would have gradually petered out. India was numbed by the violence and the harshness of repression. The nervous energy of the nation as a whole was for the moment exhausted, and it was not being recharged. Individually there were still many who could carry on civil resistance, but they functioned in a somewhat artificial atmosphere.

It was not pleasant for us in prison to learn of this slow decay of a great movement. And yet very few of us had expected a flashing success. There was always an odd chance that something flashing might happen if there was an irrepressible upheaval of the masses. But that was not to be counted upon, and so we looked forward to a long struggle with ups and downs and many a stalemate in between, and a progressive strengthening of the masses in discipline and united action and ideology. Sometimes in those early days of 1932 I almost feared a quick and spectacular success, for this seemed to lead inevitably to a compromise leaving the "Governmentarians" and opportunists at the top. The experience of 1931 had been revealing. Success to be worth while should come when the people generally were strong enough and clear enough in their ideas to take advantage of it. Otherwise the masses would fight and sacrifice, and, at the psychological moment, others would step in gracefully and gather the spoils. There was grave danger of this, because in the Congress itself there was a great deal of loose thinking and no clear ideas as to what system of government or society we were driving at. It was not merely a question of civil disobedience being countered and suppressed by the Government, but of all political life and public activity being stopped, and hardly a voice was raised against this. Those who usually stood for these liberties were involved in the struggle itself, and they took the penalties for refusing to submit to the State's coercion. Others were cowed into abject submission and hardly raised their voices in criticism. Mild criticism, when it was indulged in, was apologetic in tone and invariably accompanied by strong denunciation of the Congress and those who were carrying on the struggle.

The Indian Liberals claim to some extent to carry on the traditions

[1] "Harijan" is Gandhi's term for the depressed classes.—Ed.

of British Liberalism (although they have nothing in common with them except the name) and might have been expected to put up some intellectual opposition to the suppression of civil liberties. But they played no such part. It was not for them to say with Voltaire: "I disagree absolutely with what you say, but I will defend to the death your right to say it." It is not perhaps fair to blame them for this, for they have never stood out as the champions of democracy or liberty, and they had to face a situation in which a loose word might have got them into trouble. It is more pertinent to observe the reactions of those ancient lovers of liberty, the British Liberals, and the new socialists of the British Labour party to repression in India. They managed to contemplate the Indian scene with a certain measure of equanimity, painful as it was, and sometimes their satisfaction at the success of the "scientific application of repression," as a correspondent of the *Manchester Guardian* put it, was evident. When the National Government of Great Britain has sought to pass a sedition bill, a great deal of criticism has been directed to it, especially from Liberals and Labourites on the ground, *inter alia,* that it restricts free speech and gives magistrates the right of issuing warrants for searches. Whenever I read this criticism, I sympathized with it, and I had at the same time the picture of India before me, where the actual laws in force today are approximately a hundred times worse than the British sedition bill sought to enact. I wondered how it was that British people who strain at a gnat in England could swallow a camel in India without turning a hair. Indeed I have always wondered at and admired the astonishing knack of the British people for making their moral standards correspond with their material interests, and for seeing virtue in everything that advances their imperial designs. Mussolini and Hitler are condemned by them in perfect good faith and with righteous indignation for their attacks on liberty and democracy; and, in equal good faith, similar attacks and deprivation of liberty in India seem to them as necessary, and the highest moral reasons are advanced to show that true disinterested behavior on their part demands them.

While fire raged all over India, and men's and women's souls were put to the test, far away in London the chosen ones foregathered to draw up a constitution for India at the third Round Table Conference in 1932.

It was surprising to find how far these people had alienated themselves, not only in their day-to-day lives, but morally and mentally, from the Indian masses. Reality for these distinguished statesmen consisted of one thing—British imperial power, which could not be successfully challenged and therefore should be accepted with good or bad grace. It did not seem to strike them that it was quite impossible for them to solve India's problem or draw up a real live constitution without the good will of the masses.

In India there was an amazing growth of the spirit of violence in official circles. An inspector-general of prisons went to the length of issuing a confidential circular to all the prisons, pointing out that civil disobedience prisoners must be "dealt with grimly." [2] Whipping became a frequent jail punishment. On April 27, 1933, the Under-Secretary for India stated in the House of Commons "that Sir Samuel Hoare was aware that over 500 persons in India were whipped during 1932 for offenses in connection with the civil disobedience movement." It is not clear if this figure includes the many whippings in prisons for breaches of jail discipline. As news of frequent whippings came to us in prison in 1932, I remembered our protest and our three-day fast in December 1930 against one or two odd instances of whipping. I had felt shocked then at the brutality of it; now I was still shocked, and there was a dull pain inside me, but it did not strike me that I should protest and fast again. I felt much more helpless in the matter. The mind gets blunted to brutality after a while.

The hardest of labor was given to our men in prison—mills, oil presses, etc.—and their lot was made as unbearable as possible in order to induce them to apologize and be released on an undertaking being given to Government. That was considered a great triumph for the jail authorities.

Most of these jail punishments fell to the lot of boys and young men, who resented coercion and humiliation. A fine and spirited lot of boys they were, full of self-respect and "pep" and the spirit of adventure, the kind that in an English public school or university would have received every encouragement and praise. Here in India their youthful idealism and pride led them to fetters and solitary confinement and whipping.

The lot of our womenfolk in prison was especially hard and painful to contemplate. They were mostly middle-class women, accustomed to a sheltered life, and suffering chiefly from the many repressions and customs produced by a society dominated to his own advantage by

[2] This circular was dated June 30, 1932, and it contained the following: "The Inspector-General impresses upon superintendents and jail subordinates the fact that there is no justification for preferential treatment in favor of civil disobedience movement prisoners as such. This class require to be kept in their places and dealt with grimly."

man. The call of freedom had always a double meaning for them, and the enthusiasm and energy with which they threw themselves into the struggle had no doubt their springs in the vague and hardly conscious, but nevertheless intense, desire to rid themselves of domestic slavery also. Excepting a very few, they were classed as ordinary prisoners and placed with the most degraded of companions, and often under horrid conditions. I was once lodged in a barrack next to a female enclosure, a wall separating us. In that enclosure there were, besides other convicts, some women political prisoners, including one who had been my hostess and in whose house I had once stayed. A high wall separated us, but it did not prevent me from listening in horror to the language and curses which our friends had to put up with from the women convict warders.

It was very noticeable that the treatment of political prisoners in 1932 and 1933 was worse than it had been two years earlier, in 1930. This could not have been due merely to the whims of individual officers, and the only reasonable inference seems to be that this was the deliberate policy of the Government. Even apart from political prisoners, the United Provinces Jail Department had had the reputation in those years of being very much against anything that might savor of humanity.[3]

XXXV

## THE STRUGGLE OUTSIDE

BRAVE MEN AND women defied peacefully a powerful and entrenched government, though they knew that it was not for them to achieve what they wanted in the present or the near future. And repression without break and with ever-increasing intensity demonstrated the basis of British rule in India. There was no camouflage about it now, and this at least was some satisfaction to us. Bayonets were triumphant, but a great warrior had once said that "you can do everything with bayonets save sit on them." It was better that we should be governed thus, we thought, than that we should sell our souls and submit to spiritual prostitution. We were physically helpless in prison, but we felt we served our cause even there and served it better than many outside.

[3] In the original edition of this book, the chapters numbered I and II in the present edition followed at this point.—Ed.

Should we, because of our weakness, sacrifice the future of India to save ourselves? It was true that the limits of human vitality and human strength were narrow, and many an individual was physically disabled, or died, or fell out of the ranks, or even betrayed the cause. But the cause went on despite setbacks; there could be no failure if ideals remained undimmed and spirits undaunted. Real failure was a desertion of principle, a denial of our right, and an ignoble submission to wrong. Self-made wounds always took longer to heal than those caused by an adversary.

There was often a weariness at our weaknesses and at a world gone awry, and yet there was a measure of pride for our achievement. For our people had indeed behaved splendidly, and it was good to feel oneself to be a member of a gallant band.

During those years of civil disobedience two attempts were made to hold open Congress sessions, one at Delhi and the other at Calcutta. It was obvious that an illegal organization could not meet normally and in peace, and any attempt at an open session meant conflict with the police. The meetings were in fact dispersed forcibly with the help of the lathee by the police, and large numbers of people were arrested. The extraordinary thing about these gatherings was the fact that thousands came from all parts of India as delegates to these illegal gatherings. I was glad to learn that people from the United Provinces played a prominent part in both of them. My mother also insisted on going to the Calcutta session at the end of March 1933. She was arrested, however, together with Pandit Malaviya and others, and detained in prison for a few days at Asansol, on the way to Calcutta. I was amazed at the energy and vitality she showed, frail and ailing as she was. Prison was really of little consequence to her; she had gone through a harder ordeal. Her son and both her daughters and others whom she loved spent long periods in prison, and the empty house where she lived had become a nightmare to her.

As our struggle toned down and stabilized itself at a low level, there was little of excitement in it, except at long intervals. My thoughts traveled more to other countries, and I watched and studied, as far as I could in jail, the world situation in the grip of the great depression. I read as many books as I could find on the subject, and the more I read the more fascinated I grew. India with her problems and struggles became just a part of this mighty world drama, of the great struggle of political and economic forces that was going on everywhere, nationally and internationally. In that struggle my own sympathies went increasingly toward the communist side.

I had long been drawn to socialism and communism, and Russia had appealed to me. Much in Soviet Russia I dislike—the ruthless suppression of all contrary opinion, the wholesale regimentation, the unnecessary violence (as I thought) in carrying out various policies. But there was no lack of violence and suppression in the capitalist world, and I realized more and more how the very basis and foundation of our acquisitive society and property was violence. Without violence it could not continue for many days. A measure of political liberty meant little indeed when the fear of starvation was always compelling the vast majority of people everywhere to submit to the will of the few, to the greater glory and advantage of the latter.

Violence was common in both places, but the violence of the capitalist order seemed inherent in it; while the violence of Russia, bad though it was, aimed at a new order based on peace and co-operation and real freedom for the masses. With all her blunders, Soviet Russia had triumphed over enormous difficulties and taken great strides toward this new order. While the rest of the world was in the grip of the depression and going backward in some ways, in the Soviet country a great new world was being built up before our eyes. Russia, following the great Lenin, looked into the future and thought only of what was to be, while other countries lay numbed under the dead hand of the past and spent their energy in preserving the useless relics of a bygone age. In particular, I was impressed by the reports of the great progress made by the backward regions of Central Asia under the Soviet regime. In the balance, therefore, I was all in favor of Russia, and the presence and example of the Soviets was a bright and heartening phenomenon in a dark and dismal world.

But Soviet Russia's success or failure, vastly important as it was as a practical experiment in establishing a communist state, did not affect the soundness of the theory of communism. The Bolsheviks may blunder or even fail because of national or international reasons, and yet the communist theory may be correct. On the basis of that very theory it was absurd to copy blindly what had taken place in Russia, for its application depended on the particular conditions prevailing in the country in question and the stage of its historical development. Besides, India, or any other country, could profit by the triumphs as well as the inevitable mistakes of the Bolsheviks. Perhaps the Bolsheviks had tried to go too fast because, surrounded as they were by a world of enemies, they feared external aggression. A slower tempo might avoid much of the misery caused in the rural areas. But then the question arose if really radical results could be obtained by slowing down the rate of change. Reformism was an impossible solution of any vital problem at a critical moment when the basic structure had to be changed, and, however slow the progress might be later on, the initial step must be a complete break with the existing order, which had fulfilled its purpose and was now only a drag on future progress.

In India, only a revolutionary plan could solve the two related questions of the land and industry as well as almost every other major problem before the country. "There is no graver mistake," as Mr. Lloyd George says in his *War Memoirs,* "than to leap the abyss in two jumps."

Russia apart, the theory and philosophy of Marxism lightened up many a dark corner of my mind. History came to have a new meaning for me. The Marxist interpretation threw a flood of light on it, and it became an unfolding drama with some order and purpose, howsoever unconscious, behind it. In spite of the appalling waste and misery of the past and the present, the future was bright with hope, though many dangers intervened. It was the essential freedom from dogma and the scientific outlook of Marxism that appealed to me. It was true that there was plenty of dogma in official communism in Russia and elsewhere, and frequently heresy hunts were organized. That seemed to be deplorable, though it was not difficult to understand in view of the tremendous changes taking place rapidly in the Soviet countries when effective opposition might have resulted in catastrophic failure.

The great world crisis and slump seemed to justify the Marxist analysis. While all other systems and theories were groping about in the dark, Marxism alone explained it more or less satisfactorily and offered a real solution.

As this conviction grew upon me, I was filled with a new excitement, and my depression at the nonsuccess of civil disobedience grew much less. Was not the world marching rapidly toward the desired consummation? There were grave dangers of wars and catastrophes, but at any rate we were moving. There was no stagnation. Our national struggle became a stage in the longer journey, and it was as well that repression and suffering were tempering our people for future struggles and forcing them to consider the new ideas that were stirring the world. We would be the stronger and the more disciplined and hardened by the elimination of the weaker elements. Time was in our favor.

And so I studied carefully what was happening in Russia, Germany, England, America, Japan, China, France, Spain, Italy, and Central Europe, and tried to understand the tangled web of current affairs. I followed with interest the attempts of each country separately, and of all of them together, to weather the storm. The repeated failures of international conferences to find a solution for political and economic ills and the problem of disarmament reminded me forcibly of a little, but sufficiently troublesome, problem of our own—the communal problem. With all the good will in the world, we have so far not solved the problem; and, in spite of a widespread belief that failure would lead to world catastrophe, the great statesmen of Europe and America have failed to pull together. In either case the approach was wrong, and the people concerned did not dare to go the right way.

In thinking over the troubles and conflicts of the world, I forgot to some extent my own personal and national troubles. I would even feel buoyant occasionally at the fact that I was alive at this great revolutionary period of the world's history. Perhaps I might also have to play some little part in my own corner of the world in the great changes that were to come. At other times I would find the atmosphere of conflict and violence all over the world very depressing. Worse still was the sight of intelligent men and women who had become so accustomed to human degradation and slavery that their minds were too coarsened to resent suffering and poverty and inhumanity. Noisy vulgarity and organized humbug flourished in this stifling moral atmosphere, and good men were silent. The triumph of Hitler and the Brown Terror that followed was a great shock, though I consoled myself that it could only be temporary. Almost one had the feeling of the futility of human endeavor. The machine went on blindly; what could a little cog in it do?

But still the communist philosophy of life gave me comfort and hope. How was it to be applied to India? We had not solved yet the problem of political freedom, and the nationalistic outlook filled our minds. Were we to jump to economic freedom at the same time or take them in turn, however short the interval might be? World events as well as happenings in India were forcing the social issue to the front, and it seemed that political freedom could no longer be separated from it.

The policy of the British Government in India had resulted in ranging the socially reactionary classes in opposition to political independence. That was inevitable, and I welcomed the clearer demarcation of the various classes and groups in India. But was this fact appreciated by others? Apparently not by many. It was true that there were a handful of orthodox communists in some of the big cities, and they were hostile to, and bitterly critical of, the national movement. The organized labor movement, especially in Bombay and, to a lesser extent, in Calcutta, was also socialistic in a loose kind of way, but it was broken up into bits and suffering from the depression. Vague communistic and socialistic ideas had spread among the intelligentsia, even among intelligent Government officials. The younger men and women of the Congress, who used to read Bryce on democracies and Morley and Keith and Mazzini, were now reading, when they could get them, books on socialism and communism and Russia. The Meerut Conspiracy Case had helped greatly in directing people's minds to these new ideas, and the world crisis had compelled attention. Everywhere there was in evidence a new spirit of inquiry, a questioning and a challenge to existing institutions. The general direction of the mental wind was obvious, but still it was a gentle breeze, unsure of itself. Some people flirted with fascist ideas. A clear and definite ideology was lacking. Nationalism still was the dominating thought.

It seemed clear to me that nationalism would remain the outstanding urge, till some measure of political freedom was attained. Because of this the Congress had been, and was still (apart from certain labor circles), the most advanced organization in India, as it was far the most powerful. During the past thirteen years, under Gandhiji's leadership, it had produced a wonderful awakening of the masses, and, in spite of its vague bourgeois ideology, it had served a revolutionary purpose. It had not exhausted its utility yet and was not likely to do so till the nationalist urge gave place to a social one. Future progress, both ideological and in action, must therefore be largely associated with the Congress, though other avenues could also be used.

To desert the Congress seemed to me thus to cut oneself adrift from the vital urge of the nation, to blunt the most powerful weapon we had, and perhaps to waste energy in ineffective adventurism. And yet, was the Congress, constituted as it was, ever likely to adopt a really radical social solution? If such an issue were placed before it, the result was bound to be to split it into two or more parts, or at least to drive away large sections from it. That in itself was not undesirable or unwelcome if the issues became clearer and a strongly knit group, either a majority or minority in the Congress, stood for a radical social program.

But Congress at present meant Gandhiji. What would he do? Ideologically he was sometimes amazingly backward, and yet in action he had been the greatest revolutionary of recent times in India. He was a unique personality, and it was impossible to judge him by the usual standards, or even to apply the ordinary canons of logic to him. But, because he was a revolutionary at bottom and was pledged to political independence for India, he was bound to play an uncompromising role till that independence was achieved. And in this very process he would release tremendous mass energies and would himself, I half hoped, advance step by step toward the social goal.

The orthodox communists in India and outside have for many years past attacked Gandhiji and the Congress bitterly, and imputed all manner of base motives to the Congress leaders. Many of their theoretical criticisms of Congress ideology were able and pointed, and subsequent events partly justified them. Some of the earlier communist analyses of the general Indian political situation turned out to be remarkably correct. But, as soon as they leave their general principles and enter into details, and especially when they consider the role of the Congress, they go hopelessly astray. One of the reasons for the weakness in numbers as well as influence of the communists in India is that, instead of spreading a scientific knowledge of communism and trying to convert people's minds to it, they have largely concentrated on abuse of others. This has reacted on them and done them great injury. Most of them are used to working in labor areas, where a few slogans are usually enough to win over the workers. But mere slogans are not enough for the intellectual, and they have not realized that in India today the middle-class intellectual is the most revolutionary force. Almost in spite of the orthodox communists, many intellectuals have been drawn to communism, but even so there is a gulf between them.

According to the communists, the objective of the Congress leaders has been to bring mass pressure on the Government in order to obtain industrial and commercial concessions in the interests of Indian capitalists and zamindars. The task of the Congress is "to harness the economic and political discontent of the peasantry, the lower middle class, and the industrial working class to the chariot of the mill owners and financiers of Bombay, Ahmedabad, and Calcutta." The Indian capitalists are supposed to sit behind the scenes and issue orders to the Congress Working Committee first to organize a mass movement and, when it becomes too vast and dangerous, to suspend it or sidetrack it. Further, that the Congress leaders really do not want the British to go away, as they are required to control and exploit a starving population, and the Indian middle class do not feel themselves equal to this.

It is surprising that able communists should believe this fantastic analysis, but, believing this as they apparently do, it is not surprising that they should fail so remarkably in India. Their basic error seems to be that they judge the Indian national movement from European labor standards; and, used as they are to the repeated betrayals of the labor movement by the labor leaders, they apply the analogy to India. The Indian national movement is obviously not a labor or proletarian movement. It is a bourgeois movement, as its very name implies, and its objective so far has been, not a change of the social order, but political independence. This objective may be criticized as not far-reaching enough, and nationalism itself may be condemned as out of date. But, accepting the fundamental basis of the movement, it is absurd to say that the leaders betray the masses because they do not try to upset the land system or the capitalist system. They never claimed to do so. Some people in the Congress, and they are a growing number, want to change the land system and the capitalist system, but they cannot speak in the name of the Congress.

It is true that the Indian capitalist classes (not the big zamindars and talukdars) have profited greatly by the national movement because of British and other foreign boycotts, and the push given to Swadeshi. This was inevitable, as every national movement encourages home industries and preaches boycotts. As a matter of fact, the Bombay mill industry in a body, during the continuance of civil disobedience and when we were preaching the boycott of British goods, had the temerity to conclude a pact with Lancashire. From the point of view of the Congress, this was a gross betrayal of the national cause, and it was characterized as such. The representative of the Bombay mill owners in the Assembly also consistently ran down the Congress and "extremists" while most of us were in jail.

The part that many capitalist elements have played in India during the past few years has been scandalous, even from the Congress and nationalist viewpoint. As for the big zamindars and talukdars, they ranged themselves completely against the Congress in the Round Table Conference, and they openly and aggressively declared themselves on the side of the Government right through civil disobedience. It was with their help that Government passed repressive legislation in various provinces embodying the ordinances. And in the United Provinces Council the great majority of the zamindar members voted against the release of civil disobedience prisoners.

The idea that Gandhiji was forced to launch seemingly aggressive movements in 1921 and 1930 because of mass pressure, is also absolutely wrong. Mass stirrings there were, of course, but on both occasions it was Gandhiji who forced the pace. In 1921 he carried the Congress almost single-handed and plunged it into nonco-operation. In 1930 it would have been quite impossible to have any aggressive and effective direct action movement if he had resisted it in any way.

It is very unfortunate that foolish and ill-informed criticisms of a personal nature are made, because they divert attention from the real issues. To attack Gandhiji's *bona fides* is to injure oneself and one's own cause, for to the millions of India he stands as the embodiment of truth, and anyone who knows him at all realizes the passionate earnestness with which he is always seeking to do right.

Communists in India have associated with the industrial workers of the big towns. They have little knowledge of, or contact with, the rural areas. The industrial workers, important as they are, and likely to be more so in the future, must take second place before the peasants, for the problem of today in India is the problem of the peasantry. Congress workers, on the other hand, have spread all over these rural areas, and, in the ordinary course, the Congress must develop into a vast peasant organization. Peasants are seldom revolutionary after their immediate objective is attained, and it is likely that sometime in the future the usual problem of city versus village and industrial worker versus peasant will rise in India also.

It has been my privilege to be associated very closely with a large number of Congress leaders and workers, and I could not wish for a finer set of men and women. And yet I have differed from them on vital issues, and often I have felt a little weary at finding that they do not appreciate or understand something that seems to me quite obvious. It was not due to want of intelligence; somehow we moved in different ideological grooves. I realize how difficult it is to cross these boundaries suddenly. They constitute different philosophies of life, and we grow into them gradually and unconsciously. It is futile to blame the other party. Socialism involves a certain psychological outlook on life and its problems. It is more than mere logic. So also are the other outlooks based on heredity, upbringing, the unseen influences of the past, and our present environments. Only life itself with its bitter lessons forces us along new paths and ultimately, which is far harder, makes us think differently. Perhaps we may help a little in this process. And perhaps

> *On rencontre sa destinée*
> *Souvent par les chemins q'on prend pour l'éviter.*

## XXXVI

# WHAT IS RELIGION?

OUR PEACEFUL AND monotonous routine in jail was suddenly upset in the middle of September 1932 by a bombshell. News came that Gandhiji had decided to "fast unto death" in disapproval of the separate electorates given by Mr. Ramsay MacDonald's communal award to the depressed classes.[1] What a capacity he had to give shocks to people! Suddenly all manner of ideas rushed into my head; all kinds of possibilities and contingencies rose up before me and upset my equilibrium completely. For two days I was in darkness with no light to show the way out, my heart sinking when I thought of some results of Gandhiji's action. The personal aspect was powerful enough, and I thought with anguish that I might not see him again. It was over a year ago that I had seen him last on board ship on the way to England. Was that going to be my last sight of him?

And then I felt annoyed with him for choosing a side issue for his final sacrifice. What would be the result on our freedom movement? Would not the larger issues fade into the background, for the time being at least? And, if he attained his immediate object and got a joint electorate for the depressed classes, would not that result in a reaction and a feeling that something had been achieved and nothing more need be done for a while? And was not his action a recognition, and in part an acceptance, of the communal award and the general scheme of things as sponsored by the Government? Was this consistent with nonco-operation and civil disobedience? After so much sacrifice and

[1] A provisional decree determining the degree of representation to be held by various Indian groups in the provincial assemblies. It was opposed for many reasons by Indian nationalists, and by Gandhi particularly, because it established a separate electorate for the depressed classes and thus, in his view, widened the cleavage between these classes and other Hindus.—Ed.

brave endeavor, was our movement to tail off into something insignificant?

I felt angry with him at his religious and sentimental approach to a political question, and his frequent references to God in connection with it. He even seemed to suggest that God had indicated the very date of the fast. What a terrible example to set!

If Bapu [2] died! What would India be like then? And how would her politics run? There seemed to be a dreary and dismal future ahead, and despair seized my heart when I thought of it.

So I thought and thought, while confusion reigned in my head, with anger and hopelessness, and love for him who was the cause of this upheaval. I hardly knew what to do, and I was irritable and short-tempered with everybody, most of all with myself.

And then a strange thing happened to me. I had quite an emotional crisis, and at the end of it I felt calmer, and the future seemed not so dark. Bapu had a curious knack of doing the right thing at the psychological moment, and it might be that his action—impossible to justify as it was from my point of view—would lead to great results, not only in the narrow field in which it was confined, but in the wider aspects of our national struggle. And, even if Bapu died, our struggle for freedom would go on. So whatever happened, one had to keep ready and fit for it. Having made up my mind to face even Gandhiji's death without flinching, I felt calm and collected and ready to face the world and all it might offer.

Then came news of the tremendous upheaval all over the country, a magic wave of enthusiasm running through Hindu society, and untouchability appeared to be doomed. What a magician, I thought, was this little man sitting in Yeravda Prison, and how well he knew how to pull the strings that move people's hearts!

A telegram from him reached me. It was the first message I had received from him since my conviction, and it did me good to hear from him after that long interval. In this telegram he said:

> During all these days of agony you have been before mind's eye. I am most anxious to know your opinion. You know how I value your opinion. Saw Indu [and] Sarup's children. Indu looked happy and in possession of more flesh. Doing very well. Wire reply. Love.

[2] "Bapu" means "father" in Gujrati. Gandhi was called "Bapu" by his early followers in Gujrat, and the term has now spread all over India.—Ed.

237

It was extraordinary, and yet it was characteristic of him, that in the agony of his fast and in the midst of his many preoccupations, he should refer to the visit of my daughter and my sister's children to him, and even mention that Indira had put on flesh! (My sister was also in prison then and all these children were at school in Poona.) He never forgets the seemingly little things in life which really mean so much.

News also came to me just then that some settlement had been reached over the electorate issue. The superintendent of the jail was good enough to allow me to send an answer to Gandhiji, and I sent him the following telegram:

Your telegram and brief news that some settlement reached filled me with relief and joy. First news of your decision to fast caused mental agony and confusion, but ultimately optimism triumphed and I regained peace of mind. No sacrifice too great for suppressed downtrodden classes. Freedom must be judged by freedom of lowest but feel danger of other issues obscuring only goal. Am unable to judge from religious viewpoint. Danger your methods being exploited by others but how can I presume to advise a magician. Love.

A "pact" was signed by various people gathered in Poona; with unusual speed the British Prime Minister accepted it and varied his previous award accordingly, and the fast was broken. I disliked such pacts and agreements greatly, but I welcomed the Poona Pact apart from its contents.

The excitement was over, and we reverted to our jail routine. News of the Harijan movement and of Gandhiji's activities from prison came to us, and I was not very happy about it. There was no doubt that a tremendous push had been given to the movement to end untouchability and raise the unhappy depressed classes, not so much by the pact as by the crusading enthusiasm created all over the country. That was to be welcomed. But it was equally obvious that civil disobedience had suffered. The country's attention had been diverted to other issues, and many Congress workers had turned to the Harijan cause. Probably most of these people wanted an excuse to revert to safer activities which did not involve the risk of jail-going or, worse still, lathee blows and confiscations of property. That was natural, and it was not fair to expect all the thousands of our workers to keep always ready for intense suffering and the break-up and destruction of their homes. But still it

238

was painful to watch this slow decay of our great movement. Civil disobedience was, however, still going on, and occasionally there were mass demonstrations like the Calcutta Congress in March–April 1933. Gandhiji was in Yeravda Prison, but he had been given certain privileges to meet people and issue directions for the Harijan movements. Somehow this took away from the sting of his being in prison. All this depressed me.

Many months later, early in May 1933, Gandhiji began his twenty-one-day fast. The first news of this had again come as a shock to me, but I accepted it as an inevitable occurrence and schooled myself to it. Indeed I was irritated that people should urge him to give it up, after he had made up his mind and declared it to the public. For me the fast was an incomprehensible thing, and, if I had been asked before the decision had been taken, I would certainly have spoken strongly against it. But I attached great value to Gandhiji's word, and it seemed to me wrong for anyone to try to make him break it, in a personal matter which, to him, was of supreme importance. So, unhappy as I was, I put up with it.

A few days before beginning his fast he wrote to me, a typical letter which moved me very much. As he asked for a reply I sent him the following telegram:

Your letter. What can I say about matters I do not understand? I feel lost in strange country where you are the only familiar landmark and I try to grope my way in dark but I stumble. Whatever happens my love and thoughts will be with you.

I had struggled against my utter disapproval of his act and my desire not to hurt him. I felt, however, that I had not sent him a cheerful message, and now that he was bent on undergoing his terrible ordeal, which might even end in his death, I ought to cheer him up as much as I could. Little things make a difference psychologically, and he would have to strain every nerve to survive. I felt also that we should accept whatever happened, even his death, if unhappily it should occur, with a stout heart. So I sent him another telegram:

Now that you are launched on your great enterprise may I send you again love and greetings and assure you that I feel more clearly now that whatever happens it is well and whatever happens you win.

He survived the fast. On the first day of it he was discharged from prison, and on his advice civil disobedience was suspended for six weeks.

Again I watched the emotional upheaval of the country during the fast, and I wondered more and more if this was the right method in politics. It seemed to be sheer revivalism, and clear thinking had not a ghost of a chance against it. All India, or most of it, stared reverently at the Mahatma and expected him to perform miracle after miracle and put an end to untouchability and get *Swaraj* and so on—and did precious little itself! And Gandhiji did not encourage others to think; his insistence was only on purity and sacrifice. I felt that I was drifting further and further away from him mentally, in spite of my strong emotional attachment to him. Often enough he was guided in his political activities by an unerring instinct. He had the flair for action, but was the way of faith the right way to train a nation? It might pay for a short while, but in the long run?

And I could not understand how he could accept, as he seemed to do, the present social order, which was based on violence and conflict. Within me also conflict raged, and I was torn between rival loyalties. I knew that there was trouble ahead for me, when the enforced protection of jail was removed. I felt lonely and homeless; and India, to whom I had given my love and for whom I had labored, seemed a strange and bewildering land to me. Was it my fault that I could not enter into the spirit and ways of thinking of my countrymen? Even with my closest associates I felt that an invisible barrier came between us, and, unhappy at being unable to overcome it, I shrank back into my shell. The old world seemed to envelop them, the old world of past ideologies, hopes, and desires. The new world was yet far distant.

> *Wandering between two worlds, one dead,*
> *The other powerless to be born,*
> *With nowhere yet to rest his head.*

India is supposed to be a religious country above everything else; Hindu, Moslem, Sikh, and others take pride in their faiths and testify to their truth by breaking heads. The spectacle of what is called religion, or at any rate organized religion, in India and elsewhere has filled me with horror, and I have frequently condemned it and wished to make a clean sweep of it. Almost always it seems to stand for blind belief and reaction, dogma and bigotry, superstition and exploitation, and the preservation of vested interests. And yet I knew well that there was something else in it, something which supplied a deep inner craving of human beings. How else could it have been the tremendous power it has been and brought peace and comfort to innumerable tortured souls? Was that peace merely the shelter of blind belief and absence of questioning, the calm that comes from being safe in harbor, protected from the storms of the open sea, or was it something more? In some cases certainly it was something more.

But organized religion, whatever its past may have been, today is very largely an empty form devoid of real content. It has been filled up by some totally different substance. And, even where something of value still remains, it is enveloped by other and harmful contents.

That seems to have happened in our Eastern religions as well as in the Western. The Church of England is perhaps the most obvious example of a religion which is not a religion in any real sense of the word. Partly that applies to all organized Protestantism, but the Church of England has probably gone further because it has long been a State political department.[3]

Many of its votaries are undoubtedly of the highest character, but it is remarkable how that Church has served the purposes of British imperialism and given both capitalism and imperialism a moral and Christian covering. It has sought to justify, from the highest ethical standards, British predatory policy in Asia and Africa and given that extraordinary and enviable feeling of being always in the right to the English. Whether the Church has helped in producing this attitude of smug rectitude or is itself a product of it, I do not know. Other less favored countries on the continent of Europe and in America often accuse the English of hypocrisy—*perfide Albion* is an old taunt—but the accusation is probably the outcome of envy at British success, and certainly no other imperialist Power can afford to throw stones at England, for its own record is equally shady. No nation that is consciously hypocritical could have the reserves of strength that the British have repeatedly shown, and the brand of "religion" which they have adopted has apparently helped them in this by blunting their moral susceptibilities where their own interests were concerned. Other peoples and nations have often behaved far worse than the British have done, but they have never succeeded, quite to the same extent, in making a virtue of what profited them. All of us find it remarkably easy to spot

[3] In India the Church of England has been almost indistinguishable from the Government. The officially paid (out of Indian revenues) priests and chaplains are the symbols of the imperial power just as the higher services are.

the mote in the other's eye and overlook the beam in our own, but perhaps the British excel at this performance.

Protestantism tried to adapt itself to new conditions and wanted to have the best of both worlds. It succeeded remarkably so far as this world was concerned, but from the religious point of view it fell, as an organized religion, between two stools, and religion gradually gave place to sentimentality and big business. Roman Catholicism escaped this fate, as it stuck on to the old stool, and, so long as that stool holds, it will flourish. Today it seems to be the only living religion, in the restricted sense of the word, in the West. A Roman Catholic friend sent me in prison many books on Catholicism and papal encyclicals, and I read them with interest. Studying them, I realized the hold it had on such large numbers of people. It offered, as Islam and popular Hinduism offer, a safe anchorage from doubt and mental conflict, an assurance of a future life which will make up for the deficiencies of this life.

I am afraid it is impossible for me to seek harborage in this way. I prefer the open sea, with all its storms and tempests. Nor am I greatly interested in the afterlife, in what happens after death. I find the problems of this life sufficiently absorbing to fill my mind. The traditional Chinese outlook, fundamentally ethical and yet irreligious or tinged with religious skepticism, has an appeal for me, though in its application to life I may not agree. It is the *Tao,* the path to be followed and the way of life, that interests me; how to understand life, not to reject it but to accept it, to conform to it, and to improve it. But the usual religious outlook does not concern itself with this world. It seems to me to be the enemy of clear thought, for it is based not only on the acceptance without demur of certain fixed and unalterable theories and dogmas, but also on sentiment and emotion and passion. It is far removed from what I consider spiritual and things of the spirit, and it deliberately or unconsciously shuts its eyes to reality lest reality may not fit in with preconceived notions. It is narrow and intolerant of other opinions and ideas; it is self-centered and egotistic; and it often allows itself to be exploited by self-seekers and opportunists.

This does not mean that men of religion have not been and are not still often of the highest moral and spiritual type. But it does mean that the religious outlook does not help, and even hinders, the moral and spiritual progress of a people, if morality and spirituality are to be judged by this world's standards, and not by the hereafter. Usually religion becomes an asocial quest for God or the Absolute, and the religious man is concerned far more with his own salvation than with the good of society. The mystic tries to rid himself of self, and in the process usually becomes obsessed with it. Moral standards have no relation to social needs but are based on a highly metaphysical doctrine of sin. And organized religion invariably becomes a vested interest and thus inevitably a reactionary force opposing change and progress.

It is well known that the Christian church in the early days did not help the slaves to improve their social status. The slaves became the feudal serfs of the Middle Ages of Europe because of economic conditions. The attitude of the Church, as late as two hundred years ago (in 1727), was well exemplified in a letter written by the Bishop of London to the slave owners of the southern colonies of America.[4]

"Christianity," wrote the Bishop, "and the embracing of the gospel does not make the least alteration in Civil property or in any of the duties which belong to civil relations; but in all these respects it continues Persons just in the same State as it found them. The Freedom which Christianity gives is Freedom from the bondage of Sin and Satan and from the Dominion of Men's Lusts and Passions and inordinate Desires; but as to their outward condition, whatever that was before, whether bond or free, their being baptised and becoming Christians makes no manner of change in them."

No organized religion today will express itself in this outspoken manner, but essentially its attitude to property and the existing social order will be the same.

"No man can live without religion," Gandhiji has written somewhere. "There are some who in the egotism of their reason declare that they have nothing to do with religion. But that is like a man saying that he breathes, but that he has no nose." Again he says: "My devotion to truth has drawn me into the field of politics; and I can say without the slightest hesitation, and yet in all humility, that those who say that religion has nothing to do with politics do not know what religion means." Perhaps it would have been more correct if he had said that most of these people who want to exclude religion from life and politics mean by that word "religion" something very different from what he means. It is obvious that he is using it in a sense—probably moral and ethical more than any other—different from that of the critics of religion.

[4] This letter is quoted in Reinhold Niebuhr's *Moral Man and Immoral Society* (p. 78), a book which is exceedingly interesting and stimulating.

# XXXVII

# THE "DUAL POLICY" OF THE BRITISH GOVERNMENT

THE HARIJAN MOVEMENT was going on, guided by Gandhiji from Yeravda Prison and later from outside. There was a great agitation for removing the barriers to temple entry, and a bill to that effect was introduced in the Legislative Assembly. And then the remarkable spectacle was witnessed of an outstanding leader of the Congress going from house to house in Delhi, visiting the members of the Assembly and canvassing for their votes for this temple entry bill. Gandhiji himself sent an appeal through him to the Assembly members. And yet civil disobedience was still going on and people were going to prison; the Assembly had been boycotted by the Congress, and all our members had withdrawn from it. The rump that remained and the others who had filled the vacancies had distinguished themselves in this crisis by opposition to the Congress and support of the Government. A majority of them had helped the Government to pass repressive legislation giving some permanence to the extraordinary provisions of the ordinances.

I was amazed at Gandhiji's appeal, under the circumstances then existing, and even more so by the strenuous efforts of Rajagopalachari, who, a few weeks before, had been the acting president of the Congress. Civil disobedience, of course, suffered by these activities; but what hurt me more was the moral side. To me, for Gandhiji or any Congress leader to countenance such activities appeared immoral and almost a breach of faith with the large numbers of people in jail or carrying on the struggle. But I knew that his way of looking at it was different.

The Government attitude to this temple entry bill, then and subsequently, was very revealing. It put every possible difficulty in the way of its promoters, went on postponing it and encouraging opposition to it, and then finally declared its own opposition to it and killed it. That, to a greater or lesser extent, has been its attitude to all measures of social reform in India, and on the plea of noninterference with religion, it has prevented social progress. But this, it need hardly be said, has not prevented it from criticizing our social evils and encouraging others to do so. By a fluke, the Sarda child marriage restraint bill became law, but the subsequent history of this unhappy act showed more than anything else how much averse to enforcing any such measure the Government was. The Government that could produce ordinances over-night, creating novel offenses and providing for vicarious punishment, and could send scores of thousands of people to prison for breach of their provisions, apparently quailed at the prospect of enforcing one of its regular laws like the Sarda Act. The effect of the Act was first to increase tremendously the very evil it was intended to combat, for people rushed to take advantage of the intervening six months of grace which the Act very foolishly allowed. And then it was discovered that the Act was more or less of a joke and could be easily ignored without any steps being taken by Government. Not even the slightest attempt at propaganda was made officially, and most people in the villages never knew what the Act was. They heard distorted accounts of it from Hindu and Moslem village preachers, who themselves seldom knew the correct facts.

This extraordinary spirit of toleration of social evils in India which the British Government has shown is obviously not due to any par-tiality for them. This is due to their close association with the most reactionary elements in India. As opposition to their rule increases, they have to seek strange allies, and today the firmest champions of British rule in India are the extreme communalists and the religious reactionaries and obscurantists.

If the British Government was quiescent and took no steps to popu-larize the Sarda Act and to enforce it, why did not the Congress or other nonofficial organizations carry on propaganda in favor of it? This question is often put by British and other foreign critics. So far as the Congress is concerned, it has been engaged during the last fifteen years, and especially since 1930, in a fierce life-and-death strug-gle for national freedom with the British rulers. The other organiza-tions have no real strength or contact with the masses. Men and women of ideals and force of character and influence among the masses were drawn into the Congress and spent much of their time in British prisons.

But the real reason why the Congress and other nonofficial organi-zations cannot do much for social reform goes deeper. We suffer from the disease of nationalism; that absorbs our attention, and it will con-tinue to do so till we get political freedom.

Past experience shows us that we can make little social progress under present conditions, in spite of apparent transfers of subjects to elected ministers. I am sure that if the Congress started a nationwide propa-

ganda for the greater use of soap it would come in conflict with Gov-·
ernment in many places.

I do not think it is very difficult to convert the masses to social reform if the State takes the matter in hand. But alien rulers are always
suspect, and they cannot go far in the process of conversion. If the alien
element were removed and economic changes were given precedence,
an energetic administration could easily introduce far-reaching social
reforms.

But social reform and the Sarda Act and the Harijan movement
did not fill our minds in prison, except in so far as I felt a little irritated by the Harijan movement because it had come in the way of
civil disobedience. Early in May 1933, following Gandhiji's twenty-one-
day fast, civil disobedience had been suspended for six weeks, and we
waited anxiously for further developments. That suspension had given
a final blow to the movement, for one cannot play fast and loose with
a national struggle and switch it on and off at will. Even before the
suspension the leadership of the movement had been singularly weak
and ineffective. There were petty conferences being held, and all manner of rumors spread which militated against active work. Some of
the acting presidents of the Congress were very estimable men, but it
was unkindness to them to make them generals of an active campaign.
There was too much of a hint of tiredness about them, of a desire to
get out of a difficult position. There was some discontent against this
vacillation and indecision in high quarters, but it was difficult to express it in an organized way, as all Congress bodies were unlawful.

In the middle of June the period of suspension of civil disobedience
was extended by another six weeks. Meanwhile the Government had
in no way toned down its aggression. In the Andaman Islands, political
prisoners (those convicted in Bengal for acts of revolutionary violence
were sent there) were on hunger strike on the question of treatment,
and one or two of them died—starved to death. Others lay dying. People who addressed meetings in India in protest of what was happening
in the Andamans were themselves arrested and sentenced. We were
not only to suffer, but we were not even to complain, even though
prisoners died by the terrible ordeal of the hunger strike, having no
other means of protest open to them. Some months later, in September
1933 (when I was out of prison), an appeal was issued over a number
of signatures including Rabindranath Tagore, C. F. Andrews, and
many other well-known people, mostly unconnected with the Congress,
asking for more humanitarian treatment of the Andamans' prisoners,

and preferably for their transfer to Indian jails. The Home Member of the Government of India expressed his great displeasure at this statement, and criticized the signatories strongly for their sympathy for the prisoners. Later, as far as I can remember, the expression of such sympathy was made a punishable offense in Bengal.

Before the second six weeks of suspension of civil disobedience were over, news came to us in Dehra Dun Jail that Gandhiji had called an informal conference at Poona. Two or three hundred people met there, and, on Gandhiji's advice, mass civil disobedience was suspended, but individual civil disobedience was permitted, and all secret methods were barred. The decisions were not very inspiring, but I did not particularly object to them so far as they went. To stop mass civil disobedience was to recognize and stabilize existing conditions, for, in reality, there was no mass movement then. Secret work was merely a pretense that we were carrying on, and often it demoralized, having regard to the character of our movement. To some extent it was necessary in order to send instructions and keep contacts, but civil disobedience itself could not be secret.

What surprised me and distressed me was the absence of any real discussion at Poona of the existing situation and of our objectives. Congressmen had met together after nearly two years of fierce conflict and repression, and much had happened meanwhile in the world at large and in India, including the publication of the White Paper containing the British Government's proposals for constitutional reform. We had to put up during this period with enforced silence, and on the other side there had been ceaseless and perverted propaganda to obscure the issues. It was frequently stated, not only by supporters of the Government but by Liberals and others, that the Congress had given up its objective of independence. The least that should have been done, I thought, was to lay stress on our political objective, to make it clear again and, if possible, to add to it social and economic objectives. Instead of this, the discussion seems to have been entirely confined to the relative merits of mass and individual civil disobedience, and the desirability or otherwise of secrecy. There was also some strange talk of "peace" with the Government. Gandhiji sent a telegram to the Viceroy, as far as I remember, asking for an interview, to which the Viceroy replied with a "No," and then Gandhiji sent a second telegram mentioning something about "honorable peace." Where was this elusive peace that was being sought, when the Government was triumphantly trying to crush the nation in every way, and people were starving to death in the Andamans? But I knew that, whatever happened, it was Gandhiji's way always to offer the olive branch.

Repression was going on in full swing, and all the special laws suppressing public activities were in force. In February 1933 even a memorial meeting on my father's death anniversary was prohibited by the police, although it was a non-Congress meeting, and such a good Moderate as Sir Tej Bahadur Sapru was to have presided over it. And as a vision of future favors to come we had been presented with the White Paper.

This was a remarkable document, a perusal of which left one gasping for breath. India was to be converted into a glorified Indian state, with a dominating influence of the states' feudal representatives in the federation. But in the states themselves no outside interference would be tolerated, and undiluted autocracy would continue to prevail there. The real imperial links, the chains of debt, would bind us forever to the City of London, and the currency and monetary policy would also be controlled, through a Reserve Bank, by the Bank of England. There would be an impregnable defense of all vested rights, and additional vested interests were going to be created. Our revenues were mortgaged up to the hilt for the benefit of these vested interests. The great imperial services, which we loved so much, would continue uncontrolled and untouched, to train us for further installments of self-government. There was going to be provincial autonomy, but the Governor would be a benevolent and all-powerful dictator keeping us in order. And high above all would sit the All-Highest, the supreme Dictator, the Viceroy, with complete powers to do what he would and check when he desired. Truly, the genius of the British ruling class for colonial government was never more in evidence, and well may the Hitlers and Mussolinis admire them and look with envy on the Viceroy of India.

A constitution having been produced which tied up India hand and foot, a collection of "special responsibilities" and safeguards were added as additional fetters, making the unhappy country a prisoner incapable of movement. As Mr. Neville Chamberlain said: "They had done their best to surround the proposals with all the safeguards the wit of man could devise."

Further, we were informed that for these favors we would have to pay heavily—to begin with a lump sum of a few crores, and then annual payment. We could not have the blessings of *Swaraj* without adequate payment. We had been suffering under the delusion that India was poverty-stricken and already had too heavy a burden to carry, and we had looked to freedom to lighten it. That had been for the masses, the urge for freedom. But it now appeared that the burden was to become heavier.

This Gilbertian solution of the Indian problem was offered with true British grace, and we were told how generous our rulers were. Never before had an imperial Power of its own free will offered such power and opportunities to a subject people. And a great debate arose in England between the donors and those who, horrified at such generosity, objected to it. This was the outcome of the many comings and goings between India and England during three years, of the three Round Table Conferences, and innumerable committees and consultations.

Congress policy then was mainly one of defiance of the ordinance laws and other repressive measures, and this led to jail. Congress and the nation were exhausted after the long struggle and could not bring any effective pressure on the Government.

Naked coercion, as India was experiencing, however, is an expensive affair for the rulers. Even for them it is a painful and nerve-shaking ordeal, and they know well that ultimately it weakens their foundations. It exposes continually the real character of their rule, both to the people coerced and the world at large. They infinitely prefer to put on the velvet glove to hide the iron fist. Nothing is more irritating and, in the final analysis, harmful to a Government than to have to deal with people who will not bend to its will, whatever the consequences. So even sporadic defiance of the repressive measures had value; it strengthened the people and sapped the morale of Government.

The moral consideration was even more important to us. In a famous passage Thoreau has said: "At a time when men and women are unjustly imprisoned the place for just men and women is also in prison." Many of us often feel that a moral life under existing conditions is intolerable, when, even apart from civil disobedience, many of our colleagues are always in prison and the coercive apparatus of the State is continually repressing us and humiliating us, as well as helping in the exploitation of our people. In our own country we move about as suspects, shadowed and watched, our words recorded lest they infringe the all-pervading law of sedition, our correspondence opened, the possibility of some executive prohibition or arrest always facing us. For us the choice is: abject submission to the power of the State, spiritual degradation, the denial of the truth that is in us, and our moral prostitution for purposes that we consider base—or opposition with all the consequences thereof. No one likes to go to jail or to invite trouble. But often jail is preferable to the other alternative.

## XXXVIII

## THE END OF A LONG TERM

THE TIME FOR my discharge was drawing near. I had received the usual remissions for "good behavior," and this had reduced my two-year term by three and a half months. My peace of mind, or rather the general dullness of the mind which prison produces, was being disturbed by the excitement created by the prospect of release. What must I do outside? A difficult question, and the hesitation I had in answering it took away from the joy of going out. But even that was a momentary feeling; my long-suppressed energy was bubbling up, and I was eager to be out.

The end of July 1933 brought a painful and very disturbing piece of news—the sudden death of J. M. Sen-Gupta under detention. He had been made a State prisoner on his return from Europe early in 1932, while he was still on board ship in Bombay. Since then he had been a prisoner or a *détenu,* and his health had deteriorated. Various facilities were given to him by the Government, but evidently they could not check the course of the disease. His funeral in Calcutta was the occasion for a remarkable mass demonstration and tribute; it seemed that the long-pent-up suffering soul of Bengal had found an outlet for a while at least.

So Sen-Gupta had gone. Subhas Bose, another State prisoner whose health had broken down under years of internment and prison, had at last been permitted by the Government to go to Europe for treatment. The veteran Vithalbhai Patel also lay ill in Europe. And how many others had broken down in health or died, unable to stand the physical strain of jail life and ceaseless activity outside! How many, though outwardly not much changed, had suffered deeper mental derangements and developed complexes on account of the abnormal lives they had been made to lead!

Sen-Gupta's death made me vividly aware of all this terrible, silent suffering going on throughout the country, and I felt weary and depressed. To what end was all this? To what end?

I had been fortunate in my own health, and in spite of the strains and irregular life of Congress activity, I had, on the whole, kept well. Partly, I suppose, this was due to the good constitution I had inherited, partly to my care of the body. Illness and weak health as well as too much fat seemed to me a most unbecoming state of affairs, and, with the help of exercise, plenty of fresh air, and simple food, I managed to keep away from them.

I have cared little for food fads, and have only avoided overeating and rich foods. Like nearly all Kashmiri Brahmans, our family was a meat-eating one, and from childhood onward I had always taken meat, although I never fancied it much. With the coming of nonco-operation in 1920 I gave up meat and became a vegetarian. I remained a vegetarian till a visit to Europe six years later, when I relapsed to meat eating. On my return to India I became a vegetarian again, and since then I have been more or less a vegetarian. Meat eating seems to agree with me well, but I have developed a distaste for it, and it gives me a feeling of coarseness.

My periods of ill-health, chiefly in prison in 1932, when for many months I had a rise of temperature every day, annoyed me, because they hurt my conceit of good health. And for the first time I did not think, as I used to do, in terms of abounding life and energy, but a specter of a gradual decay and a wearing away rose up before me and alarmed me. I do not think I am particularly frightened of death. But a slow deterioration, bodily and mental, was quite another matter. However, my fears proved exaggerated, and I managed to get rid of the indisposition and bring my body under control. Long sun baths during the winter helped me to get back my feeling of well-being. While my companions in prison would shiver in their coats and shawls, I would sit, bare-bodied, delightfully warmed up by the sun's embrace. This was only possible in north India during the winter, as elsewhere the sun is usually too hot.

Among my exercises one pleased me particularly—the *shīrshāsana,* standing on the head with the palms of the hands, fingers interlocked, supporting the back of the head, elbows on the floor, body vertical, upside down. I suppose physically this exercise is very good: I liked it even more for its psychological effect on me. The slightly comic position increased my good humor and made me a little more tolerant of life's vagaries.

My usual good health and the bodily sense of well-being have been of very great help to me in getting over periods of depression, which are inevitable in prison life. They have helped me also in accommodating myself to changing conditions in prison or outside. I have had many shocks which at the time seemed to bowl me over, but to my own surprise I have recovered sooner than I expected. I suppose a test of my fundamental sobriety and sanity is the fact that I hardly know what a bad headache is, nor have I ever been troubled with insomnia. I have escaped these common diseases of civilization, as also bad eyesight, in spite of excessive use of the eyes for reading and writing, sometimes in a bad light in jail. An eye specialist expressed his amazement last year at my good eyesight. Eight years before he had prophesied that I would have to take to spectacles in another year or two. He was very much mistaken, and I am still carrying on successfully without them. Although these facts might establish my reputation for sobriety and sanity, I might add that I have a horror of people who are inescapably and unchangingly sane and sober.

While I waited for my discharge from prison, the new form of civil disobedience for individuals was beginning outside. Gandhiji decided to give the lead, and, after giving full notice to the authorities, he started on August 1 with the intention of preaching civil resistance to the Gujrat peasantry. He was immediately arrested, sentenced to one year, and sent back again to his cell in Yeravda. I was glad he had gone back. But soon a new complication arose. Gandhiji claimed the same facilities for carrying on Harijan work from prison as he had had before; the Government refused to grant them. Suddenly we heard that Gandhiji had started fasting again on this issue. It seemed an extraordinarily trivial matter for such a tremendous step. It was quite impossible for me to understand his decision, even though he might be completely right in his argument with the Government. We could do nothing, and we looked on, bewildered.

After a week of the fast his condition grew rapidly worse. He had been removed to a hospital, but he was still a prisoner, and Government would not give in on the question of facilities for Harijan work. He lost the will to live (which he had during his previous fasts) and allowed himself to go downhill. The end seemed to be near. He said good-by and even made dispositions of the few personal articles that were lying about him, giving some to the nurses. But the Government had no intention of allowing him to die on their hands, and that evening he was suddenly discharged. It was just in time to save him. Another day and perhaps it would have been too late. Probably a great deal of the credit for saving him should go to C. F. Andrews, who had rushed to India, contrary to Gandhiji's advice.

Meanwhile I was transferred from Dehra Dun Jail on August 23, and I returned to Naini Prison after more than a year and a half's residence in other jails. Just then news came of my mother's sudden illness and her removal to hospital. On August 30, 1933, I was discharged from Naini because my mother's condition was considered serious. Ordinarily I would have been released, at the latest, on September 12 when my term expired. I was thus given an additional thirteen days of remission by the Provincial Government.

Immediately after my release, I hastened to Lucknow to my mother's bedside, and I remained with her for some days. I had come out of prison after a fairly long period, and I felt detached and out of touch with my surroundings. I realized with a little shock, as we all do, that the world had gone on moving and changing while I lay stagnating in prison. Children and boys and girls growing up; marriages, births, deaths; love and hate, work and play, tragedy and comedy. New interests in life, new subjects for conversation, always there was a little element of surprise in what I saw and heard. Life seemed to have passed by, leaving me in a backwater. It was not a wholly pleasant feeling. Soon I would have adapted myself to my environment, but I felt no urge to do so. I realized that I was only having a brief outing outside prison, and would have to go back again before long. So why trouble myself about adaptation to something which I would leave soon?

Politically, India was more or less quiet; public activities were largely controlled and suppressed by the Government, and arrests occasionally took place. But the silence of India then was full of significance. It was the ominous silence which follows exhaustion after experiencing a period of fierce repression, a silence which is often very eloquent, but is beyond the ken of governments that repress. India was the ideal police state, and the police mentality pervaded all spheres of government. Outwardly all nonconformity was suppressed, and a vast army of spies and secret agents covered the land. There was an atmosphere of demoralization and an all-pervading fear among the people. Any political activity, especially in the rural areas, was immediately suppressed, and the various provincial governments were trying to hound out Congressmen from the service of municipalities and local boards. Every person who had been to prison as a civil resister was unfit, according to Government, for teaching in a municipal school or serving the municipality in any other way. Great pressure was brought to bear on municipalities, etc., and threats were held out that Government grants would be stopped if the offending Congressmen were not dismissed. The most notorious example of this coercion took place in the Calcutta Corporation. Ultimately, I believe, the Bengal Government passed a law against the employment by the Corporation of persons who had been convicted for political offenses.

Reports of Nazi excesses in Germany had a curious effect on British officials and their press in India. They gave them a justification for all they had done in India, and it was pointed out to us, with a glow of conscious virtue, how much worse our lot would have been if the Nazis had had anything to do with us. New standards and records had been set up by the Nazis, and it was certainly not an easy matter to rival them. Perhaps our lot would have been worse; it is difficult for me to judge, for I have not all the facts of the occurrences that have taken place in various parts of India during the past five years. The British Government in India believes in the charity that its right hand should not know what its left hand does, and so it has turned down every suggestion for an impartial inquiry, although such inquiries are always weighted on the official side. I think it is true that the average Englishman hates brutality, and I cannot conceive English people openly glorying in and repeating lovingly the word *Brutalität* (or its English equivalent), as the Nazis do. Even when they indulge in the deed, they are a little ashamed of it. But whether we are Germans or English or Indians, I am afraid our veneer of civilized conduct is thin enough, and, when passions are aroused, it rubs off and reveals something that is not good to look at.

I have had ample leisure in jail to read the speeches of high officials, their answers to questions in the Assembly and councils, and Government statements. I noticed, during the years 1932 to 1935, a marked change coming over them, and this change became progressively more and more obvious. They became more threatening and minatory, developing more and more the style of a sergeant-major addressing his men. A remarkable example of this was a speech delivered by the Commissioner of, I think, the Midnapur Division in Bengal in November or December 1933. *Vae victis* seems to run like a thread through these utterances. Nonofficial Europeans, in Bengal especially, go even further than the official variety, and both in their speeches and actions have shown a very decided fascist tendency.

Yet another revealing instance of brutalization was the recent public hangings of some convicted criminals in Sind. Because crime was on the increase in Sind, the authorities there decided to execute these criminals publicly, as a warning to others. Every facility was given to the public to attend and watch this ghastly spectacle, and it is said that many thousands came.

So after my discharge from prison I surveyed political and economic conditions in India, and felt little enthusiasm.

I had no desire to go back to prison. I had had enough of it. But I could not see how I could escape it under the existing circumstances, unless I decided to retire from all political activity. I had no such intention, and so I felt that I was bound to come into conflict with the Government. At any moment some order might be served on me to do something, or to abstain from doing something, and all my nature rebelled at being forced to act in a particular way. An attempt was being made to cow and coerce the people of India. I was helpless and could do nothing on the wider field, but, at any rate, I could refuse personally to be cowed and coerced into submission.

Before I went back to prison, I wanted to attend to certain matters. My mother's illness claimed my attention first of all. Very slowly she improved; the process was so slow that for a year she was bedridden. I was eager to see Gandhiji, who lay recovering from his latest fast in Poona. For over two years I had not met him. I also wanted to meet as many of my provincial colleagues as possible to discuss, not only the existing political situation in India, but the world situation as well as the ideas that filled my mind. I thought then that the world was going rapidly toward a catastrophe, political and economic, and we ought to keep this in mind in drawing up our national programs.

My household affairs also claimed my attention. I had ignored them completely so far, and I had not even examined my father's papers since his death. We had cut down our expenditure greatly, but still it was far more than we could afford. And yet it was difficult to reduce it further, so long as we lived in that house of ours. We were not keeping a car because that was beyond our means, and also because, at any moment, it could be attached by Government. Faced by financial difficulties, I was diverted by the large mail of begging letters that I received. (The censor passed the lot on.) There was a general and very erroneous impression, especially in south India, that I was a wealthy person.

Soon after my release my younger sister, Krishna, got engaged to be married, and I was anxious to have the wedding early, before my enforced departure took place. Krishna herself had come out of prison a few months earlier after serving out a year.

As soon as my mother's health permitted it, I went to Poona to see Gandhiji. I was happy to see him again and to find that, though weak, he was making good progress. We had long talks. It was obvious that we differed considerably in our outlook on life and politics and economics; but I was grateful to him for the generous way in which he tried to come as far as he could to meet my viewpoint. Our correspondence, subsequently published, dealt with some of the wider issues that filled my mind, and, though they were referred to in vague language, the general drift was clear. I was happy to have Gandhiji's declaration that there must be a de-vesting of vested interests, though he laid stress that this should be by conversion, not compulsion. As some of his methods of conversion are not far removed, to my thinking, from courteous and considerate compulsion, the difference did not seem to me very great. I had the feeling with him then, as before, that though he might be averse to considering vague theories the logic of facts would take him, step by step, to the inevitability of fundamental social changes.

For the present, I thought then, this question did not arise. We were in the middle of our national struggle, and civil disobedience was still the program, in theory, of the Congress, although it had been restricted to individuals. We had to carry on as we were and try to spread socialistic ideas among the people, and especially among the more politically conscious Congress workers, so that when the time came for another declaration of policy we might be ready for a notable advance. Meanwhile, Congress was an unlawful organization, and the British Government was trying to crush it. We had to meet that attack.

The principal problem which faced Gandhiji was a personal one. What was he to do himself? He was in a tangle. If he went to jail again, the same question of Harijan privileges would arise and, presumably, the Government would not give in, and he would fast again. Would the same round be repeated? He refused to submit to such a cat-and-mouse policy, and said that if he fasted again for those privileges, the fast would continue even though he were released. That meant a fast to death.

The second possible course before him was not to court imprisonment during the year of his sentence (ten and a half months of this remained still) and devote himself to Harijan work. But at the same time he would meet Congress workers and advise them when necessary.

A third possibility he suggested to me was that he should retire from the Congress altogether for a while, and leave it in the hands of the "younger generation," as he put it.

The first course, ending, as it seemed, in his death by starvation, was impossible for any one of us to recommend. The third seemed very undesirable when the Congress was an illegal body. It would either result in the immediate withdrawal of civil disobedience and all forms of direct action and a going back to legality and constitutional activity, or in a Congress, outlawed and isolated, now even from Gandhiji, being crushed still further by Government. Besides, there was no question of any group's taking possession of an illegal organization which could not meet and discuss any policy. By a process of exclusion we arrived thus at the second course of action suggested by him. Most of us disliked it, and we knew that it would give a heavy blow to the remains of civil disobedience. If the leader had himself retired from the fight, it was not likely that many enthusiastic Congress workers would jump into the fire. But there seemed no other way out of the tangle, and Gandhiji made his announcement accordingly.

We agreed, Gandhiji and I, though perhaps for different reasons, that the time was not yet for a withdrawal of civil disobedience and that we had to carry on even at a low ebb. For the rest, I wanted to turn people's attention to socialistic doctrines and the world situation.

I spent a few days in Bombay on my way back. I was fortunate in catching Uday Shankar there and seeing his dancing. This was an unexpected treat which I enjoyed greatly. Theaters, music, cinema, talkies, radio and broadcasting—all this had been beyond my reach for many years, for even during my intervals of freedom I had been too engrossed in other activities. I have only been once to a talkie so far, and the great names of cinema stars are names only to me. I have missed the theater especially, and I have often read with envy of new productions in foreign countries. In northern India, even when I was out of jail, there was little opportunity of seeing good plays, for there were hardly any within reach.

Recently there has been an artistic awakening, led by the brilliant Tagore family, and its influence is already apparent all over India. But how can any art flourish widely when the people of the country are hampered and restricted and suppressed at every turn and live in an atmosphere of fear?

In Bombay I met many friends and comrades, some only recently out of prison. The socialistic element was strong there, and there was much resentment at recent happenings in the upper ranks of the Congress. Gandhiji was severely critized for his metaphysical outlook applied to politics. With much of the criticism I was in agreement, but I was quite clear that, situated as we were, we had little choice in the matter and had to carry on. Any attempt to withdraw civil disobedience would have brought no relief to us, for the Government's offensive would continue and all effective work would inevitably lead to prison. Our national movement had arrived at a stage when it had to be suppressed by Government, or it would impose its will on the British Government. This meant that it had arrived at a stage when it was always likely to be declared illegal, and, as a movement, it could not go back even if civil disobedience were withdrawn. The continuance of disobedience made little difference in practice, but it was an act of moral defiance which had value. It was easier to spread new ideas during a struggle than it would be when the struggle was wound up for the time being, and demoralization ensued. The only alternative to the struggle was a compromising attitude to the British authority and constitutional action in the councils.

It was a difficult position, and the choice was not an easy one. I appreciated the mental conflicts of my colleagues, for I had myself had to face them. But I found there, as I have found elsewhere in India, some people who wanted to make high socialistic doctrine a refuge for inaction. It was a little irritating to find people who did little themselves criticizing others who had shouldered the burden in the heat and dust of the fray, as reactionaries. These parlor socialists are especially hard on Gandhiji as the archreactionary, and advance arguments which in logic leave little to be desired. But the little fact remains that this "reactionary" knows India, understands India, almost *is* peasant India, and has shaken up India as no so-called revolutionary has done. Even his latest Harijan activities have gently but irresistibly undermined orthodox Hinduism and shaken it to its foundations. The whole tribe of the Orthodox have ranged themselves against him and consider him their most dangerous enemy, although he continues to treat them with all gentleness and courtesy. In his own peculiar way he has a knack of releasing powerful forces which spread out, like ripples on the water's surface, and affect millions. Reactionary or revolutionary, he has changed the face of India, given pride and character to a cringing and demoralized people, built up strength and consciousness in the masses, and made the Indian problem a world problem. Quite apart from the objectives aimed at and its metaphysical implications, the method of nonviolent nonco-operation or civil resistance is a unique and powerful contribution of his to India and the world, and there can be no doubt that it has been peculiarly suited to Indian conditions.

I think it is right that we should encourage honest criticism and have as much public discussion of our problems as possible. It is unfortunate that Gandhiji's dominating position has to some extent prevented this discussion. There was always a tendency to rely on him and to leave the decision to him. This is obviously wrong, and the nation can only advance by reasoned acceptance of objectives and methods, and a co-operation and discipline based on them and not on blind obedience. No one, however great he may be, should be above criticism. But, when criticism becomes a mere refuge for inaction, there is something wrong with it. For socialists to indulge in this kind of thing is to invite condemnation from the public, for the masses judge by acts. "He who denies the sharp tasks of today," says Lenin, "in the name of dreams about soft tasks of the future becomes an opportunist. Theoretically it means to fail to base oneself on the developments now going on in real life, to detach oneself from them in the name of dreams."

Socialists and communists in India are largely nurtured on literature dealing with the industrial proletariat. In some selected areas, like Bombay or near Calcutta, large numbers of factory workers abound, but for the rest India remains agricultural, and the Indian problem cannot be disposed of, or treated effectively, in terms of the industrial workers. Nationalism and rural economy are the dominating considerations, and European socialism seldom deals with these. Prewar conditions in Russia were a much nearer approach to India, but there again the most extraordinary and unusual occurrences took place, and it is absurd to expect a repetition of these anywhere else. I do believe that the philosophy of communism helps us to understand and analyze existing conditions in any country, and further indicates the road to future progress. But it is doing violence and injustice to that philosophy to apply it blindfold and without due regard to facts and conditions.

Life is anyhow a complex affair, and the conflicts and contradictions of life sometimes make one despair a little. It is not surprising that people should differ, or even that comrades with a common approach to problems should draw different conclusions. But a person who tries to hide his own weakness in high-sounding phrases and noble principles is apt to be suspect. A person who tries to save himself from prison by giving undertakings and assurances to the Government, or by other dubious conduct, and then has the temerity to criticize others, is likely to injure the cause he espouses.


XXXIX

# DOMINION STATUS AND INDEPENDENCE

DURING MY VISIT to Poona to see Gandhiji, I accompanied him one evening to the Servants of India Society's home. For an hour or so questions were put to him on political matters by some of the members of the Society, and he answered them. Mr. Srinivasa Sastri was not there, nor was Pandit Hriday Nath Kunzru, probably the ablest of the other members, but some senior members were present. A few of us who were present on the occasion listened with growing amazement, for the questions related to the most trivial of happenings. Mostly they dealt with Gandhiji's old request for an interview with the Viceroy and the Viceroy's refusal. Was this the only important subject they could think of in a world full of problems, and when their own country was carrying on a hard struggle for freedom and hundreds of organizations were outlawed? There was the agrarian crisis and the industrial depression causing widespread unemployment. There were the dreadful happenings in Bengal and the Frontier and in other parts of India; the suppression of freedom of thought and speech and writing and assembly; and so many other national and international problems. But the questions were limited to unimportant happenings, and the possible reactions of the Viceroy and the Government of India to an approach by Gandhiji.

I had a strong feeling as if I had entered a monastery, the inhabitants of which had long been cut off from effective contact with the outside world. And yet our friends were active politicians, able men with long records of public service and sacrifice. They formed, with a few others, the real backbone of the Liberal party. The rest of the party was a vague, amorphous lot of people who wanted occasionally to have the sensation of being connected with political activities. Some of these, especially in Bombay and Madras, were indistinguishable from Government officials.

The questions that a country puts are a measure of that country's

260

political development. Often the failure of that country is due to the fact that it has not put the right question to itself. Our wasting our time and energy and tempers over the communal distribution of seats, or our forming parties on the communal award and carrying on a sterile controversy about it to the exclusion of vital problems, is a measure of our political backwardness. In the same way the questions that were put to Gandhiji that day in the Servants of India Society's home mirrored the strange mental state of that Society and of the Liberal party. They seemed to have no political or economic principles, no wide outlook, and their politics seemed to be of the parlor or court variety—what high officials would do or would not do.

The Indian Liberals are not liberal at all in any sense of the word, or at most they are liberal only in spots and patches. What they exactly are it is difficult to say, for they have no firm positive basis of ideas and, though small in numbers, differ from one another. They are strong only in negation. They see error everywhere and attempt to avoid it, and hope that in doing so they will find the truth. Truth for them, indeed, always lies between two extremes. By criticizing everything they consider extreme, they experience the feeling of being virtuous and moderate and good. This method helps them in avoiding painful and difficult processes of thought and in having to put forward constructive ideas.

Moderation and conservatism and a desire to avoid risks and sudden changes are often the inevitable accompaniments of old age. They do not seem quite so appropriate in the young, but ours is an ancient land, and sometimes its children seem to be born tired and weary, with all the lackluster and marks of age upon them. But even this old country is now convulsed by the forces of change, and the moderate outlook is bewildered. The old world is passing, and all the sweet reasonableness of which the Liberals are capable does not make any difference; they might as well argue with the hurricane or the flood or the earthquake.

We are all moderates or extremists in varying degrees, and for various objects. If we care enough for anything, we are likely to feel strongly about it, to be extremist about it. Otherwise we can afford a gracious tolerance, a philosophical moderation, which really hides to some extent our indifference. I have known the mildest of Moderates to grow very aggressive and extremist when a suggestion was made for the sweeping away of certain vested interests in land. Our Liberal friends represent to some extent the prosperous and well-to-do. They can afford to wait for *Swaraj* and need not excite themselves about it. But any proposal for radical social change disturbs them greatly, and they are no longer moderate or sweetly reasonable about it. Thus their moderation is really confined to their attitude toward the British Government, and they nurse the hope that if they are sufficiently respectful and compromising perhaps, as a reward for this behavior, they might be listened to. Inevitably they have to accept the British viewpoint.

I write of Liberals, but what I write applies to many of us also in the Congress. It applies even more to the Responsivists,[1] who have outdistanced the Liberals in their moderation. There is a great deal of difference between the average Liberal and the average Congressman, and yet the dividing line is not clear and definite. Ideologically there is little to choose between the advanced Liberal and the moderate Congressman. But, thanks to Gandhiji, every Congressman has kept some touch with the soil and the people of the country and has dabbled in action; because of this he has escaped some of the consequences of a vague and defective idealogy. Not so the Liberals: they have lost touch with both the old and the new. As a group they represent a vanishing species.

Most of us, I suppose, have lost the old pagan feeling and not gained the new insight. Not for us to "have sight of Proteus rising from the sea"; or "hear old Triton blow his wreathed horn." And very few of us are fortunate enough:

> To see a World in a Grain of Sand
> And a Heaven in a Wild Flower,
> Hold Infinity in the palm of your hand
> And Eternity in an hour.

Not for most of us, unhappily, to sense the mysterious life of nature, to hear her whisper close to our ears, to thrill and quiver at her touch. Those days are gone. But, though we may not see the sublime in nature as we used to, we have sought to find it in the glory and tragedy of humanity, in its mighty dreams and inner tempests, its pangs and failures, its conflicts and misery, and, over all this, its faith in a great destiny and a realization of those dreams. That has been some recompense for us for all the heartbreaks that such a search involves, and often we have been raised above the pettiness of life. But many have not undertaken this search and, having cut themselves adrift from the ancient ways, find no road to follow in the present. They neither dream

---

[1] A group which branched off from the *Swaraj* party some years before.—Ed.

nor do they act. They have no understanding of human convulsions like the great French Revolution or the Russian Revolution. The complex, swift, and cruel eruptions of human desires, long suppressed, frighten them. For them the Bastille has not yet fallen.

It is often said with righteous indignation that "patriotism is not a monopoly of Congressmen." The same phrase is repeated again and again with a lack of originality which is somewhat distressing. I hope no Congressman has ever claimed a corner on this emotion. Certainly I do not think it is a Congress monopoly, and I would be glad to make a present of it to anyone who desired it. It is often enough the refuge of the opportunist and the careerist, and there are so many varieties of it to suit all tastes, all interests, all classes. If Judas were alive today, he would no doubt act in its name. Patriotism is no longer enough: we want something higher, wider, and nobler.

Nor is moderation enough by itself. Restraint is good and is the measure of our culture, but behind that restraint there must be something to restrain and hold back. It has been, and is, man's destiny to control the elements, to ride the thunderbolt, to bring the raging fire and the rushing and tumbling waters to his use, but most difficult of all for him has been to restrain and hold in check the passions that consume him. So long as he will not master them, he cannot enter fully into his human heritage. But are we to restrain the legs that move not and the hands that are palsied?

Most of those who have shaped Congress policy during the last seventeen years have come from the middle classes. Liberal or Congressmen, they have come from the same class and have grown up in the same environment. Their social life and contacts and friendships have been similar, and there was little difference to begin with between the two varieties of bourgeois ideals that they professed. Temperamental and psychological differences began to separate them, and they began to look in different directions—one group more toward the Government and the rich, upper middle class, the other toward the lower middle classes. The ideology still remained the same, the objectives did not differ, but behind the second group there was now the push of larger numbers from the market place and the humbler professions as well as the unemployed intelligentsia. The tone changed; it was no longer respectful and polite, but strident and aggressive. Lacking strength to act effectively, some relief was found in strong language. Frightened by this new development, the moderate elements dropped out and sought safety in seclusion. Even so, the upper middle class was strongly represented in the Congress, though in numbers the lower *bourgeoisie* was predominant. They were drawn not only by the desire for success in their national struggle, but because they sought an inner satisfaction in that struggle. They sought thereby to recover their lost pride and self-respect, and to rehabilitate their shattered dignity. It was the usual nationalist urge and, though this was common to all, it was here that the temperamental differences between the Moderate and the Extremist became evident. Gradually the lower middle class began to dominate the Congress, and later the peasantry made their influence felt.

As the Congress became more and more the representative of the rural masses, the gulf that separated it from the Liberals widened, and it became almost impossible for the Liberal to understand or appreciate the Congress viewpoint. It is not easy for the upper-class drawing room to understand the humble cottage or the mud hut. Yet, in spite of these differences, both the ideologies were nationalist and bourgeois; the variation was one of degree, not of kind. In the Congress many people remained to the last who would have been quite at home in the Liberal group.

For many generations the British treated India as a kind of enormous country house (after the old English fashion) that they owned. They were the gentry owning the house and occupying the desirable parts of it, while the Indians were consigned to the servants' hall, the pantry, and the kitchen. As in every proper country house, there was a fixed hierarchy in those lower regions—butler, housekeeper, cook, valet, maid, footman, etc.—and strict precedence was observed among them. But between the upper and lower regions of the house there was, socially and politically, an impassable barrier. The fact that the British Government should have imposed this arrangement upon us was not surprising; but what does seem surprising is that we, or most of us, accepted it as the natural and inevitable ordering of our lives and destiny. We developed the mentality of a good country-house servant. Sometimes we were treated to a rare honor—we were given a cup of tea in the drawing room. The height of our ambition was to become respectable and to be promoted individually to the upper regions. Greater than any victory of arms or diplomacy was this psychological triumph of the British in India. The slave began to think as a slave, as the wise men of old had said.

Times have changed, and the country-house type of civilization is not accepted willingly now, either in England or India. But still there remain people among us who desire to stick to the servants' hall and take pride in the gold braid and livery of their service. Others, like the Liberals, accept that country house in its entirety, admire its architecture and the whole edifice, but look forward to replacing the owners, one by one, by themselves. They call this Indianization. For them the problem is one of changing the color of the administration, or at most having a new administration. They never think in terms of a new State.

For them *Swaraj* means that everything continues as before, only with a darker shade. They can only conceive of a future in which they, or people like them, will play the principal role and take the place of the English high officials; in which there are the same types of services, government departments, legislatures, trade, industry—with the Indian Civil Service at their jobs; the princes in their palaces, occasionally appearing in fancy dress or carnival attire with all their jewels glittering to impress their subjects; the landlords claiming special protection, and meanwhile harassing their tenants; the moneylender, with his moneybags, harassing both zamindar and tenant; the lawyer with his fees; and God in His heaven.

Essentially their outlook is based on the maintenance of the *status quo,* and the changes they desire can almost be termed personal changes. And they seek to achieve these changes by a slow infiltration with the good will of the British. The whole foundation of their politics and economics rests on the continuance and stability of the British Empire. Looking on this Empire as unshakable, at least for a considerable time, they adapt themselves to it and accept not only its political and economic ideology but also, to a large extent, its moral standards, which have all been framed to secure the continuance of British dominance.

The Congress attitude differs fundamentally from this because it seeks a new State and not just a different administration. What that new State is going to be may not be quite clear to the average Congressman, and opinions may differ about it. But it is common ground in the Congress (except perhaps for a moderate fringe) that present conditions and methods cannot and must not continue, and basic changes are essential. Herein lies the difference between Dominion status and independence. The former envisages the same old structure, with many bonds visible and invisible tying us to the British economic system; the latter gives us, or ought to give us, freedom to erect a new structure to suit our circumstances.

It is not a question of an implacable and irreconcilable antagonism to England and the English people, or the desire to break from them at all costs. It would be natural enough if there were bad blood between India and England after what has happened. "The clumsiness of power spoils the key and uses the pickax," says Tagore; the key to our hearts was destroyed long ago, and the abundant use of the pickax on us has not made us partial to the British. But, if we claim to serve the larger cause of India and humanity, we cannot afford to be carried away by our momentary passions. And, even if we were so inclined, the hard training which Gandhiji has given us for the last fifteen years would prevent us. I write this sitting in a British prison, and for months past my mind has been full of anxiety, and I have perhaps suffered more during this solitary imprisonment than I have done in jail before. Anger and resentment have often filled my mind at various happenings, and yet, as I sit here and look deep into my mind and heart, I do not find any anger against England or the English people. I dislike British imperialism, and I resent its imposition on India; I dislike the capitalist system; I dislike exceedingly and resent the way India is exploited by the ruling classes of Britain. But I do not hold England or the English people as a whole responsible for this; and, even if I did, I do not think it would make much difference, for it is a little foolish to lose one's temper at or to condemn a whole people. They are as much the victims of circumstances as we are.

Personally, I owe too much to England in my mental make-up ever to feel wholly alien to her. And, do what I will, I cannot get rid of the habits of mind, and the standards and ways of judging other countries as well as life generally, which I acquired at school and college in England. My predilections (apart from the political ones) are in favor of England and the English people, and, if I have become what is called an uncompromising opponent of British rule in India, it is almost in spite of these.

It is their rule, their domination, to which we object, and with which we cannot compromise willingly—not the English people. Let us by all means have the closest contacts with the English and other foreign peoples. We want fresh air in India, fresh and vital ideas, healthy co-operation; we have grown too musty with age. But, if the English come in the role of a tiger they can expect no friendship or co-operation. To the tiger of imperialism there will be only the fiercest opposition, and today our country has to deal with that ferocious animal. It may be possible to tame the wild tiger of the forest and to charm away his native ferocity, but there is no such possibility of taming capitalism and imperialism when they combine and swoop down on an unhappy land.

For anyone to say that he or his country will not compromise is, in a sense, a foolish remark, for life is always forcing us to compromise. When applied to another country or people, it is completely foolish. But there is truth in it when it is applied to a system or a particular set of circumstances, and then it becomes something beyond human power to accomplish. Indian freedom and British imperialism are two incompatibles, and neither martial law nor all the sugar coating in the world can make them compatible or bring them together. Only with the elimination of British imperialism from India will conditions be created which permit of real Indo-British co-operation.

We are told that independence is a narrow creed in the modern world, which is increasingly becoming interdependent, and therefore in demanding independence we are trying to put the clock back. Liberals and pacifists and even so-called socialists in Britain advance this plea and chide us for our narrow nationalism, and incidentally suggest to us that the way to a fuller national life is through the "British Commonwealth of Nations." It is curious how all roads in England—liberalism, pacifism, socialism, etc.—lead to the maintenance of the Empire.

I do not know what India will be like or what she will do when she is politically free. But I do know that those of her people who stand for national independence today stand also for the widest internationalism. For a socialist, nationalism can have no meaning; but even many of the nonsocialists in the advanced ranks of the Congress are confirmed internationalists. If we claim independence today, it is with no desire for isolation. On the contrary, we are perfectly willing to surrender part of that independence, in common with other countries, to a real international order. Any imperial system, by whatever high-sounding name it may be called, is an enemy of such an order, and it is not through such a system that world co-operation or world peace can be reached.

Recent developments have shown all over the world how the various imperialist systems are isolating themselves more and more by autarchy and economic imperialism. Instead of the growth of internationalism we see a reversal of the process. The reasons for this are not difficult to discover, and they indicate the growing weakness of the present economic order. One of the results of this policy is that, while it produces greater co-operation within the area of autarchy, it also means isolation from the rest of the world. For India, as we have seen by the Ottawa and other decisions, it has meant a progressive lessening of our ties and contacts with other countries. We have become, even more than we were, the hangers-on of British industry; and the dangers of this policy, apart from the immediate harm it has done in various ways, are obvious. Thus Dominion status seems to lead to isolation and not to wider international contacts.

Names are apt to mislead, but the real question before us in India is whether we are aiming at a new State or merely at a new administration. The Liberal answer is clear: they want the latter and nothing more. Not for them the full-blooded words: Power, Independence, Freedom, Liberty; they sound dangerous.

This, then, is their objective, and this is to be reached not by "direct action" or any other form of aggressive action but by a display of "wisdom, experience, moderation, power of persuasion, quiet influence, and real efficiency." It is hoped that by our good behavior and our good work we shall ultimately induce our rulers to part with power. In other words, they resist us today because either they are irritated against us on account of our aggressive attitude, or they doubt our capacity, or both. This seems a rather naïve analysis of imperialism and the present situation. That brilliant English writer, Professor R. H. Tawney, has written an appropriate and arresting passage dealing with the notion of gaining power in stages and with the co-operation of the ruling classes. He refers to the British Labour party, but his words are even more applicable to India, for in England they have at least democratic institutions, where the will of the majority can, in theory, make itself felt. Professor Tawney writes:

"Onions can be eaten leaf by leaf, but you cannot skin a live tiger paw by paw; vivisection is its trade, and it does the skinning first. . . .

"If there is any country where the privileged classes are simpletons, it is certainly not England. The idea that tact and amiability in presenting the Labour party's case can hoodwink them into the belief that it is their case also, is as hopeless as an attempt to bluff a sharp solicitor out of a property of which he holds the title deeds. The plutocracy consists of agreeable, astute, forcible, self-confident, and, when hard pressed, unscrupulous people, who know pretty well on which side their bread is buttered, and intend that the supply of butter shall not run short. . . . If their position is seriously threatened, they will use every piece on the board, political and economic—the House of Lords, the Crown, the Press, disaffection in the Army, financial crisis, international difficulties, and even, as newspaper attacks on the pound in 1931 showed, the *émigré* trick of injuring one's country to protect one's pocket."

In every democratic country today there is an argument going on as to whether radical economic changes can be brought about in the ordinary course through the constitutional machinery at their disposal. Many people are of opinion that this cannot be done, and some unusual and revolutionary method will have to be adopted. For our purpose in India the issue of this argument is immaterial, for we have no constitutional means of bringing about the changes we desire. There is no way out except by revolution or illegal action. What then is one to do? Give up all idea of change and resign oneself to fate?

The position today in India is even more extraordinary. The Executive can and does prevent or restrict all manner of public activities. Any activity that is, in its opinion, dangerous for it is prohibited. Thus all effective public activity can be stopped. Submission to this means giving up all public work. That is an impossible position to take up.

The withdrawal of civil disobedience by the Congress was naturally welcomed by the Liberals. It was also not surprising that they should take credit for their wisdom in having kept aloof from this "foolish and ill-advised movement." "Did we not say so?" they told us. It was a strange argument. When we stood up and put up a good fight, we were knocked down; therefore, the moral pointed out was that standing up is a bad thing. Crawling is best and safest. It is quite impossible to be knocked down or to fall from that horizontal position.

## XL

## INDIA OLD AND NEW

It was natural and inevitable that Indian nationalism should resent alien rule. And yet it was curious how large numbers of our intelligentsia, to the end of the nineteenth century, accepted, consciously or unconsciously, the British ideology of empire. They built their own arguments on this, and only ventured to criticize some of its outward manifestations. History and economics and other subjects that were taught in the schools and colleges were written entirely from the British imperial viewpoint, and laid stress on our numerous failings in the past and present, and the virtues and high destiny of the British

We accepted to some extent this distorted version, and, even when we resisted it instinctively, we were influenced by it. At first there was no intellectual escape from it, for we knew no other facts or arguments, and so we sought relief in religious nationalism, in the thought that at least in the sphere of religion and philosophy we were second to no other people. We comforted ourselves in our misfortune and degradation with the notion that though we did not possess the outward show and glitter of the West we had the real inner article, which was far more valuable and worth having. Vivekananda and others, as well as the interest of Western scholars in our old philosophies, gave us a measure of self-respect again and roused up our dormant pride in our past.

Gradually we began to suspect and examine critically British statements about our past and present conditions, but still we thought and worked within the framework of British ideology. If a thing was bad, it would be called "un-British"; if a Britisher in India misbehaved, the fault was his, not that of the system. But the collection of this critical material of British rule in India, in spite of the moderate outlook of the authors, served a revolutionary purpose and gave a political and economic foundation to our nationalism. Dadabhai Naoroji's *Poverty and Un-British Rule in India,* and books by Romesh Dutt and William Digby and others, thus played a revolutionary role in the development of our nationalist thought. Further researches in ancient Indian history revealed brilliant and highly civilized periods in the remote past, and we read of these with great satisfaction. We also discovered that the British record in India was very different from what we had been led to believe from their history books.

Our challenge to the British version of history, economics, and administration in India grew, and yet we continued to function within the orbit of their ideology. That was the position of Indian nationalism as a whole at the turn of the century. That is still the position of the Liberal group and other small groups as well as a number of moderate Congressmen, who go forward emotionally from time to time, but intellectually still live in the nineteenth century. Because of that the Liberal is unable to grasp the idea of Indian freedom, for the two are fundamentally irreconcilable. He imagines that step by step he will go up to higher offices and will deal with fatter and more important files. The machinery of government will go on smoothly as before, only he will be at the hub, and somewhere in the background, without intruding themselves too much, will be the British Army to give him protection in case of need. That is his idea of Dominion status within the Empire. It is a naïve notion impossible of achievement, for the price of British protection is Indian subjection. We cannot have it both ways, even if that was not degrading to the self-respect of a great country. Sir Frederick Whyte (no partisan of Indian nationalism) says in a recent book:[1] "He [the Indian] still believes that England will stand between him and disaster, and as long as he cherishes this delusion he cannot even lay the foundation of his own ideal of self-government." Evidently he refers to the Liberal or the reactionary and communal types of Indians, largely with whom he must have come into contact when he was president of the Indian Legislative Assembly. This is not the Congress belief, much less is it that of other advanced groups. They agree with Sir Frederick, however, that there can be no freedom till this delusion goes and India is left to face disaster, if that is her fate, by herself. The complete withdrawal of British military control of India will be the beginning of Indian freedom.

It is not surprising that the Indian intelligentsia in the nineteenth century should have succumbed to British ideology; what is surprising is that some people should continue to suffer that delusion even after the stirring events and changes of the twentieth century. In the nineteenth century the British ruling classes were the aristocrats of the world, with a long record of wealth and success and power behind them. This long record and training gave them some of the virtues as well as failings of aristocracy. We in India can comfort ourselves with the thought that we helped substantially during the last century and three-quarters in providing the wherewithal and the training for this superior state. They began to think themselves—as so many races and nations have done—the chosen of God, and their Empire an earthly Kingdom of Heaven. If their special position was acknowledged and their superiority not challenged, they were gracious and obliging, provided that this did them no harm. But opposition to them became opposition to the divine order, and as such was a deadly sin which must be suppressed.

If this was the general British attitude to the rest of the world, it was most conspicuous in India. There was something fascinating about the British approach to the Indian problem, even though it was singularly irritating. The calm assurance of always being in the right and of having borne a great burden worthily, faith in their racial destiny and their own brand of imperialism, contempt and anger at the unbelievers

[1] Sir Frederick Whyte: *The Future of East and West.*

271

and sinners who challenged the foundations of the true faith—there was something of the religious temper about this attitude. Like the Inquisitors of old, they were bent on saving us regardless of our desires in the matter. Incidentally they profited by this traffic in virtue, thus demonstrating the truth of the old proverb: "Honesty is the best policy." The progress of India became synonymous with the adaptation of the country to the imperial scheme and the fashioning of chosen Indians after the British mold. The more we accepted British ideals and objectives, the fitter we were for "self-government." Freedom would be ours as soon as we demonstrated and guaranteed that we would use it only in accordance with British wishes.

Indians and Englishmen are, I am afraid, likely to disagree about the record of British rule in India. That is perhaps natural, but it does come as a shock when high British officials, including Secretaries of State for India, draw fanciful pictures of India's past and present and make statements which have no basis in fact. It is quite extraordinary how ignorant English people, apart from some experts and others, are about India. If facts elude them, how much more is the spirit of India beyond their reach? They seized her body and possessed her, but it was the possession of violence. They did not know her or try to know her. They never looked into her eyes, for theirs were averted and hers downcast through shame and humiliation. After centuries of contact they face each other, strangers still, full of dislike for each other.

Yet India with all her poverty and degradation had enough of nobility and greatness about her; and, though she was overburdened with ancient tradition and present misery and her eyelids were a little weary, she had "a beauty wrought out from within upon the flesh, the deposit, little cell by cell, of strange thoughts and fantastic reveries and exquisite passions." Behind and within her battered body one could still glimpse a majesty of soul. Through long ages she had traveled and gathered much wisdom on the way, and trafficked with strangers and added them to her own big family, and witnessed days of glory and of decay, and suffered humiliation and terrible sorrow, and seen many a strange sight; but throughout her long journey she had clung to her immemorial culture, drawn strength and vitality from it, and shared it with other lands. Like a pendulum she had swung up and down; she had ventured with the daring of her thought to reach up to the heavens and unravel their mystery, and she had also had bitter experience of the pit of hell. Despite the woeful accumulations of superstition and degrading custom that had clung to her and borne her down, she had never wholly forgotten the inspiration that some of the wisest of her children, at the dawn of history, had given her in the *Upanishads.* Their keen minds, ever restless and ever striving and exploring, had not sought refuge in blind dogma or grown complacent in the routine observance of dead forms of ritual and creed. They had demanded not a personal relief from suffering in the present or a place in a paradise to come, but light and understanding: "Lead me from the unreal to the real, lead me from darkness to light, lead me from death to immortality." [2] In the most famous of the prayers recited daily even today by millions, the *gayatri mantra,* the call is for knowledge, for enlightenment.

Though often broken up politically, her spirit always guarded a common heritage, and in her diversity there was ever an amazing unity. Like all ancient lands she was a curious mixture of the good and bad, but the good was hidden and had to be sought after, while the odor of decay was evident, and her hot, pitiless sun gave full publicity to the bad.

There is some similarity between Italy and India. Both are ancient countries with long traditions of culture behind them, though Italy is a newcomer compared to India, and India is a much vaster country. Both were split up politically, and yet the conception of Italia, like that of India, never died, and in all their diversity the unity was predominant. In Italy the unity was largely a Roman unity, for that great city had dominated the country and been the fount and symbol of unity. In India there was no such single center or dominant city, although Benares might well be called the Eternal City of the East, not only for India but also for Eastern Asia. But, unlike Rome, Benares never dabbled in empire or thought of temporal power. Indian culture was so widespread all over India that no part of the country could be called the heart of that culture. From Cape Comorin to Amaranath and Badrinath in the Himalayas, from Dwarka to Puri, the same ideas coursed; and, if there was a clash of ideas in one place, the noise of it soon reached distant parts of the country.

Just as Italy gave the gift of culture and religion to Western Europe, India did so to Eastern Asia, though China was as old and venerable as India. And, even when Italy was lying prostrate politically, her life coursed through the veins of Europe.

It was Metternich who called Italy a "geographical expression," and many a would-be Metternich has used that phrase for India; strangely

[2] *Brihadaranyak Upanishad,* i, 3, 27.

enough, there is a similarity even in their geographical positions in the two continents. More interesting is the comparison of England with Austria, for has not England of the twentieth century been compared to Austria of the nineteenth, proud and haughty and imposing still, but with the roots that gave strength shriveling up and decay eating its way into the mighty fabric?

It is curious how one cannot resist the tendency to give an anthropomorphic form to a country. Such is the force of habit and early associations. India becomes *Bharat Mata,* Mother India, a beautiful lady, very old but ever youthful in appearance, sad-eyed and forlorn, cruelly treated by aliens and outsiders, and calling upon her children to protect her. Some such picture rouses the emotions of hundreds of thousands and drives them to action and sacrifice. And yet India is in the main the peasant and the worker, not beautiful to look at, for poverty is not beautiful. Does the beautiful lady of our imaginations represent the bare-bodied and bent workers in the fields and factories? Or the small group of those who have from ages past crushed the masses and exploited them, imposed cruel customs on them and made many of them even untouchable? We seek to cover truth by the creatures of our imaginations and endeavor to escape from reality to a world of dreams.

And yet, despite these different classes and their mutual conflicts, there was a common bond which united them in India, and one is amazed at its persistence and tenacity and enduring vitality. What was this strength due to? Not merely the passive strength and weight of inertia and tradition, great as these always are. There was an active sustaining principle, for it resisted successfully powerful outside influences and absorbed internal forces that rose to combat it. And yet with all its strength it could not preserve political freedom or endeavor to bring about political unity. These latter do not appear to have been considered worth much trouble; their importance was very foolishly ignored, and we have suffered for this neglect. Right through history the old Indian ideal did not glorify political and military triumph, and it looked down upon money and the professional money-making class. Honor and wealth did not go together, and honor was meant to go, at least in theory, to the men who served the community with little in the shape of financial reward.

The old culture managed to live through many a fierce storm and tempest, but, though it kept its outer form, it lost its real content. Today it is fighting silently and desperately against a new and all-powerful opponent—the *bania* civilization of the capitalist West. It will succumb to this newcomer, for the West brings science, and science brings food for the hungry millions. But the West also brings an antidote to the evils of this cut-throat civilization—the principles of socialism, of co-operation, and service to the community for the common good. This is not so unlike the old Brahman ideal of service, but it means the brahmanization (not in the religious sense, of course) of all classes and groups and the abolition of class distinctions. It may be that when India puts on her new garment, as she must, for the old is torn and tattered, she will have it cut in this fashion, so as to make it conform both to present conditions and her old thought. The ideas she adopts must become racy to her soil.


## XLI

# THE RECORD OF BRITISH RULE

WHAT HAS BEEN the record of British rule in India? I doubt if it is possible for any Indian or Englishman to take an objective and dispassionate view of this long record. And, even if this were possible, it would be still more difficult to weigh and measure the psychological and other immaterial factors. We are told that British rule "has given to India that which throughout the centuries she never possessed, a government whose authority is unquestioned in any part of the subcontinent"; it has established the rule of law and a just and efficient administration; it has brought to India Western conceptions of parliamentary government and personal liberties; and "by transforming British India into a single unitary state it has engendered amongst Indians a sense of political unity" and thus fostered the first beginnings of nationalism.[1] That is the British case, and there is much truth in it, though the rule of law and personal liberties have not been evident for many years.

The Indian survey of this period lays stress on many other factors, and points out the injury, material and spiritual, that foreign rule has brought us. The viewpoint is so different that sometimes the very thing that is commended by the British is condemned by Indians. As

[1] The quotations are from the Report of the Joint Parliamentary Committee on Indian Constitutional Reform (1934).

Dr. Ananda Coomaraswamy writes: "One of the most remarkable features of British rule in India is that the greatest injuries inflicted upon the Indian people have the outward appearance of blessings."

As a matter of fact the changes that have taken place in India during the last century or more have been world changes common to most countries in the East and West. The growth of industrialism in western Europe, and later on in the rest of the world, brought nationalism and the strong unitary state in its train everywhere. The British can take credit for having first opened India's window to the West and brought her one aspect of Western industrialism and science. But having done so they throttled the further industrial growth of the country till circumstances forced their hands. India was already the meeting place of two cultures, the western Asiatic culture of Islam and the eastern, her own product, which spread to the Far East. And now a third and more powerful impulse came from further west, and India became a focal point and a battleground for various old and new ideas. There can be no doubt that this third impulse would have triumphed and thus solved many of India's old problems, but the British, who had themselves helped in bringing it, tried to stop its further progress. They prevented our industrial growth and thus delayed our political growth, and preserved all the out-of-date feudal and other relics they could find in the country. They even froze up our changing and to some extent progressing laws and customs at the stage they found them, and made it difficult for us to get out of their shackles. It was not with their good will or assistance that the *bourgeoisie* grew in India. But after introducing the railway and other products of industrialism they could not stop the wheel of change; they could only check it and slow it down, and this they did to their own manifest advantage.

"On this solid foundation the majestic structure of the Government of India rests, and it can be claimed with certainty that in the period which has elapsed since 1858 when the Crown assumed supremacy over all the territories of the East India Company, the educational and material progress of India has been greater than it was ever within her power to achieve during any other period of her long and checkered history." [2] This statement is not so self-evident as it appears to be, and it has often been stated that literacy actually went down with the coming of British rule. But, even if the statement was wholly true, it amounts to a comparison of the modern industrial age with past ages.

[2] Report of the Joint Parliamentary Committee (1934).

In almost every country in the world the educational and material progress has been tremendous during the past century because of science and industrialism, and it may be said with assurance of any such country that progress of this kind "has been greater than was ever within her power to achieve during any other period of her long and checkered history"—though perhaps that country's history may not be a long one in comparison with Indian history. Are we needlessly cantankerous and perverse if we suggest that some such technical progress would have come to us anyhow in this industrial age, and even without British rule? And, indeed, if we compare our lot with many other countries, may we not hazard the guess that such progress might have been greater if we had not had to contend against a stifling of that progress by the British themselves? Railways, telegraphs, telephones, wireless, and the like are hardly tests of the goodness or beneficence of British rule. They were welcome and necessary, and, because the British happened to be the agents who brought them first, we should be grateful to them. But even these heralds of industrialism came to us primarily for the strengthening of British rule. They were the veins and arteries through which the nation's blood should have coursed, increasing its trade, carrying its produce, and bringing new life and wealth to its millions. It is true that in the long run some such result was likely, but they were designed and worked for another purpose—to strengthen the imperial hold and to capture markets for British goods—which they succeeded in achieving. I am all in favor of industrialization and the latest methods of transport, but sometimes, as I rushed across the Indian plains, the railway, that life-giver, has almost seemed to me like iron bands confining and imprisoning India.

The British conception of ruling India was the police conception of the State. Government's job was to protect the State and leave the rest to others. Their public finance dealt with military expenditure, police, civil administration, interest on debt. The economic needs of the citizens were not looked after, and were sacrificed to British interests. The cultural and other needs of the people, except for a tiny handful, were entirely neglected. The changing conceptions of public finance which brought free and universal education, improvement of public health, care of poor and feeble-minded, insurance of workers against illness, old age, unemployment, etc., in other countries, were almost entirely beyond the ken of the Government. It could not indulge in these spending activities, for its tax system was most regressive, taking a much larger proportion of small incomes than of the larger ones, and its expenditure on its protective and administrative functions was terribly heavy and swallowed up most of the revenue.

The outstanding feature of British rule was their concentration on everything that went to strengthen their political and economic hold on the country. Everything else was incidental. If they built up a powerful central government and an efficient police force, that was an achievement for which they can take credit, but the Indian people can hardly congratulate themselves on it. Unity is a good thing, but unity in subjection is hardly a thing to be proud of. The very strength of a despotic government may become a greater burden for a people; and a police force, no doubt useful in many ways, can be, and has been often enough, turned against the very people it is supposed to protect.

Britain's supremacy in India brought us peace, and India was certainly in need of peace after the troubles and misfortunes that followed the break-up of the Moghal empire. Peace is a precious commodity, necessary for any progress, and it was welcome to us when it came. But even peace can be purchased at too great a price, and we can have the perfect peace of the grave, and the absolute safety of a cage or of prison. Or peace may be the sodden despair of men unable to better themselves. The peace which is imposed by an alien conqueror has hardly the restful and soothing qualities of the real article.

It is a futile task to consider the "ifs" and possibilities of history. I feel sure that it was a good thing for India to come in contact with the scientific and industrial West. Science was the great gift of the West; India lacked this, and without it she was doomed to decay. The manner of our contacts was unfortunate, and yet, perhaps, only a succession of violent shocks could shake us out of our torpor. From this point of view the Protestant, individualistic, Anglo-Saxon English were suitable, for they were more different from us than most other Westerners, and could give us greater shocks.

They gave us political unity, and that was a desirable thing; but whether we had this unity or not, Indian nationalism would have grown and demanded that unity.

The political unity of India was achieved incidentally as a side product of the Empire's advance. In later years, when that unity allied itself to nationalism and challenged alien rule, we witnessed the deliberate promotion of disunity and sectarianism, formidable obstacles to our future progress.

What a long time it is since the British came here, a century and three-quarters since they became dominant! They had a free hand, as despotic governments have, and a magnificent opportunity to mold India according to their desire. During these years the world has changed out of all recognition—England, Europe, America, Japan. The insignificant American colonies bordering the Atlantic in the eighteenth century constitute today the wealthiest, the most powerful and technically the most advanced nation; the vast territories of the U.S.S.R., where till only yesterday the dead hand of the Tsar's government suppressed and stifled all growth, now pulsate with a new life and build a new world before our eyes. There have been big changes in India also, and the country is very different from what it was in the eighteenth century—railways, irrigation works, factories, schools and colleges, huge government offices, etc., etc.

And yet, in spite of these changes, what is India like today? A servile state, with its splendid strength caged up, hardly daring to breathe freely, governed by strangers from afar; her people poor beyond compare, short-lived and incapable of resisting disease and epidemic; illiteracy rampant; vast areas devoid of all sanitary or medical provision; unemployment on a prodigious scale, both among the middle classes and the masses. Freedom, democracy, socialism, communism are, we are told, the slogans of impractical idealists, doctrinaires, or knaves; the test must be one of the well-being of the people as a whole. That is indeed a vital test, and by that test India makes a terribly poor show today. We read of great schemes of unemployment relief and the alleviation of distress in other countries; what of our scores of millions of unemployed and the distress that is widespread and permanent? We read also of housing schemes elsewhere; where are the houses of hundreds of millions of our people, who live in mud huts or have no shelter at all? May we not envy the lot of other countries where education, sanitation, medical relief, cultural facilities, and production advance rapidly ahead, while we remain where we were, or plod wearily along at the pace of a snail? Russia in a brief dozen years of wonderful effort has almost ended illiteracy in her vast territories and has evolved a fine and up-to-date system of education, in touch with the life of the masses. Backward Turkey, under the Ataturk, Mustapha Kemal's, leadership, has also made giant strides toward widespread literacy.

Indians have been accused of talking too much and doing little. It is a just charge. But may we not express our wonder at the inexhaustible capacity of the British for committees and commissions, each of which, after long labor, produces a learned report—"a great State document"—which is duly praised and pigeonholed? And so we get the sensation of moving ahead, of progress, and yet have the advantage of remaining where we were. Honor is satisfied, and vested interests remain untouched and secure. Other countries discuss how to get on; we discuss checks and brakes and safeguards lest we go too fast.

"The Imperial splendor became the measure of the people's poverty," so we are told (by the Joint Parliamentary Committee, 1934) of the Moghal times. It is a just observation, but may we not apply the same measure today? What of New Delhi today with its viceregal pomp and pageantry, and the provincial governors with all their ostentation? And all this with a background of abject and astonishing poverty. The contrast hurts, and it is a little difficult to imagine how sensitive men can put up with it. India today is a poor and dismal sight behind all the splendors of the imperial frontage. There is a great deal of patchwork and superficiality, and behind it the unhappy petty *bourgeoisie,* crushed more and more by modern conditions. Further back come the workers, living miserably in grinding poverty, and then the peasant, that symbol of India, whose lot it is to be "born to Endless Night."

It would be absurd to cast the blame for all India's ills on the British. That responsibility must be shouldered by us, and we may not shirk it; it is unseemly to blame others for the inevitable consequences of our own weaknesses. An authoritarian system of government, and especially one that is foreign, must encourage a psychology of subservience and try to limit the mental outlook and horizon of the people. It must crush much that is finest in youth—enterprise, spirit of adventure, originality, "pep"—and encourage sneakiness, rigid conformity, and a desire to cringe and please the bosses. Such a system does not bring out the real service mentality, the devotion to public service or to ideals; it picks out the least public-spirited persons whose sole objective is to get on in life. We see what a class the British attract to themselves in India! Some of them are intellectually keen and capable of good work. They drift to government service or semigovernment service because of lack of opportunity elsewhere, and gradually they tone down and become just parts of the big machine, their minds imprisoned by the dull routine of work. They develop the qualities of a bureaucracy—"a competent knowledge of clerkship and the diplomatic art of keeping office." At the highest they have a passive devotion to the public service. There is, or can be, no flaming enthusiasm. That is not possible under a foreign government.

But, apart from these, the majority of petty officials are not an admirable lot, for they have learned only to cringe to their superiors and bully their inferiors. The fault is not theirs. That is the training the system gives them. And if sycophancy and nepotism flourish, as they often do, is it to be wondered at? They have no ideals in service; the haunting fear of unemployment and consequent starvation pursues them, and their chief concern is to hold on to their jobs and get other jobs for their relatives and friends. Where the spy and that most odious of creatures, the informer, always hover in the background, it is not easy to develop the more desirable virtues in a people.

Recent developments have made it even more difficult for sensitive, public-spirited men to join government service. The Government does not want them, and they do not wish to associate with it too closely, unless compelled by economic circumstance.

But, as all the world knows, it is the white man who bears the burden of Empire, not the brown. We have various imperial services to carry on the imperial tradition, and a sufficiency of safeguards to protect their special privileges—all, we are told, in the interests of India. It is remarkable how the good of India seems to be tied up with the obvious interests and advancement of these services. If any privilege or prize post of the Indian Civil Service is taken away, we are told that inefficiency and corruption will result. If the reserved jobs for the Indian Medical Service are reduced, this becomes a "menace to India's health." And of course if the British element in the Army is touched, all manner of terrible perils confront us.

I think there is some truth in this: that if the superior officials suddenly went away and left their departments in charge of their subordinates, there would be a fall in efficiency. But that is because the whole system has been built this way, and the subordinates are not by any means the best men, nor have they ever been made to shoulder responsibility. I feel convinced that there is abundant good material in India, and it could be available within a fairly short period if proper steps were taken. But that means a complete change in our governmental and social outlook. It means a new State.

As it is, we are told that whatever changes in the constitutional apparatus may come our way, the rigid framework of the great services which guard and shelter us will continue as before. Hierophants of the sacred mysteries of government, they will guard the temple and prevent the vulgar from entering its holy precincts. Gradually, as we make ourselves worthy of the privilege, they will remove the veils one after another, till, in some future age, even the holy of holies stands uncovered to our wondering and reverent eyes.

Of all these imperial services, the Indian Civil Service holds first place, and to it must largely go the credit or discredit for the functioning of government in India. We have been frequently told of the many virtues of this Service, and its greatness in the imperial scheme has almost become a maxim. Its unchallenged position of authority in India with the almost autocratic power that this gives, as well as the praise and boosting which it receives in ample measure, cannot be wholly good for the mental equilibrium of any individual or group. With all my admiration for the Service, I am afraid I must admit that it is peculiarly susceptible, both individually and as a whole, to that old and yet somewhat modern disease, paranoia.

It would be idle to deny the good qualities of the Indian Civil Service, for we are not allowed to forget them, but so much bunkum has been and is said about the Service that I sometimes feel that a little debunking would be desirable. The American economist, Veblen, has called the privileged classes the "kept classes." I think it would be equally true to call the Indian Civil Service, as well as the other imperial services, the "kept services." They are a very expensive luxury.

It is perfectly true that the Service has, as a whole, kept up a certain standard, though that standard is necessarily one of mediocrity, and has occasionally thrown up exceptional men. More could hardly be expected of any such service. As a group their power is practically absolute, subject only in theory to a control by the British Parliament. "Power corrupts," Lord Acton has told us, "and absolute power corrupts absolutely."

The members of the Indian Civil Service were intellectually and emotionally not prepared for the great changes taking place in India. They lived in a narrow, circumscribed world of their own—Anglo-India—which was neither England nor India. They had no appreciation of the forces at work in contemporary society. In spite of their amusing assumption of being the trustees and guardians of the Indian masses, they knew little about them and even less about the new aggressive *bourgeoisie*. They judged Indians from the sycophants and office seekers who surrounded them and dismissed others as agitators and knaves. Their knowledge of postwar changes all over the world, and especially in the economic sphere, was of the slightest, and they were too much in a rut to adjust themselves to changing conditions.

282

They did not realize that the order they represented was out of date under modern conditions.

Yet that order will continue so long as British imperialism continues, and this is powerful enough still and has able, resourceful leaders. The British Government in India is like a tooth that is decaying but is still strongly imbedded. It is painful, but it cannot be easily pulled out. The pain is likely to continue, and even grow worse, till the tooth is taken out or falls out itself.

The underlying assumption of the Indian Civil Service is that they discharge their duties most efficiently, and therefore they can lay every stress on their claims, which are many and varied. If India is poor, that is the fault of her social customs, her *banias* and moneylenders, and, above all, her enormous population. The greatest *bania* of all, the British Government in India, is conveniently ignored. And what they propose to do about this population I do not know, for in spite of a great deal of help received from famines, epidemics, and a high death rate generally, the population is still overwhelming. Birth control is proposed, and I, for one, am entirely in favor of the spread of the knowledge and methods of birth control. But the use of these methods itself requires a much higher standard of living for the masses, some measure of general education, and innumerable clinics all over the country. Under present conditions birth-control methods are completely out of reach for the masses. The middle classes can profit by them as, I believe, they are doing to a growing extent.

But this argument of overpopulation is deserving of further notice. The problem today all over the world is not one of lack of food or lack of other essentials, but lack of capacity to buy food, etc., for those who are in need. Even in India, the food supply has increased and can increase more than proportionately to the population.

Whenever India becomes free, and in a position to build her new life as she wants to, she will necessarily require the best of her sons and daughters for this purpose. Good human material is always rare, and in India it is rarer still because of our lack of opportunities under British rule. We shall want the help of many foreign experts in many departments of public activity, particularly in those which require special technical and scientific knowledge. Among those who have served in the Indian Civil Service or other imperial services there will be many, Indians or foreigners, who will be necessary and welcome to the new order. But of one thing I am quite sure: that no new order can be built up in India so long as the spirit of the Indian Civil Service pervades our administration and our public services. It will either succeed in crushing freedom or will be swept away itself. Only with one type of state is it likely to fit in, and that is the fascist type.

Even more mysterious and formidable are the so-called Defense Services. We may not criticize them, we may not say anything about them, for what do we know about such matters? We must only pay and pay heavily without murmuring. In 1934 Sir Philip Chetwode, Commander-in-Chief in India, told Indian politicians, in pungent military language, to mind their own business and not interfere with his. Referring to the mover of an amendment to some proposition, he said: "Do he and his friends think that a war-worn and war-wise race like the British, who won their Empire at the point of the sword and have kept it by the sword ever since, are to be talked out of war wisdom which that experience brings to a nation by armchair critics. . . .?" He made many other interesting remarks, and we were informed, lest we might think that he had spoken in the heat of the moment, that he had carefully written out his speech and spoke from a manuscript.

A politician and an armchair critic might wonder if the claims of eminent generals for freedom from interference are valid after the experiences of the World War. They had a free field then to a large extent, and from all accounts they made a terrible mess of almost everything in every army—British, French, German, Austrian, Italian, Russian. Captain Liddell Hart, the distinguished British military historian and strategist, writes in his *History of the World War* that at one stage in the war while British soldiers fought the enemy British generals fought one another.

Politicians, like all other people, err frequently, but democratic politicians have to be sensitive and responsive to men and events, and they usually realize their mistakes and try to repair them. The soldier is bred in a different atmosphere, where authority reigns and criticism is not tolerated. So he resents the advice of others, and, when he errs, he errs thoroughly and persists in error. For him the chin is more important than the mind or brain. In India we have the advantage of having produced a mixed type, for the civil administration itself has grown up and lives in a semimilitary atmosphere of authority and self-sufficiency, and possesses therefore to a great extent the soldier's chin and other virtues.

We are told that the process of "Indianization" of the Army is being pushed on, and in another thirty years or more an Indian general might even appear on the Indian stage. It is possible that in not much more than a hundred years the process of Indianization might be considerably advanced. One is apt to wonder how, in a moment of crisis, England built up a mighty army of millions within a year or two. If it had possessed our mentors, perhaps it would have proceeded more cautiously and warily. It is possible, of course, that the war would have been over long before this soundly trained army was ready for it. One thinks also of the Russian Soviet armies growing out of almost nothing and facing and triumphing over a host of enemies, and today constituting one of the most efficient fighting machines in the world. They did not apparently possess "war-worn and war-wise" generals to advise them.

What has been the record of British rule in India? Who are we to complain of its deficiencies when they were but the consequences of our own failings? If we lose touch with the river of change and enter a backwater, become self-centered and self-satisfied, and, ostrichlike, ignore what happens elsewhere, we do so at our peril. The British came to us on the crest of a wave of new impulse in the world, and represented mighty historic forces which they themselves hardly realized. Are we to complain of the cyclone that uproots us and hurls us about, or the cold wind that makes us shiver? Let us have done with the past and its bickering and face the future. To the British we must be grateful for one splendid gift of which they were the bearers, the gift of science and its rich offspring. It is difficult, however, to forget or view with equanimity the efforts of the British Government in India to encourage the disruptive obscurantist, reactionary, sectarian, and opportunist elements in the country. Perhaps that too is a needed test and challenge for us, and, before India is reborn, it will have to go through again and again the fire that cleanses and tempers and burns up the weak, the impure, and the corrupt.

## XLII

# A CIVIL MARRIAGE AND A QUESTION OF SCRIPT

AFTER SPENDING ABOUT a week in Poona and Bombay in the middle of September 1933, I returned to Lucknow. My mother was still in hospital there and improving very slowly. Kamala was also in Lucknow, trying to attend to her, although she was not very well herself. My sisters used to come over from Allahabad for the week ends. I remained in Lucknow for two or three weeks, and I had more leisure there than I was likely to have in Allahabad, my chief occupation being visits to the hospital twice daily. I utilized my spare hours in writing some articles for the press, and these were widely published all over the country. A series of articles entitled "Whither India?" in which I had surveyed world affairs in relation to the Indian situation, attracted considerable attention. I learned later that these articles were even reproduced in Persian translations in Teheran and Kabul. There was nothing novel or original in these articles for anyone in touch with recent developments and modern Western thought. But in India our people had been too engrossed in their domestic troubles to pay much attention to what was happening elsewhere. The reception given to my articles, as well as many other indications, showed that they were developing a wider outlook.

My mother was getting very tired of being in hospital, and we decided to take her back to Allahabad. One of the reasons for this was my sister Krishna's engagement, which had just been announced. We wanted to have the marriage as soon as possible, before I was suddenly removed to prison again. I had no notion how long I would be allowed to remain out, as civil disobedience was still the official program of the Congress, while the Congress itself and scores of other organizations were illegal.

We fixed the marriage for the third week of October in Allahabad. It was to be a civil ceremony. I was glad of this, though as a matter of fact we had no choice in the matter. The marriage was between two different castes, Brahman and non-Brahman, and under present British Indian law no religious ceremony had validity for such a marriage. Fortunately a recently passed Civil Marriage Act came to our rescue.

There was no fuss about my sister's wedding; it was a very simple affair. Ordinarily I dislike the fuss attendant on Indian marriages. In view of my mother's illness and, even more, the fact that civil disobedience was still going on and many of our colleagues were in prison, anything in the nature of show was singularly out of place.

The little invitation we issued for the wedding was written in Hindustani in the Latin script. Gandhiji did not approve of this. I did not use the Latin script because I had become a convert to it, although it had long attracted me. Its success in Turkey and Central Asia had impressed me, and the obvious arguments in its favor were weighty. But even so I was not convinced, and even if I had been convinced, I knew well that it did not stand the faintest chance of being adopted in present-day India. There would be the most violent opposition to it from all groups, nationalist, religious, Hindu, Moslem, old and new. And I feel that the opposition would not be merely based on emotion. A change of script is a very vital change for any language with a rich past, for a script is a most intimate part of its literature.

I have no doubt whatever that Hindustani is going to be the common language of India. Indeed it is largely so today for ordinary purposes. Its progress has been hampered by foolish controversies about the script. An effort must be made to discourage the extreme tendencies and develop a middle literary language, on the lines of the spoken language in common use. With mass education this will inevitably take place.

Some people imagine that English is likely to become the *lingua franca* of India. That seems to me a fantastic conception, except in respect of a handful of upper-class intelligentsia. It has no relation to the problem of mass education and culture. It may be, as it is partly today, that English will become increasingly a language used for technical, scientific, and business communications, and especially for international contacts. It is essential for many of us to know foreign languages in order to keep in touch with world thought and activities, and I should like our universities to encourage the learning of other languages besides English—French, German, Russian, Spanish, Italian. This does not mean that English should be neglected, but, if we are to have a balanced view of the world, we must not confine ourselves to English spectacles. We have already become sufficiently lopsided in our mental outlook because of this concentration on one aspect and ideology, and even the most rabid of our nationalists hardly realize how much they are cribbed and confined by the British outlook in relation to India.

## XLIII

## COMMUNALISM AND REACTION

ABOUT THE TIME of my sister's wedding came news of Vithalbhai J. Patel's death in Europe. He had long been ailing, and it was because of his ill-health that he had been released from prison in India. His passing away was a painful event, and the thought of our veteran leaders' leaving us in this way, one after another, in the middle of our struggle, was an extraordinarily depressing one. Many tributes were paid to Vithalbhai, and most of these laid stress on his ability as a parliamentarian and his success as president of the Assembly. This was perfectly true, and yet this repetition irritated me. Was there any lack of good parliamentarians in India or of people who could fill the speaker's chair with ability? That was the one job for which our lawyer's training had fitted us. Vithalbhai had been something much more than that—he had been a great and indomitable fighter for India's freedom.

During my visit to Benares in November I was invited to address the students of the Hindu University. I gladly accepted this invitation and addressed a huge gathering presided over by Pandit Madan Mohan Malaviya, the Vice-Chancellor. In the course of my speech I had much to say about communalism, and I denounced it in forcible language, and especially condemned the activities of the Hindu *Mahasabha*. This was not exactly a premeditated attack, but for a long time past my mind had been full of resentment at the increasingly reactionary efforts of the communalists of all groups; and, as I warmed up to my subject, some of this resentment came out. Deliberately I laid stress on the reactionary character of the Hindu communalists, for there was no point in my criticizing Moslems before a Hindu audience. At the moment, it did not strike me that it was not in the best of taste to criticize the Hindu *Mahasabha* at a meeting presided over by Malaviyaji, who had long been one of its pillars. I did not think of this, as he had not had much to do with it lately, and it almost seemed that the new aggressive leaders of the *Mahasabha* had pushed him out.

My Benares speech, briefly reported, created an uproar. Used as I was to such outcries, I was quite taken aback by the vehemence of the attack of the Hindu *Mahasabha* leaders. These attacks were largely personal and seldom touched the point at issue. It was a hornets' nest, and, though I was used to hornets, it was no pleasure to enter into controversies which degenerated into abuse. But now I had no choice, and I wrote what I considered a reasoned article on Hindu and Moslem communalism, showing how in neither case was it even *bona fide* communalism, but was political and social reaction hiding behind the communal mask.

I was very much heartened, not only by the reception of all these articles, but by the visible effect they were producing on people who tried to think. My object was to point out that the communal leaders were allied to the most reactionary elements in India and England and were in reality opposed to political, and even more so to social, advance. All their demands had no relation whatever to the masses. It was my intention to carry on with this reasoned attack when prison claimed me again.

It is interesting to trace British policy since the Rising of 1857 in its relation to the communal question. Fundamentally and inevitably it has been one of preventing the Hindu and Moslem from acting together, and of playing off one community against another. After 1857 the heavy hand of the British fell more on the Moslems than on the Hindus. They considered the Moslems more aggressive and militant, possessing memories of recent rule in India, and therefore more dangerous. The Moslems had also kept away from the new education and had few jobs under the Government.

The new nationalism then grew up from above—the upper-class, English-speaking intelligentsia—and this was naturally confined to the Hindus, for the Moslems were educationally very backward. The Government encouraged the Moslems more to keep them away from the new nationalist platform. In this task they were helped by an outstanding personality—Sir Syed Ahmad Khan. Like many of his contemporaries, he was a great admirer of the British, and a visit to Europe seems to have had a most powerful effect on him. Visiting England in 1869, he wrote letters home giving his impressions. In one of these he stated: "All good things, spiritual and worldly, which should be found in man, have been bestowed by the Almighty on Europe, and especially on England." [1]

Greater praise no man could give to the British and to Europe, and it is obvious that Sir Syed was tremendously impressed. Perhaps also he used strong language and heightened the contrasts in order to shake up his own people out of their torpor and induce them to take a step forward. He was convinced that without Western education his community would become more and more backward and powerless. English education meant Government jobs, security, influence, honor. So to this education he turned all his energy, trying to win over his community to his way of thinking. He wanted no diversions or distractions. The beginnings of a new nationalism, sponsored by the Hindu *bourgeoisie,* seemed to him to offer such a distraction, and he opposed

---

[1] This quotation has been taken from Hans Kohn's *History of Nationalism in the East.*

it. He was not going to risk the full co-operation of the Government in his educational plans by any premature step. So he turned his back on the infant National Congress, and the British Government were only too willing to encourage this attitude.

Sir Syed's decision to concentrate on Western education for Moslems was undoubtedly a right one. Without that they could not have played any effective part in the building up of Indian nationalism of the new type, and they would have been doomed to play second fiddle to the Hindus with their better education and far stronger economic position. Sir Syed's activities, therefore, although seemingly very moderate, were in the right revolutionary direction.

His dominating and forceful personality impressed itself on the Indian Moslems, and the Aligarh College became the visible emblem of his hopes and desires. His message was appropriate and necessary when it came, but it could not be the final ideal of a progressive community. It is possible that, had he lived a generation later, he would himself have given another orientation to that message. Aligarh College did fine work, produced a large number of competent men, and changed the whole tone of the Moslem intelligentsia, but still it could not wholly get out of the framework in which it was built—a feudal spirit reigned over it, and the goal of the average student's ambition was government service.

The Indian Moslems had not wholly recovered from the cramping effects of Sir Syed Ahmad Khan's political message when the events of the early years of the twentieth century helped the British Government to widen the breach between them and the nationalist movement, now clamant and aggressive. Sir Valentine Chirol wrote in 1910 in his *Indian Unrest*: "It may be confidently asserted that never before have the Mohammedans of India as a whole identified their interests and their aspirations so closely as at the present day with the consolidation and permanence of British rule." Political prophecies are dangerous. Within five years after Sir Valentine wrote, the Moslem intelligentsia was trying hard to break through from the fetters that kept it back and to range itself beside the Congress. Within a decade the Indian Moslems seemed to have outstripped the Congress and were actually giving the lead to it. But these ten years were momentous years, and the Great War had come and gone and left a broken-down world as a legacy.

And yet Sir Valentine had superficially every reason to come to the conclusion he did. The Aga Khan had emerged as the leader of the

Moslems, and that fact alone showed that they still clung to their feudal traditions, for the Aga Khan was no bourgeois leader. He was an exceedingly wealthy prince and the religious head of a sect, and from the British point of view he was very much a *persona grata* because of his close association with the British ruling classes. Sir Valentine Chirol tells us that the Aga Khan impressed upon Lord Minto, the Viceroy, "the Mohammedan view of the political situation created by the partition of Bengal, lest political concessions should be hastily made to the Hindus which would pave the way for the ascendency of a Hindu majority equally dangerous to the stability of British rule and to the interests of the Mohammedan minority whose loyalty was beyond dispute."

But behind this superficial lining up with the British Government other forces were working. Inevitably the new Moslem *bourgeoisie* was feeling more and more dissatisfied with existing conditions and was being drawn toward the nationalist movement. The Aga Khan himself had to take notice of this and to warn the British in characteristic language. He wrote in the *Edinburgh Review* of January 1914 (that is, long before the war) advising the Government to abandon the policy of separating Hindus from Moslems, and to rally the moderate of both creeds in a common camp so as to provide a counterpoise to the radical nationalist tendencies of young India—both Hindu and Moslem.

But the Aga Khan or the British Government could not stop the inevitable drift of the Moslem *bourgeoisie* toward nationalism. The World War hastened the process, and, as new leaders arose, the Aga Khan seemed to retire into the background. Gandhiji swept most of these leaders and the Moslems generally into his nonco-operation movement, and they played a leading part in the events of 1919–23.

Then came the reaction, and communal and backward elements, both among the Hindus and the Moslems, began to emerge from their enforced retirement. The outstanding fact seems to me how, on both sides, the communal leaders represent a small upper-class reactionary group, and how these people exploit and take advantage of the religious passions of the masses for their own ends.

Latterly there has been an interesting development in the speeches and statements of some of the Moslem communal leaders. This has no real importance, and I doubt if many people think so; nevertheless it is significant of the mentality of communalism, and a great deal of prominence has been given to it. Stress has been laid on the "Moslem nation" in India, on "Moslem culture," on the utter incompatibility of Hindu and Moslem "cultures." The inevitable deduction from this is (although it is not put baldly) that the British must remain in India for ever and ever to hold the scales and mediate between the two "cultures."

A few Hindu communal leaders think exactly on the same lines, with this difference, however, that they hope that, being in a majority, their brand of "culture" will ultimately prevail.

Hindu and Moslem "cultures" and the "Moslem nation"—how these words open out fascinating vistas of past history and present and future speculation! The Moslem nation in India—a nation within a nation, and not even compact, but vague, spread out, indeterminate. Politically, the idea is absurd; economically it is fantastic; it is hardly worth considering. To talk of a "Moslem nation," therefore, means that there is no nation at all but a religious bond; it means that no nation in the modern sense must be allowed to grow; it means that modern civilization should be discarded and we should go back to the medieval ways; it means either autocratic government or a foreign government; it means, finally, just nothing at all except an emotional state of mind and a conscious or unconscious desire not to face realities, especially economic realities. Emotions have a way of upsetting logic, and we may not ignore them simply because they seem so unreasonable. But this idea of a Moslem nation is the figment of a few imaginations only, and, but for the publicity given to it by the press, few people would have heard of it. And, even if many people believed in it, it would still vanish at the touch of reality.

But what is this "Moslem culture"? Is it a kind of racial memory of the great deeds of the Arabs, Persians, Turks, etc.? Or language? Or art and music? Or customs? I do not remember any one referring to present-day Moslem art or Moslem music. The two languages which have influenced Moslem thought in India are Arabic and Persian, especially the latter. But the influence of Persian has no element of religion about it. The Persian language and many Persian customs and traditions came to India in the course of thousands of years and impressed themselves powerfully all over north India. Persia was the France of the East, sending its language and culture to all its neighbors. That is a common and precious heritage for all of us in India.

I have tried hard to understand what this "Moslem culture" is, but I confess that I have not succeeded. I find a tiny handful of middle-class Moslems as well as Hindus in north India influenced by the Persian language and traditions. The Moslem peasantry and industrial workers are hardly distinguishable from the Hindu.

I must say that those Hindus and Moslems who are always looking backward, always clutching at things which are slipping away from their grasp, are a singularly pathetic sight. I do not wish to damn the past or to reject it, for there is so much that is singularly beautiful in our past. That will endure, I have no doubt. But it is not the beautiful that these people clutch at, but something that is seldom worth while and is often harmful.

If progress consists in the individual's taking a broader view of what constitutes politics, our communalists as well as our Government have deliberately and consistently aimed at the opposite of this—the narrowing of this view.

## XLIV

## IMPASSE AND EARTHQUAKE

THE POSSIBILITY OF my rearrest and conviction always hung over me. It was, indeed, more than a possibility when the land was ruled by ordinances and the like and Congress itself was an illegal organization. Constituted as the British Government was, and constituted as I was, my suppression seemed inevitable. This ever-present prospect influenced my work. I could not settle down to anything, and I was in a hurry to get through as much as possible.

Yet I had no desire to invite arrest, and to a large extent I avoided activities which might lead to it. Invitations came to me from many places in the province and outside to undertake a tour. I refused them, for any such speaking tour could only be a raging campaign which would be abruptly ended. There was no halfway house for me then. When I visited any place for some other object—to confer with Gandhiji and the Working Committee members—I addressed public meetings and spoke freely. In Jubbulpore we had a great meeting and a very impressive procession; in Delhi the gathering was one of the biggest I had seen there. Indeed, the very success of these meetings made it clear that the Government would not tolerate their frequent repetition. In Delhi, soon after the meeting, there was a very strong rumor of my impending arrest, but I survived and returned to Allahabad, breaking journey at Aligarh to address the Moslem university students there.

Twice, during those months, the members of the Working Committee met together to consider the all-India situation. The Committee itself was not functioning, not so much because it was an illegal body but because, at Gandhiji's instance after Poona, all Congress committees and offices had been suspended. I happened to occupy a peculiar position as, on coming out of jail, I refused to join this self-denying ordinance and insisted on calling myself the general secretary of the Congress. But I functioned in the air. There was no proper office, no staff, no acting president; and Gandhiji, though available for consultation, was busy with one of his tremendous all-India tours, this time for Harijan work. We managed to catch him during his tour at Jubbulpore and Delhi and held our consultations with Working Committee members. They served to bring out clearly the differences between various members. There was an impasse, and no way out of it agreeable to everybody. Gandhiji was the deciding factor between those who wanted to withdraw civil disobedience and those who were against this. As he was then in favor of the latter course, matters continued as before.

Meanwhile I continued sending articles and statements to the press. To some extent I had to tone down my writings, for they were written with a view to publication, and there was the censor and various laws whose octopuslike tentacles reached far. Even if I was prepared to take risks, the printers, publishers, and editors were not. On the whole the newspapers were good to me and stretched many a point in my favor. But not always. Sometimes statements and passages were suppressed, and once a whole long article, over which I had taken some pains, never saw the light of day. When I was in Calcutta in January 1934, the editor of one of the leading dailies came to see me. He told me that he had sent one of my statements to the editor-in-chief of all Calcutta newspapers for his opinion, and, as the editor-in-chief had disapproved of it, it had not been published. The "editor-in-chief" was the Government press censor for Calcutta.

In some of my press interviews and statements I ventured to criticize forcibly some groups and individuals. This was resented, partly because of the idea, which Gandhiji had helped to spread, that Congress could be attacked without any danger of its hitting back.

The effect of my socialist propaganda upset even some of my colleagues of the Working Committee. They would have put up with me without complaint, as they had done for several years during which I had been carrying on this propaganda, but I was now frightening to some extent the vested interests in the country, and my activities could no longer be called innocuous. I knew that some of my colleagues were no socialists, but I had always thought that, as a member of the Congress Executive, I had perfect freedom to carry on socialist propaganda without committing the Congress to it. The realization that some members of the Working Committee did not think that I had that freedom came as a surprise. I was putting them in a false position, and they resented it. But what was I to do? I was not going to give up what I considered the most important part of my work. I would much rather resign from the Working Committee if there was a conflict between the two. But how could I resign when the Committee was illegal and was not even functioning properly?

This difficulty faced me again later—I think it was toward the end of December—when Gandhiji wrote to me from Madras. He sent me a cutting from the *Madras Mail* containing an interview he had given. The interviewer had asked him about me, and he had replied almost apologizing for my activities and expressing his faith in my rectitude: I would not commit the Congress to these novel ways. I did not particularly fancy this reference to me, but what upset me much more was Gandhiji's defense, further on in the interview, of the big zamindari system. He seemed to think that this was a very desirable part of rural and national economy. This was a great surprise to me, for the big zamindaris and talukas have very few defenders today. All over the world they have been broken up, and even in India most people recognize that they cannot last long. Even talukdars and zamindars would welcome an end of the system, provided, of course, they got sufficient compensation therefor. The system is indeed sinking of its own weight. And yet Gandhiji was in favor of it and talked of trusteeship and the like. How very different was his outlook from mine, I thought again, and I wondered how far I could co-operate with him in future. Must I continue to remain in the Working Committee? There was no way out just then, and a few weeks later the question became irrelevant because of my return to prison.

My domestic affairs took up a lot of my time. My mother's health continued to improve, but very slowly. She was still bedridden, but she seemed to be out of danger. I turned to my financial affairs, which had been long neglected and were in a muddle. We had been spending much more than we could afford, and there seemed to be no obvious way of reducing our expenditure. I was not particularly anxious about making both ends meet. I almost looked forward to the time when I would have no money left. Money and possessions are useful enough in the modern world, but often they become a burden for one who wants to go on a long journey. It is very difficult for moneyed people to take part in undertakings which involve risk; they are always afraid of losing their goods and chattels. What is the good of money or property if the Government can take possession of it when it chooses, or even confiscate it? So I almost wished to get rid of what little I had. Our needs were few, and I felt confident of my ability to earn enough. My chief concern was that my mother, in the evening of her life, should not suffer discomforts or any marked lowering of the standard of living. I was also anxious that my daughter's education should not be interfered with, and this, according to my thinking, involved a stay in Europe. Apart from this, neither my wife nor I had any special need for money. Or so we thought, being unused to the real lack of it. I am quite sure that, should the time come when we lack money, we shall not be happy about it. One extravagance which I have kept up will be hard to give up, and this is the buying of books.

To improve the immediate financial situation we decided to sell off my wife's jewelry, the silver and other similar articles that we possessed, as well as many cartloads of odds and ends. Kamala did not like the idea of parting with her jewelry, although she had not worn any of it for a dozen years and it had lain in the bank. She had looked forward to handing it on to our daughter.

It was January 1934. Arrests of our workers continued in the villages of the Allahabad district. January 26—Independence Day—was coming and it could not be ignored. But who was to give the lead? And what was the lead to be? There was no one besides me who was functioning, even in theory, as an official of the All-India Congress. I consulted some friends, and almost all agreed that something should be done, but there was no agreement as to what this something should be. I found a general tendency to avoid any action which might lead to arrests on a large scale. Eventually I issued a brief appeal for the appropriate celebration of Independence Day, the manner of doing so to be decided by each local area for itself. In Allahabad we planned a fairly widespread celebration all over the district.

We felt that the organizers of this Independence Day celebration would be arrested on that day. Before I went back to prison again I wanted to pay a visit to Bengal. This was partly to meet old colleagues there, but really it was to be a gesture in the nature of tribute to the people of Bengal for their extraordinary sufferings during the past few years.

I had to go to Calcutta with Kamala to consult our doctors there about her treatment. She had been far from well, but we had both tried to overlook this to some extent and postpone recourse to a treatment which might involve a long stay in Calcutta or elsewhere. We wanted to be together as much as possible during my brief period outside prison. After I went back to jail, I thought, she would have plenty of time for doctors and treatment. Now that arrest seemed near, I decided to have these consultations at least in my presence in Calcutta; the rest could be attended to later.

So we decided to go to Calcutta, Kamala and I, on January 15. We wanted to return in good time for our Independence Day meetings.

It was the afternoon of January 15, 1934. I was standing in the veranda of our house in Allahabad addressing a group of peasants. The annual *Magh Mela* had begun, and we had crowds of visitors all day. Suddenly I became unsteady on my feet and could hardly keep my balance. I clung on to a column near by. Doors started banging, and a rumbling noise came from the adjoining Swaraj Bhawan, where many of the tiles were sliding down the roof. Being unaccustomed to earthquakes, I did not know at first what was happening, but I soon realized it. I was rather amused and interested at this novel experience, and I continued my talk to the peasants and began telling them about the earthquake. My old aunt shouted to me from some distance to run out of the building. The idea struck me as absurd. I did not take the earthquake seriously, and in any event I was not going to leave my bedridden mother upstairs, and my wife, who was probably packing, also upstairs and seek safety for myself. For what seemed quite an appreciable time the shocks continued and then passed off. They provided a few minutes' conversation and soon were almost forgotten. We did not know then, nor could we guess, what those two or three minutes had meant to millions in Behar and elsewhere.

That evening Kamala and I left for Calcutta, and, all unknowing, we were carried by our train that night through the southern earthquake area. The next day there was little news in Calcutta about the disaster. The day after bits of news began to come in. On the third day we began to have a faint notion of the calamity.

We spent three and a half days in Calcutta, and during this period I addressed three public meetings. As I had done before in Calcutta, I condemned and argued against terroristic acts, and then I passed on to the methods that the Government had adopted in Bengal. I spoke from a full heart, for I had been greatly moved by accounts of occurrences in the province. What pained me most was the manner in which human dignity had been outraged by indiscriminate suppression of whole populations. The political problem, urgent as it was, took second place before this human problem. These three speeches of mine formed the three counts in the charge against me in my subsequent trial in Calcutta. I was later sentenced on that charge.

From Calcutta we went to Santiniketan to pay a visit to the poet, Rabindranath Tagore. It was always a joy to meet him and, having come so near, we did not wish to miss him. I had been to Santiniketan twice before. It was Kamala's first visit, and she had come especially to see the place, as we were thinking of sending our daughter there. Indira was going to appear for her matriculation soon afterward, and the problem of her future education was troubling us. I was wholly against her joining the regular official or semiofficial universities, for I disliked them. The whole atmosphere that envelops them is official, oppressive, and authoritarian. They have no doubt produced fine men and women in the past, and they will continue to do so. But these few exceptions cannot save the universities from the charge of suppressing and deadening the fine instincts of youth. Santiniketan offered an escape from this dead hand, and so we fixed upon it, although in some ways it was not so up to date and well-equipped as the other universities.

On our way back we stopped at Patna to discuss with Rajendra Babu the problem of earthquake relief. He had just been discharged from prison, and, inevitably, he had taken the lead in unofficial relief work. Our arrival was unexpected, for none of our telegrams had been delivered. The house where we intended staying with Kamala's brother was in ruins; it was a big double-storied brick structure. So, like many others, we lived in the open.

The next day I paid a visit to Muzaffarpur. It was exactly seven days after the earthquake, and little had so far been done to remove the debris, except from some of the main streets. As these streets were cleaned, corpses were being discovered, some in curiously expressive attitudes, as if trying to ward off a falling wall or roof. The ruins were an impressive and terrifying sight. The survivors were thoroughly shaken up and cowed by their nerve-racking experiences.

We returned to Allahabad, and collections of funds and materials were immediately organized, and all of us, of the Congress or out of it, took this up in earnest. Some of my colleagues were of opinion that because of the earthquake the Independence Day celebrations should be called off. But other colleagues and I saw no reason why even an earthquake should interfere with our program. So on January 26 we had a large number of meetings in the villages of Allahabad district and a meeting in the city, and we met with greater success than we had anticipated.

Soon after returning from Behar I issued a statement about the earthquake, ending up with an appeal for funds. In this statement I criticized the inactivity of the Behar Government during the first few days after the earthquake. Thousands of people were killed in Monghyr city alone, and three weeks later I saw a vast quantity of debris still lying untouched, although a few miles away at Jamalpur there was a large colony of many thousands of railway workers, who could have been utilized for this purpose within a few hours of the catastrophe. Living people were unearthed even twelve days after the earthquake. The Government had taken immediate steps to protect property, but they had not been so expeditious in trying to rescue people who lay buried.

My criticism was resented, and soon afterward a few people in Behar came out with a general testimonial in favor of the Government as a kind of counterblast. The earthquake and its demands became almost a secondary matter. More important was the fact that the Government had been criticized, and it had to be defended by its loyal subjects. This was an interesting instance of a widespread phenomenon in India—the dislike of criticism of the Government, which is a commonplace in Western countries. It is the military mentality which cannot tolerate criticism. Like the King, the British Government in India and all of its superior officials can do no wrong. To hint at any such thing is *lèse majesté*.

The curious part of it is that a charge of inefficiency and incompetence is resented far more than an accusation of harsh government or tyranny. The latter might indeed land the person making it in prison, but the Government is used to it and does not really mind it. After all, in a way, it might almost be considered a compliment to an imperial race. But to be called inefficient and wanting in nerve hurts, for this strikes at the root of their self-esteem; it disturbs the messianic delusions of the English officials in India.

There is a general belief among Englishmen, frequently asserted as if it was an incontrovertible maxim, that a change of government in India, involving a reduction or elimination of British influence, would result in a much worse and more inefficient government. I believe that self-government is good for any country. But I am not prepared to accept even self-government at the cost of really good government. Self-government, if it is to justify itself, must stand ultimately for better government for the masses. It is because I believe that the British Government in India, whatever its claims in the past may have been, is incapable of providing good government and rising standards for the masses today, that I feel that it has outlived its utility, such as it was, in India. The only real justification for Indian freedom is the promise of better government, of a higher standard for the masses, of industrial and cultural growth, and of the removal of the atmosphere of fear and suppression that foreign imperialist rule invariably brings in its train.

The Allahabad Earthquake Relief Committee deputed me to visit the areas affected by the earthquake and to report on the methods of relief work adopted there. I went immediately, alone, and for ten days I wandered about those torn and ruined territories. It was a very strenuous tour, and I had little sleep during those days. From five in the morning till almost midnight we were up and about, motoring over the cracked and crumpled-up roads, or going by little boats where the bridges had collapsed and the roads were under water owing to a change in level. The towns were impressive enough with their extensive ruins, and their roads torn up and twisted sometimes as by a giant hand, or raised high above the plinth of the houses on either side. Out of huge cracks in these roads water and sand had gushed out and swept away men and cattle. More even than these towns, the plains of north Behar—the garden of Behar, they used to be called—had desolation and destruction stamped upon them. Mile upon mile of sand, and large sheets of water, and huge cracks and vast numbers of little craters out of which this sand and water had come. Some British officers who flew over this area said that it bore some resemblance to the battlefields of northern France in wartime and soon after.

The city of Monghyr was the last place in our tour. We had wandered a good deal and gone almost up to the frontier of Nepal, and we had seen many harrowing sights. We had become used to ruins and destruction on a vast scale. And yet when we saw Monghyr and the absolute destruction of this rich city, we gasped and shivered at the horror of it. I can never forget that terrible sight.

In Monghyr I indulged in a theatrical gesture to give a push to the self-help movement for digging and removing the debris. I did so with some hesitation, but it turned out to be a success. All the leaders of the relief organizations went out with spades and baskets and did a good day's digging, and we brought out the corpse of a little girl. I left Monghyr that day, but the digging went on and many local people took it up with very good results.

During my tour in the earthquake areas, or just before going there, I read with a great shock Gandhiji's statement to the effect that the earthquake had been a punishment for the sin of untouchability. This was a staggering remark, and I welcomed and wholly agreed with Rabindranath Tagore's answer to it. Anything more opposed to the scientific outlook it would be difficult to imagine.

And, if the earthquake was a divine punishment for sin, how are we to discover for which sin we are being punished?—for, alas! we have many sins to atone for. Each person can have his pet explanation; we may have been punished for submitting to alien domination, or for putting up with an unjust social system. The Maharaja of Durbhanga, the owner of enormous estates, was, financially, one of the major sufferers from the earthquake. We might as well say that this was a judgment on the zamindari system. That would be nearer the mark than to suggest that the more or less innocent people of Behar were being made to suffer vicariously for the sins of untouchability of the people of south India. Why did not the earthquake visit the land of untouchability itself? Or the British Government might call the calamity a divine punishment for civil disobedience, for, as a matter of fact, north Behar, which suffered most from the earthquake, took a leading part in the freedom movement.

I got back home in Allahabad on February 11, dead tired after my tour. Ten strenuous days had made me look ghastly, and my people were surprised at my appearance. I tried to begin writing my report of the tour for the Allahabad Relief Committee, but sleep overcame me. I spent at least twelve hours out of the next twenty-four in sleep.

Next day, in the late afternoon, Kamala and I had finished tea, and Purushottam Das Tandon had just then joined us. We were standing in the veranda when a car drove up and a police officer alighted. I knew immediately that my time had come. I went up to him and said: *"Bahut dinōn se āpkā intazār thā"*—"I have been waiting for you for a long time." He was a little apologetic and said that he was not to blame. The warrant was from Calcutta.

Five months and thirteen days I had been out, and now I went back again to seclusion and loneliness. But the real burden was not mine; it had to be shouldered, as always, by the womenfolk—by my ailing mother, my wife, my sister.

## XLV

## ALIPORE JAIL

THAT VERY NIGHT I was taken to Calcutta. From Howrah station a huge Black Maria carried me to Lal Bazaar Police Station. I had read much of this famous headquarters of the Calcutta police, and I looked round with interest. There were large numbers of European sergeants and inspectors to be seen, far more than would have been in evidence in any police headquarters in northern India. The constables seemed to be almost all from Behar or the eastern districts of the United Provinces. During the many journeys I made in the big prison lorry, to court and back or from one prison to another, a number of these constables used to accompany me inside. They looked thoroughly unhappy, disliking their job, and obviously full of sympathy for me. Sometimes their eyes glistened with tears.

I was kept in the Presidency Jail to begin with, and from there I was taken for my trial to the Chief Presidency Magistrate's court. This was a novel experience. The courtroom and building had more the appearance of a besieged fortress than of an open court. Except for a few newspapermen and the usual lawyers, no outsiders were allowed anywhere in the neighborhood. The police were present in some force. These arrangements apparently had not been made especially for me; that was the daily routine. When I was taken to the courtroom I had to march through a long passage (inside the room) which was closely wired on top and at the side. It was like going through a cage. The dock was far from the magistrate's seat. The courtroom was crowded with policemen and black-coated and -gowned lawyers.

I was used enough to court trials. Many of my previous trials had taken place in jail precincts. But there had always been some friends, relatives, familiar faces about, and the whole atmosphere had been a little easier. The police had usually kept in the background, and there had never been any cagelike structures about. Here it was very different, and I gazed at strange, unfamiliar faces between whom and me there was nothing in common. It was not an attractive crowd. I am afraid gowned lawyers en masse are not beautiful to look at, and police-court lawyers seem to develop a peculiarly unlovely look. At last I managed to spot one familiar lawyer's face in that black array, but he was lost in the crowd.

I felt very lonely and isolated even when I sat on the balcony outside before the trial began. My pulse must have quickened a little, and inwardly I was not quite so composed as I usually had been during my previous trials. It struck me then that if even I, with so much experience of trials and convictions, could react abnormally to that situation, how much more must young and inexperienced people feel the tension?

I felt much better in the dock itself. There was, as usual, no defense offered, and I read out a brief statement. The next day, February 16, I was sentenced to two years. My seventh term of imprisonment had begun.

I looked back with some satisfaction to my five and a half months' stay outside. That time had been fairly well occupied, and I had managed to get through some useful jobs. My mother had turned the corner and was out of immediate danger. My younger sister, Krishna, had married. My daughter's future education had been fixed up. I had straightened out some of my domestic and financial tangles. Many personal matters that I had been long neglecting had been attended to. In the field of public affairs I knew that no one could do much then. I had at least helped a little in stiffening up the Congress attitude and in directing it to some extent toward social and economic ways of thinking. My Poona correspondence with Gandhiji, and later my articles in the press, had made a difference. My articles on the communal question had also done some good. And then I had met Gandhiji again after more than two years, and many other friends and comrades, and had charged myself with nervous and emotional energy for another period.

One shadow remained to darken my mind—Kamala's ill-health. I had no notion then how very ill she was, for she has a habit of carrying on till she collapses. But I was worried. And yet I hoped that now I was in prison she would be free to devote herself to her treatment. It was more difficult to do so while I was out, and she was not willing to leave me for long.

I had one other regret. I was sorry that I had not visited even once the rural areas of Allahabad district. Many of my young colleagues had recently been arrested there for carrying out our instructions, and it seemed almost like disloyalty to them not to follow them in the district.

Again the Black Maria carried me back to prison. On our way we passed plenty of troops on the march with machine guns, armored cars, etc. I peeped at them through the tiny openings of our prison van. How ugly an armored car is, I thought, and a tank. They reminded me of prehistoric monsters—dinosaurs and the like.

I was transferred from the Presidency Jail to the Alipore Central Jail, and there I was given a little cell, about ten feet by nine. In front of it were a veranda and a small open yard. The wall enclosing the yard was a low one, about seven feet, and looking over it I was confronted by a strange sight. All manner of odd buildings—single-story, double-story, round, rectangular, curious roofings—rose all round, some overtopping the others. It seemed that the structures had grown one by one, being fitted in anyhow to take advantage of all the available space. Almost it looked like a jigsaw puzzle or a futurist attempt at the fantastic. And yet I was told that all the buildings had been arranged very methodically with a tower in the center (which was a church for the Christian prisoners) and radiating lines. Being a city jail, the area was limited, and every little bit of it had to be utilized.

I had hardly recovered from my first view of the seemingly fantastic structures around me when a terrifying sight greeted me. Two chimneys, right in front of my cell and yard, were belching forth dense volumes of black smoke, and sometimes the wind blew this smoke in my direction, almost suffocating me. They were the chimneys of the jail kitchens. I suggested to the superintendent later that gas masks might be provided to meet this offensive.

It was not an agreeable start, and the future was not inviting—to enjoy the unchanging prospect of the red-brick structures of Alipore Jail and to swallow and inhale the smoke of its kitchen chimneys. There were no trees or greenery in my yard. It was all paved and *pucca* and clean, except for the daily deposit of smoke, but it was also bare and cheerless. I could just see the tops of one or two trees in adjoining yards. They were barren of leaf or flower when I arrived. But gradually a mysterious change came over them, and little bits of green were peeping out all over their branches. The leaves were coming out of the buds; they grew rapidly and covered the nakedness of the branches with their pleasant green. It was a delightful change which made even Alipore Jail look gay and cheerful.

In one of these trees was a kite's nest which interested me, and I watched it often. The little ones were growing and learning the tricks of the trade, and sometimes they would swoop down with rapidity and amazing accuracy and snatch the bread out of a prisoner's hand, almost out of his mouth.

From sunset to sunrise (more or less) we were locked up in our cells, and the long winter evenings were not very easy to pass. I grew tired of reading or writing hour after hour, and would start walking up and down that little cell—four or five short steps forward and then back again. I remembered the bears at the zoo tramping up and down their cages. Sometimes when I felt particularly bored I took to my favorite remedy, the *shīrshāsana*—standing on the head!

The early part of the night was fairly quiet, and city sounds used to float in—the noise of the trams, a gramophone, or someone singing in the distance. It was pleasant to hear this faint and distant music. But there was not much peace at night, for the guards on duty tramped up and down, and every hour there was some kind of an inspection. Some officer came round with a lantern to make sure that none of us had escaped. At 3 A.M. every day, or rather night, there was a tremendous din, and a mighty sound of scraping and scrubbing. The kitchens had begun functioning.

There were vast numbers of warders and guards and officers and clerks in the Alipore Jail, as also in the Presidency. Both these prisons housed a population about equal to that of Naini Prison—2200 to 2300—but the staff in each must have been more than double that of Naini. There were many European warders and retired Indian army officers. It was evident that the British Empire functioned more intensively and more expensively in Calcutta than in the United Provinces. A sign and a perpetual reminder of the might of the Empire was the cry that prisoners had to shout out when high officials approached them. *"Sarkar salaam"* was the cry, lengthened out, and it was accompanied by certain physical movements of the body. The voices of the prisoners shouting out this cry came to me many times a day over my yard wall, and especially when the superintendent passed by daily. I could just see over my seven-foot wall the top of the huge State umbrella under which the superintendent marched.

Was this extraordinary cry—*sarkar salaam*—and the movements that went with it relics of old times, I wondered; or were they the invention of some inspired English official? I do not know, but I imagine that it was an English invention. It has a typical Anglo-Indian sound about it. Fortunately this cry does not prevail in the United Provinces jails or probably in any other province besides Bengal and Assam. The way this enforced salutation to the might of the *sarkar* is shouted out seemed to me very degrading.

The brief winter was soon over, and spring raced by, and summer began. It grew hotter day by day. I had never been fond of the Calcutta climate, and even a few days of it had made me stale and flat. In prison conditions were naturally far worse, and I did not prosper as the days went by. Lack of space for exercise and long lock-up hours in that climate probably affected my health a little, and I lost weight rapidly. How I began to hate all locks and bolts and bars and walls!

After a month in Alipore I was allowed to take some exercise outside my yard. This was an agreeable change, and I could walk up and down under the main wall, morning and evening. Gradually I got accustomed to Alipore Jail and the Calcutta climate; and even the kitchen, with its smoke and mighty din, became a tolerable nuisance. Other matters occupied my mind, other worries filled me. News from outside was not good.

I was surprised to find in Alipore that no daily paper would be allowed to me after my conviction. As an under-trial prisoner I received the daily *Statesman,* of Calcutta, but this was stopped the day after my trial was over. In the United Provinces, ever since 1932, a daily (chosen by the Government) was permitted to A-Class or first division prisoners. So also in most other provinces, and I was fully under the impression that the same rule was applicable in Bengal. Instead of the daily, however, I was supplied with the weekly *Statesman*. This was evidently meant for retired English officials or businessmen who had gone back to England, and it contained a summary of Indian news likely to interest them. No foreign news at all was given, and I missed it very much, as I used to follow it closely. Fortunately I was allowed to have the *Manchester Guardian Weekly,* and this kept me in touch with Europe and international affairs.

My arrest and trial in February coincided with upheavals and bitter conflicts in Europe. There was the ferment in France resulting in fascist riots and the formation of a "National" Government. And, far worse, in Austria, Chancellor Dollfuss was shooting down workers and putting an end to the great edifice of social democracy there. The news of the Austrian bloodshed depressed me greatly. What an awful!

and bloody place this world was, and how barbarous was man when he wanted to protect his vested interests! All over Europe and America fascism seemed to be advancing. When Hitler came into power in Germany, I had imagined that his regime could not possibly last long, as he was offering no solution of Germany's economic troubles. So also, as fascism spread elsewhere, I consoled myself that it represented the last ditch of reaction. After it must come the breaking of the shackles. But I began to wonder if my wish was not father to my thought. Was it so obvious that this fascist wave would retire so easily or so quickly? And, even if conditions became intolerable for the fascist dictatorships, would they not rather hurl their countries into devastating war rather than give in? What would be the result of such a conflict?

Meanwhile, fascism of various kinds and shapes spread. Spain, that new "Republic of Honest Men"—*los hombres honrados*—the very *Manchester Guardian* of governments, as someone called it, had gone far back and deep into reaction. All the fine phrases of its honest Liberal leaders had not kept it from sliding down. Everywhere Liberalism showed its utter ineffectiveness to face modern conditions. It clung to words and phrases, and thought that they could take the place of action. When a crisis came, it simply faded off like the end of a film that is over.

I read the leading articles of the *Manchester Guardian* on the Austrian tragedy with deep interest and appreciation.

"Austrian democracy has been destroyed, although to its everlasting glory it went down fighting and so created a legend that may rekindle the spirit of European freedom some day in years to come."

"The Europe that is unfree has ceased to breathe; there is no flow or counterflow of healthy spirits; a gradual suffocation has set in, and only some violent convulsion or inner paroxysm and a striking out to the right and left can avert the mental coma that is approaching. . . . Europe from the Rhine to the Urals is one great prison."

Moving passages which found an echo in my heart. But I wondered: what of India? How can it be that the *Manchester Guardian* or the many lovers of freedom who undoubtedly exist in England should be so oblivious to our fate? How can they miss seeing here what they condemn with such fervor elsewhere? It was a great English Liberal leader, trained in the nineteenth-century tradition, cautious by temperament, restrained in his language, who said twenty years ago, on the eve of the Great War: "Sooner than be a silent witness of the tragic triumph of force over law, I would see this country of ours blotted out of the page of history." A brave thought, eloquently put, and the gallant youth of England went in their millions to vindicate it. But if an Indian ventures to make a statement similar to Mr. Asquith's, what fate is his?

The British are an insular race, and long success and prosperity have made them look down on almost all others. For them, as some one has said, *"les nègres commencent à Calais."* But that is too general a statement. Perhaps the British upper-class division of the world would be somewhat as follows: (1) Britain—a long gap, and then (2) the British Dominions (white populations only) and America (Anglo-Saxons only, and not dagoes, wops, etc.), (3) Western Europe, (4) Rest of Europe, (5) South America (Latin races), a long gap, and then (6) the brown, yellow, and black races of Asia and Africa.

How far we of the last of these classes are from the heights where our rulers live! Is it any wonder that their vision grows dim when they look toward us, and that we should irritate them when we talk of democracy and liberty? These words were not coined for our use. Was it not a great Liberal statesman, John Morley, who declared that he could not conceive of democratic institutions in India even in the far, dim future? Democracy for India was, like Canada's fur coat, unsuited to her climate. And, later on, Britain's Labour party, the standard-bearers of socialism, the champions of the underdog, presented us, in the flush of their triumph, with a revival of the Bengal Ordinance in 1924, and during their second government our fate was even worse. I am quite sure that none of them mean us ill, and, when they address us in their best pulpit manner—"Dearly beloved brethren"—they feel a glow of conscious virtue. But, to them, we are not as they are and must be judged by other standards. It is difficult enough for an Englishman and a Frenchman to think alike because of linguistic and cultural differences; how much vaster must be the difference between an Englishman and an Asiatic?

Lord Lytton, a former governor of an Indian province, who acted as Viceroy for a while, often referred to as a liberal and sympathetic governor, is reported to have said [1] that "the Government of India was far more representative of India as a whole than the Congress politicians. The Government of India was able to speak in the name of officials, the Army, the Police, the Princes, the fighting regiments and both Moslems and Hindus, whereas the Congress politicians

[1] House of Lords, December 17, 1934.

could not even speak on behalf of one of the great Indian communities." He went on to make his meaning quite clear: "When I speak of Indian opinion, I am thinking of those on whose co-operation I had to rely and on whose co-operation the future Governors and Viceroys will have to rely."

Two interesting points emerge from his speech: the India that counts means those who help the British; and the British Government of India is the most representative and, therefore, democratic body in the country. That this argument should be advanced seriously shows that English words seem to change their meanings when they cross the Suez Canal. The next and obvious step in reasoning would be, that autocratic government is the most representative and democratic form because the King represents everybody. We get back to the divine right of kings and *"l'état, c'est moi!"*

In India we are told that our communal divisions come in the way of our democratic progress, and, therefore, with incontrovertible logic, those divisions are perpetuated. We are further told that we are not united enough. In Egypt there are no communal divisions, and it appears that the most perfect political unity prevails. And yet, this very unity becomes an obstacle in the way of democracy and freedom! Truly the path of democracy is straight and narrow. Democracy for an Eastern country seems to mean only one thing: to carry out the behests of the imperialist ruling power and not to touch any of its interests. Subject to that proviso, democratic freedom can flourish unchecked.


## XLVI

## DESOLATION

APRIL CAME. Rumors reached me in my cell in Alipore of happenings outside, rumors that were unpleasant and disturbing. The superintendent of the jail informed me casually one day that Mr. Gandhi had withdrawn civil disobedience. I knew no more. The news was not welcome, and I felt sad at this winding up of something that had meant so much to me for many years. And yet I reasoned with myself that the end was bound to come. I knew in my heart that sometime or other civil disobedience would have to be wound up, for the time being at least. Individuals may hold out almost indefinitely, regardless of the consequences, but national organizations do not behave in this manner. I had no doubt that Gandhiji had interpreted correctly the mind of the country and of the great majority of Congressmen, and I tried to reconcile myself to the new development, unpleasant as it was.

Some days later the weekly *Statesman* came to me, and I read in it the statement which Gandhiji had issued when withdrawing civil disobedience. I read it with amazement and sinking of heart. Again and again I read it; civil disobedience and much else vanished from my mind, and other doubts and conflicts filled it. "This statement," wrote Gandhiji, "owes its inspiration to a personal chat with the inmates and associates of the *Satyagraha Ashrama. . . .* More especially is it due to revealing information I got in the course of a conversation about a valued companion of long standing who was found reluctant to perform the full prison task, preferring his private studies to the allotted task. This was undoubtedly contrary to the rules of *Satyagraha.* More than the imperfection of the friend whom I love, more than ever it brought home to me my own imperfections. The friend said he had thought that I was aware of his weakness. I was blind. Blindness in a leader is unpardonable. I saw at once that I must for the time being remain the sole representative of civil resistance in action."

The imperfection or fault, if such it was, of the "friend" was a very trivial affair. I confess that I have often been guilty of it, and I am wholly unrepentant. But, even if it was a serious matter, was a vast national movement involving scores of thousands directly and millions indirectly to be thrown out of gear because an individual had erred? This seemed to me a monstrous proposition and an immoral one. I cannot presume to speak of what is and what is not *Satyagraha,* but in my own little way I have endeavored to follow certain standards of conduct, and all those standards were shocked and upset by this statement of Gandhiji's. I knew that Gandhiji usually acts on instinct (I prefer to call it that than the "inner voice" or an answer to prayer), and very often that instinct is right. He has repeatedly shown what a wonderful knack he has of sensing the mass mind and of acting at the psychological moment. The reasons which he afterward adduces to justify his action are usually afterthoughts and seldom carry one very far. A leader or a man of action in a crisis almost always acts subconsciously and then thinks of the reasons for his action. I felt also that Gandhiji had acted rightly in suspending civil resistance. But the reason he had given seemed to me an insult to intelligence and an amazing performance for a leader of a national movement. He was perfectly entitled to treat his *ashrama* inmates in any manner he liked; they had taken all kinds of pledges and accepted a certain regime. But the Congress had not done so; I had not done so. Why should we be tossed hither and thither for, what seemed to me, metaphysical and mystical reasons in which I was not interested? Was it conceivable to have any political movement on this basis? I had willingly accepted the moral aspect of *Satyagraha* as I understood it (within certain limits, I admit). That basic aspect appealed to me, and it seemed to raise politics to a higher and nobler level. I was prepared to agree that the end does not justify all kinds of means. But this new development or interpretation was something much more far-reaching, and it held forth some possibilities which frightened me.

The whole statement frightened and oppressed me tremendously. And then finally the advice he gave to Congressmen was that "they must learn the art and beauty of self-denial and voluntary poverty. They must engage themselves in nation-building activities, the spread of *khadi* through personal hand-spinning and hand-weaving, the spread of communal unity of hearts by irreproachable personal conduct toward one another in every walk of life, the banishing of untouchability in every shape or form in one's own person, the spread of total abstinence from intoxicating drinks and drugs by personal contact with individual addicts and generally by cultivating personal purity. These are services which provide maintenance on the poor man's scale. Those for whom the poor man's scale is not feasible should find a place in small unorganized industries of national importance which give a better wage."

This was the political program that we were to follow. A vast distance seemed to separate him from me. With a stab of pain I felt that the cords of allegiance that had bound me to him for many years had snapped. For long a mental tussle had been going on within me. I had not understood or appreciated much that Gandhiji had done. His fasts and his concentration on other issues during the continuance of civil disobedience, when his comrades were in the grip of the struggle, his personal and self-created entanglements, which led him to the extraordinary position that, while out of prison, he was yet pledged to himself not to take part in the political movement, his new loyalties and pledges which put in the shade the old loyalty and pledge and job, undertaken together with many colleagues, while yet that job was unfinished, had all oppressed me. During my short period out of prison I had felt these and other differences more than ever. Gandhiji had stated that there were temperamental differences between us. They were perhaps more than temperamental, and I realized that I held clear and definite views about many matters which were opposed to his. And yet in the past I had tried to subordinate them, as far as I could, to what I conceived to be the larger loyalty—the cause of national freedom for which the Congress seemed to be working. I tried to be loyal and faithful to my leader and my colleagues, for in my spiritual make-up loyalty to a cause and to one's colleagues holds a high place. I fought many a battle within myself when I felt that I was being dragged away from the anchor of my spiritual faith. Somehow I managed to compromise. Perhaps I did wrong, for it can never be right for anyone to let go of that anchor. But in the conflict of ideals I clung to my loyalty to my colleagues, and hoped that the rush of events and the development of our struggle might dissolve the difficulties that troubled me and bring my colleagues nearer to my viewpoint.

And now? Suddenly I felt very lonely in that cell of Alipore Jail. Life seemed to be a dreary affair, a very wilderness of desolation. Of the many hard lessons that I had learned, the hardest and the most painful now faced me: that it is not possible in any vital matter to rely on anyone. One must journey through life alone; to rely on others is to invite heartbreak.

Some of my accumulated irritation directed itself against religion and the religious outlook. What an enemy this was to clearness of thought and fixity of purpose, I thought; for was it not based on emotion and passion? Presuming to be spiritual, how far removed it was from real spirituality and things of the spirit. Thinking in terms of some other world, it had little conception of human values and social values and social justice. With its preconceived notions it deliberately shut its eyes to reality for fear that this might not fit in with them. It based itself on truth, and yet so sure was it of having discovered it, and the whole of it, that it did not take the trouble to search for it; all that concerned it was to tell others of it. The will to truth was not the same thing as the will to believe. It talked of peace and yet supported systems and organizations that could not exist but for violence. It condemned the violence of the sword, but what of the violence that comes quietly and often in peaceful garb and starves and kills; or, worse still, without doing any outward physical injury, outrages the mind and crushes the spirit and breaks the heart?

And then I thought of him again who was the cause of this commotion within me. What a wonderful man was Gandhiji after all, with his amazing and almost irresistible charm and subtle power over people. His writings and his sayings conveyed little enough impression of the man behind; his personality was far bigger than they would lead one to think. And his services to India, how vast they had been! He had instilled courage and manhood in her people, and discipline and endurance, and the power of joyful sacrifice for a cause, and, with all his humility, pride. Courage is the one sure foundation of character, he had said; without courage there is no morality, no religion, no love. "One cannot follow truth or love so long as one is subject to fear." With all his horror of violence, he had told us that "cowardice is a thing even more hateful than violence." And "discipline is the pledge and guarantee that a man means business. There is no deliverance and no hope without sacrifice, discipline, and self-control. Mere sacrifice without discipline will be unavailing." Words only and pious phrases perhaps, rather platitudinous, but there was power behind the words, and India knew that this little man meant business.

He came to represent India to an amazing degree and to express the very spirit of that ancient and tortured land. Almost he was India, and his very failings were Indian failings. A slight to him was hardly a personal matter, it was an insult to the nation; and Viceroys and others who indulged in these disdainful gestures little realized what a dangerous crop they were sowing. I remember how hurt I was when I first learned that the Pope had refused an interview to Gandhiji when he was returning from the Round Table Conference in December 1931. That refusal seemed to me an affront to India, and there can be no doubt that the refusal was intentional, though the affront was probably not thought of. The Catholic Church does not approve of saints or mahatmas outside its fold, and because some Protestant churchmen had called Gandhiji a great man of religion and a real Christian, it became all the more necessary for Rome to dissociate itself from this heresy.

But Gandhiji's greatness or his services to India or the tremendous debt I personally owed to him were not in question. In spite of all that, he might be hopelessly in the wrong in many matters. What, after all, was he aiming at? In spite of the closest association with him for many years, I am not clear in my own mind about his objective. I doubt if he is clear himself. One step is enough for me, he says; and he does not try to peep into the future or to have a clearly conceived end before him. Look after the means, and the end will take care of itself, he is never tired of repeating. Be good in your personal individual lives, and all else will follow. That is not a political or scientific attitude, nor is it perhaps even an ethical attitude. It is narrowly moralist, and it begs the question: What is goodness? Is it merely an individual affair or a social affair? Gandhiji lays all stress on character and attaches little importance to intellectual training and development. Intellect without character is likely to be dangerous, but what is character without intellect? How, indeed, does character develop? Gandhiji has been compared to the medieval Christian saints, and much that he says seems to fit in with this. It does not fit in at all with modern psychological experience and method.

But, however this may be, vagueness in an objective seems to me deplorable. Action to be effective must be directed to clearly conceived ends. Life is not all logic, and those ends will have to be varied from time to time to fit in with it, but some end must always be clearly envisaged.

I imagine that Gandhiji is not so vague about the objective as he sometimes appears to be. He is passionately desirous of going in a certain direction, but this is wholly at variance with modern ideas and conditions, and he has so far been unable to fit the two, or to chalk out all the intermediate steps leading to his goal. Hence the appearance of vagueness and avoidance of clarity. But his general inclination has been clear enough for a quarter of a century, ever since he started formulating his philosophy in South Africa. I do not know if those early writings still represent his views. I doubt if they do so in their entirety, but they do help us to understand the background of his thought.

"India's salvation consists," he wrote in 1909, "in unlearning what she has learned during the last fifty years. The railways, telegraphs, hospitals, lawyers, doctors, and suchlike have all to go; and the so-called upper classes have to learn consciously, religiously, and deliberately the simple peasant life, knowing it to be a life giving true happiness." And again: "Every time I get into a railway car or use a motor bus I know that I am doing violence to my sense of what is right"; "to attempt to reform the world by means of highly artificial and speedy locomotion is to attempt the impossible."

All this seems to me utterly wrong and harmful doctrine, and impossible of achievement. Behind it lies Gandhiji's love and praise of poverty and suffering and the ascetic life. For him progress and civilization consist not in the multiplication of wants, of higher standards of living, "but in the deliberate and voluntary restriction of wants, which promotes real happiness and contentment, and increases the capacity for service." If these premises are once accepted, it becomes easy to follow the rest of Gandhiji's thought and to have a better understanding of his activities. But most of us do not accept those premises, and yet we complain later on when we find that his activities are not to our liking.

Personally I dislike the praise of poverty and suffering. I do not think they are at all desirable, and they ought to be abolished. Nor do I appreciate the ascetic life as a social ideal, though it may suit individuals. I understand and appreciate simplicity, equality, self-control; but not the mortification of the flesh. Just as an athlete requires to train his body, I believe that the mind and habits have also to be trained and brought under control. It would be absurd to expect that a person who is given to too much self-indulgence can endure much suffering or show unusual self-control or behave like a hero when the crisis comes. To be in good moral condition requires at least as much training as to be in good physical condition. But that certainly does not mean asceticism or self-mortification.

Nor do I appreciate in the least the idealization of the "simple peasant life." I have almost a horror of it, and instead of submitting to it myself I want to drag out even the peasantry from it, not to urbanization, but to the spread of urban cultural facilities to rural areas. Far from this life's giving me true happiness, it would be almost as bad as imprisonment for me. What is there in "The Man with the Hoe" to idealize over? Crushed and exploited for innumerable generations, he is only little removed from the animals who keep him company.

> Who made him dead to rapture and despair,
> A thing that grieves not and that never hopes,
> Stolid and stunned, a brother to the ox?

This desire to get away from the mind of man to primitive conditions where mind does not count, seems to me quite incomprehensible. The very thing that is the glory and triumph of man is decried and discouraged, and a physical environment which will oppress the mind and prevent its growth is considered desirable. Present-day civilization is full of evils, but it is also full of good; and it has the capacity in it to rid itself of those evils. To destroy it root and branch is to remove that capacity from it and revert to a dull, sunless, and miserable existence. But even if that were desirable it is an impossible undertaking. We cannot stop the river of change or cut ourselves adrift from it, and psychologically we who have eaten of the apple of Eden cannot forget that taste and go back to primitiveness.

It is difficult to argue this, for the two standpoints are utterly different. Gandhiji is always thinking in terms of personal salvation and of sin, while most of us have society's welfare uppermost in our minds. I find it difficult to grasp the idea of sin, and perhaps it is because of this that I cannot appreciate Gandhiji's general outlook. He is not out to change society or the social structure; he devotes himself to the eradication of sin from individuals. "The follower of Swadeshi," he has written, "never takes upon himself the vain task of trying to reform the world, for he believes that the world is moved and always will be moved according to the rules set by God." And yet he is aggressive enough in his attempts to reform the world; but the reform he aims at is individual reform, the conquest over the senses and the desire to indulge them, which is sin. Probably he will agree with the definition of liberty which an able Roman Catholic writer on fascism has given: "Liberty is no more than freedom from the bondage of sin." How almost identical this is with the words of the Bishop of London written two hundred years ago: "The Freedom which Christianity gives is Freedom from the Bondage of sin and Satan and from the Dominion of Men's Lusts and Passions and inordinate Desires."

If this standpoint is once appreciated, then one begins to understand a little Gandhiji's attitude to sex, extraordinary as that seems to the average person today. For him "any union is a crime when the desire for progeny is absent," and "the adoption of artificial methods must result in imbecility and nervous prostration." "It is wrong and immoral to seek to escape the consequences of one's act. . . . It is bad for him to indulge his appetite and then escape the consequences by taking tonics or other medicines. It is still worse for a person to indulge his animal passions and escape the consequences of his acts."

Personally I find this attitude unnatural and shocking, and if he is right, then I am a criminal on the verge of imbecility and nervous prostration. The Roman Catholics have also vigorously opposed birth control, but they have not carried their argument to the logical limit, as Gandhiji has done. They have temporized and compromised with what they consider to be human nature. But Gandhiji has gone to the extreme limit of his argument and does not recognize the validity or necessity of the sexual act at any time except for the sake of children; he refuses to recognize any natural sex attraction between man and woman. "But I am told," he says, "that this is an impossible ideal, that I do not take account of the natural attraction between man and woman. I refuse to believe that the sensual affinity, referred to here, can be at all regarded as natural; in that case the deluge would soon be over us. The natural affinity between man and woman is the attraction between brother and sister, mother and son, or father and daughter. It is this natural attraction that sustains the world." And more emphatically still: "No, I must declare with all the power I can command that sensual attraction, even between husband and wife, is unnatural."

One can accept it as an act of faith or reject it. There is no halfway house, for it is a question of faith, not of reason. For my part I think Gandhiji is absolutely wrong in this matter. His advice may fit in with some cases, but as a general policy it can only lead to frustration, inhibition, neurosis, and all manner of physical and nervous ills. Sexual restraint is certainly desirable, but I doubt if Gandhiji's doctrine is likely to result in this to any widespread extent. It is too extreme, and most people decide that it is beyond their capacity and go their usual ways, or there is friction between husband and wife. Evidently Gandhiji thinks that birth-control methods necessarily mean inordinate indulgence in the sex act, and that if the sexual affinity between man and woman is admitted every man will run after every woman, and vice versa. Neither inference is justified, and I do not know why he is so obsessed by this problem of sex, important as it is. For him it is a "soot or whitewash" question; there are no intermediate shades. At either end he takes up an extreme position which seems to me most abnormal and unnatural. Perhaps this is a reaction from the deluge of literature on sexology that is descending on us in these days. I presume I am a normal individual and sex has played its part in my life, but it has not obsessed me or diverted me from my other activities. It has been a subordinate part.

I have drifted to other topics, but in those distressful days in Alipore Jail all these ideas crowded in my mind, not in logical order or sequence, but in a wild jumble which confused me and oppressed me. Above all, there was the feeling of loneliness and desolation, heightened by the stifling atmosphere of the jail and my lonely little cell. If I had been outside, the shock would have been more momentary, and I would have adjusted myself sooner to new conditions and found relief in expression and action. Inside the prison there was no such relief, and I spent some miserable days. Fortunately for myself, I am resilient and recover soon from attacks of pessimism. I began to grow out of my depression, and then I had an interview in jail with Kamala. That cheered me up tremendously, and my feeling of isolation left me. Whatever happened, I felt, we had one another.

## XLVII

## PARADOXES

PEOPLE WHO DO not know Gandhiji personally and have only read his writings are apt to think that he is a priestly type, extremely puritanical, long-faced, Calvinistic, and a kill-joy, something like the "priests in black gowns walking their rounds." But his writings do him an injustice; he is far greater than what he writes, and it is not quite fair to quote what he has written and criticize it. He is the very opposite of the Calvinistic priestly type. His smile is delightful, his laughter infectious, and he radiates light-heartedness. There is something child-like about him which is full of charm. When he enters a room, he brings a breath of fresh air with him which lightens the atmosphere

He is an extraordinary paradox. I suppose all outstanding men are so to some extent. For years I have puzzled over this problem: why with all his love and solicitude for the underdog he yet supports a system which inevitably produces it and crushes it; why with all his passion for nonviolence he is in favor of a political and social structure which is wholly based on violence and coercion? Perhaps it is not correct to say that he is in favor of such a system; he is more or less of a philosophical anarchist. But, as the ideal anarchist state is too far off still and cannot easily be conceived, he accepts the present order. It is not, I think, a question of means, that he objects, as he does, to the use of violence in bringing about a change. Quite apart from the methods to be adopted for changing the existing order, an ideal objective can be envisaged, something that is possible of achievement in the not-distant future.

Sometimes he calls himself a socialist, but he uses the word in a sense peculiar to himself which has little or nothing to do with the economic framework of society which usually goes by the name of socialism. Following his lead, a number of prominent Congressmen have taken to the use of that word, meaning thereby a kind of muddled humanitarianism. I know that Gandhiji is not ignorant of the subject, for he has read many books on economics and socialism and even Marxism, and has discussed it with others. But I am becoming more and more convinced that in vital matters the mind by itself does not carry us far.

Gandhiji underwent a tremendous conversion during his early days in South Africa, and this shook him up greatly and altered his whole outlook on life. Since then he has had a fixed basis for all his ideas, and his mind is hardly an open mind. He listens with the greatest patience and attention to people who make new suggestions to him, but behind all his courteous interest one has the impression that one is addressing a closed door. He is so firmly anchored to some ideas that everything else seems unimportant. To insist on other and secondary matters would be a distraction and a distortion of the larger scheme. To hold on to that anchor would necessarily result in a proper adjustment of these other matters. If the means are right, the end is bound to be right.

That, I think, is the main background of his thought. He suspects also socialism, and more particularly Marxism, because of their association with violence. The very words "class war" breathe conflict and violence and are thus repugnant to him. He has also no desire to raise the standards of the masses beyond a certain very modest competence, for higher standards and leisure may lead to self-indulgence and sin. It is bad enough that the handful of the well-to-do are self-indulgent; it would be much worse if their numbers were added to.

That outlook is as far removed from the socialistic, or for that matter the capitalistic, as anything can be. To say that science and industrial technique today can demonstrably feed, clothe, and house everybody and raise their standards of living very greatly, if vested interests did not intervene, does not interest him much, for he is not keen on those results, beyond a certain limit. The promise of socialism therefore holds no attraction for him, and capitalism is only partly tolerable because it circumscribes the evil. He dislikes both, but puts up with the latter for the present as a lesser evil and as something which exists and of which he has to take cognizance.

I may be wrong perhaps in imputing these ideas to him, but I do feel that he tends to think in this manner, and the paradoxes and confusions in his utterances that trouble us are really due to entirely different premises from which he starts. He does not want people to make an ideal of ever-increasing comfort and leisure, but to think of the moral life, give up their bad habits, to indulge themselves less and less, and thus to develop themselves individually and spiritually. And those who wish to serve the masses have not so much to raise them materially as to go down themselves to their level and mix with them on equal terms. In so doing inevitably they will help in raising them somewhat. That, according to him, is true democracy. "Many have despaired of resisting me," he writes in a statement he issued on September 17, 1934. "This is a humiliating revelation to me, a born democrat. I make that claim, if complete identification with the poorest of mankind, longing to live no better than they, and a corresponding conscious effort to approach that level to the best of one's ability, can entitle one to make it."

Gandhiji is always laying stress on the idea of the trusteeship of the feudal prince, of the big landlord, of the capitalist. He follows a long succession of men of religion. The Pope has declared that "the rich must consider themselves the servants of the Almighty as well as the guardians and the distributors of his wealth, to whom Jesus Christ himself entrusted the fate of the poor." Popular Hinduism and Islam repeat this idea and are always calling upon the rich to be charitable, and they respond by building temples or mosques or *dharamshalas,* or giving, out of their abundance, coppers or silver to the poor and feeling very virtuous in consequence.

This religious attitude is bound up with the world of long ago, when the only possible escape from present misery was in the hope of a world to come. But, though conditions changed and raised the human level in material prosperity beyond the wildest dreams of the past, the stranglehold of that past continued, the stress now being laid on certain vague, unmeasurable spiritual values.

Gandhiji wants to improve the individual internally, morally and spiritually, and thereby to change the external environment. He wants people to give up bad habits and indulgences and to become pure. He lays stress on sexual abstinence, on the giving up of drink, smoking, etc. Opinions may differ about the relative wickedness of these indulgences, but can there be any doubt that even from the individual point of view, and much more so from the social, these personal failings are less harmful than covetousness, selfishness, acquisitiveness, the fierce conflicts of individuals for personal gain, the ruthless struggles of groups and classes, the inhuman suppression and exploitation of one group by another, the terrible wars between nations? Of course he detests all this violence and degrading conflict. But are they not inherent in the acquisitive society of today with its law that the strong must prey on the weak, and its motto, that, as of old, "they shall take who have the power and they shall keep who can"? The profit motive today inevitably leads to conflict. The whole system protects and gives every scope to man's predatory instincts; it encourages some finer instincts, no doubt, but much more the baser instincts of man. Success means the knocking down of others and mounting on their vanquished selves. If these motives and ambitions are encouraged by society and attract the best of our people, does Gandhiji think that he can achieve his ideal—the moral man—in this environment? He wants to develop the spirit of service; he will succeed in the case of some individuals, but, so long as society puts forward as exemplars the victors of an acquisitive society and the chief urge as the personal profit motive, the vast majority will follow this course.

But the problem is no longer merely a moral or an ethical one. It is a practical and urgent problem of today, for the world is in a hopeless muddle, and some way out must be found. We cannot wait, Micawberlike, for something to turn up. Nor can we live by negation alone, criticizing the evil aspects of capitalism, socialism, communism, etc., and hoping vaguely for the golden mean, which will produce a happy compromise combining the best features of all systems, old and new. The malady has to be diagnosed and the cure suggested and worked for. It is quite certain that we cannot stand where we are, nationally and internationally; we may try to go back or we may push forward. Probably there is no choice in the matter, for going back seems inconceivable.

And yet many of Gandhiji's activities might lead one to think that he wants to go back to the narrowest autarchy, not only a self-sufficient nation, but almost a self-sufficient village. In primitive communities the village was more or less self-sufficient and fed and clothed itself and otherwise provided for its needs. Of necessity that means an extremely low standard of living. I do not think Gandhiji is permanently aiming at this, for it is an impossible objective. The huge populations of today would not be able even to subsist in some countries; they would not tolerate this reversion to scarcity and starvation. It is possible, I think, that in an agricultural country like India, so very low is our present standard, that there might be a slight improvement for the masses with the development of village industries. But we are tied up, as every country is tied up, with the rest of the world, and it seems to me quite impossible for us to cut adrift. We must think, therefore, in terms of the world, and in these terms a narrow autarchy is out of the question. Personally I consider it undesirable from every point of view.

Inevitably we are led to the only possible solution—the establishment of a socialist order, first within national boundaries, and eventually in the world as a whole, with a controlled production and distribution of wealth for the public good. How this is to be brought about is another matter, but it is clear that the good of a nation or of mankind must not be held up because some people who profit by the existing order object to the change. If political or social institutions stand in the way of such a change, they have to be removed. To compromise with them at the cost of that desirable and practical ideal would be a gross betrayal. Such a change may partly be forced or expedited by world conditions, but it can hardly take place without the willing consent or acquiescence of the great majority of the people concerned. They have therefore to be converted and won over to it. Conspiratorial violence of a small group will not help. Naturally efforts must be made to win over even those who profit by the existing system, but it is highly unlikely that any large percentage of them will be converted.

The *khadi* movement, hand-spinning and hand-weaving, which is Gandhiji's special favorite, is an intensification of individualism in production, and is thus a throwback to the preindustrial age. As a solution of any vital present-day problem it cannot be taken seriously, and it produces a mentality which may become an obstacle to growth in the right direction. Nevertheless, as a temporary measure I am convinced that it has served a useful purpose, and it is likely to be helpful for some time to come, so long as the State itself does not undertake the rightful solution of agrarian and industrial problems on a countrywide scale.

Again I think of the paradox that is Gandhiji. With all his keen intellect and passion for bettering the downtrodden and oppressed, why does he support a system, and a system which is obviously decaying, which creates this misery and waste? He seeks a way out, it is true, but is not that way to the past barred and bolted? And meanwhile he blesses all the relics of the old order which stand as obstacles in the way of advance—the feudal states, the big zamindaris and talukdaris, the present capitalist system. Is it reasonable to believe in the theory of trusteeship—to give unchecked power and wealth to an individual and to expect him to use it entirely for the public good? Are the best of us so perfect as to be trusted in this way? Even Plato's philosopher-kings could hardly have borne this burden worthily. And is it good for the others to have even these benevolent supermen over them? But there are no supermen or philosopher-kings; there are only frail human beings who cannot help thinking that their own personal good or the advancement of their own ideas is identical with the public good. The snobbery of birth, position, and economic power is perpetuated, and the consequences in many ways are disastrous.

Again, I would repeat that I am not at present considering the question of how to effect the change, of how to get rid of the obstacles in the way, by compulsion or conversion, violence or nonviolence. I shall deal with this aspect later. But the necessity for the change must be recognized and clearly stated. If leaders and thinkers do not clearly envisage this and state it, how can they expect ever to convert anybody to their way of thinking, or develop the necessary ideology in the people? Events are undoubtedly the most powerful educators, but events have to be properly understood and interpreted if their significance is to be realized and properly directed action is to result from them.

I have often been asked by friends and colleagues who have occasionally been exasperated by my utterances: Have you not come across good and benevolent princes, charitable landlords, well-meaning and amiable capitalists? Indeed I have. I myself belong to a class which mixes with these lords of the land and owners of wealth. I am a typical bourgeois, brought up in bourgeois surroundings, with all the early prejudices that this training has given me. Communists have called me a petty bourgeois with perfect justification. Perhaps they might label me now one of the "repentant *bourgeoisie*." But whatever I may be is beside the point. It is absurd to consider national, international, economic, and social problems in terms of isolated individuals. Those very friends who question me are never tired of repeating that our quarrel is with the sin and not the sinner. I would not even go so far. I would say that my quarrel is with a system and not with individuals. A system is certainly embodied to a great extent in individuals and groups, and these individuals and groups have to be converted or combated. But, if a system has ceased to be of value and is a drag, it has to go, and the classes or groups that cling to it will also have to undergo a transformation. That process of change should involve as little suffering as possible, but unhappily suffering and dislocation are inevitable. We cannot put up with a major evil for fear of a far lesser one, which in any event is beyond our power to remedy.

Every type of human association—political, social, or economic—has some philosophy at the back of it. When these associations change, this philosophical foundation must also change in order to fit in with it and to utilize it to the best advantage. Usually the philosophy lags behind the course of events, and this lag creates all the trouble. Democracy and capitalism grew up together in the nineteenth century, but they were not mutually compatible. There was a basic contradiction between them, for democracy laid stress on the power of the many, while capitalism gave real power to the few. This ill-assorted pair carried on somehow because political parliamentary democracy was in itself a very limited kind of democracy and did not interfere much with the growth of monopoly and power concentration.

Even so, as the spirit of democracy grew, a divorce became inevitable, and the time for that has come now. Parliamentary democracy is in disrepute today, and as a reaction from it all manner of new slogans fill the air. Because of this, the British Government in India becomes more reactionary still and makes it an excuse for withholding from us even the outer forms of political freedom. The Indian princes, strangely enough, make this a justification for their unchecked autocracy and stoutly declare their intention of maintaining medieval conditions in their domains such as exist nowhere else in the world. But the failure of parliamentary democracy is not that it has gone too far, but that it has not gone far enough. It was not democratic enough because it did not provide for economic democracy, and its methods were slow and cumbrous and unsuited to a period of rapid change.

The Indian states represent today probably the extremest type of autocracy existing in the world. They are, of course, subject to British suzerainty, but the British Government interferes only for the protection or advancement of British interests. A veil of mystery surrounds these states. Newspapers are not encouraged there, and at the most a literary or semiofficial weekly might flourish. Outside newspapers are often barred. Literacy is very low, except in some of the southern states—Travancore, Cochin, etc.—where it is far higher than in British India. The principal news that comes from the states is of a viceregal visit, with all its pomp and ceremonial and mutually complimentary speeches, or of an extravagantly celebrated marriage or birthday of the ruler, or an agrarian rising. Special laws protect the princes from criticism, even in British India, and within the states the mildest criticism is rigorously suppressed. Public meetings are almost unknown, and even meetings for social purposes are often banned. Leading public men from outside are frequently prevented from entering the states.

When such conditions prevail in the states, it would have been natural for the Congress to stand up for the elementary rights of the people of the states and to criticize their wholesale suppression. But Gandhiji fathered a novel policy on the Congress in regard to the states—the "policy of noninterference in the internal administration of the states." This hush-hush policy has been adhered to by him in spite of the most extraordinary and painful occurrences in the states, and in spite of wholly unprovoked attacks by the states' governments on the Congress. Apparently the fear is that Congress criticism might offend the rulers and make it more difficult to "convert" them.

More or less the same considerations apply to the talukdari and big zamindari system. It hardly seems a matter for argument that this semifeudal system is out of date and is a great hindrance to production and general progress. It conflicts even with a developing capitalism, and almost all over the world large landed estates have gradually vanished and given place to peasant proprietors. I had always imagined that the only possible question that could arise in India was one of compensation. But to my surprise I have discovered during the last year or so (1934-5) that Gandhiji approves of the talukdari system as such and wants it to continue. He said in July 1934 at Cawnpore that "better relations between landlords and tenants could be brought about by a change of hearts on both sides. If that was done, both could live in peace and harmony." He was "never in favor of abolition of the talukdari or zamindari system, and those who thought that it should be abolished did not know their own minds." (This last charge is rather unkind.)

He is further reported to have said: "I shall be no party to dispossessing propertied classes of their private property without just cause. My objective is to reach your hearts and convert you [he was addressing a deputation of big zamindars] so that you may hold all your private property in trust for your tenants and use it primarily for their welfare. . . . But supposing that there is an attempt unjustly to deprive you of your property, you will find me fighting on your side. . . . The socialism and communism of the West is based on certain conceptions which are fundamentally different from ours. One such conception is their belief in the essential selfishness of human nature. . . . Our socialism and communism should therefore be based on nonviolence and on the harmonious co-operation of labor and capital, landlord and tenant."

I do not know if there are any such differences in the basic conceptions of the East and West. Perhaps there are. But an obvious difference in the recent past has been that the Indian capitalist and landlord have ignored far more the interests of their workers and tenants than their Western prototypes. There has been practically no attempt on the part of the Indian landlord to interest himself in any social service for the tenants' welfare. Many landlords have been deprived of their lands by moneylenders, and the smaller ones have sunk to the position of tenants on the land they once owned. These moneylenders from the city advanced money on mortgages and foreclosed, thus blossoming out into zamindars; according to Gandhiji, they are now the trustees for the unhappy people whom they have themselves dispossessed of their lands, and are expected to devote their income primarily to the welfare of their tenantry.

If the talukdari system is good, why should it not be introduced all over India? Large tracts of India have peasant proprietors. I wonder if Gandhiji would be agreeable to the creation of large zamindaris and talukas in Gujrat? I imagine not. But then why is one land system good for the United Provinces or Behar or Bengal, and another for Gujrat and the Punjab? Presumably there is not any vital difference between the people of the north and east and west and south of India, and their basic conceptions are the same. It comes to this, then, that whatever is should continue, the *status quo* should be maintained. There should be no economic inquiry as to what is most desirable or beneficial for the people, no attempts to change present conditions; all that is necessary is to change the people's hearts. That is the pure religious attitude to life and its problems. It has nothing to do with politics or economics or sociology. And yet Gandhiji goes beyond this in the political, national sphere.

Such are some of the paradoxes that face India today. We have managed to tie ourselves up into a number of knots, and it is difficult to get on till we untie them. That release will not come emotionally. What is better, Spinoza asked long ago, "freedom through knowledge and understanding, or emotional bondage?" He preferred the former.

## XLVIII

## DEHRA JAIL AGAIN

I WAS NOT flourishing in Alipore Jail. My weight had gone down considerably, and the Calcutta air and increasing heat were distressing me. There were rumors of my transfer to a better climate. On May 7 I was told to gather my belongings and to march out of the jail. I was being sent to Dehra Dun Jail. The drive through Calcutta in the cool evening air was very pleasant after some months of seclusion, and the crowds at the big Howrah station were fascinating.

I was glad of my transfer and looked forward to Dehra Dun with its near-by mountains. On arrival I found that all was not as it used to be nine months earlier, when I had left it for Naini. I was put in a new place, an old cattle shed cleaned up and fitted out.

As a cell it was not bad, and there was a little veranda attached to it. There was also a small yard adjoining, about fifty feet in length. The cell was better than the ancient one I had had previously in Dehra, but soon I discovered that other changes were not for the better. The surrounding wall, which had been ten feet high, had just been raised, especially for my benefit, by another four or five feet. The view of the hills I had so looked forward to was completely cut off, and I could just see a few treetops. I was in this jail for over three months, and I never had even a glimpse of the mountains. I was not allowed to walk outside in front of the jail gate, as I used to, and my little yard was considered quite big enough for exercise.

These and other new restrictions were disappointing, and I felt irritated. I grew listless and disinclined to take even the little exercise that my yard allowed. I had hardly ever felt quite so lonely and cut off from the world. The solitary confinement began to tell on my nerves, and physically and mentally I declined. On the other side of the wall, only a few feet away, I knew there was freshness and fragrance, the cool smell of grass and soft earth, and distant vistas. But they were all out of reach, and my eyes grew weary and heavy, faced always by those walls. There was not even the usual movement of prison life, for I was kept apart and by myself.

After six weeks the monsoon broke and it rained in torrents; we had twelve inches of rain during the first week. There was a change in the air and whisperings of new life; the temperature came down, and the body felt relaxed and relieved. But there was no relief for the eyes or the mind. Sometimes the iron door of my yard would open to allow a warder to come in or go out, and for a few seconds I had a sudden glimpse of the outside world—green fields and trees, bright with color and glistening with pearly drops of rain—for a moment only, and then it all vanished like a flash of lightning. The door was hardly ever fully opened. Apparently the warders had instructions not to open it if I was anywhere near and, even when they opened it, to do so just a little. These brief glimpses of greenery and freshness were hardly welcome to me. That sight produced in me a kind of nostalgia, a heartache, and I would even avoid looking out when the door opened.

But all this unhappiness was not really the fault of the jail, though it contributed to it. It was the reaction of outside events—Kamala's illness and my political worries. I was beginning to realize that Kamala was again in the grip of her old disease, and I felt helpless and unable to be of any service to her. I knew that my presence by her side would have made a difference.

Unlike Alipore, Dehra Dun Jail allowed me a daily newspaper, and I could keep in touch with political and other developments outside. In Patna the All-India Congress Committee met after nearly three years (for most of this time it had been unlawful), and its proceedings were depressing. It surprised me that no attempt was made at this first meeting, after so much that had happened in India and the world, to analyze the situation, to have full discussions, to try to get out of old ruts. Gandhiji seemed to be, from a distance, his old dictatorial self— "If you choose to follow my lead, you have to accept my conditions," he said. He told the All-India Congress Committee to be businesslike and to adopt the resolutions placed before them by the Working Committee with speed, and then he went away.

It is probably true that prolonged discussions would not have improved matters. Two groups took shape: one desiring purely constitutional activities through the legislatures, the other thinking rather vaguely along socialistic lines. The majority of the members belonged to neither of these groups. They disliked a reversion to constitutionalism, and at the same time socialism frightened them a little and seemed to them to introduce an element which might split their ranks. They had no constructive ideas, and the one hope and sheet anchor they possessed was Gandhiji. As of old, they turned to him and followed his lead, even though many of them did not wholly approve of what he said. Gandhiji's support of the moderate constitutional elements gave them dominance in the Committee and the Congress.

The reaction took the Congress further back than I had thought. At no time during the last fifteen years, ever since the advent of noncooperation, had Congress leaders talked in this ultraconstitutional fashion.

The proscription of the Congress was ended by the Government, and it became a legal organization. But many of its associated and subsidiary bodies continued to be illegal, such as its volunteer department, the Seva Dal, as also a number of *kisan sabhas,* which were semi-independent peasant unions, and several educational institutions and youth leagues, including a children's organization. In particular the *Khudai Khidmatgars,* or the Frontier Redshirts, as they are called, were still outlawed. This organization had become a regular part of the Congress in 1931, and represented it in the Frontier Province. Thus, although the Congress had completely drawn off the direct action part of the struggle and had reverted to constitutional ways, the Government kept on all the special laws meant for civil disobedience and even continued the proscription of important parts of the Congress organization. Special attention was also paid to the suppression of peasant organizations and labor unions, while, it was interesting to note, high Government officials went about urging the zamindars and landlords to organize themselves. Every facility was offered to these landlords' organizations. The two major ones in the United Provinces were having their subscriptions collected for them by official agency, together with the revenue or taxes.

One of the secretaries of the Hindu *Mahasabha* actually went out of his way to approve of the continuation of the ban on the "Redshirts," and to pat Government on the back for it. This amazed me. Apart from this question of principle, it was well known that these Frontier people had behaved wonderfully during the years of struggle; and their leader, Khan Abdul Ghaffar Khan, one of the bravest and straightest men in India, was still in prison—a State prisoner kept confined without any trial. It seemed to me that communal bias could hardly go further.

I was much upset by this Hindu *Sabha* secretary's statement. It was bad enough in itself, but to my mind it appeared as a symbol of the new state of affairs in the country. In the heat of that summer afternoon I dozed off, and I remember having a curious dream. Abdul Ghaffar Khan was being attacked on all sides, and I was fighting to defend him. I woke up in an exhausted state, feeling very miserable, and my pillow was wet with tears. This surprised me, for in my waking state I was not liable to such emotional outbursts.

My nerves were obviously in a bad way in those days. My sleep became troubled and disturbed, which was very unusual for me, and all manner of nightmares came to me. Sometimes I would shout out in my sleep. Once evidently the shouting had been more vigorous than usual, and I woke up with a start to find two jail warders standing near my bed, rather worried at my noises. I had dreamed that I was being strangled.

About this time a resolution of the Congress Working Committee had also a painful effect on me. This resolution was passed, it was stated, "in view of the loose talk about the confiscation of private property and necessity of class war," and it proceeded to remind Congressmen that the Karachi resolution "neither contemplates confiscation of private property without just cause or compensation, nor advocacy of class war. The Working Committee is further of the opinion that confiscation and class war are contrary to the Congress creed of nonviolence." The resolution was loosely worded and exhibited a certain amount of ignorance on the part of the framers as to what class war was. It was obviously aimed at the newly formed Congress Socialist party. There had, as a matter of fact, been no talk of confiscation on the part of any responsibile member of this group; there had, however, been frequent reference to the existence of class war under present conditions. The Working Committee's resolution seemed to hint that any person believing in the existence of this class conflict could not even be an ordinary member of the Congress.

The Working Committee subsequently tried to explain its resolution on class war. The importance of that resolution lay not so much in its language or what it definitely laid down, as in the fact that it was yet another indication of the way Congress was going. The resolution had obviously been inspired by the new parliamentary wing of the Congress aiming at gaining the support of men of property in the coming election to the Legislative Assembly. At their instance the Congress was looking more and more to the Right and trying to win over the moderate and conservative elements in the country. Soothing words were being addressed even to those who had been hostile to the Congress movements in the past and had sided with the Government during the continuance of civil disobedience. A clamorous and critical Left wing was felt to be a handicap in this process of conciliation and "conversion," and the Working Committee's resolution, as well as many other individual utterances, made it clear that the Congress Executive were not going to be moved from their new path by this nibbling from the Left. If the Left did not behave, it would be sat upon and eliminated from the Congress ranks. The manifesto issued by the Parliamentary Board of the Congress contained a program which was far more cautious and moderate than any that the Congress had sponsored during the past fifteen years.

On the Government side there was an air of triumph, in no way concealed, at what they considered the success of their policy in suppressing civil disobedience and its offshoots. The operation had been successful, and for the moment is mattered little whether the patient lived or died. They proposed to continue the same policy, with minor variations, even though the Congress had been for the moment brought round to some extent. Perhaps they also thought that in continuing to suppress the more advanced elements in the Congress or in the labor and peasant ranks, they would not greatly offend the more cautious leaders of the Congress.

To some extent my thoughts in Dehra Dun Jail ran along these channels. I was really not in a position to form definite opinions about the course of events, for I was out of touch. In Alipore I had been almost completely out of touch; in Dehra a newspaper of the Government's choice brought me partial and sometimes one-sided news. It is quite possible that contacts with my colleagues outside and a closer study of the situation would have resulted in my varying my opinions in some degree.

Distressed with the present, I began thinking of the past, of what had happened politically in India since I began to take some part in public affairs. How far had we been right in what we had done? How far wrong? It struck me that my thinking would be more orderly and helpful if I put it down on paper. This would also help in engaging my mind in a definite task and so diverting it from worry and depression. So in the month of June 1934 I began this "autobiographical narrative" in Dehra Jail, and for the last eight months I have continued it when the mood to do so has seized me. Often there have been intervals when I felt no desire to write; three of these gaps were each of them nearly a month long. But I managed to continue, and now I am nearing the end of this personal journey. Most of this has been written under peculiarly distressing circumstances when I was suffering from depression and emotional strain. Perhaps some of this is reflected in what I have written, but this very writing helped me greatly to pull myself out of the present with all its worries. As I wrote, I was hardly thinking of an outside audience; I was addressing myself, framing questions and answering them for my own benefit, sometimes even drawing some amusement from it. I wanted as far as possible to think straight, and I imagined that this review of the past might help me to do so.

Toward the end of July, Kamala's condition rapidly deteriorated, and within a few days became critical. On August 11 I was suddenly asked to leave Dehra Jail, and that night I was sent under police escort to Allahabad. The next evening we reached Prayag station in Allahabad, and there I was informed by the district magistrate that I was being released temporarily so that I might visit my ailing wife. It was six months to a day from the time of my arrest.

## XLIX

## ELEVEN DAYS

*For the Sword outwears its sheath,*
*And the soul wears out the breast.*
*—*BYRON.

MY RELEASE WAS temporary. I was given to understand that it was for a day or two or for such longer period as the doctors might think absolutely necessary. It was a peculiar position, full of uncertainty, and it was not possible for me to settle down to anything. A fixed period would have enabled me to know how I stood, and I would have tried to adjust myself to it. As it was, any day, at any moment, I might be taken back to prison.

The change was sudden, and I was wholly unprepared for it. From solitary confinement to a crowded house with doctors, nurses, and relatives. My daughter Indira had also come from Santiniketan. Many friends were continually coming to see me and inquire after Kamala's health. The style of living was quite different; there were home comforts, better food. And coloring all this background was anxiety for Kamala's serious condition.

There she lay, frail and utterly weak, a shadow of herself, struggling feebly with her illness, and the thought that she might leave me became an intolerable obsession. It was eighteen and a half years since our marriage, and my mind wandered back to that day and to all that these succeeding years had brought us. I was twenty-six at the time, and she was about seventeen, a slip of a girl, utterly unsophisticated in the ways of the world. The difference in our ages was considerable, but greater still was the difference in our mental outlook, for I was far more grown-up than she was. And yet with all my appearance of worldly wisdom I was very boyish, and I hardly realized that this

332

delicate, sensitive girl's mind was slowly unfolding like a flower and required gentle and careful tending. We were attracted to each other and got on well enough, but our backgrounds were different, and there was a want of adjustment. These maladjustments would sometimes lead to friction, and there were many petty quarrels over trivialities, boy-and-girl affairs which did not last long and ended in a quick reconciliation. We both had quick tempers, sensitive natures, and childish notions of keeping our dignity. In spite of this our attachment grew, though the want of adjustment lessened only slowly. Twenty-one months after our marriage, Indira, our daughter and only child, arrived.

Our marriage had almost coincided with new developments in politics, and my absorption in them grew. They were the home-rule days, and soon after came martial law in the Punjab and nonco-operation, and more and more I was involved in the dust and tumble of public affairs. So great became my concentration in these activities that, all unconsciously, I almost overlooked her and left her to her own resources, just when she required my full co-operation. My affection for her continued and even grew, and it was a great comfort to know that she was there to help me with her soothing influence. She gave me strength, but she must have suffered and felt a little neglected. An unkindness to her would almost have been better than this semiforgetful, casual attitude.

And then came her recurring illness and my long absences in prison, when we could only meet at jail interviews. The civil disobedience movement brought her in the front rank of our fighters, and she rejoiced when she too went to prison. We grew ever nearer to each other. Our rare meetings became precious, and we looked forward to them and counted the days that intervened. We could not get tired of each other or stale, for there was always a freshness and novelty about our meetings and brief periods together. Each of us was continually making fresh discoveries in the other, though sometimes perhaps the new discoveries were not to our liking. Even our grown-up disagreements had something boyish and girlish about them.

After eighteen years of married life she had still retained her girlish and virginal appearance; there was nothing matronly about her. Almost she might have been the bride that came to our house so long ago. But I had changed vastly, and, though I was fit and supple and active enough for my age—and, I was told, I still possessed some boyish traits—my looks betrayed me. I was partly bald, and my hair was gray; lines and furrows crossed my face, and dark shadows surrounded my eyes. The last four years with their troubles and worries had left many a mark on me. Often, in these later years, when Kamala and I had gone out together in a strange place, she was mistaken, to my embarrassment, for my daughter. She and Indira looked like two sisters.

Eighteen years of married life! But how many long years out of them had I spent in prison cells, and Kamala in hospitals and sanatoria? And now again I was serving a prison sentence and out just for a few days, and she was lying ill, struggling for life. I felt a little irritated at her for her carelessness about her health. And yet how could I blame her, for her eager spirit fretted at her inaction and her inability to take her full share in the national struggle? Physically unable to do so, she could neither take to work properly nor to treatment, and the fire inside her wore down the body.

Surely she was not going to leave me now when I needed her most? Why, we had just begun to know and understand each other, really; our joint life was only now properly beginning. We relied so much on each other; we had so much to do together.

So I thought as I watched her from day to day and hour to hour.

Colleagues and friends came to see me. They told me of much that had happened of which I was unaware. They discussed current political problems and asked me questions. I found it difficult to answer them. It was not easy for my mind to get away from Kamala's illness, and after the isolation and detachment of jail I was not in a position to face concrete questions suddenly. Long experience had taught me that it is not possible to appraise a situation from the limited information available in jail. Personal contacts were necessary for a proper mental reaction, otherwise the expression of opinion was likely to be purely academic and divorced from reality. It seemed also unfair to Gandhiji and my old colleagues of the Congress Working Committee for me to say anything definite regarding Congress policy before I had had the opportunity to discuss everything with them. My mind was full of criticisms of much that had been done, but I was not prepared to make any positive suggestions. Not expecting to come out of prison just then, I had not thought along these lines.

I had also a feeling that, in view of the courtesy shown by the Government in allowing me to come to my wife, it would not be proper for me to take advantage of this for political purposes. I had given no undertaking or assurance to avoid any such activity; nevertheless I was continually being pulled back by this idea.

I avoided issuing any public statements except to contradict false rumors. Even in private I refrained from committing myself to any definite line of policy, but I was free enough with my criticisms of past events. The Congress Socialist party had recently come into existence, and many of my intimate colleagues were associated with it. So far as I had gathered, its general policy was agreeable to me, but it seemed a curious and mixed assemblage, and, even if I had been completely free, I would not have suddenly joined it. Local politics took up some of my time, for in Allahabad, as in several other places, there had been an extraordinarily virulent campaign during the elections for the local Congress committees. No principles were involved —it was purely a question of personalities—and I was asked to help in settling some of the personal quarrels that had arisen.

I felt disgusted with the local squabble and the kind of politics which were rapidly developing. I felt out of tune with them and a stranger in my own city of Allahabad. What could I do, I wondered, in this environment when the time came for me to attend to such matters?

I wrote to Gandhiji about Kamala's condition. As I thought I would be going back to prison soon and might have no other chance to do so, I gave him also some glimpse into my mind. Recent events had embittered and distressed me greatly, and my letter carried a faint reflection of this. I did not attempt to suggest what should be done or what should not be done; all I did was to interpret some of my reactions to what had happened. It was a letter full of barely suppressed emotions, and I learned subsequently that it pained Gandhiji considerably.

Day after day went by, and I waited for the summons to prison or some other intimation from Government. From time to time I was informed that further directions would be issued the next day or the day after. Meanwhile the doctors were asked to send a daily bulletin of my wife's condition to the Government. Kamala had slightly improved since my arrival.

It was generally believed, even by those who are usually in the confidence of the Government, that I would have been fully discharged but for two impending events—the fall session of the Congress that was taking place in October in Bombay and the Assembly elections in November. Out of prison I might be a disturbing factor at these, and so it seemed probable that I might be sent back to prison for another three months and then discharged. There was also the possibility of my not being sent back to jail, and this possibility seemed to grow as the days went by. I almost decided to settle down.

It was the eleventh day after my release, August 23. The police car drove up, and the police officer came up to me and told me that my time was up and I had to accompany him to Naini Prison. I bade good-by to my people. As I was getting into the police car, my ailing mother ran up again to me with arms outstretched. That face of hers haunted me for long.

## L

## BACK TO PRISON

*Shadow is itself unrestrained in its path while sunshine, as an incident of its very nature, is pursued a hundredfold by nuance. Thus is sorrow from happiness a thing apart; the scope of happiness, however, is hampered by the aches and hurts of endless sorrows.*

—RAJATARANGINI.[1]

I WAS BACK again in Naini Prison, and I felt as if I were starting a fresh term of imprisonment. In and out, out and in; what a shuttlecock I had become! This switching on and off shook up the whole system emotionally and it was not easy to adjust oneself to repeated changes. I had expected to be put in my old cell at Naini, to which a previous long stay had accustomed me. There were some flowers there, originally planted by my brother-in-law, Ranjit Pandit, and a good veranda. But this old Barrack No. 6 was occupied by a *détenu,* a State prisoner, kept confined without trial or conviction. It was not considered desirable for me to associate with him, and I was therefore placed in another part of the jail which was much more closed in and was devoid of flowers or greenery.

But the place where I spent my days and nights mattered little, for my mind was elsewhere. I feared that the little improvement that had taken place in Kamala's condition would not stand the shock of my rearrest. And so it happened. For some days it was arranged to supply me in prison with a very brief doctor's bulletin daily. This came by a devious route. The doctor had to telephone it to the police headquarters, and the latter then sent it on to the prison. It was not considered

[1] R. S. Pandit's translation. ("River of Kings." *Taranga,* viii verse, 1913.)

desirable to have any direct contacts between the doctors and the jail staff. For two weeks these bulletins came to me, sometimes rather irregularly, and then they were stopped although there was a progressive deterioration in Kamala's condition.

Bad news and the waiting for news made the days intolerably long, and the nights were sometimes worse. Time seemed almost to stand still or to move with desperate slowness, and every hour was a burden and a horror. I had never before had this feeling in this acute degree. I thought then that I was likely to be released within two months or so, after the Bombay Congress session, but those two months seemed an eternity.

Exactly a month after my rearrest a police officer took me from prison on a brief visit to my wife. I was told that I would be allowed to visit her in this way twice a week, and even the time for it was fixed. I waited on the fourth day—no one came for me; and on the fifth, sixth, seventh. I became weary of waiting. News reached me that her condition was becoming critical again. What a joke it was, I thought, to tell me that I would be taken to see her twice a week!

At last the month of September was over. They were the longest and most damnable thirty days that I had ever experienced.

Suggestions were made to me through various intermediaries that if I could give an assurance, even an informal assurance, to keep away from politics for the rest of my term I would be released to attend on Kamala. Politics were far enough from my thoughts just then, and the politics I had seen during my eleven days outside had disgusted me, but to give an assurance! And to be disloyal to my pledges, to the cause, to my colleagues, to myself! It was an impossible condition, whatever happened. To do so meant inflicting a mortal injury on the roots of my being, on almost everything I held sacred. I was told that Kamala's condition was becoming worse and worse, and my presence by her side might make all the difference between life and death. Was my personal conceit and pride greater than my desire to give her this chance? It might have been a terrible predicament for me, but fortunately that dilemma did not face me in that way at least. I knew that Kamala herself would strongly disapprove of my giving any undertaking, and, if I did anything of the kind, it would shock her and harm her.

Early in October I was taken to see her again. She was lying almost in a daze with a high temperature. She longed to have me by her, but, as I was leaving her, to go back to prison, she smiled at me bravely

337

and beckoned to me to bend down. When I did so, she whispered: "What is this about your giving an assurance to Government? Do not give it!"

During the eleven days I was out of prison it had been decided to send Kamala, as soon as she was a little better, to a more suitable place for treatment. Ever since then we had waited for her to get better, but instead she had gone downhill, and now, six weeks later, the change for the worse was very marked. It was futile to continue waiting and watching this process of deterioration, and it was decided to send her to Bhowali in the hills even in her present condition.

The day before she was to leave for Bhowali I was taken from prison to bid her good-by. When will I see her again? I wondered. And will I see her at all? But she looked bright and cheerful that day, and I felt happier than I had done for long.

Nearly three weeks later I was transferred from Naini Prison to Almora District Jail so as to be nearer to Kamala. Bhowali was on the way, and my police escort and I spent a few hours there. I was greatly pleased to note the improvement in Kamala, and I left her, to continue my journey to Almora, with a light heart. Indeed, even before I reached her, the mountains had filled me with joy.

I was glad to be back in these mountains, and, as our car sped along the winding road, the cold morning air and the unfolding panorama brought a sense of exhilaration. Higher and higher we went; the gorges deepened; the peaks lost themselves in the clouds; the vegetation changed till the firs and pines covered the hillsides. A turn of the road would bring to our eyes suddenly a new expanse of hills and valleys with a little river gurgling in the depths below. I could not have my fill of the sight, and I looked on hungrily, storing my memory with it, so that I might revive it in my mind when actual sight was denied.

Clusters of little mountain huts clung to the hillsides, and round about them were tiny fields made by prodigious labor on every possible bit of slope. They looked like terraces from a distance, huge steps which sometimes went from the valley below right up almost to the mountain top. What enormous labor had gone to make nature yield a little food to the sparse population! How they toiled unceasingly, only to get barely enough for their needs! Those plowed terraces gave a domesticated look to the hillsides, and they contrasted strangely with the bleaker or the more wooded slopes.

It was very pleasant in the daytime, and, as the sun rose higher, the growing warmth brought life to the mountains, and they seemed to lose their remoteness and become friendly and companionable. But how they change their aspect with the passing of day! How cold and grim they become when "Night with giant strides stalks o'er the world" and life hides and protects itself and leaves wild nature to its own! In the semidarkness of the moonlight or starlight the mountains loom up mysterious, threatening, overwhelming, and yet almost insubstantial, and through the valleys can be heard the moaning of the wind. The poor traveler shivers as he goes his lonely way and senses hostility everywhere. Even the voice of the wind seems to mock him and challenge him. And at other times there is no breath of wind or other sound, and there is an absolute silence that is oppressive in its intensity. Only the telegraph wires perhaps hum faintly, and the stars seem brighter and nearer than ever. The mountains look down grimly, and one seems to be face to face with a mystery that terrifies. With Pascal one thinks: *"Le silence éternel de ces espaces infinis m'effraie."* In the plains the nights are never quite so soundless; life is still audible there, and the murmuring and humming of various animals and insects break the stillness of the night.

But the night with its chill and inhospitable message was yet distant as we motored along to Almora. As we neared the end of our journey, a turn in the road and a sudden lifting of the clouds brought a new sight which I saw with a gasp of surprised delight. The snowy peaks of the Himalayas stood glistening in the far distance, high above the wooded mountains that intervened. Calm and inscrutable they seemed, with all the wisdom of past ages, mighty sentinels over the vast Indian plain. The very sight of them cooled the fever in the brain, and the petty conflicts and intrigues, the lusts and falsehoods of the plains and the cities seemed trivial and far away before their eternal ways.

The little jail of Almora was perched up on a ridge. I was given a lordly barrack to live in. This consisted of one huge hall, fifty-one feet by seventeen, with a *katcha,* very uneven floor, and a worm-eaten roof which was continually coming down in little bits. There were fifteen, windows and a door, or rather there were so many barred openings in the walls, for there were no doors or windows. There was thus no lack of fresh air. As it grew colder some of the window openings were covered with coir matting. In this vast expanse (which was bigger than my yard at Dehra Dun) I lived in solitary grandeur. But I was not quite alone, for at least two score sparrows had made their home in the broken-down roof. Sometimes a wandering cloud would visit me, its many arms creeping in through the numerous openings and filling the place with a damp mist.

Here I was locked up every evening at about five, after I had taken my last meal, a kind of high tea, at four-thirty; and at seven in the morning my barred door would be unlocked. In the daytime I would sit either in my barrack or outside in an adjoining yard, warming myself in the sun. I could just see over the enclosing walls the top of a mountain a mile or so away, and above me I had a vast expanse of blue sky dotted with clouds. Wonderful shapes these clouds assumed, and I never grew tired of watching them. I fancied I saw them take the shape of all manner of animals, and sometimes they would join together and look like a mighty ocean. Or they would be like a beach, and the rustling of the breeze through the deodars would sound like the coming in of the tide on a distant sea front. Sometimes a cloud would advance boldly on us, seemingly solid and compact, and then dissolve in mist as it came near and finally enveloped us.

I preferred the wide expanse of my barrack to a narrow cell, though it was lonelier than a smaller place would have been. Even when it rained outside, I could walk about in it. But, as it grew colder, its cheerlessness became more marked, and my love for fresh air and the open abated when the temperature hovered about the freezing point. The new year brought a good fall of snow to my delight, and even the drab surroundings of prison became beautiful. Especially beautiful and fairylike were the deodar trees just outside the jail walls with their garment of snow.

I was worried by the ups and downs of Kamala's condition, and a piece of bad news would upset me for a while, but the hill air calmed me and soothed me, and I reverted to my habit of sleeping soundly. As I was on the verge of sleep, I often thought what a wonderful and mysterious thing was sleep. Why should one wake up from it? Suppose I did not wake at all?

Yet the desire to be out of jail was strong in me, more than I had ever felt before. The Bombay Congress was over, and November came and went by, and the excitement of the Assembly elections also passed away. I half expected that I might be released soon.

But then came the surprising news of the arrest and conviction of Khan Abdul Ghaffar Khan and the amazing orders passed on Subhas Bose during his brief visit to India. These orders in themselves were devoid of all humanity and consideration; they were applied to one who was held in affection and esteem by vast numbers of his country-

340

men, and who had hastened home, in spite of his own illness, to the deathbed of his father—to arrive too late. If that was the outlook of the Government, there could be no chance of my premature release. Official announcements later made this perfectly clear.

After I had been a month in Almora jail I was taken to Bhowali to see Kamala. Since then I have visited her approximately every third week. Sir Samuel Hoare, the Secretary of State for India, has repeatedly stated that I am allowed to visit my wife once or twice a week. He would have been more correct if he had said once or twice a month. During the last three and a half months that I have been at Almora I have paid five visits to her. I do not mention this as a grievance, because I think that in this matter the Government have been very considerate to me and have given me quite unusual facilities to visit Kamala. I am grateful to them for this. The brief visits I have paid her have been very precious to me and perhaps to her also. The doctors suspended their regime for the day of my visit to some extent, and I was permitted to have fairly long talks with her. We came ever nearer to each other, and to leave her was a wrench. We met only to be parted. And sometimes I thought with anguish that a day might come when the parting was for good.

My mother had gone to Bombay for treatment, for she had not recovered from her ailment. She seemed to be progressing. One morning in mid-January a telegram brought a wholly unexpected shock. She had had a stroke of paralysis. There was a possibility of my being transferred to a Bombay prison to enable me to see her, but, as there was a little improvement in her condition, I was not sent.

January gave place to February, and there was the whisper of spring in the air. The bulbul and other birds were again to be seen and heard, and tiny shoots were mysteriously bursting out of the ground and gazing at this strange world. Rhododendrons made blood-red patches on the hillsides, and peach and plum blossoms were peeping out. The days passed and I counted them as they passed, thinking of my next visit to Bhowali. I wondered what truth there is in the saying that life's rich gifts follow frustration and cruelty and separation. Perhaps the gifts would not be appreciated otherwise. Perhaps suffering is necessary for clear thought, but excess of it may cloud the brain. Jail encourages introspection, and my long years in prison have forced me to look more and more within myself. I am not by nature an introvert, but prison life, like strong coffee or strychnine, leads to introversion. Sometimes, to amuse myself, I drew an outline of Professor McDougall's cube for the measurement of introversion and extroversion, and I gazed at it to find out how frequent were the changes from one interpretation to another. They seemed to be rapid.

## LI

## REFLECTIONS ON SOCIAL CHANGE

*Dawn reddens in the wake of night, but the days of our life return not.*
*The eye contains a far horizon, but the wound of spring lies deep in the heart.*

—Li T'ai-Po.

I FOLLOWED FROM the newspapers supplied to me the proceedings of the Bombay session of the Congress. The two outstanding features of this, as far as I could make out from my distant and secluded abode on the mountains, were: the dominant personality of Gandhiji and the exceedingly poor show that the communal opposition under Pandit Madan Mohan Malaviya and Mr. Aney put up.

Gandhiji's retirement from the Congress was a striking feature of the session, and outwardly it marked the end of a great chapter in Congress and Indian history. But, essentially, its significance was not great, for he cannot rid himself, even if he wanted to, of his dominating position.

I was glad that the Congress had adopted the idea of a Constituent Assembly for settling the constitution of the country. It seemed to me that there was no other way of solving the problem, and I am sure that sometime or other some such assembly will have to meet. Manifestly it cannot do so without the consent of the British Government, unless there has been a successful revolution. It is equally manifest that this consent is not likely to be forthcoming under present circumstances. A real assembly can therefore not meet till enough strength has been evolved in the country to force the pace. This inevitably means that even the political problem will remain unsolved till then.

It was interesting to watch the reactions of Simla and London to this idea. It was made known semiofficially that Government would have no objection; they gave it a patronizing approval, evidently looking upon it as an old type of All-Parties Conference, foredoomed to failure, which would strengthen their hands. Later they seem to have realized the dangers and possibilities of the idea, and they began opposing it vigorously.

Soon after the Bombay Congress came the Assembly elections. With all my lack of enthusiasm for the Congress parliamentary program, I was greatly interested, and I wished the Congress candidates success, or to put it more correctly, I hoped for the defeat of their opponents. Among these opponents was a curious assortment of careerists, communalists, renegades, and people who had stanchly supported the Government in its policy of repression. The Congress met with remarkable success, and I was pleased that a good number of undesirables had been kept out.

The Assembly elections threw a revealing light on the people at the back of the reactionary communal bodies. They were the big landlords, the feudal elements and the banker class.

Soon after the Assembly elections the Report of the Joint Parliamentary Committee on Indian Constitutional Reform was issued. Among the varied and widespread criticisms to which it was subjected, stress was often laid on the fact that it showed "distrust" and "suspicion" of the Indian people. This seemed to me a very strange way of looking at our national and social problems. Were there no vital conflicts of interest between British imperial policy and our national interests? The question was which was to prevail. Did we want freedom merely to continue that imperial policy? Apparently that was the British Government's notion, for we were informed that the "safeguards" would not be used so long as we behaved and demonstrated our fitness for self-rule by doing just what British policy required. If British policy was to be continued in India, why all this shouting about getting the reins in our own hands?

The measure of liberty that this proposed gift of Britain offers to India can be taken from the fact that even the most moderate and politically backward groups in India have condemned it as reactionary. The habitual and persistent supporters of Government have had to combine criticisms of it with their usual genuflections. Others have been more vehement.

In view of these proposals the Liberals found it difficult to retain in full measure their abiding faith in the inscrutable wisdom of Providence in placing India under British dominion.

A certain hopeful reliance is placed by Liberal leaders, and probably by many others including some Congressmen, on the victory of the Labour party in Britain and the formation of a Labour Government there. There is absolutely no reason why India should not endeavor to go ahead with the co-operation of advanced groups in Britain, or should not try to profit by the advent of a Labour Government. But to rely helplessly on a change in fortune's wheel in England is hardly dignified or in consonance with national honor. Dignity apart, it is not good common sense. Why should we expect much from the British Labour party? We have had two Labour Governments already, and we are not likely to forget their gifts to India. At the South-port Conference in 1934, a resolution was submitted by Mr. V. K. Krishna Menon "expressing the conviction that it is imperative that the principle of self-determination for the establishment of full self-government for India should be implemented forthwith." Mr. Arthur Henderson urged the withdrawal of the resolution and, very frankly, refused to give an undertaking on behalf of the Executive to carry out its policy of self-determination for India. He said: "We have laid down very clearly that we are going to consult if possible all sections of the Indian people. That ought to satisfy anybody." The satisfaction will perhaps be tempered by the fact that exactly this was the declared policy of the last Labour Government and the National Government, resulting in the Round Table Conference, the White Paper, the Joint Committee Report, and the India Act.

It is perfectly clear that in matters of imperial policy there is little to choose between Tory or Labour in England. It is true that the Labour rank and file is far more advanced, but it has little influence on its very conservative leadership. It may be that the Labour Left wing will gather strength, for conditions change rapidly nowadays; but do national or social movements curl themselves up and go to sleep, waiting for problematical changes elsewhere?

One of the notable consequences of the Round Table Conference and the proposal to have a federation, is to push the Indian princes very much to the forefront. The solicitude of the Tory die-hards for them and their "independence" has put new life into them. Never before have they had so much importance thrust on them. Previously they had dared not say no to a hint from the British Resident, and the Government of India's attitude to the numerous highnesses was openly disdainful. There was continual interference in their internal affairs, and often this was justified. Even today a large number of the states are directly or indirectly being governed by British officers "lent" to the states. But Mr. Churchill's and Lord Rothermere's campaign seems to have unnerved the Government of India a little, and it has

344

grown cautious about interfering with their decisions. The princes also now talk in a much more superior way.

I have tried to follow these superficial developments in the Indian political scene, but I cannot help feeling that they are unreal, and the background in India oppresses me. The background is one of continual repression of every kind of freedom, of enormous suffering and frustration, of distortion of good will, and encouragement of many evil tendencies. Large numbers lie in prison and spend their young lives, year after year, eating their hearts out. Their families and friends and connections and thousands of others grow bitter, and a nauseating sense of humiliation and powerlessness before brute strength takes possession of them. Numerous organizations are outlawed even in normal times, while "Emergency Powers" and "Tranquillity Acts" make for themselves almost a permanent home in the Government's armory. Exceptions in the matter of restrictions of liberties rapidly become the general rule. Large numbers of books and periodicals are proscribed or prevented entry by a "Sea Customs Act," and the possession of "dangerous" literature may lead to a long term of imprisonment. A frank expression of opinion on the political or economic problems of the day, or a favorable report of social and cultural conditions in Russia meets with the strong disapproval of the censor. The *Modern Review* was warned by the Bengal Government because it published an article by Dr. Rabindranath Tagore on Russia, an article written after a personal visit to that country. We are informed by the Under-Secretary for India in Parliament that "the article gave a distorted view of the achievements of British rule in India," and hence action was taken against it.[1] The judge of these achievements is the censor, and we may not have a contrary opinion or give expression to it. Objection was also taken by Government to the publication of a brief message from Rabindranath Tagore to the Dublin Society of Friends. This is a strange background for the introduction of reforms and responsible government and the like.

Far-reaching changes are taking place before our eyes, and the future, whatever shape it might take, is not a remote, far-off thing which arouses a purely academic interest in the detached minds of philosophers, sociologists, and economists. It is a matter which affects every human being for better or for worse, and surely it is every citizen's duty to try to understand the various forces at play and decide on his own course of action. A world is coming to an end, and a new world

[1] November 12, 1934.

345

is taking shape. To find an answer to a problem it is necessary to know what it is. Indeed it is as important to know the problem as to seek a solution for it.

Even more important are the economic changes that are rapidly taking place the world over. We must realize that the nineteenth-century system has passed away and has no application to present-day needs.

We have to face many questions, and we must face them boldly. Has the present social or economic system a right to exist if it is unable to improve greatly the condition of the masses? Does any other system give promise of this widespread betterment? How far will a mere political change bring radical improvement? If vested interests come in the way of an eminently desirable change, is it wise or moral to attempt to preserve them at the cost of mass misery and poverty? Surely the object is not to injure vested interests, but to prevent them from injuring others. If it was possible to come to terms with these vested interests, it would be most desirable to do so. People may disagree with the justice or injustice of this, but few will doubt the expediency of a settlement. Such a settlement obviously cannot be the removal of one vested interest by the creation of another. Whenever possible and desirable, reasonable compensation might be given, for a conflict is likely to cost far more. But, unhappily, all history shows that vested interests do not accept such compromises. Classes that have ceased to play a vital part in society are singularly lacking in wisdom. They gamble for all or nothing, and so they fade away.

In considering a method for changing the existing order we have to weigh the costs of it in material as well as spiritual terms. We cannot afford to be too shortsighted. We have to see how far it helps ultimately in the development of human happiness and human progress, material and spiritual. But we have always to bear in mind the terrible costs of not changing the existing order, of carrying on as we do today with our enormous burden of frustrated and distorted lives, starvation and misery, and spiritual and moral degradation.

It is obvious that the vast changes that socialism envisages cannot be brought about by the sudden passing of a few laws. But the basic laws and power are necessary to give the direction of advance and to lay the foundation of the structure. If the great building-up of a socialized society is to proceed, it cannot be left to chance nor can it be done in fits and starts with intervals of destruction of what has been built. The major obstructions have thus to be removed. The object is not to deprive, but to provide; to change the present scarcity to future abundance. But in doing so the path must necessarily be cleared of impediments and selfish interests which want to hold society back. And the path we take is not merely a question of what we like or dislike or even of abstract justice, but of what is economically sound, capable of progress, adaptation to changing conditions, and likely to do good to the largest number of human beings.

A clash of interests seems inevitable. There is no middle path. Each one of us will have to choose his side. Before we can choose, we must know and understand. The emotional appeal of socialism is not enough. This must be supplemented by an intellectual and reasoned appeal based on facts and arguments and detailed criticism. In the West a great deal of this kind of literature exists, but in India there is a tremendous lack of it, and many good books are not allowed entry here. But to read books from other countries is not enough. If socialism is to be built up in India, it will have to grow out of Indian conditions, and the closest study of these conditions is essential. We want experts in the job who study and prepare detailed plans. Unfortunately our experts are mostly in Government service or in the semiofficial universities, and they dare not go far in this direction.

An intellectual background is not enough to bring socialism. Other forces are necessary. But I do feel that without that background we can never have a grip of the subject or create a powerful movement. At the present moment the agrarian problem is far the most important in India, and it is likely to remain so. But industry is of little less importance, and it grows. What is our objective: a peasant state or an industrial one? Of course we are bound to remain predominantly agricultural, but one can and, I think, must push industry.

Our captains of industry are quite amazingly backward in their ideas; they are not even up-to-date capitalists. The masses are so poor that they do not look upon them as potential consumers and fight bitterly against any proposal to increase wages or lower hours of work. The whole outlook of the industry is an early nineteenth-century one. They make stupendous profits when they have the chance and the worker continues as before; if there is a slump, the owners complain that they cannot carry on without reducing wages. Not only have they the help of the State, but also usually the sympathy of our middle-class politicians. To compare the magnificent palaces of the jute millionaires and the cotton lords, with their ostentatious display of pomp and luxury, to the wretched hovels where their seminaked workers live, should be an education of the most impressive kind. But we take these contrasts for granted and pass them by, unaffected and unimpressed.

Bad as is the lot of the Indian industrial worker, it is, from the income point of view, far better than the peasant's lot. The peasant has one advantage: he lives in fresh air and escapes the degradation of the slums. But so low has he sunk that he often converts even his open-air village into a "dung heap," as Gandhiji has called it. There is no sense of co-operation in him or of joint effort for the good of the community. It is easy to condemn him for this, but what is the unhappy creature to do when life presents itself to him as a bitter and unceasing individual struggle with every man's hand raised against him? How he lives at all is an almost incredible wonder. It has been found that the average daily income of typical farmers in the Punjab was about nine annas (roughly ninepence) per head in 1928-29. This fell in 1930-31 to nine pies (three farthings) per head! The Punjab peasant is considered to be far more prosperous than the peasantry of Behar and Bengal in the United Provinces. In some of the eastern districts of the United Provinces (Gorakhpur, etc.) in prosperous times before the slump, the daily field wage was two annas (twopence). To talk of improving these staggering conditions by philanthropy or local efforts in rural uplift is a mockery of the peasant and his misery.

How are we to get out of this quagmire? Means can no doubt be devised, although it is a difficult task to raise masses of people who have sunk so low. But the real difficulty comes from interested groups who oppose change, and under imperialist domination the change seems to be out of the question. In what direction will India look in the coming years? Communism and fascism seem to be the major tendencies of the age, and intermediate tendencies and vacillating groups are gradually being eliminated.

As between fascism and communism my sympathies are entirely with communism. As these pages will show, I am very far from being a communist. My roots are still perhaps partly in the nineteenth century, and I have been too much influenced by the humanist liberal tradition to get out of it completely. This bourgeois background follows me about and is naturally a source of irritation to many communists. I dislike dogmatism, and the treatment of Karl Marx's writings or any other books as revealed scripture which cannot be challenged, and the regimentation and heresy hunts which seem to be a feature of modern communism. I dislike also much that has happened in Russia, and especially the excessive use of violence in normal times. But still I incline more and more toward a communist philosophy.

Marx may be wrong in some of his statements, or his theory of value; this I am not competent to judge. But he seems to me to have possessed quite an extraordinary degree of insight into social phenomena, and this insight was apparently due to the scientific method he adopted. This method, applied to past history as well as current events, helps us in understanding them far more than any other method of approach, and it is because of this that the most revealing and keen analyses of the changes that are taking place in the world today come from Marxist writers. It is easy to point out that Marx ignored or underrated certain subsequent tendencies, like the rise of a revolutionary element in the middle class, which is so notable today. But the whole value of Marxism seems to me to lie in its absence of dogmatism, in its stress on a certain outlook and mode of approach, and in its attitude to action. That outlook helps us in understanding the social phenomena of our own times and points out the way of action and escape.

Even that method of action was no fixed and unchangeable road but had to be suited to circumstances. That, at any rate, was Lenin's view, and he justified it brilliantly by fitting his action to changing circumstances. He tells us: "To attempt to answer 'yes' or 'no' to the question of the definite means of struggle, without examining in detail the concrete situation of a given moment at a given stage of its development, means to depart altogether from the Marxian ground." And again he says: "Nothing is final; we must always learn from circumstances."

Because of this wide and comprehensive outlook, the really understanding communist develops to some extent an organic sense of social life. Politics for him cease to be a mere record of opportunism or a groping in the dark. The ideals and objectives he works for give a meaning to the struggle and to the sacrifices he willingly faces. He feels that he is part of a grand army marching forward to realize human fate and destiny, and he has the sense of "marching step by step with history."

Probably most communists are far from feeling all this. Perhaps only a Lenin had this organic sense of life in its fullness which made his action so effective. But to a small extent every communist, who has understood the philosophy of his movement, has it.

It is difficult to be patient with many communists; they have developed a peculiar method of irritating others. But they are a sorely tried people, and, outside the Soviet Union, they have to contend against enormous difficulties. I have always admired their great courage and capacity for sacrifice. They suffer greatly, as, unhappily, untold millions suffer in various ways, but not blindly before a malign and all-powerful fate. They suffer as human beings, and there is a tragic nobility about such suffering.

The success or failure of the Russian social experiments does not directly affect the validity of the Marxian theory. It is conceivable, though it is highly unlikely, that a set of untoward circumstances or a combination of powers might upset those experiments. But the value of those mighty social upheavals will still remain. With all my instinctive dislike for much that has happened there, I feel that they offer the greatest hope to the world. I do not know enough, and I am not in a position to judge their actions. My chief fear is that the background of too much violence and suppression might bring an evil trail behind them which it may be difficult to get rid of. But the greatest thing in favor of the present directors of Russia's destiny is that they are not afraid to learn from their mistakes. They can retrace their steps and build anew. And always they keep their ideal before them. Their activities in other countries, through the Communist International, have been singularly futile, but apparently those activities have been reduced to a minimum now.

Coming back to India, communism and socialism seem a far cry, unless the rush of external events forces the pace here. We have to deal not with communism but, with the addition of an extra syllable, with communalism. And communally India is in a dark age. Men of action waste their energies on trivial things and intrigue, and maneuver and try to overreach each other. Few of them are interested in trying to make the world a better, brighter place. Perhaps this is a temporary phase that will pass soon.

The Congress has at least largely kept out of this communal darkness, but its outlook is petty bourgeois, and the remedy it seeks for this as for other problems is in terms of the petty *bourgeoisie*. It is not likely to succeed that way. It represents today this lower middle class, for that is the most vocal and revolutionary at present. But it is nevertheless not as vital as it appears to be. It is pressed on either side by two forces—one entrenched, the other still weak but growing rapidly. It is passing through a crisis of its existence at present; what will happen to it in the future it is difficult to say. It cannot go over to the side of the entrenched forces before it has fulfilled its historic mission of attaining national freedom. But, before it succeeds in that, other forces may grow powerful and influence it in their direction, or gradually displace it. It seems likely, however, that so long as a large measure of national freedom is not obtained, the Congress will play a dominant role in India.

Any violent activity seems to be out of the question, injurious, and waste of effort. That, I think, is generally recognized in India, in spite of rare instances of futile and sporadic violence. That way cannot lead us anywhere except into a hopeless maze of violence and counter-violence out of which it will be difficult to emerge.

I write vaguely and somewhat academically about current events and try to play the part of a detached onlooker. I am not usually considered a looker-on when action beckons; my offense, I am often told, is that I rush in foolishly without sufficient provocation. What would I do now? What would I suggest to my countrymen to do? Perhaps the instinctive caution of a person who dabbles in public affairs comes in the way of my committing myself prematurely. But, if I may confess the truth, I really do not know, and I do not try to find out. When I cannot act, why should I worry? I do worry to a large extent, but that is inevitable. At least, so long as I am in prison, I try to save myself from coming to grips with the problem of immediate action.

All activity seems to be far away in prison. One becomes the object of events, not the subject of action. And one waits and waits for something to happen. I write of political and social problems of India and the world, but what are they to this little self-contained world of jail which has long been my home? Prisoners have only one major interest: the date of their release.

## LII

## A CONCLUSION

*We are enjoined to labor; but it is not granted to us to complete our labors.*—The Talmud.

I HAVE REACHED the end of the story. This egotistical narrative of my adventures through life, such as they are, has been brought up to today, February 14, 1935, District Jail, Almora. Three months ago today I celebrated in this prison my forty-fifth birthday, and I suppose

I have still many years to live. Sometimes a sense of age and weariness steals over me; at other times I feel full of energy and vitality. I have a fairly tough body, and my mind has a capacity for recovering from shock, so I imagine I shall yet survive for long unless some sudden fate overtakes me. But the future has to be lived before it can be written about.

The adventures have not been very exciting perhaps; long years in prison can hardly be termed adventurous. Nor have they been in any way unique, for I have shared these years with their ups and downs with tens of thousands of my countrymen and countrywomen; and this record of changing moods, of exaltations and depressions, of intense activity and enforced solitude, is our common record. I have been one of a mass, moving with it, swaying it occasionally, being influenced by it; and yet, like the other units, an individual, apart from the others, living my separate life in the heart of the crowd. We have posed often enough and struck up attitudes, but there was something very real and intensely truthful in much that we did, and this lifted us out of our petty selves and made us more vital and gave us an importance that we would otherwise not have had. Sometimes we were fortunate enough to experience that fullness of life which comes from attempting to fit ideals with action. And we realized that any other life involving a renunciation of these ideals and a tame submission to superior force, would have been a wasted existence, full of discontent and inner sorrow.

To me these years have brought one rich gift, among many others. More and more I have looked upon life as an adventure of absorbing interest, where there is so much to learn, so much to do. I have continually had a feeling of growing up, and that feeling is still with me and gives a zest to my activities as well as to the reading of books, and generally makes life worth while.

In writing this narrative I have tried to give my moods and thoughts at the time of each event, to represent as far as I could my feelings on the occasion. It is difficult to recapture a past mood, and it is not easy to forget subsequent happenings. Later ideas, thus, must inevitably have colored my account of earlier days; but my object was, primarily for my own benefit, to trace my own mental growth. Perhaps what I have written is not so much an account of what I have been but of what I have sometimes wanted to be or imagined myself to be.

Indeed, I often wonder if I represent anyone at all, and I am inclined to think that I do not, though many have kindly and friendly feelings toward me. I have become a queer mixture of the East and the West, out of place everywhere, at home nowhere. Perhaps my thoughts and approach to life are more akin to what is called Western than Eastern, but India clings to me, as she does to all her children, in innumerable ways; and behind me lie, somewhere in the subconscious, racial memories of a hundred, or whatever the number may be, generations of Brahmans. I cannot get rid of either that past inheritance or my recent acquisitions. They are both part of me, and, though they help me in both the East and the West, they also create in me a feeling of spiritual loneliness not only in public activities but in life itself. I am a stranger and alien in the West. I cannot be of it. But in my own country also, sometimes, I have an exile's feeling.

The distant mountains seem easy of access and climbing, the top beckons, but, as one approaches, difficulties appear; and the higher one goes the more laborious becomes the journey, and the summit recedes into the clouds. Yet the climbing is worth the effort and has its own joy and satisfaction. Perhaps it is the struggle that gives value to life, not so much the ultimate result. Often it is difficult to know which is the right path; it is easier sometimes to know what is not right, and to avoid that is something after all. If I may quote, with all humility, the last words of the great Socrates: "I know not what death is—it may be a good thing, and I am not afraid of it. But I do know that it is a bad thing to desert one's post, and I prefer what may be good to what I know to be bad."

The years I have spent in prison! Sitting alone, wrapped in my thoughts, how many seasons I have seen go by, following one another into oblivion! How many moons I have watched wax and wane, and the pageant of the stars moving along inexorably and majestically! How many yesterdays of my youth lie buried here! Sometimes I see the ghosts of these dead yesterdays rise up, bringing poignant memories, and whispering to me: "Was it worth while?" There is no hesitation about the answer. If I were given the chance to go through my life again, with my present knowledge and experience added, I would no doubt try to make many changes in my personal life; I would endeavor to improve in many ways on what I had previously done, but my major decisions in public affairs would remain untouched. Indeed, I could not vary them, for they were stronger than myself, and a force beyond my control drove me to them.

It is almost exactly a year since my conviction; a year has gone by out of the two years of my sentence. Another full year remains, for there are no remissions this time, as simple imprisonment carries no such deductions. Even the eleven days that I was out in August last have been added on to the period of my sentence. But this year too will pass, and I shall go out—and then? I do not know, but I have a feeling that a chapter of my life is over and another chapter will begin. What this is going to be I cannot clearly guess. The leaves of the book of life are closed.

## POSTSCRIPT

BADENWEILER, SCHWARZWALD,
*October 25, 1935*

IN MAY LAST my wife left Bhowali for further treatment in Europe. After her departure there were no more visits to Bhowali for me, no more fortnightly outings and drives on the mountain roads. I missed them, and Almora Jail seemed to be drearier than before.

News came of the Quetta earthquake, and for a while all else was forgotten. But not for long, for the Government of India does not allow us to forget it or its peculiar ways. Soon we learned that Rajendra Prasad, the Congress president, and the man who knew more about earthquake relief work than almost any other person in India, was not permitted to go to Quetta and help in relief. Nor could Gandhiji or any other public man of note. Many Indian newspapers had their securities confiscated for writing articles on Quetta.

Everywhere the military mentality, the police outlook—in the Assembly, in civil government, in bombing on the Frontier. Almost it would seem that the British Government in India is permanently at war with large sections of the Indian people.

The police are a useful and necessary force, but a world full of policemen and the police bludgeon may not, perhaps, be a desirable place to live in. It has often been said that an unrestrained use of force degrades the user of it as it humiliates and degrades the object of it. Few things are more striking today in India than the progressive deterioration, moral and intellectual, of the higher services, more especially the Indian Civil Service. This is most in evidence in the superior officials, but it runs like a thread throughout the services. Whenever occasion arises for making a fresh appointment to the higher ranks, the person who fits in easily with this moral and intellectual deterioration is inevitably chosen.

On September 4 I was suddenly discharged from Almora Jail as news had come that my wife's condition was critical. She was under treatment in Badenweiler in the Schwarzwald in Germany. My sentence was "suspended," I was told, and I was released five and a half months before my time. I hurried to Europe by air.

Europe in turmoil, fearful of war and tumult and with economic crises always on the horizon; Abyssinia invaded and her people bombed; various imperialist systems in conflict and threatening each other; and England, the greatest of the imperialist Powers, standing up for peace and the League Covenant while it bombs and ruthlessly oppresses its subject peoples. But here in the Black Forest it is calm and peaceful, and even the swastika is not much in evidence. I watch the mists steal up the valley and hide the distant frontier of France and cover the landscape, and I wonder what lies behind them.

## LIII

## FIVE YEARS LATER

FIVE AND A half years ago, sitting in my prison barrack in the Almora District Jail, I wrote the last line of my autobiography. Eight months later I added a postscript from Badenweiler in Germany. That autobiography, published in England, had a kindly reception from all manner of people in various countries, and I was glad that what I had written had brought India nearer to many friends abroad, and had made them appreciate, to some extent, the inner significance of our struggle for freedom. Unfortunately this book did not reach the American public, and various happenings conspired to delay an American edition. I am happy that at last it is going to appear in a new garb in America.

My publisher has asked me to add to it in order to bring it up to date. His demand is reasonable, and I could not deny it. And yet I have found it no easy matter to comply with it. We live in strange times, when life's normal course has been completely upset, and it is difficult for me even to communicate with my publisher. With my approval, my autobiography has now been abridged considerably, for much that it contained is perhaps of little interest today, especially to American readers. And yet I do not know what this abridgement is, what has been taken out, what remains. We have been unable to overcome the difficulties of communication which war brings in its train. America seems to be very far away from India now, and sometimes it takes many months for letters to cross the oceans. And then there is the censor.

But a more serious difficulty confronted me. I wrote my autobiography entirely in prison, cut off from outside activity. I suffered from various humors in prison, as every prisoner does; but gradually I developed a mood of introspection and some peace of mind. How am I to capture that mood now, how am I to fit in with that narrative? As I glance through my book again, I feel almost as if some other person had written a story of long ago. The five years that have gone by have changed the world and left their impress upon me. Physically I am older, of course, but it is the mind that has received shock and sensation again and again and has hardened, or perhaps matured. My wife's death in Switzerland ended a chapter of my existence and took away much from my life that had been part of my being. It was difficult for me to realize that she was no more, and I could not adjust myself easily. I threw myself into my work, seeking some satisfaction in it, and rushed about from end to end of India. Even more than in my earlier days, my life became an alternation of huge crowds and intensive activity and loneliness. My mother's death later broke a final link with the past. My daughter was away studying at Oxford, and later under treatment in a sanatorium abroad. I would return to my home from my wanderings almost unwillingly and sit in that deserted house all by myself, trying even to avoid interviews there. I wanted peace after the crowds.

But there was no peace in my work or my mind, and the responsibility that I had to shoulder often oppressed me very greatly. I could not align myself with various parties and groups; I did not even fit in with my closest colleagues. I could not function as I wanted to, and at the same time I prevented others from functioning as they wanted to. A sense of suppression and frustration grew, and I became a solitary figure in public life, though vast crowds came to hear me and enthusiasm surrounded me.

I was affected more than others by the development of events in Europe and the Far East. Munich was a shock hard to bear, and the tragedy of Spain became a personal sorrow to me. As these years of horror succeeded one another, the sense of impending catastrophe overwhelmed me, and my faith in a bright future for the world became dim.

And now the catastrophe has come. The volcanoes in Europe spit fire and destruction, and here in India I sit on the edge of another volcano, not knowing when it may burst. It is difficult to tear myself away from the problem of the moment, to develop the mood of retrospection and survey these five years that have gone by, and write calmly about them. And, even if I could do so, I would have to write another big book, for there is so much to say. I shall endeavor, therefore, as best I may, to refer briefly only to certain events and developments in which I have played a part or which have affected me.

I was with my wife when she died in Lausanne on February 28, 1936. A little while before, news had reached me that I had been elected president of the Indian National Congress for the second time. I returned to India by air soon after, and on my way, in Rome, I had a curious experience. Some days before my departure a message was conveyed to me that Signor Mussolini would like to meet me when I passed through Rome. In spite of my strong disapproval of the fascist regime, I would ordinarily have liked to meet Signor Mussolini and to find out for myself what a person who was playing such an important part in the world's affairs was like. But I was in no mood for interviews then. What came in my way even more was the continuance of the Abyssinian campaign and my apprehension that such an interview would inevitably be used for purposes of fascist propaganda. No denial from me would go far. I remembered how Mr. Gandhi, when he passed through Rome in 1931, had a bogus interview in the *Giornale d'Italia* fastened on to him. I remembered also several other instances of Indians visiting Italy being used, against their wishes, for fascist propaganda. I was assured that nothing of the kind would happen to me and that our interview would be entirely private. Still, I decided to avoid it, and I conveyed my regrets to Signor Mussolini.

I could not avoid going through Rome, however, as the Dutch K.L.M. airplane I was traveling on spent a night there. Soon after my arrival in Rome, a high official called upon me and gave me an invitation to meet Signor Mussolini that evening. It had all been fixed up, he told me. I was surprised and pointed out that I had already asked to be excused. We argued for an hour, till the time fixed for the interview itself, and then I had my way. There was no interview.

I returned to India and plunged into my work. Within a few days of my return I had to preside over the annual session of the National Congress. For some years, which I had spent mainly in prison, I had been out of touch with developments. I found many changes, new alignments, a hardening on party lines within the Congress. There was an atmosphere of suspicion and bitterness and conflict. I treated this lightly, having confidence in my own capacity to deal with the situation. For a short while I seemed to carry the Congress in the direction I wanted it to go. But I realized soon that the conflict was deep-rooted, and it was not so easy to charm away the suspicion of each other and the bitterness that had grown in our ranks. I thought seriously of resigning from the presidency, but, realizing that this would only make matters worse, I refrained.

Again and again, during the next few months, I considered this question of resignation. I found it difficult to work smoothly with my own colleagues in the Congress executive, and it became clear to me that they viewed my activities with apprehension. It was not so much that they objected to any specific act, but they disliked the general trend and direction. They had justification for this, as my outlook was different. I was completely loyal to Congress decisions, but I emphasized certain aspects of them, while my colleagues emphasized other aspects. I decided finally to resign, and I informed Gandhiji of my decision. In the course of my letter to him I wrote: "Since my return from Europe I have found that the meetings of the Working Committee exhaust me greatly; they have a devitalizing effect on me, and I have almost the feeling of being much older in years after every fresh experience. I should not be surprised if this feeling was also shared by my colleagues of the Committee. It is an unhealthy experience, and it comes in the way of effective work."

Soon afterward a far-away occurrence, unconnected with India, affected me greatly and made me change my decision. This was the news of General Franco's revolt in Spain. I saw this rising, with its background of German and Italian assistance, developing into a European or even a world conflict. India was bound to be drawn into this, and I could not afford to weaken our organization and create an internal crisis by resigning just when it was essential for us to pull together. I was not wholly wrong in my analysis of the situation, though I was premature and my mind rushed to conclusions which took some years to materialize.

The reaction of the Spanish War on me indicates how, in my mind, the problem of India was tied up with other world problems. More and more I came to think that these separate problems, political or economic, in China, Abyssinia, Spain, Central Europe, India, or elsewhere, were facets of one and the same world problem. There could be no final solution of any one of them till this basic problem was solved. And in all probability there would be upheaval and disaster before the final solution was reached. As peace was said to be indivisible in the present-day world, so also freedom was indivisible, and the world could not continue for long part free, part unfree. The challenge of fascism and Nazi-ism was in essence the challenge of imperialism. They were twin brothers, with this variation, that imperialism functioned abroad in colonies and dependencies while fascism and Nazi-ism functioned in the same way in the home country also. If freedom was to be established in the world, not only fascism and Nazi-ism had to go, but imperialism had to be completely liquidated.

This reaction to foreign events was not confined to me. Many others in India began, to some extent, to feel that way, and even the public was interested. This public interest was kept up by thousands of meetings and demonstrations that the Congress organized all over the country in sympathy with the people of China, Abyssinia, Palestine, and Spain. Some attempts were also made by us to send aid, in the shape of medical supplies and food, to China and Spain. This wider interest in international affairs helped to raise our own national struggle to a higher level and to lessen somewhat the narrowness which is always a feature of nationalism.

But, inevitably, foreign affairs did not touch the life of the average person, who was absorbed in his own troubles. The peasant was full of his growing difficulties, his appalling poverty, and of the many burdens that crushed him. The agrarian problem was, after all, the major problem of India, and the Congress had gradually evolved an agrarian program which, though going far, yet accepted the present structure. The industrial worker was little better off, and there were frequent strikes. Politically minded people discussed the new constitution that had been imposed upon India by the British Parliament. This constitution, though giving some power in the provinces, kept the reality of power in the hands of the British Government and their representatives. For the Central Government a federation was proposed which tied up feudal and autocratic states with semidemocratic provinces, and was intended to perpetuate the British imperialist structure. It was a fantastic affair, which could never work, and which had every safeguard that the wit of man could devise to protect British vested interests. This constitution was indignantly rejected by the Congress, and in fact there was hardly anyone in India who had a good word for it.

At first the provincial part of it was applied. In spite of our rejection of the constitution, we decided to contest elections, as this brought us into intimate touch not only with millions of voters, but also others. This general election was a memorable affair for me. I was not a candidate myself, but I toured all over India on behalf of Congress candidates, and I imagine that I created some kind of a record in the way of election campaigns. In the course of about four months I traveled about fifty thousand miles, using every kind of convenience for this purpose, and often going into remote rural areas where there were no proper means of transport. I traveled by airplane, railway, automobile, motor truck, horse carriages of various kinds, bullock cart, bicycle, elephant, camel, horse, steamer, paddle-boat, canoe, and on foot.

I carried about with me microphones and loud-speakers and addressed a dozen meetings a day, apart from impromptu gatherings by the roadside. Some mammoth gatherings approached a hundred thousand; the average audience was usually twenty thousand. The daily total of persons attending was frequently a hundred thousand, and sometimes it was much greater. On a rough estimate it can be said that ten million persons actually attended the meetings I addressed, and probably several million more were brought into some kind of touch with me during my journeying by road.

I rushed about from place to place, from the northern frontiers of India to the southern seas, taking little rest, kept up by the excitement of the moment and the enormous enthusiasm that met me. It was an extraordinary feat of physical endurance which surprised me. This election campaign, in which large numbers of people took part on our behalf, stirred up the whole countryside, and a new life was visible everywhere. For us it was something much more than an election campaign. We were interested not only in the thirty million voters but also in the hundreds of millions of others who had no votes.

There was another aspect of this extensive touring which gripped me. For me it was a voyage of discovery of India and her people. I saw a thousand facets of this country of mine in all their rich diversity, and yet always with the unifying impress of India upon them. I gazed at the millions of friendly eyes that looked up at me and tried to understand what lay behind them. The more I saw of India, the more I felt how little I knew of her infinite charm and variety, how much more there was for me to find out. She seemed to smile at me often, and sometimes to mock at me and elude me.

Sometimes, though rarely, I took a day off and visited some famous sight near by—the Ajanta Caves or Mohenjo Daro in the Indus Valley. For a brief while I lived in the past, and the Bodhisatvas and the beautiful women of the Ajanta Frescoes filled my mind. Some days later I would start with surprise as I looked at some woman, working in the fields or drawing water from a village well, for she would remind me of the women of Ajanta.

The Congress triumphed in the general election, and there was a great argument as to whether we should accept ministries in the provinces. Ultimately it was decided that we should do so but on the understanding that there would be no interference from the Viceroy or the governors.

In the summer of 1937 I visited Burma and Malaya. It was no holiday, as crowds and engagements pursued me everywhere, but the change was pleasant, and I loved to see and meet the flowery and youthful people of Burma, so unlike in many ways the people of India with the stamp of long ages past upon them.

New problems faced us in India. In most of the provinces Congress governments were in power, and many of the ministers had spent years in prison previously. My sister, Vijaya Lakshmi Pandit, became one of the ministers in the United Provinces—the first woman minister in India. The immediate effect of the coming of the Congress ministries was a feeling of relief in the countryside, as if a great burden had been lifted. A new life coursed through the whole country, and the peasant and the worker expected big things to happen immediately. Political prisoners were released, and a large measure of civil liberty, such as had not been known previously, was established. The Congress ministers worked hard and made others work hard also. But they had to work with the old apparatus of government, which was wholly alien to them and often hostile. Even the services were not under their control. Twice there was a conflict with the governors, and the ministers offered their resignations. Thereupon the governors accepted the viewpoint of the ministers, and the crisis ended. But the power and influence of the old services—the civil service, the police, and others— backed by the governor and buttressed by the constitution itself, were great and could make themselves felt in a hundred ways. Progress was slow, and dissatisfaction arose.

This dissatisfaction found expression in the Congress itself, and the more advanced elements grew restive. I was myself unhappy at the trend of events as I noticed that our fine fighting organization was being converted gradually into just an electioneering organization. A struggle for independence seemed to be inevitable, and this phase of provincial autonomy was just a passing one. In April 1938 I wrote to Gandhiji expressing my dissatisfaction at the work of the Congress ministries. "They are trying to adapt themselves far too much to the old order and trying to justify it. But all this, bad as it is, might be tolerated. What is far worse is that we are losing the high position that we have built up, with so much labor, in the hearts of the people. We are sinking to the level of ordinary politicians."

I was perhaps unnecessarily hard on the Congress ministers; the fault lay much more in the situation itself and in the circumstances. The record of these ministries was in fact a formidable one in numerous fields of national activity. But they had to function within certain limits, and our problems required going outside these limits. Among the many good things that they did were the agrarian legislation they passed, giving considerable relief to the peasantry, and the introduction of what is called basic education. This basic education is intended to be made free and compulsory for every child in the country for seven years, from the age of seven to fourteen. It is based on the modern method of teaching through a craft, and it has been so evolved as to reduce the capital and recurring cost very greatly, without in any way impairing the efficiency of education. For a poor country like India, with scores of millions of children to educate, the question of cost is important. This system has already revolutionized education in India and is full of promise.

Higher education was also tackled vigorously, and so also public health, but the efforts of the Congress governments had not borne much fruit when they finally resigned. Adult literacy, however, was pushed with enthusiasm and yielded good results. Rural reconstruction also had a great deal of attention paid to it.

The record of the Congress governments was impressive, but all this good work could not solve the fundamental problems of India. That required deeper and more basic changes and an ending of the imperialistic structure which preserved all manner of vested interests.

So conflict grew within the Congress between the more moderate and the more advanced sections. The first organized expression of this took place in a meeting of the All-India Congress Committee in October 1937. This distressed Gandhiji greatly, and he expressed himself strongly in private. Subsequently he wrote an article in which he disapproved of some action I had taken as Congress president.

I felt that I could no longer carry on as a responsible member of

362

the Executive, but I decided not to do anything to precipitate a crisis. My term of office as Congress president was drawing to an end, and I could drop out quietly then. I had been president for two successive years and three times in all. There was some talk of my being elected for another term, but I was quite clear in my own mind that I should not stand. About this time I played a little trick which amused me greatly. I wrote an article, which was published anonymously in the *Modern Review* of Calcutta, in which I opposed my own re-election.[1] No one, not even the editor, knew who had written it, and I watched with great interest its reaction on my colleagues and others. All manner of wild guesses were made about the writer, but very few people knew the truth till John Gunther mentioned it in his book *Inside Asia*.

Subhas Bose was elected president of the next Congress session, which was held at Haripura, and soon afterward I decided to go to Europe. I wanted to see my daughter, but the real reason was to freshen up my tired and puzzled mind.

But Europe was hardly the place for peaceful contemplation or for light to illumine the dark corners of the mind. There was gloom there and the apparent stillness that comes before the storm. It was the Europe of 1938 with Mr. Neville Chamberlain's appeasement in full swing and marching over the bodies of nations, betrayed and crushed, to the final scene that was staged at Munich. I entered into this Europe of conflict by flying straight to Barcelona. There I remained for five days and watched the bombs fall nightly from the air. There I saw much else that impressed me powerfully; and there, in the midst of want and destruction and ever-impending disaster, I felt more at peace with myself than anywhere else in Europe. There was light there, the light of courage and determination and of doing something worth while.

I went to England and spent a month there and met people of all degrees and all shades of opinion. I sensed a change in the average man, a change in the right direction. But there was no change at the top where Chamberlainism sat triumphantly. And then I went to Czechoslovakia and watched at close quarters the difficult and intricate game of how to betray your friend and the cause you are supposed to stand for on the highest moral grounds. I followed this game during the Munich crisis from London, Paris, and Geneva and came to many strange conclusions. What surprised me most was the utter collapse, in the moment of crisis, of all the so-called advanced people and groups.

[1] See Appendix E.

Geneva gave me the impression of archaeological remains, with the dead bodies of the hundreds of international organizations that had their headquarters there, lying about. London exhibited tremendous relief that war had been averted and cared for little else. Others had paid the price, and it did not matter; but it was going to matter very much before a year was out. The star of Mr. Chamberlain was in the ascendant, though protesting voices were heard. Paris distressed me greatly, especially the middle-class section of it, which did not even protest overmuch. This was the Paris of the Revolution, the symbol of liberty the world over.

I returned from Europe sad at heart with many illusions shattered. On my way back I stopped in Egypt, where Mustafa Nahas Pasha and the other leaders of the Wafd party gave me a warm welcome. I was glad to meet them again and to discuss our common problems in the light of the fast-developing world situation. Some months later a deputation from the Wafd party visited us in India and attended our annual Congress session.

In India the old problems and conflicts continued, and I had to face the old difficulty of how to fit in with my colleagues. It distressed me to see that on the eve of a world upheaval many Congressmen were wrapped up in these petty rivalries. Yet there was some sense of proportion and understanding among Congressmen in the upper circles of the organization. Outside the Congress, the deterioration was much more marked. Communal rivalry and tension had increased, and the Moslem League, under Mr. M. A. Jinnah's leadership, was aggressively antinationalist and narrow-minded and continued to pursue an astonishing course. There was no constructive suggestion, no attempt even to meet halfway, no answers to questions as to what exactly they wanted. It was a negative program of hatred and violence, reminiscent of Nazi methods. What was particularly distressing was the growing vulgarity of communal organizations which was affecting our public life. There were, of course, many Moslem organizations and large numbers of Moslems who disapproved of the activities of the Moslem League and favored the Congress.

Following this course, the Moslem League inevitably went more and more astray till it stood openly against democracy in India and even for the partition of the country. They were encouraged in these fantastic demands by British officials, who wanted to exploit the Moslem League, as all other disruptive forces, in order to weaken the Congress influence. It was astonishing that just when it became obvious that small nations had no further place in the world, except as parts of a federation of nations, there should be this demand for a splitting up of India. Probably the demand was not seriously meant, but it was the logical consequence of the two-nation theory that Mr. Jinnah had advanced. The new development of communalism had little to do with religious differences. These admittedly could be adjusted. It was a political conflict between those who wanted a free, united, and democratic India and certain reactionary and feudal elements who, under the guise of religion, wanted to preserve their special interests. Religion, as practiced and exploited in this way by its votaries of different creeds, seemed to me a curse and a barrier to all progress, social and individual. Religion, which was supposed to encourage spirituality and brotherly feeling, became the fountainhead of hatred, narrowness, meanness, and the lowest materialism.

Matters came to a head in the Congress at the presidential election early in 1939. Unfortunately Maulana Abul Kalam Azad refused to stand, and Subhas Chandra Bose was elected after a contest. This gave rise to all manner of complications and deadlocks which persisted for many months. At the Tripuri Congress there were unseemly scenes. I was at that time very low in spirits, and it was difficult for me to carry on without a breakdown. Political events, national and international happenings, affected me, of course; but the immediate causes were unconnected with public affairs. I was disgusted with myself, and in a press article I wrote: "I fear I give little satisfaction to them [my colleagues], and yet that is not surprising, for I give even less satisfaction to myself. It is not out of this stuff that leadership comes, and the sooner my colleagues realize this the better for them and me. The mind functions efficiently enough, the intellect is trained to carry on through habit, but the springs that give life and vitality to that functioning seem to dry up."

Subhas Bose resigned from the presidency and started the Forward Bloc, which was intended to be almost a rival organization to the Congress. It petered out after a while, as it was bound to do, but it added to the disruptive tendencies and the general deterioration. Under cover of fine phrases, adventurist and opportunist elements found platforms, and I could not help thinking of the rise of the Nazi party in Germany. Their way had been to mobilize mass support for one program and then to utilize this for an entirely different purpose.

Deliberately I kept out of the new Congress Executive. I felt I could not fit in, and I did not like much that had been done. Gandhiji's fast in connection with Rajkot and the subsequent developments upset me. I wrote then that the "sense of helplessness increases after the Rajkot events. I cannot function where I do not understand, and I do not understand at all the logic of what has taken place." "More and more," I added, "the choice before many of us becomes difficult, and this is no question of Right or Left or even of political decisions. The choice is of unthinking acceptance of decisions which sometimes contradict one another and have no logical sequence, or opposition, or inaction. Not one of these courses is easily commendable. To accept unthinkingly what one cannot appreciate or willingly agree to produces mental flabbiness and paralysis. No great movement can be carried on on this basis; certainly not a democratic movement. Opposition is difficult when it weakens us and helps the adversary. Inaction produces frustration and all manner of complexes when from every side comes the call for action."

Soon after my return from Europe at the end of 1938, two other activities claimed my attention. I presided over the All-India States' Peoples' Conference at Ludhiana and thus became even more intimately connected with the progressive movements in the semifeudal Indian states. In large numbers of these states there had been a growing ferment, occasionally leading to clashes between the peoples' organizations and the authorities, which were often helped by British troops. It is difficult to write in restrained language about those states or about the part that the British Government has played in maintaining these relics of the Middle Ages. A recent writer has rightly called them Britain's Fifth Column in India. There are some enlightened rulers who want to side with their people and introduce substantial reforms, but the paramount power comes in the way. A democratic state will not function as a fifth column.

It is clear that these five hundred and fifty-odd states cannot function separately as political or economic units. They cannot remain as feudal enclaves in a democratic India. A few large ones may become democratic units in a federation; the others must be completely absorbed. No minor reforms can solve this problem. The states system will have to go, and it will go when British imperialism goes.

My other activity was the chairmanship of a National Planning Committee which was formed under Congress auspices with the co-operation of the provincial governments. As we proceeded with this work, it grew and grew, till it embraced almost every phase of national activity. We appointed twenty-nine subcommittees for various groups of subjects—agricultural, industrial, social, economic, financial—and tried to co-ordinate their activities so as to produce a scheme of planned economy for India. Our scheme will necessarily be in outline which will have to be filled in later. The Planning Committee is still functioning and is not likely to finish its labors for some months more. For me this has been fascinating work, and I have learned much from it. It is clear that any scheme that we may produce can only be given effect to in a free India. It is also clear that any effective planning must involve a socialization of the economic structure.

In the summer of 1939 I paid a brief visit to Ceylon, as friction had grown there between the Indian residents and the Government. I was happy to be back again in that beautiful island, and my visit, I think, laid the foundations for closer relations between India and Ceylon. I had the most cordial of welcomes from everybody, including the Ceylonese members of the Government. I have no doubt that in any future order Ceylon and India must hang together. My own picture of the future is a federation which includes China and India, Burma and Ceylon, Afghanistan, and possibly other countries. If a world federation comes, that will be welcome.

The situation in Europe in August 1939 was threatening, and I did not want to leave India at a moment of crisis. But the desire to visit China, even for a short while, was strong. So I flew to China, and within two days of my leaving India I was in Chungking. Very soon I had to rush back to India, as war had at last descended upon Europe. I spent less than two weeks in free China, but these two weeks were memorable ones both personally for me and for the future relations of India and China.

As I flew to China, my mind went back to the long line of illustrious pilgrims and travellers who had journeyed between India and China for thousands of years. Across vast deserts and mighty mountains, they had marched for many months and sometimes for years, encountering dangers and perils, but full of enthusiasm and the spirit of adventure, for they were the bearers of the treasures of thought and culture from one country to another. In those far-off days they had forged the imperishable links which bound India and China together. I imagined myself as one of a long line, yet another link joining together these two Ancients in history and civilization, who had found re-birth and youthful vitality again, and were facing the future with hope and confidence.

Almost my first experience in Chungking was of an air-raid, and these were repeated nightly while I was there. I was interested in the behavior of the Chinese crowds and I watched with admiration how calm and untroubled they were when death threatened them from the skies. I saw the life in the city being carried on almost normally in spite of the terrible strain of the war. I visited factories, summer schools, military academies, youth camps, and universities, torn from their ancient roots, finding a new life and vitality under bamboo shelters. I was fascinated by the growth of the village co-operative movement and cottage industries. I met scholars, statesmen and generals, the leaders of the new China, and, above all, I had the privilege of meeting on several occasions the supreme leader of China, Generalissimo Chiang-Kai-shek, who embodies in himself the unity of China and her determination to be free. It was my privilege also to meet the first lady of the land, Madame Chiang, who has been a continuous source of inspiration to the nation.

But though I met men and women of note and distinction, I was always trying to understand the people of China. I had read much about them and of their magnificent record of culture, and I was eager to sense the reality. I found not only a race wise and profound, deep in the lore of its own great past, but also a vital people, full of life and energy, adapting themselves to modern conditions. On the face of even the man in the street there was the imprint of ages of culture.

I found, to my joy, that my desire that China and India should draw closer to each other was fully reciprocated by China's leaders. Often, as we sat in a dug-out and enemy planes were bombing the city, we discussed the past and the present of our two countries and the bright promise of their future co-operation.

I returned to India full of this thought, and the vague ideas I had nourished for many years now began to take definite shape in my mind. There had been much talk in the West of a Federation of Europe, and of a Federal Union which seemed to exclude India and China. I had dreamed of a wider federation, comprising all of the nations and peoples of the world. Perhaps the time for that was not yet. But if there were to be regional federations, then surely there must be an Eastern Federation of China and India and other eastern countries.

I returned in haste.

War and India. What were we to do? For years past we had thought about this and proclaimed our policy. Yet in spite of all this the British

Government declared India to be a belligerent country without any reference to our people, to the Central Assembly, or to the provincial governments. That was a slight hard to get over, for it signified that imperialism functioned as before. The Congress Working Committee issued a long statement in the middle of September 1939, in which our past and present policy was defined and the British Government was invited to explain their war aims, more particularly in regard to British imperialism. We had frequently condemned fascism and Nazi-ism. but we were more intimately concerned with the imperialism that dominated over us. Was this imperialism to go? Did they recognize the independence of India and her right to frame her own constitution through a Constituent Assembly? What immediate steps would be taken to introduce popular control of the Central Government? Later, in order to meet every possible objection of any minority group, the idea behind the Constituent Assembly was further amplified. It was stated that minority claims would be settled in this Assembly with the consent of the minority concerned, and not by a majority vote. If such agreement was not possible in regard to any issue, then this was to be referred to an impartial tribunal for final decision. This was an unsafe proposal from a democratic point of view, but the Congress was prepared to go to almost any length in order to allay the suspicions of minorities.

The British Government's answer was clear. It left no doubt that they were not prepared to clarify their war aims or to hand over control of the Government to the people's representatives. The old order continued and was to continue, and British interests in India could not be left unprotected. The Congress ministries in the provinces thereupon resigned, as they were not prepared to co-operate on these terms in the prosecution of the war. The constitution was suspended, and autocratic rule was re-established. The old constitutional conflict of Western countries between an elected parliament and the king's prerogative, which had cost the heads of two kings in England and France, took shape in India. But there was something much more than this constitutional aspect. The volcano was not in action, but it was there and rumblings were heard.

The impasse continued, and, meanwhile, new laws and ordinances descended upon us by decree, and Congressmen and others were arrested in ever-growing numbers. Resentment grew and a demand for action on our side. But the course of the war and the peril of England itself made us hesitate, for we could not wholly forget the old lesson which Gandhiji had taught us, that our objective should not be to embarrass the opponent in his hour of need.

As the war progressed, new problems arose, or the old problems took new shape, and the old alignments seemed to change, the old standards to fade away. There were many shocks, and adjustment was difficult. The Russo-German Pact, the Soviet's invasion of Finland, the friendly approach of Russia toward Japan. Were there any principles, or any standards of conduct in this world, or was it all sheer opportunism?

April came and the Norwegian debacle. May brought the horrors of Holland and Belgium. June, the sudden collapse of France, and Paris, that proud and fair city, nursery of freedom, lay crushed and fallen. Not only military defeat came to France but, what was infinitely worse, spiritual submission and degradation. How did all this come about, I wondered, unless there was something rotten at the core? Was it that England and France were the outstanding representatives of an old order that must pass, and therefore they were unable to hold out? Was it that imperialism, though apparently giving them strength, really weakened them in a struggle of this nature? They could not fight for freedom if they denied it themselves, and their imperialism would turn to unabashed fascism, as it had done in France. The shadow of Mr. Neville Chamberlain and his old policy still fell on England despite a change in premiers. The Burma-China route was being closed for three months in order to appease Japan. And here in India there was no hint at change, and our self-imposed restraint was understood to mean an incapacity to do anything effective. The lack of any vision in the British Government amazed me, their utter incapacity to read the signs of the times and to understand what was happening and adapt themselves to it. Was this some law of nature that in international happenings, as in other fields, cause must inexorably be followed by effect; that a system that had ceased to have any useful function could not even defend itself intelligently?

If the British Government were slow of understanding and could not learn even from experience, what can one say about the Government of India? There is something comic and something tragic about the functioning of this Government, for nothing seems to shake them out of their age-long complacency; neither logic nor reason, neither peril nor disaster. Like Rip Van Winkle, they sleep, even though waking, on Simla hill.

The development in the war situation posed new questions before the Congress Working Committee. Gandhiji wanted the Committee to extend the principle of nonviolence, to which we had adhered in our struggle for freedom, to the functioning of a free state. A free India must rely on this principle to guard itself against external aggression or internal disorder. This question did not rise for us at the time, but it occupied his own mind, and he felt that the time had come for a clear enunciation. Every one of us was convinced that we must adhere to our policy of nonviolence, as we had so far done, in our own struggle. The war in Europe had strengthened this conviction. But to commit the future state was another and a more difficult matter, and it was not easy to see how anyone moving on the plane of politics could do it.

Mr. Gandhi felt, and probably rightly, that he could not give up or tone down a message which he had for the world. He must have freedom to give it as he liked and must not be kept back by political exigencies. So, for the first time, he went one way and the Congress Working Committee another. There was no break with him, for the bond was too strong, and he will no doubt continue to advise in many ways and often to lead. Yet it is perhaps true that by his partial withdrawal, a definite period in the history of our national movement has come to an end. In recent years I have found a certain hardness creeping into him, a lessening of the adaptability that he possessed. Yet the old spell is there, the old charm works, and his personality and greatness tower over others. Let no one imagine that his influence over India's millions is any the less. He has been the architect of India's destiny for twenty years and more, and his work is not completed.

During the last few weeks, the Congress, at the instance of C. Rajagopalachari, made yet another offer to Britain. Rajagopalachari is said to belong to the Right in the Congress. His brilliant intellect, selfless character, and penetrating powers of analysis have been a tremendous asset to our cause. He was the Prime Minister of Madras during the functioning of the Congress Government there. Eager to avoid conflict, he put forward a proposal which was hesitatingly accepted by some of his colleagues. This proposal was the acknowledgment of India's independence by Britain and the immediate formation at the center of a Provisional National Government, which would be responsible to the present Central Assembly. If this were done, this Government would take charge of defense and thus help in the war effort.

This Congress proposal was eminently feasible and could be given effect to immediately without upsetting anything. The National Government was inevitably going to be a composite affair with full representation of minority groups. The proposal was definitely a moderate one. From the point of view of defense and war effort, it is patent that any serious effort involves the confidence and co-operation of the people. Only a national government has the chance to get this. It is not possible through imperialism.

But imperialism thinks otherwise and imagines that it can continue to function and to coerce people to do its will. Even when danger threatens, it is not prepared to get this very substantial help if this involves a giving up of political and economic control over India. It does not care even for the tremendous moral prestige which would come to it if it did the right thing in India, and the rest of the Empire. So the Viceroy gave reply on behalf of the British Government and rejected the Congress proposal. The alternative proposal that he put forward was identical with what he had suggested nine months before. This was to add some popular leaders by nomination to his council and to have an amorphous war advisory council. The Viceroy's council is not a cabinet, and all power is concentrated in the Viceroy. So the addition of a few persons to this council made no essential difference.

The Viceroy made it further clear that no major change would take place even after the war unless this was approved of by various groups in India. Thus he gave a power of veto, not only to any minority group, but to the feudal princes and even to British vested interests. This was a complete negation of democracy. It was much worse. For he laid down conditions which were impossible of fulfillment and which made Indian independence even in the future impossible. What came as a peculiar shock to us was the deliberate attempt made by the British Government to encourage every disruptive and reactionary tendency and thus to break the unity of India.

The British Government's proposals had to be rejected, and the Congress had no other course left open but to defend itself and the people from the onslaughts that were being made upon it. Thousands of Congressmen had been arrested and forced collections were being made even from the poor peasantry.

The All India Congress Committee withdrew the previous offer made by it and decided in favour of Civil Disobedience. Mr. Gandhi was appointed as the leader of this movement. As I write this we stand on the verge of this new adventure.

For more than thirteen months now we have given earnest and painful thought to the war developments and to their effect on the Indian situation. We had often proclaimed our faith in democracy and we had condemned aggression. The fate of Denmark, Norway, Holland, Belgium, and France distressed us exceedingly, and we disliked the prospect of a Nazi order's being established all over Europe and possibly elsewhere. Our sympathies went out to the peoples being ruthlessly bombed in the great cities of Europe and elsewhere. And yet, in spite of a world changing before our eyes, we saw the old face of imperialism still in India, and we continued to hear its old and harsh voice. The language was the same and the content changed in no way. The sands of time ran out in India, as in Europe and the world, but wisdom and foresight did not come to those who might have checked catastrophe.

More and more this terrible war seemed to me something much more than a war between mighty powers. It was a prelude to vast change in the world, a revolution not only of the political map but of the social and economic structure. Unless this basic fact was grasped, governments and armies would function in vain. The old world had ended and was dying before our eyes. What would the new world be like? Unless we had that vision of the future before us, for what were we fighting? It was the old question put by us to the British Government in September, 1939, and to which there had been no answer. The people of Britain, suffering so grievously and facing constant danger bravely, would perhaps understand our plight in India and help in solving our problem. But governments come in the way, and no government in the world can be so blind to change as the present Government of India. Victory and defeat have little meaning unless we know whose victory and for what.

The world of today hangs together, and it will survive or perish together. Only a world order of free nations co-operating together for the common good, and based on social justice, can solve the problems that overwhelm us. It is fantastic to imagine that India or China can be excluded from this order or can be given a subordinate place. The full freedom of India and China is an essential prerequisite to a world settlement. There will be no peace or stability otherwise, whatever may happen in the battlefields of Europe.

So the Indian Congress is again going into the wilderness. With no desire to embarrass the people of Britain, we are being compelled by the imperialism that dominates over us to defend our elementary rights and to insist on our independence. We cannot be willing parties to our humiliation and subjection.

Most of us look upon this question from a political point of view, though all of us are ardently desirous of ending wars and insuring peace. Mr. Gandhi, as an apostle of non-violence, and many others who agree with him, are opposed to all wars. For him it is also a matter of conscience not to participate in this or any war. For others the reason is mainly a political one—the denial of the right of India to decide for herself in regard to the war, and the denial of freedom to her. Both avenues of approach lead to the same conclusion. Though the immediate issue is the war issue in India, the real question remains, and must remain, the independence of India.

So many of my colleagues have gone back to prison, and I envy them somewhat. Perhaps it is easier to develop an organic sense of life in the solitude of confinement than in this mad world of war and politics, of fascism and imperialism.

But sometimes there is an escape for a while at least from this world. Three months ago I went back to Kashmir after an absence of twenty-three years. I was only there for twelve days, but these days were filled with beauty, and I drank in the loveliness of that land of enchantment. I wandered about the glorious valley and the higher mountains and climbed a glacier, and forgot for a while the pain and torment of soul which are the lot of humanity today. Life seemed to be worth while.

JAWAHARLAL NEHRU

*Allahabad, October 17, 1940.*

# THE PARTING OF THE WAYS

To SAY THAT anything has happened in India which leads to a parting of the ways as between Britain and India is incorrect. For their ways have been separate as they were bound to be, so long as England was the dominating imperialist Power and India was subject to her will. Such a relation could only be based on coercion, and coercion cannot lead to a marching together, hand in hand. It can only lead to the dominant party's chaining and pulling the other and dragging it against its will, or to a breaking of this chain.

So our ways have lain in different directions, and a continuous tug of war has resulted; sometimes the conflict has been psychological and wordy, sometimes it has been rebellion. In 1857 a bloody rebellion took place, and it was suppressed in a ghastly manner. The conflict continued, bitter and persistent, though it was not so obvious on the surface. It took shape in the organization of the national movement, which spoke softly for a while but whose voice grew harder as it came to represent the real feelings of the people. Another rebellion against the dominating authority took shape, a peaceful one, discarding all methods of violence, but more powerful and widespread than any previous one. The hundreds of millions of India, weary of their long subjection and poverty and exploitation, shed their fear and, looking the dominating imperialism in the face, demanded freedom.

There were many ups and downs, and much suffering and sorrow came to these millions, but there was no looking back for them. The conflict continued in various ways, and, meanwhile, the world rushed toward the abyss of self-destruction. India's problem began to be viewed in a larger perspective and in relation to the difficulties that encompassed the world. Though our vision became broader and deeper, and though it tried to peep into the future, yet that problem remained essentially one of Indian nationalism versus British imperialism. India's freedom and independence were the prerequisites for us in order to play our part in the larger world. And, in that larger world also, it seemed to us a sham and a mockery to talk of freedom and democracy and yet hold on to imperialism.

Fascism and Nazi-ism were anathema to us, and the horrors of central Europe produced a powerful reaction on India. Yet we remembered (how can we ever forget?) the horrors we had witnessed in

India. Yet we saw and felt, to the innermost core of our being, the day-to-day humiliation and exploitation of our own people. We were not wise nor clever enough to understand that, though fascism and Nazi-ism were definitely bad, imperialism was not so bad after all.

War came in Europe, and we discovered that India had also been declared a belligerent country, without so much as a formal reference or intimation to any representatives of the people of India. The Congress might be considered an unofficial organization, but there was the General Assembly, there were the provincial governments enjoying, it was said, provincial autonomy. None of these was told or asked for its opinion.

The air resounded with loud cries invoking freedom and asserting the sanctity of democracy. They sounded good. But we had heard these cries so often before and experienced for ourselves the aftermath. We could not be easily swept away; we were cautious, doubly so because of the way in which the war had been imposed upon us, despite our repeated warnings. Was this freedom and democracy meant for us also, or only for the favored mortals who lived in Europe and its extensions? Did it mean that imperialism would go from here and elsewhere?

We inquired from the British Government and asked to be enlightened, so that we might know what course we should pursue. Our inquiries were considered irrelevant and impertinent. Yet the answers that they gave indicated sufficiently clearly that there was no intention and, so far as they were concerned, no possibility of the ending of the imperialist structure in India, no question of power being transferred to the people's representatives. The National Congress had not asked anything for itself. It wanted no jobs in high places, which it could have had even without asking for them. It wanted a declaration of independence for India and a Constituent Assembly, elected by the people, to frame the constitution of a free India, with full safeguards for the protection of all minority rights.

In the mind and heart of India there was a conflict. There was an intense dislike of fascism and Nazi-ism and no desire to see them win. If India could but be convinced that this war was being fought for a new world order, for real freedom, then indeed India would throw all her weight and strength into it. But imperialism and we were old acquaintances, very old, with many generations of contact. We knew each other, suspected each other, and disliked each other thoroughly. There was this background of one hundred and eighty years of hostility, of exploitation, of bitterness, of promises unfulfilled, of disruption and reactionary movements encouraged, and attempts to break up the national unity of India. It was no easy matter for us to get over these tremendous hurdles, or remove the complexes that had grown up. Yet we said we would do it, but we could not even attempt it unless a great psychological shock was given to the people, a pleasant shock, which would suddenly change the air of India and get rid of the fears and complexes. That pleasant shock could only come by an unequivocal declaration of independence and immediate steps to give effect to the popular will in the carrying on of the administration. Unless this was done, no man in India, no group, could make the people move in the direction of willing association with the war.

Wars today require mass support, and even authoritarian countries have to whip up their people by ceaseless propaganda. No war can be fought effectively by a professional army in an atmosphere of public ill will or indifference. So even from the narrower point of view of organizing India's defense or India's participation in the war effort, a popular representative government was essential. Imperialism can coerce; it cannot win public approval and good will.

The Viceroy and the British Government said no to us, and our course seemed to be clear. The Congress governments in the provinces resigned, and parliamentary government in these provinces ceased, because it was not prepared to submit to the British Government's fiat against the wishes of the people it represented. It was the old conflict between king and parliament taking a new shape; the Viceroy and the governors represented the King's veto, our elected assemblies the will of the people. In America a proud and freedom-loving people resisted the authority of a distant king and his ministers and, after a long struggle, established their own freedom.

But in India, in the twentieth century, on the eve of the new order that was promised, in the face of loud declarations in favor of freedom and democracy, in India, parliamentary government, such as it existed in the provinces, was suspended. The Viceroy's authority was supreme; he could make laws and unmake them, tax people and coerce them without the slightest reference to any representative body.

The Congress ministries had resigned, it is true, though they had the great majority of the members of the assemblies behind them. They resigned because they could not accept the Viceroy's mandates or the British Government's policy. But the assemblies were still there. The Viceroy or the governors could have dissolved them and had a fresh election. But they knew well that such an election would result in an overwhelming majority in favor of the Congress governments that had resigned. No other ministry was possible, as it could not command a majority. So the only course was for the provincial assemblies to be suspended, no fresh elections, and the Viceroy and governors to exercise dictatorial powers. It was a clear case of conflict between the people and parliament on the one side and the King's representatives on the other. One party had to be suppressed or to give in. Parliament was suppressed. It was as if Mr. Neville Chamberlain, unable to carry Parliament with him, had advised the King to suspend it and to rule by decree; or President Roosevelt, in a like predicament, had ignored the House of Representatives and the Senate and constituted himself the dictator. We hear a great deal about authoritarianism and dictators, and England's chiefs condemn both in resonant and forcible language. Yet in India today there is a full-blooded dictatorship and authoritarianism.

Our course was clear. Yet we restrained and held ourselves, even though many among us were indignant with us, even though many colleagues of ours found their way to prisons for the offense of explaining our policy to the people. We were hesitant because we hoped against hope that England's Government, including some progressive and labor elements, might, in this hour of supreme trial, shake itself out of its deadening imperialism and act according to its professions. We had no desire to encourage the Nazi rulers in any way; the thought of their domination over Europe and elsewhere was a painful one. We who had suffered as a subject people knew well what this would mean for others. We, of all people, could not tolerate the racial views and racial oppression of the Nazis. The horror that enveloped Holland and Belgium, the supreme tragedy of France deeply moved us. The imminent peril of England made us feel that we should not add to her difficulties and embarrassments. Though England's ruling classes may have treated us badly and her imperialism may have crushed us, we had no ill will for her people, who were bravely facing peril and extreme danger. We tried hard to find a way out honorable and advantageous to both India and England. We made new proposals, even going beyond our own mandate given at the last sessions of the Congress at Ramgarh. We pledged ourselves for the organization of Indian defense and help in the war effort. But we could only do so as free people, with the good will and co-operation of India's millions. That freedom had to be declared and a provisional national government formed, which would represent not one party only but various important elements. The fundamental basis for this proposal was the recognition that the imperialist structure had to go.

The Viceroy and the British Government have said a final no to us and to India. On the eve of the French collapse, Britain's rulers were unorthodox enough to propose a union of England and France. That was an astonishing proposal. It came too late. But it showed that the British Government had got out of the rut and could take a big step if the situation demanded it. But where their own interests are so vitally concerned, as in India, they still live in the rut, and not all the shock of war and danger has taken them out. Even an obvious advantage in this war cannot make them give up the special position that imperialism has conferred upon them. They talk complacently still of their Empire and of their desire to maintain it, forgetting perhaps that the word, which sounds so good to them, is a symbol to us of our own subjection, degradation, and poverty.

I repeat that it is incorrect to say that there is any new parting of the ways, for our ways never lay together. But this declaration of the British Government means the final breaking of such slender bonds as held our minds together; it means the ending of all hope that we shall ever march together. I am sorry, for in spite of my hostility to British imperialism and all imperialisms, I have loved much that was England, and I should have liked to keep the silken bonds of the spirit between India and England. Those bonds can only exist in freedom. I wanted India's freedom for India's sake, of course; but I also wanted it for England's sake. That hope is shattered, and fate seems to have fashioned a different future for us. The way of co-operation does not lie for us; the hundred-year-old hostility will remain and grow in future conflicts, and the breach, when it comes, as come it must, will also not be in friendship but in hostility.

I am told that the British Government has been led to believe that we shall tamely submit to their decrees because so far we have been quiescent. Our very restraint appears to have made them think that we were incapable of any action. In this world of force, of bombing airplanes, tanks, and armed men, how weak we are! Why trouble about us? But perhaps, even in this world of armed conflict, there is such a thing as the spirit of man, and the spirit of a nation, which is neither ignoble nor weak, and which may not be ignored, save at peril.

To those of us who are intimately connected with Indian politics, the British Government's reply needs no analysis or clarification. To do them justice, it is clear enough, and there is no ambiguity. Yet others perhaps might miss its significance and be misled by the use of resounding words into thinking that something worth while was offered, that the people of India were getting some power in her government.

It is proposed to appoint some nonofficial Indians to the Viceroy's Executive Council. This Council is no real Executive or Cabinet; it is more advisory. Real power rests with the Viceroy, who does not always take members of his Council into his confidence. They are heads of departments, advising the Viceroy about their special subjects. All policy emanates from the Viceroy. In fact, his is the responsibility, and he is answerable to the Secretary of State for India in the British Parliament. If this legal, constitutional, and conventional structure remains, it makes little difference who or how many people are added to the Council. They do not make an atom of difference to the Viceroy's position, power, or authority, except in so far as they might try to influence him by their powers of persuasion.

Apart from this, the addition of a few nonofficials to the Executive Council does not make an essential difference to it; the majority continues to be of the nominated official and service members, who may have their virtues (which are not very obvious) but who represent the hundred per cent imperialistic bureaucratic type. They are completely dependent on the Viceroy for their position and are obsequious to him. They are wholly cut off from the life, thought, and activities of the people, and live in an official world of their own. Such efficiency as they have consists in running the old type of police state. They are remote from the modern world and its problems and do not understand them. They belong to an order which has passed elsewhere and which must pass in India.

Then again the so-called "representative Indians" who may be appointed to the Viceroy's Executive Council will be chosen presumably from all manner of odd groups, some completely reactionary. All of them will not even represent the progressive elements in India, and in the Council they will either neutralize each other or make matters worse. They will not be elected by the people in any way and will not be responsible to them. They will be chosen by the Viceroy in their individual capacity.

It is obvious that the addition of these few odd Indians to the Viceroy's Executive Council means less than nothing from any national point of view, or from the viewpoint of any power being transferred to the people.

The second proposal is the creation of a War Advisory Council composed of an odd assortment of people, including some representatives of the semifeudal Indian states. This will meet from time to time, apparently to listen to good advice and to act as recruiting sergeants and the like. They will have no executive power of any kind or indeed any other power. It will be just a show body of no relevance or importance.

These are the two proposals for the present, and, as the Viceroy has made perfectly clear, the British Government do not contemplate the transfer of any power or responsibility that they possess. Further, it has been stated by the Secretary of State for India that when he refers to "the principal elements in India's national life," he includes the European vested interests in India. Probably the conception of India's national life that Mr. Amery and the Viceroy cherish is one which consists chiefly of British vested interests, Indian feudal princes, big landlords, communalists, and other reactionaries. According to them, these national interests form the warp and woof of our national life and deserve protection and representation. The three or four hundred-odd millions of people who live and labor and often starve are an excrescence.

So much for the present and so long as the war lasts. The golden future of our dreams, that new order of freedom of which we hear so much, is envisaged as follows: After the conclusion of the war, "a body representative of the principal elements in India's national life" will be set up to devise the framework of the new constitution. We have seen what, in the opinion of Mr. Amery and the Viceroy, these elements in India's national life are. We shall have (or so it is proposed, but destiny may dispose otherwise) a noble company of bejeweled maharajahs, belted knights, European industrial and commercial magnates, big landlords and talukdars, Indian industrialists, representatives of the imperial services, and a few commoner mortals, all sitting together, possibly under the presidency of the Viceroy himself, drawing up India's constitution. Thus will India exercise her right to self-determination. It will be a pretty pattern that this assembly will produce, with a flower for every vested interest and feudal relic and with the background of British imperialism. Above all, British interests, which are so important a part of India's national life, will have been preserved and given their rightful due. We shall call this Dominion status so that everyone may be pleased.

But let it not be forgotten that even this assembly cannot have it all its own way. The British Government cannot divest themselves of their high responsibility to protect British vested interests whatever happens. So whatever this assembly decides must be "subject to the due fulfillment of the obligations which Great Britain's long connection with India has imposed upon her and for which His Majesty's Government cannot divest themselves of responsibility."

Meanwhile, it is suggested that the Government will welcome every sincere and practical step taken by representative Indians to reach a basis of friendly agreement on the form that the postwar representative body should take and the principles and outlines of the constitution. These representative Indians must, of course, come from the principal elements of India's national life as outlined above.

If some of us in the outer darkness do not approve of this pattern or fancy this picture, it is no doubt our misfortune. If we wonder sometimes how any British Government can presume to make this offer to the Indian people in this age of change and revolution, when empires are disappearing and the old structure collapses all over the world, it must indicate how simple and naïve we are. We ought to have known that imperialisms do not abdicate; they hold on even when it is manifest folly to endeavor to do so. But in our simplicity we cannot help feeling a mild surprise at the fact that leaders of the British Labour party, those champions of freedom and socialism, should be responsible for this "offer" to India. But it is no offer. It is a decision announced and going to be imposed upon us whether we like it or not.

The Congress had ventured to suggest another way—that the constitution should be framed by a Constituent Assembly elected by adult franchise by the people. This had the misfortune of being a democratic way and of giving an equal importance to each individual. It is true that "the principal elements of India's national life," as conceived by the Viceroy and the Secretary of State, might have found some difficulty in getting elected. Democratic elections are not always just to these important elements, like those representing British or Indian vested interests.

The Viceroy has further stated that: "It goes without saying that they [the British Government] could not contemplate the transfer of their present responsibilities for the peace and welfare of India to any system of government whose authority is directly denied by large and powerful elements in India's national life. Nor could they be parties to the coercion of such elements into submission to such a government."

This statement is worthy of close consideration. It is obvious that any system of government that might be proposed for India will find many odd groups and interests opposed to it. No system can possibly be devised which meets with unanimity from all these groups and interests and from the four hundred millions of India. Every agrarian legislation has to deal with the inherent conflicts between the landlord and the tenant; every labor legislation is looked upon with disfavor by the captains of industry. Even among industrialists in India, there is a continuing conflict between British vested interests and the rising Indian industry, which has been deliberately prevented from expanding so that the former might not suffer. So the conflicts of interests run through the whole of national life as it is constituted today, because there are different classes with conflicting interests. Some of us would like to have a classless society, and I have no doubt that it will ultimately come. Meanwhile the only known method of resolving these conflicts, other than that of force and coercion, is the democratic method. If any group can hold up a political or economic change, even though this is desired by the great majority, this must lead to a disruption of the State and possibly to civil conflict.

The British Government's statement means that there can be no far-reaching political or economic changes, for some group is bound to object to them. Even if no Indian group objects, British vested interests will do so. But there are Indian reactionary groups that will play that role. This means that the *status quo* will largely remain to the great advantage of British imperialism. This is the way to perpetuate the present order, to make India safe for British vested interests.

The idea that the British Government should be asked to coerce any group is absurd. No one has ever hinted at this, except the reactionaries and communalists who want the coercion of the progressive elements. The British Government are asked to put an end to all their present coercion; in fact, to retire from the Indian scene as a government. Only then will conditions be produced in India which will induce various elements in India to seek a basis of agreement among themselves, for the alternative is civil war. So long as the British Government remains, it plays off one against the other and produces an unhealthy desire in the minds of some to seek its favor as against their own compatriots.

The British Government say they will not coerce an important group to impose a system of government which this does not like. The alternative surely is that they will coerce other groups who want that particular system of government. What exactly has the function of the

British Government been, and is today, in India? It is to coerce the Indian people as a whole, every group, in order to maintain their own hold and special position. It is to suppress Indian industry in favor of British industry in India. It is to maintain an army of occupation whose chief function is to coerce the Indian people. It is to uphold Indian princes by coercing their subjects into submission. It is strange to be told that the British Government do not want to use coercion. What else do they use in India?

Again, how is one to tell that an important group does not want a particular system of government? Ordinarily that group votes, and other groups vote, and then it is possible to know what the feelings or intentions of various groups are. They come to a mutual arrangement, trying to find some common measure of agreement, or, unhappily, they do not, and there is conflict.

The British proposal is ideally suited to prevent any progress or major change. Even British interests will bar the way. As a matter of fact the Government have gone further and stated that in any event they are not going to divest themselves of responsibility for the protection of these interests. Whatever happens, these interests remain; and so, whatever happens, the British financial and industrial structure dominates India. It so happens that this is exactly what we want to get rid of. There is no progress or lessening of India's appalling poverty till we succeed in this. All else is secondary.

We have an intimate glimpse from the Viceroy's statement of the blessings of Dominion status that is held out to us as a lure. Many of us, I fear, are not attracted by this picture.

It may be said that the Viceroy's statement about not coercing any large element which disapproves of a system of government applies chiefly to the religious minorities. Certainly let us agree that there must be no such coercion, and the British Government must on no account do it. Nor should others. But where does coercion come in? Who suggests it?

The Congress proposal was not that the Congress or any party or religious groups should be given power. It asked for power for the Indian people as a whole and wanted the Indian people to decide what they wanted in a democratic manner. It went further, in its desire to protect all minority interests. It agreed to separate electorates for such minorities as desired it and laid down that matters relating to minority rights must not be settled by a majority vote. They must be settled by agreement or, if unhappily this is not possible in regard to any particular matter, through an impartial tribunal. It is difficult to conceive any more comprehensive or effective method for minority protection short of throwing overboard all pretense at democracy and establishing a dictatorship of the minority.

So far as the Moslems in India are concerned, they are only technically a minority. They are vast in numbers and powerful in other ways, and it is patent that they cannot be coerced against their will. Just as the Hindus cannot be coerced against their will. If the two can not agree as organized groups, it will be unfortunate for India, and no one can say what the consequence will be. But let us always remember that in political and economic matters people do not function as religious groups. The lines of cleavage are different.

The real question of minority protection arises for others, who are neither Hindu nor Moslem. It seems amazing to me that any Indian, whether he is a Hindu, Moslem, Sikh, Christian, or adherent of any other faith, should seek protection against his own compatriots from a foreign authority. As a matter of fact they do not, except a few, who do it not because of religion but because of vested interests.

Let us be clear about it. This communal question is essentially one of protection of vested interests, and religion has always been a useful stalking horse for this purpose. Those who have feudal privileges and vested interests fear change and become the camp followers of British imperialism. The British Government, on the other hand delight in using the communal argument to deny freedom, democracy, or any major change, and to hold on to power and privilege in India. That is the *raison d'être* and the justification of communalism in India. If, as has been said, the Indian princes may be described as Britain's Fifth Column in India, communalism and its champions might well be included in this Fifth Column. It is not surprising, therefore, that communalists and princes get on well together and co-operate with each other. They have a common purpose to serve—to obstruct India's freedom so that vested interests might flourish.

It is not, of course, enough to dispose of communalism by this simple analysis, although this is the basic explanation. There are so many other factors, and it is perfectly true that mass elements, who may be affected by communalism, have neither vested interests to preserve nor any love for British imperialism. To understand how they have been influenced by communalism, and have often acted against their own interests, is to understand how Hitler came to influence mass elements among the German people. The analogy is not complete, but it helps.

385

People are swept away by slogans which appeal to them, and then they are used for entirely different purposes. There has been a strange similarity in the recent development of the communal technique in India to Nazi methods.

Communalism began in India as a demand for a specified share in services and in representation in the legislatures. It has now developed into an openly antinational, antidemocratic movement, hinting at the partition of India. For a long while it had no constructive or any other program. It lived on invective, violence, and general offensiveness. It is amazing how it vulgarized our public life. It discovered that what it had valued most in the past—separate electorates—brought little good. In fact, they weakened a minority group. Then, by the very force of the logic of hatred and separation that it had pursued, it had to go to the extreme of demanding a partition of India. The medieval theory of religious groups constituting a political community, which collapsed before an advancing nationalism in Europe, was revived. An idea similar to that of the Crusades, of Christendom versus Islam, suddenly appeared (it is said with British inspiration) in India. It was an astonishing throwback. Whoever else benefited or suffered from it, it was clear that British imperialism was the gainer.

It is curious that even in early and medieval India, this theory never functioned in the Western way. Other religions were welcomed and accommodated. The early Christians came in the first century and found a home. Jews were accommodated, Moslems were welcome to spread their religion and settle down (till invasion brought political conflicts), Parsis came and were absorbed. Later Moslem rulers thought in terms of building up a single nation of the Moslem newcomers and the Hindus and others. The great Akbar laid the foundations for this. The new cultural elements were absorbed, and a common culture gradually developed, especially in northern India.

And now we are told to go back to the pre-Akbar days, to reverse the process of history, to think in terms of medievalism. When nationalism is giving place to internationalism, an even narrower creed than nationalism is advanced, and this finds favor and protection with our British rulers. When the world is groping blindly toward a real federation of nations, it is suggested that India should be split up into various parts.

Moslem countries—Turkey, Egypt, Iraq, Syria, Persia—have long discarded this medieval theory. They are intensely nationalist and are proud of their ancient culture. Some of them deliberately go to their pre-Islamic days to find cultural inspiration. The Chinese Moslems are proud of their Chinese culture and fight for China's freedom. That is the course of history. Indeed, it is a course that has already been run, and the mighty revolution that is taking place in the world today will lay down another course—the way to world federation based on national freedom and a juster economic system. Privilege and vested interest will have to go.

That is the goal of India—a united, free, democratic country, closely associated in a world federation with other free nations. We want independence, but not the old type of narrow, exclusive independence. We believe that the day of separate warring national states is over.

We want independence and not Dominion or any other status. Every thinking person knows that the whole conception of Dominion status belongs to past history; it has no future. It cannot survive this war, whatever the result of the war. But, whether it survives or not, we want none of it. We do not want to be bound down to a group of nations which has dominated and exploited over us; we will not be in an Empire in some parts of which we are treated as helots and where racialism runs riot. We want to cut adrift from the financial domination of the City of London. We want to be completely free with no reservations or exceptions, except such as we ourselves approve, in common with others, in order to join a Federation of Nations, or a new World Order. If this new World Order or Federation does not come in the near future, we should like to be closely associated in a federation with our neighbors—China, Burma, Ceylon, Afghanistan, Persia. We are prepared to take risks and face dangers. We do not want the so-called protection of the British Army or Navy. We shall shift for ourselves.

If the past had not been there to bear witness, the present would have made us come to this final decision. For even in this present of war and peril, there is no change in the manner of treatment accorded to our people by British imperialism. Let those who seek the favor and protection of this imperialism go its way. We go ours. The parting of the ways has come.

# APPENDIX A

WE BELIEVE THAT it is the inalienable right of the Indian people, as of any other people, to have freedom and to enjoy the fruits of their toil and have the necessities of life, so that they may have full opportunities of growth. We believe also that if any government deprives a people of these rights and oppresses them the people have a further right to alter it or to abolish it. The British Government in India has not only deprived the Indian people of their freedom but has based itself on the exploitation of the masses, and has ruined India economically, politically, culturally, and spiritually. We believe, therefore, that India must sever the British connection and attain *Purna Swaraj,* or complete independence.

India has been ruined economically. The revenue derived from our people is out of all proportion to our income. Our average income is seven pice (less than twopence) per day, and of the heavy taxes we pay, 20 per cent are raised from the land revenue derived from the peasantry and 3 per cent from the salt tax, which falls most heavily on the poor.

Village industries, such as hand-spinning, have been destroyed, leaving the peasantry idle for at least four months in the year, and dulling their intellect for want of handicrafts, and nothing has been substituted, as in other countries, for the crafts thus destroyed.

Customs and currency have been so manipulated as to heap further burdens on the peasantry. British manufactured goods constitute the bulk of our imports. Customs duties betray clear partiality for British manufactures, and revenue from them is used not to lessen the burden on the masses but for sustaining a highly extravagant administration. Still more arbitrary has been the manipulation of the exchange ratio, which has resulted in millions being drained away from the country.

Politically, India's status has never been so reduced as under the British regime. No reforms have given real political power to the people. The tallest of us have to bend before foreign authority. The rights of free expression of opinion and free association have been denied to us, and many of our countrymen are compelled to live in exile abroad and cannot return to their homes. All administrative talent is killed, and the masses have to be satisfied with petty village offices and clerkships.

Culturally, the system of education has torn us from our moorings, and our training has made us hug the very chains that bind us.

Spiritually, compulsory disarmament has made us unmanly, and the presence of an alien army of occupation, employed with deadly effect to crush in us the spirit of resistance, has made us think that we cannot look after ourselves or put up a defense against foreign aggression, or even defend our homes and families from the attacks of thieves, robbers, and miscreants.

We hold it to be a crime against man and God to submit any longer to a rule that has caused this fourfold disaster to our country. We recognize, however, that the most effective way of gaining our freedom is not through violence. We will therefore prepare ourselves by withdrawing, so far as we can, all voluntary association from the British Government, and will prepare for civil disobedience, including nonpayment of taxes. We are convinced that if we can but withdraw our voluntary help and stop payment of taxes without doing violence, even under provocation, the end of this inhuman rule is assured. We therefore hereby solemnly resolve to carry out the Congress instructions issued from time to time for the purpose of establishing *Purna Swaraj.*

## APPENDIX B

PRESIDENTIAL ADDRESS BY JAWAHARLAL NEHRU AT 49TH SESSION OF INDIAN NATIONAL CONGRESS, AT LUCKNOW, APRIL 1936

COMRADES,

After many years I face you again from this tribune—many weary years of strife and turmoil and common suffering. It is good for us to meet again; it is good for me to see this great host of old comrades and friends, linked together by strong bonds that cannot break, to sense the old brave spirit yet again, to feel your overwhelming kindness and good will to one whose greatest privilege it is to have been a comrade and a soldier with all of you in a mighty struggle for freedom. I am heartened and strengthened by you, though even in this great gathering I feel a little lonely. Many a dear comrade and friend has left us, worn out, long before the normal length of our earthly days, by the stress and strain of conflict. One by one they go, leaving a void in our hearts and a dull misery in our minds. They find peace from this turmoil perhaps, and it is well, for they deserved it. They rest after their labors.

But what of us who remain behind with a heavier burden to carry? There is no rest for us or for those who languish in prison or in detention camp. We cannot rest, for rest is betrayal of those who have gone and in going handed the torch of freedom to us to keep alight; it is betrayal of the cause we have espoused and the pledge we have taken; it is betrayal of the millions who never rest.

I am weary and I have come back like a tired child yearning for solace in the bosom of our common mother, India. That solace has come to me in overflowing measure; thousands of hands have been stretched out to me in love and sympathy; millions of silent voices have carried their message of affection to my heart. How can I thank you, men and women of India? How can I express in words feelings that are too deep for utterance?

For many years now I have been a distant looker-on on this Indian scene where once I was an actor, and many a thing has happened that has filled me with distress and anguish. I do not wish to survey this recent past of ours, which must be fresh in your memory, and which has left a sorry trail behind and many knots which are difficult to unravel. But we may not ignore it, for out of that past as well as the present, we have to build our future. We have followed high ideals, and we have taken pride in the fact that our means are worthy of those ideals. We have been witnesses of many a miracle in this old and battered land of ours, and yet our very success has been followed by failure and disillusion. Temporary failure has little significance when the aim is high and the struggle bound to be a long one; it is but the incentive to further effort. Often it teaches us more than a victory easily won and becomes a prelude to a greater success. But we profit by it only if we learn its lesson and search our minds for an explanation of that failure. Only by constant self-questioning, individual and national, can we keep on the right path. An easy and unthinking confidence is almost as bad as a weak submission to helpless dejection. Real failure comes only when we forget our ideals and objectives and principles and begin to wander away from the road which leads to their realization.

In this crisis of our history, therefore, let us look into ourselves and examine, without pity or prejudice, what we have done and what others have done to us, and seek to find out where we stand today. We dare not delude ourselves or evade real issues for fear of offending others, even though some of these others are comrades whom we respect. That is the way of self-deception which none who seek great and vital changes can follow except at their peril.

Sixteen years ago, under the inspiration of our leader, we took a new and long step converting this Congress from an ineffective body, feebly functioning among the upper classes, into a powerful democratic organization with its roots in the Indian soil and the vast masses who live on it. A handful of our old friends, representing an age and a class which had had its day, left us, fearful of this democratic upsurge, and preferring the shelter and protection of British imperialism to joining hands with the new vital forces which convulsed the country and struggled for freedom. Historically, they lapsed into the past. But we heard the rumbling of those forces and, for the moment, lined up with them and played a not unworthy part in current history. We sensed the new spirit of mass release, of psychological escape from the cramping effects of long subjection; we gloried in the breaking of the mental bonds that encompassed us. And, because our minds became free, we felt that political freedom could not be far, for it is often harder to break the bonds of the spirit than physical bonds and chains of iron and steel. We represented the Spirit of the Age and were marching step by step with countless others in our country and outside. The exhilaration of being in tune with the masses and with the world forces came upon us and the feeling that we were the agents of historic destiny.

We were engrossed in our national struggle, and the turn it took bore the powerful impress of our great leader and of our national genius. We were hardly conscious then of what was happening outside. And yet our struggle was but part of a far wider struggle for freedom, and the forces that moved us were moving millions of people all over the world and driving them into action. All Asia was astir from the Mediterranean to the Far East, from the Islamic West to the Buddhist East; Africa responded to the new spirit; Europe, broken up by the war, was struggling to find a new equilibrium. And right across a vast area in Europe and Asia, in the Soviet territories, a new conception of human freedom and social equality fought desperately against a host of enemies. There were great differences in the many aspects of this freedom struggle all over the world, and we were misled by them and did not see the common background. Yet, if we are to understand these varied phenomena and derive a lesson from them for our own national struggle, we must try to see and understand the whole picture, And, if we do so, we cannot fail to observe an organic connection between them which endures through changing situations. If once we grasp this organic bond, the world situation becomes easier to understand, and our own national problems take their proper places in the wider picture. We realize then that we cannot isolate India or the Indian problem from that of the rest of the world. To do so is to ignore the real forces that are shaping events and to cut ourselves adrift from the vital energy that flows from them. To do so, again, is to fail to understand the significance of our own problems, and, if we do not understand this, how can we solve them? We are apt to lose ourselves, as we have indeed done, in petty conflicts and minor questions, like the communal problem, and forget the major issues; we are apt to waste our energy (like our moderate friends do) in interminable discussions over legal quibbles and constitutional questions.

During the troubled aftermath of the Great War came revolutionary changes in Europe and Asia, and the intensification of the struggle for social freedom in Europe, and a new aggressive nationalism in the countries of Asia. There were ups and downs, and sometimes it appeared as if the revolutionary urge had exhausted itself and things were settling down. But economic and political conditions were such that there could be no settling down, the existing structure could no longer cope with these new conditions, and all its efforts to do so were vain and fruitless. Everywhere conflicts grew, and a great depression overwhelmed the world, and there was a progressive deterioration, everywhere except in the wide-flung Soviet territories of the U.S.S.R., where, in marked contrast with the rest of the world, astonishing progress was made in every direction. Two rival economic and political systems faced each other in the world, and, though they tolerated each other for a while, there was an inherent antagonism between them, and they played for mastery on the stage of the world. One of them was the capitalist order which had inevitably developed into vast imperialisms, which, having swallowed the colonial world, were intent on eating each other up. Powerful still and fearful of war, which might endanger their possessions, yet they came into inevitable conflict with each other and prepared feverishly for war. They were quite unable to solve the problems that threatened them, and helplessly they submitted to slow decay. The other was the new socialist order of the U.S.S.R., which went from progress to progress, though often at terrible cost, and where the problems of the capitalist world had ceased to exist.

Capitalism, in its difficulties, took to fascism with all its brutal suppression of what Western civilization had apparently stood for; it became, even in some of its homelands, what its imperialist counterpart had long been in the subject colonial countries. Fascism and imperialism thus stood out as the two faces of the now decaying capitalism, and, though they varied in different countries according to national characteristics and economic and political conditions, they represented the same forces of reaction and supported each other, and at the same time came into conflict with each other, for such conflict was inherent in their very nature. Socialism in the west and the rising nationalisms of the Eastern and other dependent countries opposed this combination of fascism and imperialism. Nationalism in the East, it must be remembered, was essentially different from the new and terribly narrow nationalism of fascist countries; the former was the historical urge to freedom, the latter the last refuge of reaction.

Thus we see the world divided up into two vast groups today—the imperialist and fascist on one side, the socialist and nationalist on the other. There is some overlapping of the two, and the line between them is difficult to draw, for there is mutual conflict between the fascist and imperialist Powers, and the nationalism of subject countries has sometimes a tendency to fascism. But the main division holds, and, if we keep it in mind, it will be easier for us to understand world conditions and our own place in them.

Where do we stand then, we who labor for a free India? Inevitably we take our stand with the progressive forces of the world which are ranged against fascism and imperialism. We have to deal with one imperialism in particular, the oldest and the most far-reaching of the modern world; but, powerful as it is, it is but one aspect of world imperialism. And that is the final argument for Indian independence and for the severance of our connection with the British Empire. Between Indian nationalism, Indian freedom, and British imperialism there can be no common ground, and, if we remain within the imperialist fold, whatever our name or status, whatever outward semblance of political power we might have, we remain cribbed and confined and allied to and dominated by the reactionary forces and the great financial vested interests of the capitalist world. The exploitation of our masses will still continue, and all the vital social problems that face us will remain unsolved. Even real political freedom will be out of our reach, much more so radical social changes.

With the development of this great struggle all over the world we have seen the progressive deterioration of many of the capitalist-imperialist countries and an attempt at consolidation of the reactionary forces under fascism or Nazi-ism or so-called "national" governments. In India the same process has been evident to us during these past years, and the stronger the nationalist movement has grown, the more have efforts been made by our imperialist rulers to break our ranks and to gather together under their banner the reactionary elements in the country. The Round Table Conferences were such attempts, and, though they helped our rulers in some measure, they served a useful purpose by showing us clearly the division between the imperialist and the anti-imperialist forces in the country. Unhappily we did not fully profit by this lesson, and we still imagine that we can win over some of these imperialist groups to the side of Indian freedom and anti-imperialism, and in a vain attempt to do so we suppress our ideals, blush for our objectives, and tone down our activities.

Meanwhile the decay of British imperialism in India becomes ever more apparent. It cannot, by its very nature, solve our economic problems and rid us of our terrible poverty, which it has largely itself created. It subsists on a normal fare of the fiercest repression and a denial of civil and even personal liberty. It surrounds us with a wide network of spies, and, among the pillars of its administration, are the tribe of informers and *agents provocateurs* and the like. Its services try to seek comfort for their obvious deterioration and incompetence by perpetually singing songs of mutual adulation. Argument gives place to the policeman's baton and the soldier's bayonet and prison and detention camp, and even our extraordinary finances are justified by the methods of the bully. It is astonishing to find to what depths of vulgarity our rulers have descended in their ardent desire to hold on to what they have got, and it is depressing, though perhaps inevitable, that some of our own countrymen, more interested in British imperialism than the British themselves, should excel at this deplorable game. So wanting in mental equilibrium are they, so obsessed by fear of the Congress and the national movement it represents, that their wishes become thoughts, their thoughts inferences, and their inferences facts, solemnly stated in official publications, and on which the majesty of the British Government rests in India, and people are kept in prison and detention camp without charge or trial. Being interested in psychology, I have watched this process of moral and intellectual decay and realized, even more than I did previously, how autocratic power corrupts and degrades and vulgarizes. I have read sometimes the reports of the recent Assembly meetings and noted the great difference in tone and content between them and the Assembly of ten years ago. I have observed the forced attempts made to discredit the Congress by a reference to the Tilak *Swaraj* Fund with which I was connected for many years as secretary of the Congress. But, prepared as I was for much, even I was surprised at the insinuations made against our much-loved chief, Rajendra Babu, and the charges brought against the Behar Relief Fund. A mild criticism by me of official incompetence soon after the Behar earthquake was deeply resented, probably because the truth of it was realized. Newspapers that criticized the official arrangements at a subsequent earthquake were heavily penalized or suppressed. All criticism hurts the sensitive skin of the Government, and its reactions are quick and far-reaching. The more incompetent it grows, the less it likes being told so. But this does not prevent it from indulging in reckless allegations about others.

This psychological aspect interests me even more than the more aggressive manifestations of British authority in India, for its throws light on much that has happened. It shows us how a clear and definite fascist mentality has developed among our rulers and how closely allied is imperialism to fascism. How this fascist mentality has functioned in the recent past and is functioning today, I shall not go into now. You know well the horror of these years and of the nightmare that we have all experienced. We shall not easily forget it, and, if there are some who have been cowed by it, there are others who have steeled themselves to a greater resolve to end this infamy in India.

But of one thing I must say a few words, for to me it is one of the most vital things that I value. That is the tremendous deprivation of civil liberties in India. A government that has to rely on the Criminal Law Amendment Act and similar laws, that suppress the press and literature, that ban hundreds of organizations, that keep people in prison without trial, and that do so many other things that are happening in India today, is a government that has ceased to have even a shadow of a justification for its existence. I can never adjust myself to these conditions; I find them intolerable. And yet I find many of my own countrymen complacent about them, some even supporting them, some, who have made the practice of sitting on a fence into a fine art, being neutral when such questions are discussed. And I have wondered what there was in common between them and me and those who think as I do. We in the Congress welcome all co-operation in the struggle for Indian freedom; our doors are ever open to all who stand for that freedom and are against imperialism. But they are not open to the allies of imperialism and the supporters of repression and those who stand by the British Government in its suppression of civil liberty. We belong to opposite camps.

Recently, as you know, we have had a typical example of the way Government functions in India in the warning issued to a dear and valued comrade of ours, Subhas Chandra Bose. We who know him also know how frivolous are the charges brought against him. But, even if there was substance in them, we could not tolerate willingly the treatment to which he has long been subjected. He did me the honor to ask me for advice, and I was puzzled and perplexed, for it is no easy thing to advise another in such a matter, when such advice might mean prison. Subhas Bose has suffered enough at the cost of his health. Was I justified in adding to this mental and physical agony? I hesitated and at first suggested to him to postpone his departure. But this advice made me unhappy, and I consulted other friends and then advised him differently. I suggested that he should return to his homeland as soon as he could. But it appears that even before my advice reached him he had started on his journey back to India.

This instance leads us to think of the larger problem, of the way the bogey of terrorism has been exploited by the Government to crush political activity and to cripple physically and mentally the fair province of Bengal. You know that terrorism as such is practically nonexistent now in Bengal or any part of India. Terrorism is always a sign of political immaturity in a people, just as so-called constitutionalism, where there is no democratic constitution, is a sign of political senility. Our national movement has long outgrown that immature stage, and even the odd individuals who have in the past indulged in terrorist acts have apparently given up that tragic and futile philosophy. The Congress, by its stress on peaceful and effective action, has drawn the youth of the country into its fold, and all traces of terroristic activity would long have vanished but for the policy of the Government, which feeds the roots out of which a helpless violence grows. But, terrorism or no terrorism, a government which adopts the methods which have long prevailed in Midnapore and elsewhere in Bengal stands self-condemned. Similar methods have also long prevailed in the Frontier Province, although there is no hint of terroristic activity there, and that fine man and true, beloved of millions, Abdul Ghaffar Khan, still lies in prison. Excuses differ, but the real reason is the ever-growing fascist mentality of our rulers.

That is one side of the picture. What of us? I have found a spirit of disunion spreading over the land, a strange malaise, and petty conflicts among old comrades growing ever bigger and interfering with all activity. We have forgotten for the moment the larger ideals we stood for, and we quarrel over petty issues. We have largely lost touch with the masses, and, deprived of the life-giving energy that flows from them, we dry up and weaken, and our organization shrinks and loses the power it had. First things must always come first, and, because we have forgotten this and argue and dispute over secondary matters, we are in danger of losing our bearings.

Every great struggle has its ups and downs and temporary failures. When such a setback occurs, there is a reaction when the fund of national energy is exhausted and has to be recharged. That happens again and again, and yet that is not an adequate explanation of all that has taken place. Our direct-action struggles in the past were based on the masses, and especially the peasantry, but the backbone and leadership were always supplied by the middle classes, and this, under the circumstances, was inevitable. The middle classes are a vague group or groups; at the top, a handful of them are closely allied to British imperialism; at the bottom are the dispossessed and other groups who have been progressively crushed by economic circumstances and out of whose ranks come the advanced political workers and revolutionaries; in between are the center groups, which tend often to side with the advanced elements, but which also have alliances with the upper groups and live in the hope of joining their superior ranks. A middle-class leadership is thus often a distracted leadership, looking in two directions at the same time. In times of crisis and struggle, when unity of aim and activity is essential, this two-faced leadership is bound to injure the cause and to hold back when a forward move is called for. Being too much tied up with property and the goods of this world, it is fearful of losing them, and it is easier to bring pressure on it and to exhaust its stamina. And yet, paradoxically, it is only from the middle-class intellectuals that revolutionary leadership comes, and we in India know that our bravest leaders and our stoutest comrades have come from the ranks of the middle classes. But by the very nature of our struggle, these front-rank leaders are taken away, and the others who take their places tire and are influenced more by the static element of their class. That has been very evident during our recent struggle, when our propertied classes were hit hard by the Government's drastic policy of seizure and confiscation of moneys and properties, and were thus induced to bring pressure for the suspension of the struggle.

How is this problem to be solved, then? Inevitably, we must have middle-class leadership, but this must look more and more toward the masses and draw strength and inspiration from them. The Congress must be not only *for* the masses, as it claims to be, but *of* the masses; only then will it really be for the masses. I have a feeling that our relative weakness today is due to a certain decay of our middle-class elements and our divorce from the people at large. Our policies and ideas are governed far more by this middle-class outlook than by a consideration of the needs of the great majority of the population. Even the problems that trouble us are essentially middle-class problems, like the communal problem, which have no significance for the masses.

This is partly due, I think, to a certain historical growth during the last fifteen years to which we have failed to adapt ourselves, to a growing urgency of economic problems affecting the masses, and to a rising mass consciousness which does not find sufficient outlet through the Congress. This was not so in 1920 and later when there was an organic link between Congress and the masses, and their needs and desires, vague as they were, found expression in the Congress. But, as those needs and desires have taken more definite shape, they have not been so welcome to other elements in the Congress, and that organic connection has gone. That, though regrettable, is really a sign of growth, and, instead of lamenting it, we must find a new link and a new connection on a fresh basis which allows for growth of mass consciousness within the Congress. The middle-class claim to represent the masses had some justification in 1920; it has much less today, though the lower middle classes have still a great deal in common with the masses.

Partly also our divorce from the people at large is due to a certain narrowness of our Congress constitution. The radical changes made in it fifteen years ago brought it in line with existing conditions then, and it drew in large numbers and became an effective instrument of national activity. Though the control and background were essentially middle-class and city, it reached the remotest village and brought with it political and economic consciousness to the masses, and there was widespread discussion of national issues in city and village alike. One could feel the new life pulsating through this vast land of ours, and, as we were in harmony with it, we drew strength from it. The intense repression by the Government during later years broke many of our physical and outward bonds with our countryside. But something more than that happened. The vague appeal of earlier days no longer sufficed, and on the new economic issues that were forcing themselves on us, we hesitated to give a definite opinion. Worse even than the physical divorce, there was a mental divorce between the middle-class elements and the mass elements. Our constitution no longer fitted in with changing conditions; it lost its roots in the soil and became a matter of small committees functioning in the air. It still had the mighty prestige of the Congress name behind it, and this carried it a long way, but it had lost the living democratic touch. It became a prey to authoritarianism and a battleground for rival cliques fighting for control, and, in doing so, stooping to the lowest and most objectionable of tactics. Idealism disappeared, and in its place there came opportunism and corruption. The constitutional structure of the Congress was unequal to facing the new situation; it could be shaken up anywhere almost by a handful of unscrupulous individuals. Only a broad democratic basis could have saved it, and this was lacking.

Last year an attempt was made to revise the constitution in order to get rid of some of these evils. How far that attempt has succeeded or not I am not competent to judge. Perhaps it has made the organization more efficient, but efficiency means little if it has no strength behind it, and strength, for us, can come only from the masses. The present constitution stresses still further the authoritarian side of the organization, and in spite of stressing rural representation does not provide effective links with the masses.

The real problem for us is, how in our struggle for independence we can join together all the anti-imperialist forces in the country, how we can make a broad front of our mass elements with the great majority of the middle classes which stands for independence. There has been some talk of a joint front, but, so far as I can gather, this refers to some alliance among the upper classes, probably at the expense of the masses. That surely can never be the idea of the Congress, and, if it favors it, it betrays the interests it has claimed to represent and loses the very reason for its existence. The essence of a joint popular front must be uncompromising opposition to imperialism, and the strength of it must inevitably come from the active participation of the peasantry and workers.

Perhaps you have wondered at the way I have dealt at some length with the background of international and national affairs and not touched so far the immediate problems that fill your minds. You may have grown impatient. But I am convinced that the only right way of looking at our own problems is to see them in their proper place in a world setting. I am convinced that there is intimate connection between world events, and our national problem is but a part of the world problem of capitalist imperialism. To look at each event apart from the others and without understanding the connection between them must lead us to the formation of erratic and erroneous views. Look at the vast panorama of world change today, where mighty forces are at grips with each other and dreadful war darkens the horizon. Subject peoples struggling for freedom and imperialism crushing them down; exploited classes facing their exploiters and seeking freedom and equality. Italian imperialism bombing and killing the brave Ethiopians; Japanese imperialism continuing its aggression in north China and Mongolia; British imperialism piously objecting to other countries misbehaving, yet carrying on in much the same way in India and the Frontier; and behind it all a decaying economic order which intensifies all these conflicts. Can we not see an organic connection in all these various phenomena? Let us try to develop the historic sense so that we can view current events in proper perspective and understand their real significance. Only then can we appreciate the march of history and keep step with it.

I realize that in this address I am going a little beyond the usual beat of the Congress president. But I do not want you to have me under any false pretenses, and we must have perfect frankness with each other. Most of you must know my views on social and economic matters, for I have often given expression to them. Yet you chose me as president. I do not take that choice to mean an endorsement by you all, or by a majority, of those views, but I take it that this does mean that those views are spreading in India and that most of you will be indulgent in considering them at least.

I am convinced that the only key to the solution of the world's problems and of India's problems lies in socialism, and, when I use this word, I do so not in a vague humanitarian way but in the scientific, economic sense. Socialism is, however, something even more than an economic doctrine; it is a philosophy of life, and as such also it appeals to me. I see no way of ending the poverty, the vast unemployment, the degradation and the subjection of the Indian people except through socialism. That involves vast and revolutionary changes in our political and social structure, the ending of vested interests in land and industry, as well as the feudal and autocratic Indian states system. That means the ending of private property, except in a restricted sense, and the replacement of the present profit system by a higher ideal of co-operative service. It means ultimately a change in our instincts and habits and desires. In short, it means a new civilization, radically different from the present capitalist order. Some glimpse we can have of this new civilization in the territories of the U.S.S.R. Much has happened there which has pained me greatly and with which I disagree, but I look upon that great and fascinating unfolding of a new order and a new civilization as the most promising feature of our dismal age. If the future is full of hope, it is largely because of Soviet Russia and what it has done, and 1 am convinced that, if some world catastrophe does not intervene, this new civilization will spread to other lands and put an end to the wars and conflicts which capitalism feeds.

I do not know how or when this new order will come to India. I imagine that every country will fashion it after its own way and fit it in with its national genius. But the essential basis of that order must remain and be a link in the world order that will emerge out of the present chaos.

Socialism is thus for me not merely an economic doctrine which I favor; it is a vital creed which I hold with all my head and heart. I work for Indian independence because the nationalist in me cannot tolerate alien domination; I work for it even more because for me it is the inevitable step to social and economic change. I should like the Congress to become a socialist organization and to join hands with the other forces in the world who are working for the new civilization. But I realize that the majority in the Congress, as it is constituted today, may not be prepared to go thus far. We are a nationalist organization, and we think and work on the nationalist plane. It is evident enough now that this is too narrow even for the limited objective of political independence, and so we talk of the masses and their economic needs. But still most of us hesitate, because of our nationalist backgrounds, to take a step which might frighten away some vested interests. Most of those interests are already ranged against us, and we can expect little from them except opposition even in the political struggle.

Much as I wish for the advancement of socialism in this country, 1 have no desire to force the issue in the Congress and thereby create difficulties in the way of our struggle for independence. I shall co-operate gladly and with all the strength in me with all those who work for independence even though they do not agree with the socialist solution. But I shall do so stating my position frankly and hoping in course of time to convert the Congress and the country to it, for only thus can I see it achieving independence. It should surely be possible for all of us who believe in independence to join our ranks together even though we might differ on the social issue. The Congress has been in the past a broad front representing various opinions joined together by that common bond. It must continue as such even though the difference of those opinions becomes more marked.

How does socialism fit in with the present ideology of the Congress? I do not think it does. I believe in the rapid industrialization of the country; and only thus, I think, will the standards of the people rise substantially and poverty be combated. Yet I have co-operated wholeheartedly in the past with the *khadi* program, and I hope to do so in the future because I believe that *khadi* and village industries have a definite place in our present economy. They have a social, a political, and an economic value which is difficult to measure but which is apparent enough to those who have studied their effects. But I look upon them more as temporary expedients of a transition stage than as solutions of our vital problems. That transition stage might be a long one, and in a country like India, village industries might well play an important, though subsidiary, role even after the development of industrialism. But, though I co-operate in the village-industries program, my ideological approach to it differs considerably from that of many others in the Congress who are opposed to industrialization and socialism.

The problem of untouchability and the Harijans again can be approached in different ways. For a socialist it presents no difficulty, for under socialism there can be no such differentiation or victimization. Economically speaking, the Harijans have constituted the landless proletariat, and an economic solution removes the social barriers that custom and tradition have raised.

I come now to a question which is probably occupying your minds —the new Act passed by the British Parliament and our policy in regard to it. This Act has come into being since the last Congress met, but even at that time we had had a foretaste of it in the shape of the White Paper, and I know of no abler analysis of those provisions than that contained in the presidential address of my predecessor in this high office. The Congress rejected that proposed constitution and resolved to have nothing to do with it. The new Act, as is well known, is an even more retrograde measure and has been condemned by even the most moderate and cautious of our politicians. If we rejected the White Paper, what then are we to do with this new charter of slavery to strengthen the bonds of imperialist domination and to intensify the exploitation of our masses? And, even if we forget its content for a while, can we forget the insult and injury that have accompanied it, the contemptuous defiance of our wishes, the suppression of civil liberties, and the widespread repression that has been our normal lot? If they had offered to us the crown of heaven with this accompaniment and with dishonor, would we not have spurned it as inconsistent with our national honor and self-respect? What then of this?

A charter of slavery is no law for the slave, and, though we may perforce submit for a while to it and to the humiliation of ordinances and the like, inherent in that enforced submission are the right and the desire to rebel against it and to end it.

Our lawyers have examined this new constitution and have condemned it. But constitutions are something much more than legal documents. "The real constitution," said Ferdinand Lassalle, consists of "the actual relationships of power," and the working of this power we see even today, after the Act has been passed. That is the constitution we have to face, not the fine phrases which are sometimes presented to us, and we can only deal with it with the strength and power generated by the people of the country.

To this Act our attitude can only be one of uncompromising hostility and a constant endeavor to end it. How can we do this?

Since my return from Europe I have had the advantage of full and frank discussion with my colleagues of the Working Committee. All of us have agreed that the Act has to be rejected and combated, but all of us have not been able to agree to the manner of doing so. We have pulled together in the past, and I earnestly hope that we shall do so in the future, but in order to do so effectively we must recognize that there are marked differences in our outlooks. I do not yet know, as I write, what the final recommendation of the Working Committee will be on this issue. I can only, therefore, venture to put before you my own personal views on the subject, not knowing how far they represent the views of Congressmen. I should like to make it clear, however, in fairness to my old colleagues of the Working Committee, that the majority of them do not agree with all the views I am going to express. But, whether we agree or disagree, or whether we agree to differ, there is a strong desire on our part to continue to co-operate together, laying stress on our many points of agreement rather than on the differences. That is the right course for us, and, as a democratic organization, that is the only course open to us.

I think that, under the circumstances, we have no choice but to contest the election to the new provincial legislatures, in the event of their taking place. We should seek election on the basis of a detailed political and economic program, with our demand for a Constituent Assembly in the forefront. I am convinced that the only solution of our political and communal problems will come through such an assembly, provided it is elected on an adult franchise and a mass basis. That Assembly will not come into existence till at least a semirevolutionary situation has been created in this country and the actual relationships of power, apart from paper constitutions, are such that the people of India can make their will felt. When that will happen, I cannot say, but the world is too much in the grip of dynamic forces today to admit of static conditions in India or elsewhere for long. We may thus have to face this issue sooner than we might expect. But, obviously, a Constituent Assembly will not come through the new Act or the new legislatures. Yet we must press this demand and keep it before our country and the world, so that when the time comes we may be ripe for it.

A Constituent Assembly is the only proper and democratic method for the framing of our constitution, and for its delegates then to negotiate a treaty with the representatives of the British Government. But we cannot go to it with blank minds in the hope that something good will emerge out of it. Such an assembly, in order to be fruitful, must have previous thought behind it and a definite scheme put forward by an organized group. The actual details, as to how the Assembly is to be convened, must depend on the circumstances then existing and need not trouble us now. But it will be our function as the Congress to know exactly what we are after, to place this clearly and definitely before the Assembly, and to press for its acceptance.

One of the principal reasons for our seeking election will be to carry the message of the Congress to the millions of voters and to the scores of millions of the disfranchised, to acquaint them with our future program and policy, to make the masses realize that we not only stand for them but that we are of them and seek to co-operate with them in removing their social and economic burdens. Our appeal and message will not be limited to the voters, for we must remember that hundreds of millions are disfranchised and they need our help most, for they are at the bottom of the social ladder and suffer most from exploitation. We have seen in the past widespread official interference in the elections; we shall have to face that, as well as the serried and moneyed ranks of the reactionaries. But the real danger will come from our toning down our program and policy in order to win over the hesitating and compromising groups and individuals. If we compromise on principles, we shall fall between two stools and deserve our fall. The only right way and the only safe way is to stand four-square on our own program and to compromise with no one who has opposed the national struggle for freedom in the past, or who is in any way giving support to British imperialism.

When we have survived the election, what then are we to do? Office or no office? A secondary matter perhaps, and yet behind that issue lie deep questions of principle and vital differences of outlook, and a decision on that, either way, has far-reaching consequences. Behind it lies, somewhat hidden, the question of independence itself and whether we seek revolutionary changes in India or are working for petty reforms under the aegis of British imperialism. We go back again in thought to the clash of ideas which preceded the changes in the Congress in 1920. We made a choice then deliberately and with determination discarded the old sterile creed of reformism. Are we to go back again to that blind and suffocating lane, after all these years of brave endeavor, and to wipe out the memory of what we have done and achieved and suffered? That is the issue, and let none of us forget it when we have to give our decision. In this India, crying aloud for radical and fundamental change, in this world pregnant with revolutionary and dynamic possibility, are we to forget our mission and our historic destiny, and slide back to static futility? And, if some of us feel tired and hunger for rest and quiet, do we imagine that India's masses will follow our lead, when elemental forces and economic necessity are driving them to their inevitable goal? If we enter the backwaters, others will take our place on the bosom of the flowing stream and will dare to take the rapids and ride the torrent.

How has this question arisen? If we express our hostility to the Act and reject the entire scheme, does it not follow logically that we should have nothing to do with the working of it and should prevent its functioning, in so far as we can? To accept office and ministry under the conditions of the Act, is to negate our rejection of it and to stand self-condemned. National honor and self-respect cannot accept this position, for it would inevitably mean our co-operation in some measure with the repressive apparatus of imperialism, and we would become partners in this repression and in the exploitation of our people. Of course we would try to champion the rights of the people and would protest against repression, but as ministers under the Act we could do very little to give relief, and we would have to share responsibility for the administration with the apparatus of imperialism, for the deficit budgets, for the suppression of labor and the peasantry. It is always dangerous to assume responsibility without power, even in democratic countries; it will be far worse with this undemocratic constitution, hedged in with safeguards and reserved powers and mortgaged funds, where we have to follow the rules and regulations of our opponents' making. Imperialism sometimes talks of co-operation, but the kind of co-operation it wants is usually known as surrender, and the ministers who accept office will have to do so at the price of surrender of much that they might have stood for in public. That is a humiliating position which self-respect itself should prevent one from accepting. For our great national organization to be party to it is to give up the very basis and background of our existence.

Self-respect apart, common sense tells us that we can lose much and gain little by acceptance of office in terms of the Act. We cannot get much out of it, or else our criticism of the Act itself is wrong, and we know that it is not so. The big things for which we stand will fade into the background, and petty issues will absorb our attention, and we shall lose ourselves in compromises and communal tangles, and disillusion with us will spread over the land. If we have a majority, and only then can the question of acceptance of office arise, we shall be in a position to dominate the situation and to prevent reactionaries and imperialists from profiting by it. Office will not add to our real strength; it will only weaken us by making us responsible for many things that we utterly dislike.

Again, if we are in a minority, the question of office does not arise. It may be, however, that we are on the verge of a majority and with the co-operation of other individuals and groups we can obtain office. There is nothing inherently wrong in our acting together with others on specific issues of civil liberty or economic or other demands, provided we do not compromise on any principle. But I can imagine few things more dangerous and more likely to injure us than the acceptance of office on the sufferance of others. That would be an intolerable position.

It is said that our chances at the elections would increase if we announced that we were prepared to accept offices and ministries. Perhaps that might be so, for all manner of other people, eager for the spoils and patronage that office gives, would then hurry to join us. Does any Congressman imagine that this would be a desirable development or that we would gain strength thereby? Again, it is said more voters would vote for us if they knew that we were going to form ministries. That might happen if we deluded them with false promises of what we might do for them within the Act, but a quick nemesis would follow our failure to give effect to those promises, and failure would be inevitable if the promises were worth while.

There is only one straight course open to us: to go to the people with our program and make it clear to them that we cannot give effect to the major items in it under present conditions, and therefore, while we use the platform of the legislatures to press that program, we seek to end these imperialist bodies by creating deadlocks in them whenever we are in a position to do so. Those deadlocks should preferably take place on those programs so that the masses might learn how ineffective for their purposes are these legislatures.

One fact is sometimes forgotten—the provision for second chambers in many of the provinces. These chambers will be reactionary and will be exploited by the Governor to check any forward tendencies in the lower house. They will make the position of a minister who seeks advance even more difficult and unenviable.

Some people have suggested, though their voices are hushed now, that provincial autonomy might be given on this office issue and each Provincial Congress Committee should be empowered to decide it for its own province. An astonishing and fatal suggestion playing into the hands of our imperialist rulers. We who have labored for Indian unity can never be parties to any proposal which tends to lessen that unity. That way lies disaster and a disruption of the forces working for freedom. If we agree to this, why then should we also not agree to the communal issue being decided provincially, or many other issues where individual provinces might think differently? First issues will sink into the background, independence itself will fade away, and the narrowest provincialism raise its ugly head. Our policy must be uniform for the whole of India, and it must place first things first, and independence is the first thing of all.

So that I am convinced that for the Congress to favor the acceptance of office, or even to hesitate and waver about it, would be a vital error. It will be a pit from which it would be difficult for us to come out. Practical statesmanship is against it, as well as the traditions of the Congress and the mentality we have sought to develop in the people. Psychologically, any such lead might have disastrous consequences. If we stand for revolutionary changes, as we do, we have to cultivate a revolutionary mentality among our people, and anything that goes against it is harmful to our cause.

This psychological aspect is important. For we must never forget, and never delude our masses into imagining, that we can get any real power or real freedom through working these legislatures. We may use them certainly to advance our cause to some extent, but the burden of the struggle for freedom must fall on the masses, and primarily, therefore, our effective work must lie outside these legislatures. Strength will come from the masses and from our work among them and our organization of them.

Of secondary importance though the work in the legislatures is, we may not treat it casually and allow it to become a hindrance to our other work. Therefore it is necessary for the Congress, through its executive, to have direct control over the elections and the program placed before the country, as well as the activity in the legislatures. Such control will inevitably be exercised through committees and boards appointed for the purpose, but the continued existence of semi-autonomous parliamentary boards seems to be undesirable. Provision should also be made for a periodical review of all such activities so that Congressmen in general and the country should keep in touch with them and should influence them.

We have considered the provincial elections which, it is said, may take place early next year. The time is far off yet, and it is by no means impossible that these elections may not take place for a much longer time, or may not take place at all, and the new Act may take its rightful place in oblivion. Much may happen in the course of the next year, and war is ever on the horizon, to upset the schemes and timetables of our rulers. But we cannot speculate on this, and we have to make provision for contingencies. That decision might even have been delayed, but dangerous and compromising tendencies seek to influence Congress policy, and the Congress cannot remain silent when the issue is raised and its whole future is in the balance.

The provincial legislatures may come, but few persons, I imagine, are confident about the coming of the federal part of this unholy structure. So far as we are concerned, we shall fight against it to our utmost strength, and the primary object of our creating deadlocks in the provinces and making the new Act difficult of functioning, is to kill the federation. With the federation dead, the provincial end of the Act will also go and leave the slate clean for the people of India to write on. That writing, whatever it be, can never admit the right of the Indian states to continue as feudal and autocratic monarchies. They have long survived their day, propped up by an alien Power, and have become the strangest anomalies in a changing world. The future has no place for autocracy or feudalism; a free India cannot tolerate the subjection of many of her children and their deprivation of human rights, nor can it ever agree to a dissection of its body and a cutting up of its limbs. If we stand for any human, political, social, or economic rights for ourselves, we stand for those identical rights for the people of the states.

I have referred to the terrible suppression of civil liberties by the British Government in India. But in the states matters are even worse, and, though we know that the real power behind those states is that of British imperialism, this tragic suppression of our brothers by their own countrymen is of painful significance. Indian rulers and their ministers have spoken and acted increasingly in the approved fascist manner, and their record during the past few years especially has been one of aggressive opposition to our national demands. States which are considered advanced ban the Congress organization and offer insult to our national flag and decree new laws to suppress the press. What shall we say of the more backward and primitive states?

There is one more matter concerning the Constitution Act which has given rise to much controversy. This is the communal decision. Many people have condemned it strongly and, I think, rightly; few have a good word for it. My own viewpoint is, however, somewhat different from that of others. I am not concerned so much with what it gives to this group or that but more so with the basic idea behind it. It seeks to divide India into numerous separate compartments, chiefly on a religious basis, and thus makes the development of democracy and economic policy very difficult. Indeed, the communal decision and democracy can never go together. We have to admit that, under present circumstances, and so long as our politics are dominated by middle-class elements, we cannot do away with communalism altogether. But to make a necessary exception in favor of our Moslem or Sikh friends is one thing, to spread this evil principle to numerous other groups and thus to divide up the electoral machinery and the legislature into many compartments is a far more dangerous proposition. If we wish to function democratically, the proposed communal arrangement will have to go, and I have no doubt that it will go. But it will not go by the methods adopted by the aggressive opponents of the decision. These methods result inevitably in perpetuating the decision, for they help in continuing a situation which prevents any reconsideration.

I have not been enamored of the past Congress policy in regard to the communal question and its attempts to make pacts and compromises. Yet essentially I think it was based on a sound instinct. First of all, the Congress always put independence first and other questions, including the communal one, second, and refused to allow any of those other questions to take pride of place. Secondly, it argued that the communal problem had arisen from a certain set of circumstances which enabled the third party to exploit the other two. In order to solve it, one had either to get rid of the third party (and that meant independence), or get rid of that set of circumstances, which meant a friendly approach by the parties concerned and an attempt to soften the prejudice and fear that filled them. Thirdly, that the majority community must show generosity in the matter to allay the fear and suspicion that minorities, even though unreasonably, might have.

That analysis is, I think, perfectly sound. I would add that, in my opinion, a real solution of the problem will only come when economic issues, affecting all religious groups and cutting across communal boundaries, arise. Apart from the upper middle classes, who live in hopes of office and patronage, the masses and the lower middle classes have to face identical political and economic problems. It is odd and significant that all the communal demands of any group, of which so much is heard, have nothing whatever to do with these problems of the masses and the lower middle classes.

It is also significant that the principal communal leaders, Hindu or Moslem or others, are political reactionaries, quite apart from the communal question. It is sad to think how they have sided with British imperialism in vital matters, how they have given their approval to the suppression of civil liberty, how during these years of agony they have sought to gain narrow profit for their group at the expense of the larger cause of freedom. With them there can be no co-operation, for that would mean co-operation with reaction. But I am sure that with the larger masses and the middle classes, who may have temporarily been led away by the specious claims of their communal leaders, there must be the fullest co-operation, and out of that co-operation will come a fairer solution of this problem.

I am afraid I cannot get excited over this communal issue, important as it is temporarily. It is, after all, a side issue, and it can have no real importance in the larger scheme of things. Those who think of it as the major issue think in terms of British imperialism continuing permanently in this country. Without that basis of thought, they would not attach so much importance to one of its inevitable offshoots. I have no such fear, and so my vision of a future India contains neither imperialism nor communalism.

Yet the present difficulty remains and has to be faced. Especially our sympathy must go to the people of Bengal, who have suffered most from these communal decisions, as well as from the heavy hand of the Government. Whenever opportunity offers to improve their situation in a friendly way, we must seize it. But always the background of our action must be the national struggle for independence and the social freedom of the masses.

I have referred previously to the growing divorce between our organization and the masses. Individually many of us still have influence with the masses and our word carries weight with them, and who can measure the love and reverence of India's millions for our leader, Gandhiji? And yet organizationally we have lost that intimate touch that we had. The social reform activities of the *khadi* and village industries and Harijan organizations keep large numbers of our comrades in touch with the masses, and those contacts bear fruit. But they are essentially nonpolitical, and so, politically, we have largely lost touch. There are many reasons for this, and some are beyond our control. Our present Congress constitution is, I feel, not helpful in developing these contacts or in encouraging enough the democratic spirit in its primary committees. These committees are practically rolls of voters who meet only to elect delegates or representatives, and take no part in discussion or the formation of policy.

It is interesting to read in that monumental and impressive record, the Webbs' new book on Russia, how the whole Soviet structure is based on a wide and living democratic foundation. Russia is not supposed to be a democratic country after the Western pattern, and yet we find the essentials of democracy present in far greater degree among the masses there than anywhere else. The six hundred thousand towns and villages there have a vast democratic organization, each with its own soviet, constantly discussing, debating, criticizing, helping in the formulation of policy, electing representatives to higher committees. This organization of citizens covers the entire population over 18 years of age. There is yet another vast organization of the people as producers, and a third, equally vast, as consumers. And thus scores of millions of men and women are constantly taking part in the discussion of public affairs and actually in the administration of the country. There has been no such practical application of the democratic process in history.

All this is, of course, utterly beyond us, for it requires a change in the political and economic structure and much else before we can experiment that way. But we can profit by that example still and try in our own limited way to develop democracy on the lowest rungs of the Congress ladder and make the primary committee a living organization.

An additional method for us to increase our contacts with the masses is to organize them as producers and then affiliate such organizations to the Congress or have full co-operation between the two. Such organizations of producers as exist today, such as trade-unions and peasant unions, as well as other anti-imperialist organizations, could be brought within this sphere of mutual co-operation for the good of the masses and the struggle for national freedom. Thus Congress could have an individual as well as a corporate membership and, retaining its individual character, could influence, and be influenced by, other mass elements.

These are big changes that I have hinted at, and I am by no means sure how they can be brought about, or whether it is possible to go far in this direction in the near future. Still, we must move to some extent at least if we are to have our roots in the soil of India and draw life and strength from its millions. The subject is fascinating but complicated and can only be tackled by an expert committee, which I trust will be appointed on behalf of the Congress. The report of that committee must be freely discussed so as to get the widest backing for it.

All this will take us to the next Congress. Meanwhile perhaps some urgent changes are needed in our constitution to remove anomalies and avoid difficulties. Owing to my absence, I have had little experience of the working of the new constitution and cannot make any concrete suggestions. The reduction in the numbers of delegates and All-India Congress Committee members would be, to some extent, desirable if there was a background of widespread activity in the primary and secondary committees. Without it, it makes us even less responsive to mass opinion, and, therefore, an increase seems desirable. But the real solution is to increase the interest and day-to-day activity of the lower committees.

I have been told that the manual-labor franchise has not been a success and has led to a great deal of evasion. If that is so, a change is desirable, for a constitution must be such as can be worked easily and without subterfuge.

The Congress is an all-inclusive body and represents many interests, but essentially it is a political organization with various subsidiary and allied organizations, like the Spinners' Association and the Village Industries Association. These allied organizations work in the economic field, but they do not seek directly to remove the burdens of the peasantry under the present system of land tenure. Nor can the Congress, situated as it is, wholly function as a peasant organization, although in many provinces it has espoused the cause of the peasantry and brought them much relief. It seems to me necessary that the Congress should encourage the formation of peasant unions as well as workers' unions, and co-operate with such as already exist, so that the day-to-day struggle of the masses might be continued on the basis of their economic demands and other grievances. This identification of the Congress with the economic struggle of the masses will bring us nearer to them and nearer to freedom than anything else. I would welcome also the organization of other special interests, like those of the women, in the general framework of our national struggle for freedom. The Congress would be in a position to co-ordinate all these vital activities and thus to base itself on the widest possible mass foundation.

There has been some talk of a militant program and militant action. I do not know what exactly is meant, but, if direct action on a national scale or civil disobedience are meant, then I would say that I see no near prospect of them. Let us not indulge in tall talk before we are ready for big action. Our business today is to put our house in order, to sweep away the defeatist mentality of some people, and to build up our organization with its mass affiliations, as well as to work among the masses. The time may come, and that sooner perhaps than we expect, when we might be put to the test. Let us get ready for that test. Civil disobedience and the like cannot be switched on and off when we feel like doing so. It depends on many things, some of which are beyond our control, but in these days of revolutionary change and constantly recurring crises in the world, events often move faster than we do. We shall not lack for opportunities.

The major problem of India today is that of the land—of rural poverty and unemployment and a thoroughly out-of-date land system. A curious combination of circumstances has held back India during the past few generations, and the political and economic garments it wears no longer fit it and are torn and tattered. In some ways our agrarian conditions are not unlike those of France a hundred and fifty years ago, prior to the great revolution. They cannot continue so for long. At the same time we have become parts of international capitalism, and we suffer the pains and crises which afflict this decaying system. As a result of these elemental urges and conflicts of world forces, what will emerge in India none can say. But we can say with confidence that the present order has reached the evening of its day, and it is up to us to try to mold the future as we would like it to be.

The world is filled with rumors and alarms of war. In Abyssinia bloody and cruel war has already gone on for many months, and we have watched anew how hungry and predatory imperialism behaves in its mad search for colonial domains. We have watched also with admiration the brave fight of the Ethiopians for their freedom against heavy odds. You will permit me, I feel sure, to greet them on your behalf and express our deep sympathy for them. Their struggle is something more than a local struggle. It is one of the first effective checks by an African people on an advancing imperialism, and already it has had far-reaching consequences.

In the Far East also war hovers on the horizon, and we see an Eastern imperialism advancing methodically and pitilessly over ancient China and dreaming of world empire. Imperialism shows its claws wherever it may be, in the West or in the East.

In Europe an aggressive fascism or Nazi-ism steps continuously on the brink of war, and vast armed camps arise in preparation for what seems to be the inevitable end of all this. Nations join hands to fight other nations, and progressive forces in each country ally themselves to fight the fascist menace.

Where do we come in in this awful game? What part shall we play in this approaching tragedy? It is difficult to say. But we must not permit ourselves to be passive tools exploited for imperialist ends. It must be our right to say whether we join a war or not, and without that consent there should be no co-operation from us. When the time comes, we may have little say in the matter, and so it becomes necessary for the Congress to declare clearly now its opposition to India's participation in any imperialist war, and every war that will be waged by imperialist Powers will be an imperialist war, whatever the excuses put forward might be. Therefore we must keep out of it and not allow Indian lives and Indian money to be sacrificed.

To the progressive forces of the world, to those who stand for human freedom and the breaking of political and social bonds, we offer our full co-operation in their struggle against imperialism and fascist reaction, for we realize that our struggle is a common one. Our grievance is not against any people or any country as such, and we know that even in imperialist England, which throttles us, there are many who do not love imperialism and who stand for freedom.

During this period of difficulty and storm and stress, inevitably our minds and hearts turn to our great leader who has guided us and inspired us by his dynamic personality these many years. Physical ill-health prevents him now from taking his full share in public activities. Our good wishes go out to him for his rapid and complete recovery, and with those wishes is the selfish desire to have him back again among us. We have differed with him in the past, and we shall differ with him in the future about many things, and it is right that each one of us should act up to his convictions. But the bonds that hold us together are stronger and more vital than our differences, and the pledges we took together still ring in our ears. How many of us have that passionate desire for Indian independence and the raising of our poverty-stricken masses which consumes him? Many things he taught us long years ago, it seems now—fearlessness and discipline and the will to sacrifice ourselves for the larger cause. That lesson may have grown dim, but we have not forgotten it, nor can we ever forget him who has made us what we are and raised India again from the depths. The pledge of independence that we took together still remains to be redeemed, and we await again for him to guide us with his wise counsel.

But no leader, however great he be, can shoulder the burden single-handed; we must all share it to the best of our ability and not seek helplessly to rely on others to perform miracles. Leaders come and go; many of our best-loved captains and comrades have left us all too soon, but India goes on, and so does India's struggle for freedom. It may be that many of us must suffer still and die so that India may live and be free. The promised land may yet be far from us, and we may have to march wearily through the deserts, but who will take

415

away from us that deathless hope which has survived the scaffold and immeasurable suffering and sorrow; who will dare to crush the spirit of India which has found rebirth again and again after so many crucifixions?

## APPENDIX C

COMRADES,

Eight and a half months ago I addressed you from this tribune, and now, at your bidding, I am here again. I am grateful to you for this repeated expression of your confidence, deeply sensible of the love and affection that have accompanied it, somewhat overburdened by this position of high honor and authority that you would have me occupy again; and yet I am fearful of this responsibility. Men and women who have to carry the burden of responsible positions in the world today have a heavy and unenviable task, and many are unable to cope with it. In India that task is as heavy as anywhere else, and, if the present is full of difficulty, the veil of the future hides perhaps vaster and more intricate problems. Is it surprising then that I accept your gracious gift with hesitation?

Before we consider the problems that face us, we must give thought to our comrades—those who have left us during these past few months and those who languish year after year, often with no end in prospect, in prison and detention camp. Two well-beloved colleagues have gone —Mukhtar Ahmad Ansari and Abbas Tyabji, the bearers of names honored in Congress history, dear to all of us as friends and comrades, brave and wise counselors in times of difficulty.

To our comrades in prison or in detention we send greeting. Their travail continues and it grows, and only recently we have heard with horror of the suicide of three *détenus* who found life intolerable for them in the fair province of Bengal, whose young men and women in such large numbers live in internment without end. We have an analogy elsewhere, in Nazi Germany, where concentration camps flourish and suicides are not uncommon.

Soon after the last Congress I had to nominate the Working Committee, and I included in this our comrade, Subhas Chandra Bose. But you know how he was snatched away from us on arrival at Bombay, and ever since then he has been kept in internment despite failing health. Our Committee has been deprived of his counsel, and I have missed throughout the year this brave comrade on whom we all counted so much. Helplessly we watch this crushing of our men and women, but this helplessness in the present steels our resolve to end this intolerable condition of our people.

One who was not with us at Lucknow has come back to us after long internment and prison. We offer cordial welcome to Khan Abdul Ghaffar Khan for his own brave self as well as for the sake of the people of the Frontier Province, whom he has so effectively and gallantly led in India's struggle for freedom. But, though he is with us, he may not, so the orders of the British Government in India run, go back home or enter his province or even the Punjab. And in that province of his the Congress organization is still illegal and most political activities prevented.

I must also offer on your behalf warm welcome to one who, though young, is an old and well-tried soldier in India's fight for freedom. Comrade M. N. Roy has just come to us after a long and most distressing period in prison, but, though shaken up in body, he comes with fresh mind and heart, eager to take his part in that old struggle that knows no end till it ends in success.

The elements have been unusually cruel to us during these past few months, and famine and floods and droughts have afflicted many provinces and brought great suffering to millions of our people. Recently a great cyclone descended on Guntur district in the South, causing tremendous damage and rendering large numbers homeless, with all their belongings destroyed. We may not complain of this because the elements are still largely beyond human control. But the wit of man can find a remedy for recurring floods due to known causes, and make provision for the consequences of droughts and the like, and organize adequate relief for the victims of natural catastrophes. But that wit is lacking among those who control our destinies, and our people, always living on the verge of utter destitution, can face no additional shock without going under.

We are all engrossed in India at present in the provincial elections that will take place soon. The Congress has put up over a thousand candidates, and this business of election ties us up in many ways, and yet I would ask you, as I did at Lucknow, to take heed of the terrible and fascinating drama of the world. Our destinies are linked up with it, and our fate, like the fate of every country, will depend on the outcome of the conflicts of rival forces and ideas that are taking place everywhere. Again I would remind you that our problem of national freedom as well as social freedom is but a part of this great world problem, and to understand ourselves we must understand others also.

Even during these last eight months vast changes have come over the international situation, the crisis deepens, the rival forces of progress and reaction come to closer grips with each other, and we go at a terrific pace toward the abyss of war. In Europe fascism has been pursuing its triumphant course, speaking ever in a more strident voice, introducing an open gangsterism in international affairs. Based as it is on hatred and violence and dreams of war, it leads inevitably, unless it is checked in time, to world war. We have seen Abyssinia succumb to it; we see today the horror and tragedy of Spain.

How has this fascism grown so rapidly, so that now it threatens to dominate Europe and the world? To understand this, one must seek a clue in British foreign policy. This policy, in spite of its outward variations and frequent hesitations, has been one of consistent support of Nazi Germany. The Anglo-German Naval Treaty threw France into the arms of Italy and led to the rape of Abyssinia. Behind all the talk of sanctions against Italy later on, there was the refusal by the British Government to impose any effective sanction. Even when the United States of America offered to co-operate in imposing the oil sanction, Britain refused and was content to see the bombing of Ethiopians and the breaking up of the League of Nations system of collective security. True, the British Government always talked in terms of the League and in defense of collective security, but its actions belied its words and were meant to leave the field open to fascist aggression. Nazi Germany took step after step to humiliate the League and upset the European order, and ever the British "National" Government followed meekly in its trail and gave it its whispered blessing.

Spain came then as an obvious and final test, a democratic government assailed by a fascist-military rebellion aided by mercenary foreign troops. Here again while fascist Powers helped the rebels, the League Powers proclaimed a futile policy of nonintervention, apparently designed to prevent the Spanish democratic government from combating effectively the rebel menace.

So we find British imperialism inclining more and more toward the fascist Powers, though the language it uses, as is its old habit, is democratic in texture and pious in tone. And because of this contradiction between words and deeds, British prestige has sunk in Europe and the world and is lower today than it has ever been for many generations.

So in the world today these two great forces strive for mastery—those who labor for democratic and social freedom and those who wish to crush this freedom under imperialism and fascism. In this struggle Britain, though certainly not the mass of the British people, inevitably joins the ranks of reaction. And the struggle today is fiercest and clearest in Spain; on the outcome of that depends war or peace in the world in the near future, fascist domination or the scotching of fascism and imperialism. That struggle has many lessons for us, and perhaps the most important of these is the failure of the democratic process in resolving basic conflicts and introducing vital changes to bring social and economic conditions in line with world conditions. That failure is not caused by those who desire or work for these changes. They accept the democratic method, but, when this method threatens to affect great vested interests and privileged classes, these classes refuse to accept the democratic process and rebel against it. For them democracy means their own domination and the protection of their special interests. When it fails to do this, they have no further use for it and try to break it up. And in their attempt to break it, they do not scruple to use any and every method to ally themselves with foreign and anti-national forces. Calling themselves nationalists and patriots, they employ mercenary armies of foreigners to kill their own kith and kin and enslave their own people.

In Spain today our battles are being fought, and we watch this struggle not merely with the sympathy of friendly outsiders, but with the painful anxiety of those who are themselves involved in it. We have seen our hopes wither, and a blank despair has sometimes seized us at this tragic destruction of Spain's manhood and womanhood. But in the darkest moments the flame that symbolizes the hope of Spanish freedom has burned brightly and proclaimed to the world its eventual triumph. So many have died, men and women, boys and girls, that the Spanish Republic might live and freedom might endure. We see in Spain, as so often elsewhere, the tragic destruction of the walls of the citadel of freedom. How often they have been lost and then retaken, how often destroyed and rebuilt!

I wish, and many of you will wish with me, that we could give some effective assistance to our comrades in Spain, something more than sympathy, however deeply felt. The call for help has come to us from those sorely stricken people, and we cannot remain silent to that appeal. And yet I do not know what we can do in our helplessness when we are struggling ourselves against an imperialism that binds and crushes.

So I would like to stress before you, as I did before, this organic connection between world events, this action and interaction between one and the other. Thus we shall understand a little this complicated picture of the world today, a unity in spite of its amazing diversity and conflicts. In Europe, as in the Far East, there is continuous trouble, and everywhere there is ferment. The Arab struggle against British imperialism in Palestine is as much part of this great world conflict as India's struggle for freedom. Democracy and fascism, nationalism and imperialism, socialism and a decaying capitalism, combat each other in the world of ideas, and this conflict develops on the material plane, and bayonets and bombs take the place of votes in the struggle for power. Changing conditions in the world demand a new political and economic orientation, and, if this does not come soon, there is friction and conflict. Gradually this leads to a revolution in the minds of men, and this seeks to materialize, and every delay in this change-over leads to further conflict. The existing equilibrium having gone, giving place to no other, there is deterioration, reaction, and disaster. It is this disaster that faces us in the world today, and war on a terrible scale is an ever-present possibility. Except for the fascist Powers, every country and people dreads this war, and yet they all prepare for it feverishly, and in doing so they line up on this side or that. The middle groups fade out or, ghostlike, they flit about, unreal, disillusioned, self-tortured, ever-doubting. That has been the fate of the old liberalism everywhere, though in India perhaps those who call themselves Liberals, and others who think in their way, have yet to come out of the fog of complacency that envelops them. But we

> Move with new desires.
> For where we used to build and love
> Is no man's land, and only ghosts can live
> Between two fires.

What are these new desires? The wish to put an end to this mad world system which breeds war and conflict and which crushes millions; to abolish poverty and unemployment and release the energies of vast numbers of people and utilize them for the progress and betterment of humanity; to build where today we destroy. During the past eight months I have wandered a great deal in this vast land of ours, and I have seen again the throbbing agony of India's masses, the call of their eyes for relief from the terrible burdens they carry. That is our problem; all others are secondary and merely lead up to it. To solve that problem we shall have to end the imperialistic control and exploitation of India. But what is this imperialism of today? It is not merely the physical possession of one country by another; its roots lie deeper. Modern imperialism is an outgrowth of capitalism and cannot be separated from it.

It is because of this that we cannot understand our problems without understanding the implications of imperialism and socialism. The disease is deep-seated and requires a radical and revolutionary remedy, and that remedy is the socialist structure of society. We do not fight for socialism in Indian today, for we have to go far before we can act in terms of socialism, but socialism comes in here and now to help us to understand our problem and point out the path to its solution, and to tell us the real content of the *Swaraj* to come. With no proper understanding of the problem, our actions are likely to be erratic, purposeless, and ineffective.

The Congress stands today for full democracy in India and fights for a democratic state, not for socialism. It is anti-imperialist and strives for great changes in our political and economic structure. I hope that the logic of events will lead it to socialism, for that seems to me the only remedy for India's ills. But the urgent and vital problem for us today is political independence and the establishment of a democratic state. And because of this, the Congress must line up with all the progressive forces of the world and must stand for world peace. Recently there has taken place in Europe a significant development in the peace movement. The World Peace Congress, held at Brussels in September last, brought together numerous mass organizations on a common platform and gave an effective lead for peace. Whether this lead will succeed in averting war, no one can say, but all lovers of peace will welcome it and wish it success. Our Congress was ably represented at Brussels by Shri V. K. Krishna Menon, and the report that he has sent us is being placed before you. I trust that the Congress will associate itself fully with the permanent peace organization that is being built up and assist with all its strength in this great task. In doing so we must make our own position perfectly clear. For us, and we think for the world, the problem of peace cannot be separated from imperialism, and in order to remove the root causes of war, imperialism must go. We believe in the sanctity of treaties, but we cannot consider ourselves bound by treaties in the making of which the people of

India had no part, unless we accept them in due course. The problem of maintaining peace cannot be isolated by us, in our present condition, from war resistance. The Congress has already declared that we can be no parties to an imperialist war, and we will not allow the exploitation of India's man power and resources for such a war. Any such attempt will be resisted by us.

The League of Nations has fallen very low, and there are few who take it seriously as an instrument for the preservation of peace. India has no enthusiasm for it whatever, and the Indian membership of the League is a farce, for the selection of delegates is made by the British Government. We must work for a real League of Nations, democratically constructed, which would in effect be a League of Peoples. If even the present League, ineffective and powerless as it is, can be used in favor of peace, we shall welcome it.

With this international background in view, let us consider our national problems. The Government of India Act of 1935, the new Constitution, stares at us offensively, this new charter of bondage which has been imposed upon us despite our utter rejection of it; and we are preparing to fight elections under it. Why we have entered into this election contest and how we propose to follow it up has been fully stated in the Election Manifesto of the All-India Congress Committee, and I commend this manifesto for your adoption. We go to the legislatures not to co-operate with the apparatus of British imperialism, but to combat the Act and seek to end it, and to resist in every way British imperialism in its attempt to strengthen its hold on India and its exploitation of the Indian people. That is the basic policy of the Congress, and no Congressman, no candidate for election, must forget this. Whatever we do must be within the four corners of this policy. We are not going to the legislatures to pursue the path of constitutionalism or a barren reformism.

There is a certain tendency to compromise over these elections, to seek a majority at any cost. This is a dangerous drift and must be stopped. The elections must be used to rally the masses to the Congress standard, to carry the message of the Congress to the millions of voters and nonvoters alike, to press forward the mass struggle. The biggest majority in a legislature will be of little use to us if we have not got this mass movement behind us, and a majority built on compromises with reactionary groups or individuals will defeat the very purpose of the Congress.

With the effort to fight the Act, and as a corollary to it, we have to stress our positive demand for a Constituent Assembly elected under adult suffrage. That is the very cornerstone of Congress policy today, and our election campaign must be based on it. This Assembly must not be conceived as something emanating from the British Government or as a compromise with British imperialism. If it is to have any reality, it must have the will of the people behind it and the organized strength of the masses to support it, and the power to draw up the constitution of a free India. We have to create that mass support for it through these elections and later through our other activities.

The Working Committee has recommended to this Congress that a convention of all Congress members of all the legislatures, and such other persons as the Committee might wish to add to them, should meet soon after the election to put forward the demand for the Constituent Assembly, and determine how to oppose, by all feasible methods, the introduction of the federal structure of the Act. Such a Convention, which must include the members of the All-India Congress Committee, should help us greatly in focusing our struggle and giving it proper direction in the legislatures and outside. It will prevent the Congress members of the legislatures from developing provincialism and getting entangled in minor provincial matters. It will give them the right perspective and a sense of all-India discipline, and it should help greatly in developing mass activities on a large scale. The idea is full of big possibility, and I trust that the Congress will approve of it.

Next to this demand for the Constituent Assembly, our most important task will be to oppose the federal structure of the Act. Utterly bad as the Act is, there is nothing so bad in it as this federation, and so we must exert ourselves to the utmost to break this and thus end the Act as a whole. To live not only under British imperialist exploitation but also under Indian feudal control, is something that we are not going to tolerate whatever the consequences. It is an interesting and instructive result of the long period of British rule in India that when, as we are told, it is trying to fade off, it should gather to itself all the reactionary and obscurantist groups in India, and endeavor to hand partial control to the feudal elements.

The development of this federal scheme is worthy of consideration. We are not against the conception of a federation. It is likely that a free India may be a federal India, though in any event there must be a great deal of unitary control. But the present federation that is being thrust upon us is a federation in bondage and under the control, politically and socially, of the most backward elements in the country. The present Indian states took shape early in the nineteenth century in the unsettled conditions of early British rule. The treaties with their autocratic rulers, which are held up to us so often now as sacred documents which may not be touched, date from that period.

It is worth while comparing the state of Europe then with that of India. In Europe then there were numerous tiny kingdoms and princedoms; kings were autocratic, holy alliances and royal prerogatives flourished. Slavery was legal. During these hundred years and more Europe has changed out of recognition. As a result of numerous revolutions and changes the princedoms have gone and very few kings remain. Slavery has gone. Modern industry has spread, and democratic institutions have grown up with an ever-widening franchise. These in their turn have given place in some countries to fascist dictatorships. Backward Russia, with one mighty jump, has established a Soviet Socialist state and an economic order which has resulted in tremendous progress in all directions. The world has gone on changing and hovers on the brink of yet another vast change. But not so the Indian states; they remain static in this ever-changing panorama, staring at us with the eyes of the early nineteenth century. The old treaties are sacrosanct, treaties made not with the people or their representatives but with their autocratic rulers.

This is a state of affairs which no nation, no people can tolerate. We cannot recognize these old settlements of more than a hundred years ago as permanent and unchanging. The Indian states will have to fit into the scheme of a free India, and their peoples must have, as the Congress has declared, the same personal, civil, and democratic liberties as those of the rest of India.

Till recent years little was heard of the treaties of the states or of paramountcy. The rulers knew their proper places in the imperial scheme of things, and the heavy hand of the British Government was always in evidence. But the growth of the national movement in India gave them a fictitious importance, for the British Government began to rely upon them more and more to help it in combating this nationalism. The rulers and their ministers were quick to notice the change in the angle of vision and to profit by it. They tried to play, not without success, the British Government and the Indian people against each other and to gain advantages from both. They have succeeded to a remarkable degree and have gained extraordinary power under the federal scheme. Having preserved themselves as autocratic units, which are wholly outside the control of the rest of India, they have gained power over other parts of India. Today we find them talking as if they were independent and laying down conditions for their adherence to the federation. There is talk even of the abolition of the viceregal paramountcy, so that these states may remain, alone in the whole world, naked and unchecked autocracies, which cannot be tampered with by any constitutional means. A sinister development is the building up of the armies of some of the bigger states on an efficient basis.

Thus our opposition to the federal part of the Constitution Act is not merely a theoretical one, but a vital matter which affects our freedom struggle and our future destiny. We have got to make it a central pivot of our struggle against the Act. We have got to break this federation.

Our policy is to put an end to the Act and have a clean slate to write afresh. We are told by people who can think only in terms of action taken in the legislatures, that it is not possible to wreck it and there are ample provisions and safeguards to enable the Government to carry on despite a hostile majority. We are well aware of these safeguards; they are one of the principal reasons why we reject the Act. We know also that there are second chambers to obstruct us. We can create constitutional crises inside the legislatures, we can have deadlocks, we can obstruct the imperialist machine, but always there is a way out. The Constitution cannot be wrecked by action inside the legislatures only. For that, mass action outside is necessary, and that is why we must always remember that the essence of our freedom struggle lies in mass organization and mass action.

The policy of the Congress in regard to the legislatures is perfectly clear; only in one matter it still remains undecided—the question of acceptance or not of office. Probably the decision of this question will be postponed till after the elections. At Lucknow I ventured to tell you that, in my opinion, acceptance of office was a negation of our policy of rejection of the Act; it was further a reversal of the policy we had adopted in 1920 and followed since then. Since Lucknow the Congress has further clarified its position in the Election Manifesto and declared that we are not going to the legislatures to co-operate in any way with the Act but to combat it. That limits the field of our decision in regard to offices, and those who incline to acceptance of them must demonstrate that this is the way to nonco-operate with the Act, and to end it.

It seems to me that the only logical consequence of the Congress policy, as defined in our resolutions and in the Election Manifesto, is to have nothing to do with office and ministry. Any deviation from this would mean a reversal of that policy. It would inevitably mean a kind of partnership with British imperialism in the exploitation of the Indian people, an acquiescence, even though under protest and subject to reservations, in the basic ideas underlying the Act, an association to some extent with British imperialism in the hateful task of the repression of our advanced elements. Office accepted on any other basis is hardly possible, and, if it is possible, it will lead almost immediately to deadlock and conflict. That deadlock and impasse does not frighten us; we welcome it. But then we must think in terms of deadlocks and not in terms of carrying on with the office.

There seems to be a fear that if we do not accept office others will do so and they will put obstacles in the way of our freedom movement. But, if we are in a majority, we can prevent others from misbehaving; we can even prevent the formation of any ministry. If our majority is a doubtful one, then office for us depends on compromises with non-Congress elements, a policy full of danger for our cause and one which would inevitably lead to our acting in direct opposition to the Congress mandate of rejection of the Act. Whether we are in a majority or in a minority, the real thing will always be the organized mass backing behind us. A majority without that backing can do little in the legislatures; even a militant minority with conscious and organized mass support can make the functioning of the Act very difficult.

We have put the Constituent Assembly in the forefront of our program, as well as the fight against the federal structure. With what force can we press these two vital points and build up a mass agitation around them if we wobble over the question of office and get entangled in its web?

We have great tasks ahead, great problems to solve both in India and in the international sphere. Who can face and solve these problems in India but this great organization of ours, which has, through fifty years' effort and sacrifice, established its unchallengeable right to speak for the millions of India? Has it not become the mirror of their hopes and desires, their urge to freedom, and the strong arm that will wrest this freedom from unwilling and resisting hands? It started in a small way with a gallant band of pioneers, but even then it represented a historic force, and it drew to itself the good will of the Indian people. From year to year it grew, faced inner conflicts whenever it wanted to advance and was held back by some of its members. But the urge to go ahead was too great, the push from below increased; and, though a few left us, unable to adjust themselves to changing conditions, vast numbers of others joined the Congress. It became a great propaganda machine dominating the public platform of India. But it was an amorphous mass; its organizational side was weak, and effective action on a large scale was beyond its powers. The coming of Gandhiji brought the peasant masses to the Congress, and the new constitution that was adopted at his instance in Nagpur in 1920 tightened up the organization, limited the number of delegates according to population, and gave it strength and capacity for joint and effective action. That action followed soon after on a countrywide scale and was repeated in later years. But the very success and prestige of the Congress often drew undesirable elements to its fold and accentuated the defects of the constitution. The organization was becoming unwieldy and slow of movement and capable of being exploited in local areas by particular groups. Two years ago radical changes were made in the constitution again at Gandhiji's instance. One of these was the fixation of the number of delegates according to membership, a change which has given a greater reality to our elections and strengthened us organizationally. But still our organizational side lags far behind the great prestige of the Congress, and there is a tendency for our committees to function in the air, cut off from the rank and file.

It was partly to remedy this that the Mass Contacts resolution was passed by the Lucknow Congress, but unhappily the committee that was in charge of this matter has not reported yet. The problem is a wider one than was comprised in that resolution, for it includes an overhauling of the Congress constitution with the object of making it a closer-knit body, capable of disciplined and effective action. That action to be effective must be mass action, and the essence of the strength of the Congress has been this mass basis and mass response to its calls. But, though that mass basis is there, it is not reflected in the organizational side, and hence an inherent weakness in our activities. We have seen the gradual transformation of the Congress from a small upper-class body to one representing the great body of the lower middle classes, and later the masses of this country. As this drift to the masses continued, the political role of the organization changed and is changing, for this political role is largely determined by the economic roots of the organization.

We are already and inevitably committed to this mass basis, for without it there is no power or strength in us. We have now to bring

427

that into line with the organization, so as to give our primary members greater powers of initiative and control and opportunities for day-to-day activities. We have, in other words, to democratize the Congress still further.

Another aspect of this problem that has been debated during the past year has been the desirability of affiliating other organizations, of peasants, workers, and others, which also aim at the freedom of the Indian people, and thus to make the Congress the widest possible joint front of all the anti-imperialist forces in the country. As it is, the Congress has an extensive direct membership among these groups; probably 75% of its members come from the peasantry. But, it is argued, that functional representation will give far greater reality to the peasants and workers in the Congress. This proposal has been resisted because of a fear that the Congress might be swamped by new elements, sometimes even politically backward elements. As a matter of fact, although this question is an important one for us, any decision of it will make little difference at present; its chief significance will be as a gesture of good will. For there are few well-organized workers' or peasants' unions in the country which are likely to profit by Congress affiliation. There is not the least possibility of any swamping, and, in any event, this can easily be avoided. I think that now or later some kind of functional representation in the Congress is inevitable and desirable. It is easy for the Congress to lay down conditions for such affiliation, so as to prevent bogus and mushroom growths or undesirable organizations from profiting by it. A limit might also be placed on the number of representatives that such affiliated organizations can send. Some such recommendation, I believe, has been made by the Provincial Congress Committee of the United Provinces.

The real object before us is to build up a powerful joint front of all the anti-imperialist forces in the country. The Congress has indeed been in the past, and is today, such a united popular front, and inevitably the Congress must be the basis and pivot of united action. The active participation of the organized workers and peasants in such a front would add to its strength and must be welcomed. Co-operation between them and the Congress organization has been growing and has been a marked feature of the past year. This tendency must be encouraged. The most urgent and vital need of India today is this united national front of all forces and elements that are ranged against imperialism. Within the Congress itself most of these forces are represented, and in spite of their diversity and difference in outlook, they have co-operated and worked together for the common good. That is a healthy sign both of the vitality of our great movement and the unity that binds it together. The basis of it is anti-imperialism and independence. Its immediate demand is for a Constituent Assembly leading to a democratic state where political power has been transferred to the mass of the people. An inevitable consequence of this is the withdrawal of the alien army of occupation.

These are the objectives before us, but we cannot ignore the present-day realities and the day-to-day problems of our people. These ever-present realities are the poverty and unemployment of our millions, appalling poverty and an unemployment which has even the middle classes in its grip and grows like a creeping paralysis. The world is full of painful contrasts today, but surely nowhere else are these contrasts so astounding as in India. Imperial Delhi stands, visible symbol of British power, with all its pomp and circumstance and vulgar ostentation and wasteful extravagance; and within a few miles of it are the mud huts of India's starving peasantry, out of whose meager earnings these great palaces have been built, huge salaries and allowances paid. The ruler of a state flaunts his palaces and his luxury before his wretched and miserable subjects, and talks of his treaties and his inherent right to autocracy. And the new Act and Constitution have come to us to preserve and perpetuate these contrasts, to make India safe for autocracy and imperialist exploitation.

As I write, a great railway strike is in progress. For long the world of railway workers has been in ferment because of retrenchment and reduction in wages and against them is the whole power of the State. Some time ago there was a heroic strike in the Ambernath Match Factory near Bombay, owned by a great foreign trust. But behind that trust and supporting it, we saw the apparatus of Government functioning in the most extraordinary way. The workers in our country have yet to gain elementary rights; they have yet to have an eight-hour day and unemployment insurance and a guaranteed living wage.

But a vaster and more pressing problem is that of the peasantry, for India is essentially a land of the peasants. In recognition of this fact, and to bring the Congress nearer to the peasant masses, we are meeting here today at the village of Faizpur and not, as of old, in some great city. The Lucknow Congress laid stress on this land problem and called on the provincial committees to frame agrarian programs. This work is still incomplete, for the vastness and intricacy of it has demanded full investigation. But the urgency of the problem calls for immediate solution. Demands for radical reforms in the rent and revenue and the abolition of feudal levies have been made from most of the provinces. The crushing burden of debt on the agricultural classes has led to a widespread cry for a moratorium and a substantial liquidation of debt. In the Punjab, *karza* (Debt) committees have grown up to protect the peasantry. All these and many other demands are insistently made, and vast gatherings of peasants testify to their inability to carry their present burdens. Yet it is highly doubtful if this problem can be solved piecemeal and without changing completely the land system. That land system cannot endure, and an obvious step is to remove the intermediaries between the cultivator and the State. Co-operative or collective farming must follow.

The reform of the land system is tied up with the development of industry, both large-scale and cottage, in order to give work to our scores of millions of unemployed and raise the pitiful standards of our people. That again is connected with so many other things—education, housing, roads and transport, sanitation, medical relief, social services, etc. Industry cannot expand properly because of the economic and financial policy of the Government, which, in the name of Imperial Preference, encourages British manufactures in India, and works for the profit of Big Finance in the City of London. The currency ratio continues in spite of persistent Indian protest; gold has been pouring out of India continuously now for five years at a prodigious rate, though all India vehemently opposes this outflow. And the new Act tells us that we may do nothing which the Viceroy or the Governor might consider as an unfair discrimination against British trade or commercial interests. The old order may yield place to the new, but British interests are safe and secure.

And so one problem runs into another, and all together form that vast complex that is India today. Are we going to solve this by petty tinkering and patchwork with all manner of vested interests obstructing us and preventing advance? Only a great planned system for the whole land and dealing with all these various national activities, co-ordinating them, making each serve the larger whole and the interests of the mass of our people—only such a planned system, with vision and courage to back it, can find a solution. But planned systems do not flourish under the shadow of monopolies and vested interests and imperialist exploitation. They require the air and soil of political and social freedom.

These are distant goals for us today though the rapid march of events may bring us face to face with them sooner than we imagine. The immediate goal—independence—is nearer and more definite, and that is why perhaps we escape, to a large extent, that tragic disillusion and hopelessness which affect so many in Europe.

We are apparently weak, not really so. We grow in strength, the Empire of Britain fades away. Because we are politically and economically crushed, our civil liberties taken away, hundreds of our organizations made illegal, thousands of our young men and women always kept in prison or in detention camp, our movements continually watched by hordes of secret service men and informers, our spoken word taken down, lest it offend the law of sedition—because of all this and more we are not weaker but stronger, for all this intense repression is the measure of our growing national strength. War and revolution dominate the world, and nations arm desperately. If war comes or other great crisis, India's attitude will make a difference. We hold the keys of success in our hands if we but turn them rightly. And it is the increasing realization of this that has swept away the defeatist mentality of our people.

Meanwhile the general election claims our attention and absorbs our energy. Here too we find official interference, in spite of denial, and significant attempts to prevent secrecy of voting in the case of illiterate voters. The United Provinces have been singled out for this purpose, and the system of colored boxes, which will be used everywhere else, has been ruled out for the United Provinces. But we shall win in these elections in spite of all the odds—State pressure, vested interest, money.

That will be but a little step in a long journey, and we shall march on, with danger and distress as companions. We have long had these for our fellow travelers, and we have grown used to them. And, when we have learned how to dominate them, we shall also know how to dominate success.

# APPENDIX D

STATEMENT ISSUED BY THE CONGRESS WORKING COMMITTEE ON
SEPTEMBER 15, 1939

THE WORKING COMMITTEE has given its earnest consideration to the grave crisis that has developed owing to the declaration of war in Europe. The principles which should guide the nation in the event of war have been repeatedly laid down by the Congress, and only a month ago this Committee reiterated them and expressed its displeasure at the flouting of Indian opinion by the British Government in India.

As a first step to dissociate itself from this policy of the British Government, the Committee called upon the Congress members of the Central Legislative Assembly to refrain from attending the next session. Since then the British Government has declared India a belligerent country and promulgated ordinances, passed the Government of India Act Amending Bill, and taken other far-reaching measures which affect the Indian people vitally, and circumscribe and limit the powers and activities of the Provincial Governments. This has been done without the consent of the Indian people, whose declared wishes, in such matters, have been deliberately ignored by the British Government. The Working Committee must take the gravest view of these developments.

The Congress has repeatedly declared its entire disapproval of the ideology and practice of fascism and Nazi-ism and their glorification of war and violence and the suppression of the human spirit. It has condemned aggression, in which they repeatedly indulged, and their sweeping away of well-established principles and recognized standards of civilized behavior. It has seen in fascism and Nazi-ism the intensification of the principle of imperialism, against which the Indian people have struggled for many years. The Working Committee must therefore unhesitatingly condemn the aggression of the Nazi Government in Germany against Poland and sympathize with those who resist.

The Congress has further laid down that the issue of war and peace for India must be decided by the Indian people, and no outside authority can impose this decision upon them, nor can the Indian people permit their resources to be exploited for imperialist ends. Any imposed decision, or an attempt to use Indian resources, for purposes not approved by them, will necessarily have to be opposed by them. If co-operation is desired in a worthy cause, this cannot be obtained by compulsion and imposition, and the Committee cannot agree to the carrying out by the Indian people of orders issued by an external authority. Co-operation must be between equals by mutual consent for a cause which both consider to be worthy.

The people of India have in the recent past faced great risks and willingly made great sacrifices to secure their own freedom and establish a free and democratic state in India, and their sympathy is entirely on the side of democracy and freedom; but India cannot associate herself in a war said to be for democratic freedom, when that very freedom is denied her, and such limited freedom as she possesses is taken away from her.

The Committee is aware that the Governments of Great Britain and France have declared that they are fighting for democracy and freedom and to put an end to aggression; but the history of the recent past is full of examples showing constant divergence between the spoken word, the ideals proclaimed, and the real motives and objectives. During the war of 1914-18, the declared war aims were the preservation of democracy, self-determination and freedom of small nations; and yet the very Governments which solemnly proclaimed these aims entered into secret treaties embodying imperialist designs for the carving out of the Ottoman empire.

While stating that they did not want any acquisition of territory, the victorious Powers added largely to their colonial domains. The present European war itself signifies an abject failure of the Treaty of Versailles and of its makers, who broke their pledged word and imposed an imperialist peace on the defeated nations. The one hopeful outcome of that Treaty, the League of Nations, was muzzled and strangled at the outset and later on killed by its parent States.

Subsequent history demonstrated afresh how even a seemingly fervent declaration of faith may be followed by an ignoble desertion. In Manchuria the British Government connived at aggression; in Abyssinia they acquiesced in it; in Czechoslovakia and Spain, where democracy was in peril, it was deliberately betrayed, and the whole system of collective security was sabotaged by the very Powers who had previously declared their firm faith in it.

Again it is asserted that democracy is in danger and must be defended, and with this statement the Committee is in entire agreement. The Committee believes that the peoples in the West are moved by this ideal and objective, and for these they are prepared to make sacrifices; but again and again the ideals and the sentiments of the people and of those who have sacrificed themselves in the struggle have been ignored and faith has not been kept with them.

If the war is to defend the *status quo,* imperialist possessions, colonies, vested interests and privilege, then India can have nothing to do with it. If, however, the issue is democracy and a world order based on democracy, then India is intensely interested in it. The Committee is convinced that the interests of Indian democracy do not conflict with

433

the interests of British democracy or world democracy. But there is an inherent and ineradicable conflict between democracy for India, or elsewhere, and imperialism and fascism. If Great Britain fights for the maintenance and extension of democracy, then she must necessarily end imperialism in her own possessions and establish full democracy in India, and the Indian people must have the right of self-determination to frame their own constitution through a Constituent Assembly without external interference, and must guide their own policy. A free and democratic India will gladly associate herself with other free nations for mutual defense against aggression and for economic co-operation. She will work for the establishment of a real world order based on freedom and democracy, utilizing the world's knowledge and resources for the progress and advancement of humanity.

The crisis that has overtaken Europe is not of Europe only, but of humanity, and will not pass, like other crises or wars, leaving the essential structure of the present-day world intact. It is likely to refashion the world for good; for politically, socially, and economically this crisis is an inevitable consequence of the social and political conflicts and contradictions which have grown alarmingly since the last Great War, and it will not be finally resolved till these conflicts and contradictions are removed and a new equilibrium established. That equilibrium can be based only on the ending of the domination and exploitation of one country by another, and on the reorganization of economic relations on a juster basis for the common good of all. India is the crux of the problem, for India has been an outstanding example of modern imperialism, and no refashioning of the world can succeed which ignores this vital problem. With her vast resources she must play an important part in any scheme of world reorganization. But she can only do so as a free nation whose energies have been released to work for this great end. Freedom today is indivisible, and every attempt to retain imperialist domination in any part of the world will lead inevitably to a fresh disaster.

The Working Committee has noted that many rulers of Indian states have offered their services and resources, and expressed their desire to support the cause of democracy in Europe. If they must make their professions in favor of democracy abroad, the Committee suggests that their first concern should be the introduction of democracy within their own states, in which today undiluted autocracy reigns. The British Government in India is more responsible for this autocracy than even rulers themselves, as has been made painfully evident during the past year. This policy is the very negation of democracy and of the new world order for which Great Britain claims to be fighting in Europe.

As the Committee views past events in Europe, Africa, and Asia, and more particularly the past and present occurrences in India, it fails to find any attempt to advance the cause of democracy, self-determination, or any evidence that the present war declarations of the British Government are being, or are going to be, acted upon. The true measure of democracy is the ending of imperialism and fascism alike and the aggression that has accompanied them in the past and the present. Only on that basis can the new order be built up.

In the struggle for that new world order, the Committee is eager and desirous to help in every way; but the Committee cannot associate itself, or offer any co-operation in a war which is conducted on imperialist lines, and which is a means to consolidate imperialism in India and elsewhere.

In view, however, of the gravity of the occasion, and the fact that the pace of events during the last few days has often been swifter than the working of men's minds, the Committee desires to take no final decision at this stage, so as to allow for a full elucidation of the issues at stake, the real objectives aimed at, and the position of India in the present and in the future. But a decision cannot long be delayed, as India is being committed from day to day to a policy to which she is not a party, and of which she disapproves. The Working Committee, therefore, invites the British Government to declare in unequivocal terms what their war aims are in regard to democracy and imperialism and the new order that is envisaged, in particular how these aims are going to apply to India and to be given effect to at present. Do they include the elimination of imperialism and the treatment of India as a free nation whose policy will be guided in accordance with the wishes of her people? A clear declaration about the future pledging the Government to the ending of imperialism and fascism alike, will be welcomed by the people of all countries; but it is far more important to give immediate effect to it to the largest possible extent, for only this will convince the people that the declaration is meant to be honored. The real test of any declaration is its application in the present, for it is the present that will govern action today and will give shape to the future.

War has broken out in Europe, and the prospect is terrible to contemplate. But war has been taking its heavy toll of human life during the past years in Abyssinia, Spain, and China. Innumerable innocent men, women, and children have been bombed to death from the air in open cities. Cold-blooded massacres, torture and utmost humiliation have followed each other in quick succession during these years of horror. That horror grows; violence and the threat of violence shadow the world, and, unless checked and ended, will destroy the previous inheritance of past ages. That horror has to be checked in Europe and China, but it will not end till its root causes, fascism and imperialism, are removed. To that end, the Working Committee is prepared to give its co-operation; but it will be infinite tragedy if even this terrible war is carried on in the spirit of imperialism and for the purpose of retaining this structure which is itself the cause of war and human degradation.

The Working Committee wishes to declare that the Indian people have no quarrel with the German people, or the Japanese people, or any other people; but they have a deep-rooted quarrel with the systems which deny freedom and are based on violence and aggression. They do not look forward to the victory of one people over another, or to a dictated peace, but a victory of real democracy for all people in all countries, and a world freed from the nightmare of violence and imperialist oppression.

The Committee earnestly appeals to the Indian people to end all internal conflict and controversy at this grave hour of peril, and keep in readiness and hold together as a united nation, calm of purpose, and determined to achieve freedom for India within the larger freedom of the world.

# APPENDIX E

EXCERPT FROM THE ARTICLE ABOUT HIMSELF WRITTEN ANONYMOUSLY
BY JAWAHARLAL NEHRU IN THE "MODERN REVIEW" OF CALCUTTA

*Jawaharlal ki jai!* (Hail Jawaharlal!). The Rashtrapati looked up as he passed swiftly through the waiting crowds; his hands went up, and his pale, hard face was lit up with a smile. . . . The smile passed away and the face became stern and sad. Almost it seemed that the smile and the gesture accompanying it had little reality; they were just tricks of the trade to gain the goodwill of the crowd whose darling he had become. Was it so? Watch him again.

Is all this natural, or the carefully thought out trickery of the public man? Perhaps it is both, and long habit has become second nature now. The most effective pose is one in which there seems to be least posing, and Jawaharlal has learned well to act without the paint and powder of the actor. . . . Whither is this going to lead him and the country? What is he aiming at with all his apparent lack of aim?

For nearly two years now he has been President of Congress. Steadily and persistently he goes on increasing his personal prestige and influence. . . . From the Far North to Cape Comorin he has gone like some triumphant Caesar, leaving a trail of glory and a legend behind him. Is all this just a passing fancy which amuses him . . . or is it his will to power that is driving him from crowd to crowd and making him whisper to himself, "I drew these tides of men into my hands and wrote my will across the sky in stars."

What if the fancy turns? Men like Jawaharlal, with all their great capacity for great and good work, are unsafe in a democracy. He calls himself a democrat and socialist, and no doubt he does so in all earnestness . . . but a little twist and he might turn into a dictator. He might still use the language of democracy and socialism, but we all know how fascism has fattened on this language and then cast it away as useless lumber.

Jawaharlal cannot become a fascist. . . . He is too much an aristocrat for the crudity and vulgarity of fascism. His very face and voice tell us that. His face and voice are definitely private. . . . And yet he has all the makings of a dictator in him—vast popularity, a strong will, energy, pride . . . and with all his love of the crowd, an intolerance of others and a certain contempt for the weak and inefficient. His flashes of temper are well known. His overwhelming desire to get things done, to sweep away what he dislikes and build anew, will hardly brook for long the slow processes of democracy. . . . His conceit is already formidable. It must be checked. We want no Caesars. . . . It is not through Caesarism that India will attain freedom, and though she might prosper a little under a benevolent and efficient despotism, she will remain stunted and the day of the emancipation of her people will be delayed.

# APPENDIX F

THE working committee have given full and earnest consideration to
the proposals made by the British War Cabinet with regard to India
and the elucidation of them by Sir Stafford Cripps.

These proposals, which have been made at the very last hour because of the compulsion of events, have to be considered not only in
relation to India's demand for independence, but more especially in
the present grave war crisis with a view to meeting effectively the
perils and dangers that confront India and envelop the world.

The Congress has repeatedly stated ever since commencement of
the war in September, 1939, that the people of India would line themselves up with the progressive forces of the world and assume full
responsibility to face new problems and shoulder new burdens that
had arisen, and it asked that the necessary conditions to enable them
to do so be created.

The essential condition was freedom of India, for only the realization of present freedom could light the flame which would illuminate
millions of hearts and move them to action.

## Previous Argument Cited

At the last meeting of the All-India Congress Committee after
commencement of war in the Pacific it was stated that:

"Only a free and independent India can be in a position to undertake
the defense of the country on a national basis and be able to help in
furtherance of larger causes that are emerging from the war."

The British War Cabinet's new proposals relate principally to the
future upon cessation of hostilities.

The committee, while recognizing that self-determination for the people of India is accepted in principle in that uncertain future, regret that
this is fettered and circumscribed and that certain provisions have been
introduced which gravely imperil the development of a free and united
national government and establishment of a democratic State.

Even the constitution-making body is so constituted that the people's
right of self-determination is vitiated by the introduction of non-
representative elements.

The people of India have as a whole clearly demanded full inde-

438

pendence, and Congress has repeatedly declared that no other status except that of independence for the whole of India could be agreed to or could meet the essential requirements of the present situation. The committee recognize that future independence may be implicit in the proposals, but the accompanying provisions and restrictions are such that real freedom may well become an illusion.

The complete ignoring of 90,000,000 of people in the Indian States and their treatment as commodities at the disposal of their rulers is a negation both of democracy and self-determination.

### Holds People Ignored

While the representation of an Indian State in the constitution-making body is fixed on a population basis the people of the State have no voice in choosing those representatives, nor are they to be consulted at any stage while decisions vitally affecting them are being taken.

Such States may in many ways become barriers to the growth of Indian freedom. Enclaves where foreign authority still prevails and where the possibility of maintaining foreign armed forces, it has been stated, would be a likely contingency and a perpetual menace to the freedom of the people of the States as well as of the rest of India.

Acceptance beforehand of the novel principle of non-accession for a province is also a severe blow to the conception of Indian unity and an apple of discord likely to generate growing trouble in the provinces and which may well lead to further difficulties in the way of the Indian States merging themselves into an Indian union.

Congress has been wedded to Indian freedom and unity, and any break of that unity, especially in the modern world when people's minds inevitably think in terms of ever larger federations, would be injurious to all concerned and exceedingly painful to contemplate.

Nevertheless, the committee cannot think in terms of compelling the people of any territorial unit to remain in an Indian union against their declared and established will. While recognizing this principle, the committee feel that every effort should be made to create conditions which would help the different units in developing a common and cooperative national life.

Acceptance of this principle inevitably involves that no changes should be made which would result in fresh problems being created and compulsion being exercised on other substantial groups within that area. Each territorial unit should have the fullest possible autonomy within the union consistent with a strong national state.

The proposal now made on the part of the British War Cabinet encourages and will lead to attempts at separation at the very inception of union, and thus create friction just when the utmost cooperation and good-will are most needed.

This proposal has been made presumably to meet communal demand, but it will have other consequences also and lead to politically reactionary and obscurantist groups among the different communities and create trouble and divert public attention from vital issues before the country.

Any proposal concerning the future of India must demand attention and scrutiny, but in today's grave crisis it is the present that counts and even proposals for the future in so far as they affect the present.

The committee necessarily attached greatest importance to this aspect of the question and on this ultimately depends what advice they should give to those who look to them for guidance. For this the present British War Cabinet's proposals are vague and altogether incomplete, and there would appear to be no vital changes in the present structure contemplated.

It has been made clear that the defense of India will in any event remain under British control. At any time defense is a vital subject. During wartime it is all-important and covers almost every sphere of life and administration.

To take away defense from the sphere of responsibility at this stage is to reduce that responsibility to a farce and nullity and make it perfectly clear that India is not going to be free in any way and her government is not going to function as a free and independent government during pendency of the war.

The committee would repeat that an essential, fundamental prerequisite for the assumption of responsibility by the Indian people in the present is their realization as a fact that they are free and are in charge of maintaining and defending their freedom.

### See War Response Involved

What is most wanted is an enthusiastic response of the people which cannot be evoked without the fullest trust in them and the devolution of responsibility on them in the matter of defense. It is only thus that even in this grave eleventh hour it may be possible to galvanize the people of India to rise to the height of the occasion.

It is manifest that the present government of India, as well as its provincial agencies, are lacking in competence and are incapable of shouldering the burden of India's defense. It is only the people of India through their popular representatives who may shoulder this burden worthily. But that can only be done by present freedom and full responsibility being cast upon them.

The committee are, therefore, unable to accept the proposals put forward on behalf of the British War Cabinet.

# GLOSSARY

ALUM—A standard paraded at the Moharram festival and other celebrations.

ASHRAMA—Hermitage; a retreat for retired devotees or sages.

BANIA—Trader, shopkeeper; a caste.

BHIKKU—A Buddhist monk.

CHAPPAL—Leather sandal; slipper.

CHARKHA—Spinning wheel.

COIR—Stiff, elastic fiber from the coconut husk, used for making rope.

DHARAMSHALA—A house or shelter used for various religious and charitable purposes.

GAEKWAR—Title of the Maharaja, the ruling prince of Baroda.

GAYATRI MANTRA—A prayer for the illumination of the intellect.

GHAT—Landing place; steps leading down to a river.

HARTAL—A concerted cessation of work as a protest; nonco-operation.

JAGIR—A grant of public revenues of a district to an administrator for personal and public use; also, the revenues, the district, or its tenure.

KARZA—Debt.

KHADI—Homespun cloth.

LATHEE—Heavy stick bound with iron.

MAIDAN—Open space or esplanade.

MANTRAM—A ritualistic or devotional formula.

MELA—A fair held in connection with a religious festival.

NEWAR—Tape.

PANCHAYAT—A communal or village court.

PANDIT—A learned man, a teacher, especially a Brahman versed in Hindu religion, science, and laws.

PAN SUPARI—Areca nut rolled in betel leaf with a little shell-lime for chewing.

PRAYASHCHIT—Expiation; penance.

PUCCA—Good, substantial, solid.

PUJA—Hindu religious rite.

PURDAH—Seclusion of women.

PURDANASHIN—A woman who practices *purdah*.

SABHA—A meeting; an assembly.

SAMVAT—The era which began with the first year of the legendary king Vikramaditya (on February 23, 57 B.C.).

SANYASI—One devoted to asceticism and meditation.

SARKAR—Government; also, as a title, master.

SATYAGRAHA—Civil disobedience.

SAWAR—Rider, cavalier, cavalryman.

SITA-RAM—Invocation in memory of Sita, legendary idol of womanhood, and Rama, her husband, idol of manhood.

SWADESHI—Home manufacture and boycott of foreign goods.

SWARAJ—Political independence; self-government.

TALUK—A large estate.

TALUKA—A very large estate in the United Provinces (in Oudh).

TALUKADAR—A semi-feudal land-owner in Oudh.

TALUKDAR—The holder of a large estate.

VAKIL—Attorney.

ZAMINDAR—Landlord.

# INDEX